# Business Marketing Strategy

## Strategy

Concepts and Applications

# Business Marketing Strategy

## Concepts and Applications

**V. Kasturi Rangan**
*Harvard University*

**Benson P. Shapiro**
*Harvard University*

**Rowland T. Moriarty, Jr.**
*Chairman, Cubex Corporation*

**IRWIN**

Chicago • Bogotá • Boston • Buenos Aires • Caracas
London • Madrid • Mexico City • Sydney • Toronto

| | |
|---|---|
| Senior sponsoring editor: | Stephen M. Patterson |
| Editorial assistant: | Christine Scheid |
| Marketing manager: | Jim Lewis |
| Project editor: | Paula M. Buschman |
| Production manager: | Ann Cassady |
| Designer: | Michael Warrell |
| Graphics supervisor: | Heather Burbridge |
| Compositor: | Graphic Sciences Corporation |
| Typeface: | 10/12 Times Roman |
| Printer: | R. R. Donnelley & Sons Company |

**Library of Congress Cataloging-in-Publication Data**

Rangan, V. Kasturi.
    Business marketing strategy  :  concepts and applications /
V. Kasturi Rangan, Benson P. Shapiro, Rowland T. Moriarty, Jr.
      p.  cm. — (The Irwin series in marketing)
    Includes index.
    ISBN 0-256-16910-1
    1. Marketing—Management.  2. Product management.  3. Industrial
marketing—Management.  4. Marketing—Management—Cases studies.
I. Shapiro, Benson P.  II. Moriarty, Rowland T.  III. Title.
IV. Series.
HF5415.13.R269   1995
658.8′02—dc20                  94–22562

*Printed in the United States of America*
1 2 3 4 5 6 7 8 9 0 DO 1 0 9 8 7 6 5 4

# The Irwin Series in Marketing

Gilbert A. Churchill, Jr., Consulting Editor
*University of Wisconsin, Madison*

Alreck & Settle
*The Survey Research Handbook, 2/E*

Arens & Bovee
*Contemporary Advertising, 5/E*

Bearden, Ingram, & LaForge
*Marketing: Principles & Perspectives, 1/E*

Belch & Belch
*Introduction to Advertising and Promotion:
An Integrated Marketing Communications
Perspective, 3/E*

Berkowitz, Kerin, Hartley, & Rudelius
*Marketing, 4/E*

Bernhardt & Kinnear
*Cases in Marketing Management, 6/E*

Bonoma & Kosnik
*Marketing Management: Text & Cases, 1/E*

Boyd, Walker, & Larréché
*Marketing Management: A Strategic
Approach, 2/E*

Burstiner
*Basic Retailing, 2/E*

Cadotte
*The Market Place: A Strategic Marketing
Simulation, 1/E*

Cateora
*International Marketing, 8/E*

Churchill, Ford, & Walker
*Sales Force Management, 4/E*

Cole & Mishler
*Consumer and Business Credit Management, 10/E*

Cravens
*Strategic Marketing, 4/E*

Cravens & Lamb
*Strategic Marketing Management Cases, 4/E*

Crawford
*New Products Management, 4/E*

Dillon, Madden, & Firtle
*Essentials of Marketing Research, 1/E*

Dillon, Madden, & Firtle
*Marketing Research in a Marketing
Environment, 3/E*

Engel, Warshaw, & Kinnear
*Promotional Strategy, 8/E*

Faria, Nulsen, & Roussos
*Compete!, 4/E*

Futrell
*ABC's of Selling, 4/E*

Futrell
*Fundamentals of Selling, 4/E*

Hawkins, Best, & Coney
*Consumer Behavior, 6/E*

Lambert & Stock
*Strategic Logistics Management, 3/E*

Lehmann & Winer
*Analysis for Marketing Planning, 3/E*

Lehmann & Winer
*Product Management, 1/E*

Levy & Weitz
*Retailing Management, 2/E*

Mason, Mayer, & Ezell
*Retailing, 5/E*

Mason, Mayer, & Wilkinson
*Modern Retailing, 6/E*

Mason & Perreault
*The Marketing Game!, 2/E*

McCarthy & Perreault
*Basic Marketing: A Global-Managerial
Approach, 11/E*

McCarthy & Perreault
*Essentials of Marketing: A Global-Managerial Approach, 6/E*

Meloan & Graham
*International and Global Marketing Concepts and Cases, 1/E*

Patton
*Sales Force: A Sales Management Simulation Game, 1/E*

Peter & Donnelly
*A Preface to Marketing Management, 6/E*

Peter & Donnelly
*Marketing Management: Knowledge and Skills, 4/E*

Peter & Olson
*Consumer Behavior and Marketing Strategy, 3/E*

Peter & Olson
*Understanding Consumer Behavior, 1/E*

Quelch
*Cases in Product Management, 1/E*

Quelch, Dolan, & Kosnik
*Marketing Management: Text & Cases, 1/E*

Quelch & Farris
*Cases in Advertising and Promotion Management, 4/E*

Quelch, Kashani, & Vandermerwe
*Cases in European Marketing Management, 1/E*

Smith & Quelch
*Ethics in Marketing, 1/E*

Stanton, Buskirk, & Spiro
*Management of a Sales Force, 9/E*

Thompson & Stappenbeck
*The Marketing Strategy Game, 1/E*

Walker, Boyd, & Larréché
*Marketing Strategy: Planning and Implementation, 1/E*

Weitz, Castleberry, & Tanner
*Selling: Building Partnerships, 2/E*

# Preface

This book is based on the extremely successful industrial marketing course at the Harvard Business School. We three co-authors have taught the course for over a decade and a half, from the mid 70s to the early 90s, and almost every year it has been among the best rated of the second-year MBA electives.

In organizing the book, we mulled over the several frameworks used in the past years. The most obvious way to organize the material appeared to be by marketing mix topics, such as market segmentation, customer selection, product policy, pricing, channels of distribution, and so on. What we found, however, was that second-year MBA students, having studied the principles of marketing by the marketing mix framework in the core course, realize that it is highly interactive and are anxious and eager to jump ahead and take a holistic view of the marketing function. Moreover, we have seen from our various consulting experiences that marketing decisions made by managers in the real world are integrative and rarely can decisions be compartmentalized as solely relating to pricing or distribution or sales, and the like. So from both a pedagogical point of view and a practitioner point of view, the classic marketing mix organization did not appeal to us very much.

At the other extreme, we were also aware of business-to-business marketing books that have tended to specialize by distinctive topic areas. The notion of industrial buying behavior, for example, was quite important and widely researched and taught in the late 70s and early 80s. The topic of distribution channels rose in prominence in the mid-80s. Then in the late 80s high-tech marketing became the rage. We did not want to specialize this book by any such interest focus either, because its primary purpose is to serve students, professionals, and practitioners who practice industrial marketing across a wide range of industry settings. What we sought was a pedagogically wholesome and managerially motivating framework that would appeal to a broad cross section of industrial marketers. Our organization of the book, therefore, has a very simple logic: the product life cycle.

Business-to-business marketing concepts and challenges vary in importance over the life cycle of the product. While the process of new product development is critical early on, the task of managing the order fulfillment cycle is more important at the tail end of the life cycle. Similarly, while the task of selecting and building a sales-and-distribution channel is of paramount importance in the early stage, issues of channel management and distribution cost efficiency become more important in the later stage. The book, therefore, has three core modules—"Managing New Products," "Managing Mature Products," and "Managing Product Market Diversity"—to reflect the market maturation process. Within each of these core sections there are a variety of conceptual issues that cut across the entire spectrum of the marketing mix. The organizing framework is simple, it is holistic, and it treats the marketing mix as interactive and integrative, yet at the same time the special topics and issues facing industrial marketers are picked up at an appropriate point in the product life cycle. The challenges and scope of business-to-business marketing are set out and the basic concepts in customer segmentation and organization buying behavior are reviewed in the opening section.

While each of the four sections has been written to represent a cogent collection of challenging conceptual and practical material, the articles may be read as stand-alone pieces and are intended to be of value to graduate students as well as practicing managers who think and deal daily with issues and problems such as those portrayed in the book. The readings are almost evenly split between practical applications and thoughtful conceptual frameworks. We provide a brief overview of each of the readings in the book in Reading 1 (see Table 1 on page 13).

As is obvious from the table of contents, in a venture of this magnitude several people contribute to the product. We would like to thank Tom Bonoma for "Major Sales, Who Really Does the Buying?," and also his coauthored piece, "Industrial Market Segmentation." We are grateful to our colleagues Steven Wheelwright and Kim Clark for allowing us to use their article "Creating Project Plans to Focus Product Development"; to Dorothy Leonard-Barton, Edith Wilson, and John Doyle for releasing "Commercializing Technology: Understanding User Needs"; to Robert Dolan for his article "Industrial Marketing Research: Beta Test Site Management"; and to Frank Cespedes for our use of "Once More: How Do You Improve Customer Service?" We would like to thank our other colleagues who co-authored several of the articles that are contained in this book, namely, George Bowman, Bruce Isaacson, Barbara Jackson, Thomas Kosnik, Ernie Maier, Melvyn Menezes, Ursula Moran, Elliott Ross, John Sviokla, and Gordon Swartz. While many people contributed to it, the manuscript itself was put together by Susan Brumfield and Morgan McCurdy, our cheerful assistants. A special thanks to them, especially Susan Brumfield for painstakingly proofreading the manuscript and coordinating with the project editor at Richard D. Irwin.

Our gratitude in no small measure is due to Dean John McArthur for encouraging field research, the backbone of several of the articles we have written. We appreciate the Division of Research at the Harvard Business School for so generously funding our field research and for giving us permission to use the articles. We thank the *Harvard Business Review* for granting permission to use a number of articles that were originally published in its pages. We thank the *Journal of Marketing* for allowing us to revise two articles: "New Product Channel Selection" and the "Segmenting Customers in Mature Industrial Markets". We thank *Industrial Marketing Management* for allowing us to revise "Beating the Commodity Magnet," and *Business Horizons* for letting us use "Once More: How Do You Improve Customer Service?" And last but not least we would like to thank our students over the various years who have helped us refine our thinking by their active class participation. This helped us work through the concepts carefully and helped in clarifying and enhancing our communication of them.

The book itself, however, would not have been possible without the help of the practitioners and managers who kept us challenged by directing us to topical issues and problems. We are forever indebted to them for their time and their willingness to share a slice of their professional lives with us.

This book is dedicated with affection to our spouses and our children.

Jayanthi Rangan and our kids Vikram and Mallika

V. Kasturi Rangan

Norma L. Shapiro

Benson P. Shapiro

Jerry Moriarty and our kids Anna, Thomas, and Caroline

Rowland T. Moriarty

# Contents

**Preface**

SECTION I

## Introduction

1  **Scope and Challenge of Business-to-Business Marketing**   3
V. Kasturi Rangan and Bruce Isaacson

2  **How to Segment Industrial Markets**   15
Benson P. Shapiro and Thomas V. Bonoma

3  **Major Sales: Who *Really* Does the Buying?**   26
Thomas V. Bonoma

SECTION II

## Managing New Products

4  **New Product Commercialization**   43
V. Kasturi Rangan

5  **Creating Project Plans to Focus Product Development**   56
Steven C. Wheelwright and Kim B. Clark

6  **Commercializing Technology: Understanding User Needs**   73
Dorothy Leonard-Barton, Edith Wilson, and John Doyle

7    **Industrial Pricing to Meet Customer Needs    98**
     Benson P. Shapiro and Barbara B. Jackson

8    **Industrial Market Research: Beta Test Site Management    112**
     Robert J. Dolan

9    **Designing Channels of Distribution    122**
     V. Kasturi Rangan, Melvyn A. J. Menezes, and Ernie P. Maier


SECTION III
_____

**Managing Mature Products**


10   **Beating the Commodity Magnet    137**
     V. Kasturi Rangan and George T. Bowman

11   **Manage Customers for Profits (Not Just Sales)    152**
     Benson P. Shapiro, V. Kasturi Rangan, Rowland T. Moriarty,
     and Elliot B. Ross

12   **Close Encounters of the Four Kinds: Managing Customers
     in a Rapidly Changing Environment    164**
     Benson P. Shapiro

13   **Segmenting Customers in Mature Industrial Markets    187**
     V. Kasturi Rangan, Rowland T. Moriarty, and
     Gordon Swartz

14   **Once More: How Do You Improve
     Customer Service?    198**
     Frank V. Cespedes

15   **Automation to Boost Sales and Marketing    212**
     Rowland T. Moriarty and Gordon S. Swartz

16   **Reorienting Channels of Distribution    225**
     V. Kasturi Rangan

17   **Managing Hybrid Marketing Systems    238**
     Rowland T. Moriarty and Ursula Moran


SECTION IV
_____

**Managing Product Market Diversity**


18   **Managing Market Complexity: A Three-Ring Circus    257**
     V. Kasturi Rangan

**19 Variety versus Value: Two Generic Approaches to Product Policy 270**
Benson P. Shapiro

**20 What the Hell Is "Market Oriented"? 288**
Benson P. Shapiro

**21 Staple Yourself to an Order 297**
Benson P. Shapiro, V. Kasturi Rangan, and John J. Sviokla

**22 High-Tech Marketing: Concepts, Continuity, and Change 311**
Rowland T. Moriarty and Thomas J. Kosnik

**23 The Logic of Global Business: An Interview with ABB's Percy Barnevik 328**
William Taylor

**Index 347**

# SECTION I Introduction

# Scope and Challenge of Business-to-Business Marketing

*This reading identifies six key linkages that distinguish business-to-business market-ing: three with respect to the external environment (i.e., derived demand, complex buying process, and concentrated customer base) and three with respect to the in-ternal organization (emphasis on technology, high level of customization, and order fulfillment mechanism). These linkages give rise to unique challenges in the analysis and execution of marketing decisions. After these challenges are discussed, the or-ganization of the book is explained. The three core sections, following this introduc-tory section, reflect the product life cycle theme: managing new products, managing mature products, and managing product market diversity.*

Industrial or business-to-business marketing is the marketing of goods and services to commercial enterprises, governments, and other nonprofit institutions for use in the goods and services that they, in turn, produce for resale to other industrial cus-tomers.[1] Implicit in this definition is the type of customer in business-to-business markets as well as the use of the goods purchased. In industrial markets, goods are usually bought for enhancement and subsequent resale, whereas in consumer mar-kets, goods are bought for their final consumption or use.

Because most economic activity is directly or indirectly geared to serving con-sumers' needs, it is hard to estimate the size of the economy for industrial products and services. Certain activities, however, do predominate in the industrial sector, for example, chemicals, primary metals, and machinery manufacturing. One estimate suggests that business-to-business activity represents about one-third of the U.S. 1989 GNP of $5,200 billion.[2] In less-developed economies, the percentage can be

V. Kasturi Rangan and Bruce Isaacson prepared this note.
Copyright © 1994 by the President and Fellows of Harvard College.
Harvard Business School note 594–125.

[1]E. Raymond Corey, *Industrial Marketing Cases and Concepts,* 4th ed. (Englewood Cliffs, N.J.: Prentice Hall, 1991), p. xi.
[2]V. Kasturi Rangan and Bruce Isaacson, "What Is Industrial Marketing?" Harvard Business School note No. 592-012.

even higher, because a thriving industrial sector, be it manufacturing or trading, is needed first, so consumers will get products of acceptable quality and value.

Products sold in industrial markets are usually classified as:[3]

- *Heavy equipment* such as radiology instrumentation or diesel engines.
- *Light equipment* such as hand tools or personal computers.
- *Systems* such as database networks, where the equipment is of secondary importance to the solution being delivered.
- *Raw materials* such as crude oil or cotton fiber.
- *Processed materials* such as rolled steel or plastic polymer that have undergone further processing from raw materials.
- *Consumable supplies* such as coolants, abrasives, or medical syringes.
- *Components* such as electrical motors or disk drives.
- *Services* such as management consulting and contract maintenance.

The above categories are neither exhaustive nor mutually exclusive. They are listed merely to suggest the scope and range of industrial products.

## Aspects Distinguishing Industrial Marketing

The industrial marketing system can be considered in terms of two key linkages. The first is the external interface between the seller's marketing/sales function and the end user. The second is the internal interface between the seller's marketing/sales function and its manufacturing operations (see Figure 1).

While each of these linkages is highly complex (e.g., the role of research and development [R&D] in the internal interface and the role of distribution channels in the external interface), the two sets of linkages serve as convenient handles to explore the major challenges of business-to-business marketing.

### The External Linkages

The three important considerations with respect to external linkages are derived demand, complex buying/selling process, and concentrated customer base.

**Derived Demand.**    The demand for industrial products tends to be driven by the primary demand for consumer goods. For example, an automobile is built from hundreds of components—engines, wheels, the exterior body, the dashboard, and so forth. Each of these in turn is the end result of a supply chain consisting of many other components and raw materials. The dashboard, for

---

[3]This classification scheme is based on one offered by Robert W. Haas, *Industrial Marketing Management* (Boston: Kent Publishing Company, 1982), chap. 1.

### *Framework for the Book*

While the concepts and frameworks offered in the book are meant to illuminate the six management challenges described above, the organization of the book reflects the dynamics of the product life cycle (PLC). The fundamental task of reading the market and developing a new product is significantly different from that of maintaining or increasing share in a mature market.[6] The former involves creativity in interpreting customers' latent needs, while the latter requires the sensitivity to listen to customers' manifest needs. The former might require customer education and market development, while the latter might require product differentiation and market segmentation. New products might require a value-enhancing pricing approach, while mature products might need a price/service adjustment. Each of the six management challenges described above has a somewhat different flavor for new product-markets as compared to mature product-markets. It is a fact of life that products, markets, and functional departments, rather than elements of the marketing mix, are the more commonly used units of decision making at many firms. Taking a longitudinal PLC view encourages and reinforces this holistic orientation. We have therefore chosen to organize the book on the model of the product life cycle. Within each stage of the PLC, we present concepts, frameworks, and readings that best illustrate the six management challenges described above.

## The Three Core Sections of the Book

The introductory Section I is meant to provide readers a basic understanding of how industrial marketing differs from consumer marketing, and to reinforce classic concepts in market segmentation and organizational buying behavior. Sections II, III, and IV comprise the core of the book.

Industrial markets, like all other markets, naturally mature along the product life cycle. At the start of the PLC, manufacturers must face and overcome a considerable amount of uncertainty. Some of the uncertainty may be caused by the new product configuration or technology itself and how to valuate its true benefits. But a large part of the variance may also be market driven, for example, a lack of product knowledge and acceptance in the targeted markets. Only as the product-market context matures is information available to plan and approach marketing activities with greater deliberation. For instance, in the early part of the PLC so little information is

---

[6]While the concept of managing the product over its life cycle is not new, as can be seen from Theodore Levitt, "Exploit the Product Life Cycle," *Harvard Business Review,* November–December 1965, and Philip Kotler, "Marketing Strategies for Different Stages of the Product Life Cycle," chap. 12, pp. 347–76, *Marketing Management: Analysis, Planning, Implementation, and Control,* 6th ed. (Englewood Cliffs, N.J.: Prentice Hall, 1988), our approach of emphasizing the conceptual differences is unique. We not only explore the differences in management prescriptions, but we attempt to understand the rationale for the underlying differences.

available on how customers buy and use the product that firms usually target markets by clearly identifiable demographic variables such as company size or industry type. But, as the PLC advances, better information begins to emerge on customer usage and buying behavior patterns. Firms able to use this information to their advantage are likely to be more successful.

As the product matures, a similar increase in knowledge of several marketing facets, such as product positioning and channel networks, becomes available, enabling firms to be more thoughtful in their marketing options. But that does not mean that decisions are any less complicated because by now competition is keen, customers are more knowledgeable and demanding, and prices and margins are usually declining. This raises a different set of management challenges; maintaining market share and profits becomes an arduous task. Early in the PLC, a firm's success depends on how skillfully its management is able to anticipate the product-market trends and absorb the associated uncertainties and risks. By contrast, when the PLC matures, management success depends on how accurately it is able to read the already available product-market information and deploy resources to retain strengths and overcome weaknesses. This difference leads to different emphases on the various aspects of the marketing mix. Two of the three core modules, Section II, "Managing New Products," and Section III, "Managing Mature Products," are organized to cover this spectrum of issues and challenges facing industrial marketers as the product-market evolves from new to mature.

The evolution of the PLC is usually accompanied by other related changes in the product-market context. Customers, who are by now completely familiar with and knowledgeable about the product, demand special services to fulfill their unique requirements. As manufacturers scramble to differentiate their products in different segments, product variety, customer segments, buying behavior, and channel arrangements begin to proliferate. Managing this complexity requires one to view the industrial marketing system in its entirety and not by specific product lines or channels. Coordination among products, markets, and channels becomes a significant management task. The third core module, Section IV, "Managing Product Market Diversity," takes a macro view of an organization's entire marketing activity whereby marketing decisions are integrated and synchronized with general management's resources, constraints, and objectives. Product decisions have to be viewed in the context of the business units' other products, sales force decisions must be harmonized in the context of a firm's overall distribution channels, and marketing decisions have to be made in the context of a firm's corporate strategy. Table 1 provides a reading-by-reading plan of the book organized by the PLC theme. We also provide a brief description of the major topics and challenges covered in each reading.

## TABLE 1    Readings

| Reading | Theme |
|---|---|
| **Introduction** | |
| 1. Scope and Challenge of Business-to-Business Marketing | Highlights distinctive aspects of business-to-business marketing. |
| 2. How to Segment Industrial Markets | Proposes the concept of nested indicators to understand and implement industrial market segmentation. |
| 3. Major Sales: Who *Really* Does the Buying? | Discusses the nature and scope of the buying decision-making unit. |
| **Managing New Products** | |
| 4. New Product Commercialization: Common Mistakes | Discusses four common mistakes in new product development and launch. |
| 5. Creating Project Plans to Focus Product Development | Discusses ways to plan and prepare a portfolio of new product development projects. |
| 6. Commercializing Technology: Understanding User Needs | Discusses several methods of incorporating customer needs in new product development. |
| 7. Industrial Pricing to Meet Customer Needs | Discusses pricing strategies ranging from "cost plus" to "customer's valuation of benefits." |
| 8. Industrial Market Research: Beta Test Site Management | Beta test site management. |
| 9. Designing Channels of Distribution | Offers a systematic six-step methodology for designing new product channels. |
| **Managing Mature Products** | |
| 10. Beating the Commodity Magnet | Discusses four generic strategies to avoid the commodity pull. |
| 11. Manage Customers for Profit (Not Just Sales) | Offers a framework for managing customer profitability. |
| 12. Close Encounters of the Four Kinds: Managing Customers in a Rapidly Changing Environment | Proposes models for obtaining and sustaining customer relationships. |
| 13. Segmenting Customers in Mature Industrial Markets | A practical application of buying behavior segmentation. |
| 14. Once More: How Do You Improve Customer Service? | Offers a framework for constructing and managing service activities after the sale is over. |
| 15. Automation to Boost Sales and Marketing | Discusses productivity enhancements made possible by marketing/sales automation systems. |
| 16. Reorienting Channels of Distribution | Projects trends and challenges in managing distribution channels. |
| 17. Managing Hybrid Marketing Systems | Provides guidance on how to compose hybrid channels. |
| **Managing Product Market Diversity** | |
| 18. Managing Market Complexity: A Three-Ring Circus | Highlights the organizational difficulties of managing product-market diversity. |
| 19. Variety versus Value: Two Generic Approaches to Product Policy | Discusses two generic, somewhat opposite, approaches to product policy. |
| 20. What the Hell Is "Market Oriented"? | Looks at interfunctional aspects of market orientation. |
| 21. Staple Yourself to an Order | A practical approach to reengineering the order generation and fulfillment process. |
| 22. High-Tech Marketing: Concepts, Continuity, and Change | Looks at how managers can adapt fundamental marketing techniques to address high-tech environments. |
| 23. The Logic of Global Business: An Interview with ABB's Percy Barnevik | An interview with Asea Brown Boveri's CEO, Percy Barnevik, on the logic of its global organization structure. |

# How to Segment Industrial Markets

*The difficulty of segmenting industrial markets has dissuaded companies from try-ing, despite the benefits they could gain in terms of market selection and focus. The problem is to identify the most useful variables. One way to do this is to arrange the five general segmentation criteria—demographics, operating variables, customer purchasing approaches, situational factors, and personal buyer characteristics—into a nested hierarchy. The segmentation criteria of the largest, outermost nest are general characteristics about industries and companies. Innermost nests are spe-cific, subtle, and hard-to-assess traits.*

As difficult as segmenting consumer markets is, it is much simpler and easier than segmenting industrial markets. Often the same industrial products have multiple ap-plications; likewise, several different products can be used in the same application. Customers differ greatly and it is hard to discern which differences are important and which are trivial for developing a marketing strategy.

Little research has been done on industrial market segmentation. None of the 10 articles in the *Journal of Marketing Research*'s special August 1978 section, "Mar-ket Segmentation Research," for instance, deals with industrial market segmentation in more than a passing manner. Our research indicates that most industrial marketers use segmentation as a way to explain results rather than as a way to plan.

In fact, industrial segmentation can assist companies in several areas:

- **Analysis of the market.** Better understanding of the total marketplace, including how and why customers buy.

---

This reading was prepared by Benson P. Shapiro and Thomas V. Bonoma.

- **Selection of key markets.** Rational choice of market segments that best fit the company's capabilities.
- **Management of marketing.** The development of strategies, plans, and programs to profitably meet the needs of different market segments and to give the company a distinct competitive advantage.

In this article we integrate and build on previous schemes for segmenting industrial markets and offer a new approach that enables not only the simple grouping of customers and prospects, but also more complex grouping of purchase situations, events, and personalities. It thus serves as an important new analytical tool.

Consider the dilemma of one skilled and able industrial marketer who observed recently:

"I can't see any basis on which to segment my market. We have 15 percent of the market for our type of plastics fabrication equipment. There are 11 competitors who serve a large and diverse set of customers, but there is no unifying theme to our customer set or to anyone else's."

His frustration is understandable, but he should not give up, for at least he knows that 15 percent of the market purchases one product and that knowledge, in itself, is a basis for segmentation. Segments exist, even when the only apparent basis for differentiation is brand choice.

At other times, a marketer may be baffled by a profusion of segmentation criteria. Customer groups and even individual customers within these groups may differ in demographics (including industry and company size), operating differences (production technology is an example), purchasing organization, "culture," and personal characteristics. Usually, a marketer can group customers, prospects, and purchase situations in different ways depending on the variables used to segment the market. The problem is to identify relevant segmentation bases.

We have identified five general segmentation criteria, which we have arranged as a *nested* hierarchy—like a set of boxes that fit one into the other or a set of wooden Russian dolls. Moving from the outer nest toward the inner, these criteria are: demographics, operating variables, customer purchasing approaches, situational factors, and personal characteristics of the buyers.

Exhibit 1 shows how the criteria relate to one another as nests. The segmentation criteria of the largest, outermost nest are demographics—general, easily observable characteristics about industries and companies. Those of the smallest, inmost nest are personal characteristics—specific, subtle, hard-to-assess traits. The marketer moves from the more general, easily observable segmentation characteristics to the more specific, subtle ones. This approach will become clearer as we explain each criterion.

We should note at this point that it may not be necessary or even desirable for every industrial marketer to use every stage of the nested approach for every product. Although it is possible to skip irrelevant criteria, it is important that the marketer completely understand the approach before deciding on omissions and shortcuts.

---

**EXHIBIT 1   Nested Approach**

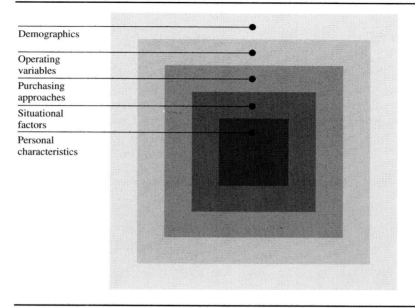

Demographics

Operating
variables

Purchasing
approaches

Situational
factors

Personal
characteristics

---

# Demographics

We begin with the outermost nest, which contains the most general segmentation criteria, demographics. These variables give a broad description of the company and relate to general customer needs and usage patterns. They can be determined without visiting the customer and include industry and company size, and customer location.

**The Industry.**   Knowledge of the industry affords a broad understanding of customer needs and perceptions of purchase situations. Some companies, such as those selling paper, office equipment, business-oriented computers, and financial services, market to a wide range of industries. For these, industry is an important basis for market segmentation. Hospitals, for example, share some computer needs with retail stores and yet differ markedly from them as a customer group.

Marketers may wish to subdivide individual industries. For example, although financial services are in a sense a single industry, commercial banks, insurance companies, stockbrokerage houses, and savings and loan associations all differ dramatically. Their differences in terms of product and service needs, such as specialized peripherals and terminals, data handling, and software requirements, make a more detailed segmentation scheme necessary to sell computers to the financial services market.

**Company Size.**    The fact that large companies justify and require specialized programs affects market segmentation. It may be, for example, that a small supplier of industrial chemicals, after segmenting its prospective customers on the basis of company size, will choose not to approach large companies whose volume requirements exceed its own production capacity.

**Customer Location.**    The third demographic factor, location, is an important variable in decisions related to deployment and organization of sales staff. A manufacturer of heavy-duty pumps for the petrochemical industry, for example, would want to provide good coverage in the Gulf Coast, where customers are concentrated, while putting little effort into New England. Customer location is especially important when proximity is a requirement for doing business, as in marketing products of low value per unit weight or volume (corrugated boxes or prestressed concrete), or in situations where personal service is essential, as in job shop printing.

As noted, a marketer can determine all of these demographic variables easily. Industry-oriented and general directories are useful in developing lists of customers in terms of industry, size, and location. Government statistics, reports by market research companies, and industry and trade association publications provide a great deal of demographic data.

Many companies base their industrial marketing segmentation approach on demographic data alone. But while demographics are useful and easily obtained, they do not exhaust the possibilities of segmentation. They are often only a beginning.

# Operating Variables

The second segmentation nest contains a variety of segmentation criteria called operating variables. Most of these enable more precise identification of existing and potential customers within demographic categories. Operating variables are generally stable and include technology, user-nonuser status (by product and brand), and customer capabilities (operating, technical, and financial).

**Company Technology.**    A company's technology, involving either its manufacturing process or its product, goes a long way toward determining its buying needs. Soda ash, for example, can be produced by two methods that require different capital equipment and supplies. The production of Japanese color televisions is highly automated and uses a few, large integrated circuits. In the United States, on the other hand, color TV production once involved many discrete components, manual assembly, and fine-tuning. In Europe, production techniques made use of a hybrid of integrated circuits and discrete components. The technology used affects companies' requirements for test gear, tooling, and components and, thus, a marketer's most appropriate marketing approach.

**Product and Brand-Use Status.**    One of the easiest ways, and in some situations the only obvious way, to segment a market is by product and brand use. Users of a particular product or brand generally have some characteristics in common; at the very least, they have a common experience with a product or brand.

Manufacturers who replace metal gears with nylon gears in capital equipment probably share perceptions of risk, manufacturing process or cost structure, or marketing strategy. They probably have experienced similar sales presentations. Having used nylon gears, they share common experiences, including, perhaps, similar changes in manufacturing approaches.

One supplier of nylon gears might argue that companies that have already committed themselves to replace metal gears with nylon gears are better customer prospects than those that have not yet done so, since it is usually easier to generate demand for a new brand than for a new product. But another supplier might reason that manufacturers that have not yet shifted to nylon are better prospects because they have not experienced its benefits and have not developed a working relationship with a supplier. A third marketer might choose to approach both users and nonusers with different strategies.

Current customers are a different segment from prospective customers using a similar product purchased elsewhere. Current customers are familiar with a company's product and service, and company managers know something about customer needs and purchasing approaches. Some companies' marketing approaches focus on increasing sales volume from existing customers, via either customer growth or gaining a larger share of the customer's business, rather than on additional sales volume from new customers. In these cases, industrial sales managers often follow a two-step process: First, they seek to gain an initial order on trial, and then to increase the share of the customer's purchases. Banks are often more committed to raising the share of major customers' business than to generating new accounts.

Sometimes it is useful to segment customers not only on the basis of whether they buy from the company or from its competitors, but also, in the latter case, on the identity of competitors. This information can be useful in several ways. Sellers may find it easier to lure customers from competitors that are weak in certain respects. When Bethlehem Steel opened its state-of-the-art Burns Harbor plant in the Chicago area, for example, it went after the customers of one local competitor known to offer poor quality.

**Customer Capabilities.**    Marketers might find companies with known operating, technical, or financial strengths and weaknesses to be an attractive market. For example, a company operating with tight materials inventories would greatly appreciate a supplier with a reliable delivery record. And customers unable to perform quality-control tests on incoming materials might be willing to pay for supplier quality checks. Some raw materials suppliers might choose to develop a thriving business among less-sophisticated companies, for which lower-than-usual average discounts well compensate added services.

Technically weak customers in the chemical industry have traditionally depended on suppliers for formulation assistance and technical support. Some suppliers have been astute in identifying customers needing such support and in providing it in a highly effective manner.

Technical strength can also differentiate customers. Digital Equipment Corporation for many years specialized in selling its minicomputers to customers able to develop their own software, and Prime Computer sells computer systems to business users who do not need the intensive support and "hand holding" offered by IBM and other manufacturers. Both companies use segmentation for market selection.

Many operating variables are easily researched. In a quick drive around a soda ash plant, for example, a vendor might be able to identify the type of technology being used. Data on financial strength is at least partially available from credit-rating services. Customer personnel may provide other data, such as the name of current suppliers; "reverse engineering" (tearing down or disassembly) of a product may yield information on the type and even the producers of components, as may merely noting the names on delivery trucks entering the prospect's premises.

## Purchasing Approaches

One of the most neglected but valuable methods of segmenting an industrial market involves consumers' purchasing approaches and company philosophy. The factors in this middle segmentation nest include the formal organization of the purchasing function, the power structure, the nature of buyer–seller relationships, the general purchasing policies, and the purchasing criteria.

**Purchasing Function Organization.**    The organization of the purchasing function to some extent determines the size and operation of a company's purchasing unit. A centralized approach may merge individual purchasing units into a single group, and vendors with decentralized manufacturing operations may find it difficult to meet centralized buying patterns.[1] To meet these differing needs, some suppliers handle sales to centralized purchasers through so-called national account programs, and those to companies with a decentralized approach through field-oriented sales forces.

**Power Structures.**    These also vary widely among customers. The impact of influential organizational units varies and often affects purchasing approaches. The powerful financial analysis units at General Motors and Ford may, for example, have made those companies unusually price-oriented in their purchasing decisions. A company may have a powerful engineering department, for instance, that strongly influences purchases; a supplier with strong technical skills would suit such a customer. A vendor might find it useful to adapt its marketing program to customer strengths, using one approach for customers with strong engineering operations and another for customers lacking these.

---

[1] See E. Raymond Corey, "Should Companies Centralize Procurement?" *Harvard Business Review,* November–December 1978, p. 102.

**Buyer–Seller Relationships.**    A supplier probably has stronger ties with some customers than others. The link may be clearly stated. A lawyer, commercial banker, or investment banker, for example, might define as an unattractive market segment all companies having as a board member the representative of a competitor.

**General Purchasing Policies.**    A financially strong company that offers a lease program might want to identify prospective customers who prefer to lease capital equipment or who have meticulous asset management. When AT&T could lease but not sell equipment, this was an important segmentation criterion for it. Customers may prefer to do business with long-established companies or with small independent companies, or may have particularly potent affirmative action purchasing programs (minority-owned businesses were attracted by Polaroid's widely publicized social conscience program, for example). Or they may prefer to buy systems rather than individual components.

A prospective customer's approach to the purchasing process is important. Some purchasers require an agreement based on supplier cost, particularly the auto companies, the U.S. government, and the three large general merchandise chains, Sears Roebuck, Montgomery Ward, and J.C. Penney. Other purchasers negotiate from a market-based price and some use bids. Bidding is an important method for obtaining government and quasi-government business; but because it emphasizes price, bidding tends to favor suppliers that, perhaps because of a cost advantage, prefer to compete on price. Some vendors might view purchasers that choose suppliers via bidding as desirable, while others might avoid them.

**Purchasing Criteria.**    The power structure, the nature of buyer–seller relationships, and general purchasing policies all affect purchasing criteria. Benefit segmentation in the consumer goods market is the process of segmenting a market in terms of the reasons why customers buy. It is, in fact, the most insightful form of consumer goods segmentation because it deals directly with customer needs. In the industrial market, consideration of the criteria used to make purchases and the application for these purchases, which we consider later, approximate the benefit segmentation approach.

# Situational Factors

Up to this point we have focused on the grouping of customer companies. Now we consider the role of the purchase situation, even single-line entries on the order form.

Situational factors resemble operating variables but are temporary and require a more detailed knowledge of the customer. They include the urgency of order fulfillment, product application, and the size of order.

**Urgency of Order Fulfillment.**    It is worthwhile to differentiate between products to be used in routine replacement or for building a new plant and emergency replacement of existing parts. Some companies have found a degree of urgency useful for market selection and for developing a focused marketing-manufacturing approach leading to a "hot-order shop"—a factory that can supply small, urgent orders quickly.

A supplier of large-size, heavy-duty stainless steel pipe fittings, for example, defined its primary market as fast-order replacements. A chemical plant or paper mill needing to replace a fitting quickly is often willing to pay a premium price for a vendor's application engineering, for flexible manufacturing capacity, and for installation skills that would be unnecessary in the procurement of routine replacement parts.

**Product Application.**    The requirements for a 5-horsepower motor used in intermittent service in a refinery will differ from those of a 5-horsepower motor in continuous use. Requirements for an intermittent-service motor would vary depending on whether its reliability was critical to the operation or safety of the refinery. Product application can have a major impact on the purchase process, purchase criteria, and thus on the choice of vendor.

**Size of Order.**    Market selection can be based at the level of individual line entries on the order form. A company with highly automated equipment might segment the market so that it can concentrate only on items with large unit volumes. A nonautomated company, on the other hand, might want only small quantity, short-run items. Ideally, these vendors would like the order split up into long-run and short-run items. In many industries, such as paper and pipe fittings, distributors break up orders in this way.

Marketers can differentiate individual orders in terms of product uses as well as users. The distinction is important as users may seek different suppliers for the same product under different circumstances. The pipe-fittings manufacturer that focused on urgent orders is a good example of a marketing approach based on these differences.

Situational factors can greatly affect purchasing approaches. General Motors, for example, makes a distinction between product purchases—that is, raw materials or components for a product being produced—and nonproduct purchases. Urgency of order fulfillment is so powerful that it can change both the purchase process and the criteria used. An urgent replacement is generally purchased on the basis of availability, not price.

The interaction between situational factors and purchasing approaches is an example of the permeability of segmentation nests. Factors in one nest affect those in other nests. Industry criteria, for instance, an outer-nest demographic description, influence but do not determine application, a middle-nest situational criterion. The nests are a useful mental construct but not a clean framework of independent units because in the complex reality of industrial markets, criteria are interrelated.

The nesting approach cannot be applied in a cookbook fashion but requires, instead, careful, intelligent judgment.

# Buyers' Personal Characteristics

People, not companies, make purchase decisions, although the organizational framework in which they work and company policies and needs may constrain their choices. Marketers for industrial goods, like those for consumer products, can segment markets according to the individuals involved in a purchase in terms of buyer–seller similarity, buyer motivation, individual perceptions, and risk-management strategies.

Some buyers are risk averse, others risk receptive. The level of risk a buyer is willing to assume is related to other personality variables such as personal style, intolerance for ambiguity, and self-confidence. The amount of attention a purchasing agent will pay to cost factors depends not only on the degree of uncertainty about the consequences of the decision but also on whether credit or blame for these will accrue to him or her. Buyers who are risk averse are not good prospects for new products and concepts. Risk-averse buyers also tend to avoid untested vendors.

Some buyers are meticulous in their approach to buying—they shop around, look at a number of vendors, and then split their order to assure delivery. Others rely on old friends and past relationships, and seldom make vendor comparisons.[2] Companies can segment a market in terms of these preferences.

Data on personal characteristics are expensive and difficult to gather. It is often worthwhile to develop good, formal, sales information systems to ensure that salespeople transmit the data they gather to the marketing department for use in developing segmented marketing strategies. One chemical company attributes part of its sales success to its sales information system's routine collection of data on buyers. Such data-gathering efforts are most justified in the case of customers with large sales potential.

# Reassembling the Nest

Marketers are interested in purchase decisions that depend on company variables, situational factors, and the personal characteristics of the buyers. The three outer nests, as Exhibit 2 shows, cover company variables, the fourth inner-middle nest, situational factors, and the inmost nest, personal characteristics.

As we move from the outer nests to the inner nests, the segmentation criteria change in terms of visibility, permanence, and intimacy. The data in the outer nests are generally highly visible, even to outsiders, are more or less permanent, and require little intimate knowledge of customers. But situational factors and personal characteristics are less visible, are more transient, and require extensive vendor research.

---

[2]For further discussion of these, see Thomas V. Bonoma, "Major Sales: Who *Really* Does the Buying?" *Harvard Business Review,* May–June 1982, p. 111, and Benson P. Shapiro and Ronald Posner, "Making the Major Sale," *Harvard Business Review,* March–April 1976, p. 68.

---

**EXHIBIT 2     Classification of Nests**

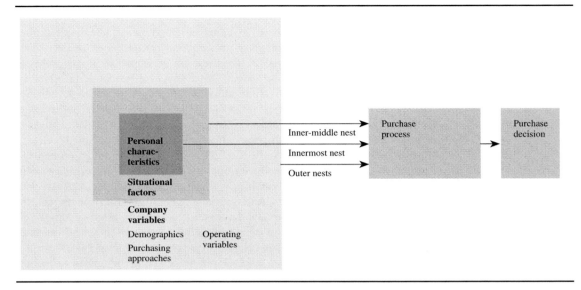

---

An industrial marketing executive can choose from a wide range of segmentation approaches other than the nested approach and, in fact, the myriad of possibilities often has one of the four following outcomes:

- No segmentation. "The problem is too large to approach."
- After-the-fact segmentation. "Our market research shows that we have captured a high share of the distribution segment and low shares of the others; thus we must be doing something right for customers in high-share segments."
- Superficial segmentation. "While we know all banks are different, it's easier to organize marketing plans around banks because we can identify them and tell the salespeople whom to call on." This dangerous outcome gives a false sense of security.
- Obtuse, convoluted, and disorganized segmentation. "We have a 300-page report on market segmentation and customer buying patterns, but there is just too much data in there. So we have decided to focus on insurance companies and hospitals to avoid another two-day market planning meeting."

Our approach using a hierarchical structure is easy to use. Marketers can, in most cases, work systematically from the outer nests to the inner nests. They can run through the whole set of criteria and identify important factors that otherwise might be neglected. And they can balance between reliance on the easily acquired data of the outer nests and the detailed analyses of the inner nests.

We suggest that a marketer begin at the outside nest and work inward because data are more available and definitions clearer in the outer nests. On the other hand, the situational and personal variables of the inner nests are often the most useful. In our experience, managers most frequently neglect situational criteria. In situations where knowledge and analysis exist, a marketer might decide to begin at a middle nest and work inward or, less probably, outward.

After several attempts at working completely through the process, companies will discover which segmentation criteria are likely to yield greater benefits than others and which cannot be considered carefully without better data. A warning is necessary, however. A company should not decide that an approach is *not* useful because data are lacking. The segmentation process requires that assessments of analytic promise and data availability be made independently. The two steps should not be confused. When the necessary data are gathered, managers can weigh segmentation approaches.

A fine line exists between minimizing the cost and difficulty of segmentation by staying in the outer nests on the one hand and gaining the useful data of the inner nests at appreciable direct and indirect cost on the other. The outer-nest criteria are generally inadequate when used by themselves in all but the most simple or homogeneous markets because they ignore buying differences among customers. Overemphasis on the inner-nest factors, however, can be too expensive and time-consuming for small markets. We suggest achieving a sense of balance between the simplicity and low cost of the outer nests and the richness and expense of the inner ones by making the choices explicit and the process clear and disciplined.

---

### Executive Decision Making

"Unless we admit that rules of thumb, the limited experience of the executives in each individual business, and the general sentiment of the street are the sole possible guides for executive decisions of major importance, it is pertinent to inquire how the representative practices of businessmen generally may be made available as a broader foundation for such decisions, and how a proper theory of business is to be obtained. The theory of business, to meet the need, must develop to such a point that the executive, who will make the necessary effort, may learn effectively from the experiences of others in the past what to avoid and how to act under the conditions of the present. Otherwise, business will continue unsystematic, haphazard, and, for many men, a pathetic gamble, with the failures of each serious business depression made up largely of the best moral risks.

"No amount of theory can be a substitute for energy, enthusiasm, initiative, creative ability, and personality, nor will it take the place of technical knowledge. Now, however, all of these personal qualities may be coupled with an adequate technical equipment, and yet the executive of wide experience may fail through our inability to grasp the broad underlying forces controlling business, a knowledge of which would give a sound basis for judgment. It is a serious criticism of our business structure that it so long lacked an adequate method by which these broad forces may be appraised, their probable course charted, and their applications to individual executive problems made reasonably clear."

---

From Wallace B. Donham, "Essential Groundwork for a Broad Executive Theory," *Harvard Business Review,* October 1922, p. 1.

# Major Sales: Who *Really* Does the Buying?

*Seemingly well-planned, well-executed selling strategies may fail if management does not understand the human side of selling. Marketing managers can get at the human factors of purchasing decisions by answering four questions: Who is in the buying center? Who are the powerful buyers? What does each buying-center member want? How do they perceive us? Sales managers should listen to the sales force, emphasize homework and details, and make productive sales calls the norm.*

> You don't understand: Willy was a salesman. . . . He don't put a bolt to a nut. He don't tell you the law or give you medicine. He's a man way out there in the blue, riding on a smile and a shoeshine. And when they start not smiling back—that's an earthquake.
>
> Arthur Miller
> *Death of a Salesman*

Many companies' selling efforts are models of marketing efficiency. Account plans are carefully drawn, key accounts receive special management attention, and substantial resources are devoted to the sales process, from prospect identification to postsale service. Even such well-planned and well-executed selling strategies often fail, though, because management has an incomplete understanding of buying psychology—the human side of selling. Consider the following two examples:

• A fast-growing maker and seller of sophisticated graphics computers had trouble selling to potentially major customers. Contrary to the industry practice of quoting high list prices and giving large discounts to users who bought in quantity, this company priced 10 to 15 percent lower than competitors and gave smaller quantity discounts. Even though its net price was often the lowest, the company met

This reading was prepared by Thomas V. Bonoma.
Copyright © 1982 by the President and Fellows of Harvard College.
Reprinted with permission from *Harvard Business Review* 60, no. 3, May-June 1982, pp. 111–19.

resistance from buyers. The reason, management later learned, was that purchasing agents measured themselves and were measured by their superiors less by the net price of the sophisticated computers they bought than by the amount deducted from the price during negotiations. The discount had a significance to buyers that sound pricing logic could not predict.

• Several years ago, at AT&T's Long Lines division, an account manager was competing against a vendor with possibly better technology who threatened to lure away a key account. Among the customer's executives who might make the final decision about whether to switch from Bell were a telecommunications manager who had once been a Bell employee, a vice president of data processing who was known as a "big-name system buster" in his previous job because he had replaced all the IBM computers with other vendors' machines, and an aggressive telecommunications division manager who seemed to be unreachable by the AT&T team.

AT&T's young national account manager was nearly paralyzed by the threat. His team had never seriously considered the power, motivations, or perceptions of the various executives in the customer company, which had been buying from AT&T for many years. Without such analysis, effective and coordinated action on short notice—the usual time available for response to sales threats—was impossible.

# Getting at the Human Factors

How can psychology be used to improve sales effectiveness? My contention is that seller awareness of and attention to the human factors in purchasing will produce higher percentages of completed sales and fewer unpleasant surprises in the selling process.

It would be inaccurate to call the human side of selling an emerging sales concern; only the most advanced companies recognize the psychology of buying as a major factor in improving account selection and selling results. Yet in most industries, the bulk of a company's business comes from a small minority of its customers. Retaining these key accounts is getting increasingly difficult as buyers constantly look not only for the best deal but also for the vendor that best understands them and their needs. It is this understanding and the targeted selling that results from it that can most benefit marketing managers.

## Buying a Corporate Jet

The personal aspects and their complexities become apparent when one looks closely at an example of the buying process: the purchase of a business jet, which carries a price tag in excess of $3 million. The business-jet market splits obviously into two segments: those companies that already own or operate a corporate aircraft and those that do not.

In the owner market, the purchase process may be initiated by the chief executive officer, a board member (wishing to increase efficiency or security), the company's chief pilot, or through vendor efforts like advertising or a sales visit. The CEO will be central in deciding whether to buy the jet, but he or she will be heavily influenced by the company's pilot, financial officer, and perhaps by the board itself.

Each party in the buying process has subtle roles and needs. The salesperson who tries to impress, for example, both the CEO with depreciation schedules and the chief pilot with minimum runway statistics will almost certainly not sell a plane if he or she overlooks the psychological and emotional components of the buying decision. "For the chief executive," observes one salesperson, "you need all the numbers for support, but if you can't find the kid inside the CEO and excite him or her with the raw beauty of the new plane, you'll never sell the equipment. If you sell the excitement, you sell the jet."

The chief pilot, as an equipment expert, often has veto power over purchase decisions and may be able to stop the purchase of one or another brand of jet by simply expressing a negative opinion about, say, the plane's bad weather capabilities. In this sense, the pilot not only influences the decision but also serves as an information gatekeeper by advising management on the equipment to select. Though the corporate legal staff will formulate the purchase agreement and the purchasing department will acquire the jet, these parties may have little to say about whether or how the plane will be obtained, and which type. The users of the jet—middle and upper management of the buying company, important customers, and others—may have at least an indirect role in choosing the equipment.

The involvement of many people in the purchase decision creates a group dynamic that the selling company must factor into its sales planning. Who makes up the buying group? How will the parties interact? Who will dominate and who submit? What priorities do the individuals have?

It takes about three months for those companies that already own or operate aircraft to reach a decision. Because even the most successful vendor will sell no more than 90 jets a year, every serious prospect is a key account. The nonowners, not surprisingly, represent an even more complex market, since no precedent or aviation specialists exist.

The buying process for other pieces of equipment and for services will be more or less similar, depending on the company, product, and people involved. The purchase of computer equipment, for example, parallels the jet decision, except that sales prospects are likely to include data processing and production executives and that the market is divided into small and large prospects rather than owners and nonowners. In other cases (such as upgrading the corporate communications network, making a fleet purchase, or launching a plant expansion), the buying process may be very different. Which common factors will reliably steer selling-company management toward those human considerations likely to improve selling effectiveness?

Different buying psychologies exist that make effective selling difficult. On the one hand, companies don't buy, people do. This knowledge drives the seller to analyze who the important buyers are and what they want. On the other hand, many individuals, some of whom may be unknown to the seller, are involved in most major purchases. Even if all the parties are identified, the outcome of their interaction may be unpredictable from knowledge of them as individuals. Effective selling requires usefully combining the individual and group dynamics of buying to predict what the buying "decision-making unit" will do. For this combination to be practical, the selling company must answer four key questions.

# 1.  Who's in the "Buying Center"?

The set of roles, or social tasks, buyers can assume is the same regardless of the product or participants in the purchase decision. This set of roles can be thought of as a fixed set of behavioral pigeonholes into which different managers from different functions can be placed to aid understanding. Together, the buying managers who take on these roles can be thought of as a "buying center."[1]

Exhibit 1 shows six buying roles encountered in every selling situation. I have illustrated these roles by using the purchase or upgrading of a telecommunications system as an example. Let's consider each triangle, representing a buying role, in turn.

The *initiator* of the purchase process, whether for a jet, paper towels, or communication services, recognizes that some company problem can be solved or avoided by acquiring a product or service. A company's turboprop aircraft may provide neither the speed nor the range to get top management quickly to and from scattered operations. The prospective buyer of communications equipment may want to take advantage of technological improvements or to reduce costs through owning instead of leasing.

One or more *gatekeepers* are involved in the purchase process. These individuals, who may have the title of buyer or purchasing manager, usually act as problem or product experts. They are paid to keep up on the range of vendor offerings. In the jet example, the chief pilot will ordinarily fill this role. In the telecommunications example given in Exhibit 1, corporate purchasing, the corporate telecommunications staff, or, increasingly, data processing experts may be consulted. By controlling (literally keeping the gate open or shut for) information and, sometimes, vendor access to corporate decision makers, the gatekeepers largely determine which vendors get the chance to sell. For some purchases the gatekeeping process is formalized through the use of an approved-vendors list, which constitutes a written statement of who can (and who, by absence, cannot) sell to the company.

*Influencers* are those who "have a say" in whether a purchase is made and about what is bought. The range of influencers becomes increasingly broad as major purchases are contemplated, because so many corporate resources are involved and so many people affected. In important decisions, board committees, stockholders of a public company, and even lowly mechanics can become influencers. One mining-machinery company encountered difficulty selling a new type of machine to its

---

[1]The concept of the buying center was proposed in its present form by Frederick E. Webster, Jr. and Yoram Wind in *Organizational Buying Behavior* (Englewood Cliffs, N.J.: Prentice Hall, 1972), pp. 75–87.

Unfortunately, power does not correlate perfectly with organizational rank. As the case of the mine maintenance personnel illustrates, those with little formal power may be able to stop a purchase or hinder its completion. A purchasing manager who will not specify a disfavored vendor or the secretary who screens one vendor's salespeople because of a real or imagined slight also can dramatically change the purchasing outcome. Sales efforts cannot be directed through a simple reading of organizational charts; the selling company must identify the powerful buying-center members.

In Exhibit 2, I outline five major power bases in the corporation. In addition, I have categorized them according to whether their influence is positive (champion power) or negative (veto power).

*Reward power* refers to a manager's ability to encourage purchases by providing others with monetary, social, political, or psychological benefits. In one small company, for instance, the marketing vice president hoped to improve marketing decisions by equipping the sales force with small data-entry computers. Anticipating objections that the terminals were unnecessary, he felt forced to offer the sales vice president a computer of his own. The purchase was made.

*Coercive power* refers to a manager's ability to impose punishment on others. Of course, threatening punishment is not the same thing as having the power to impose it. Those managers who wave sticks most vigorously are sometimes the least able to deliver anything beyond a gentle breeze.

*Attraction power* refers to a person's ability to charm or otherwise persuade people to go along with his or her preferences. Next to the ability to reward and punish, attraction is the most potent power base in managerial life. Even CEOs find it difficult to rebut a key customer with whom they have flown for 10 years who says, "Joe, as your friend, I'm telling you that buying this plane would be a mistake."

---

**Exhibit 2    Bases of Power**

| *Type of Power* | *Champion* | *or* | *Veto* |
|---|:---:|:---:|:---:|
| **Reward:** Ability to provide monetary, social, political, or psychological rewards to others for compliance | ● | | |
| **Coercive:** Ability to provide monetary or other punishments for noncompliance | ● | | |
| **Attraction:** Ability to elicit compliance from others because they like you | ● | | ● |
| **Expert:** Ability to elicit compliance because of technical expertise, either actual or reputed | | | ● |
| **Status:** Compliance-gaining ability derived from a legitimate position of power in a company | | | ● |

NOTE: These five power bases were originally proposed over 20 years ago by psychologists J.R.P. French, Jr. and Bertram Raven. See "The Bases of Social Power" in D. Cartwright, ed., *Studies in Social Power* (Ann Arbor: University of Michigan Press, 1959).

When a manager gets others to go along with his judgment because of real or perceived expertise in some area, *expert power* is being invoked. A telecommunications manager will find it difficult to argue with an acknowledged computer expert who contends that buying a particular telephone switching system is essential for the "office of the future"—or that not buying it now eventually will make effective communication impossible. With expert power, the skills need not be real, if by *real* we mean that the individual actually possesses what is attributed to him or her. It is enough that others believe that the expert has special skills or are willing to respect his or her opinion because of accomplishments in a totally unrelated field.

*Status power* comes from having a high position in the corporation. This notion of power is most akin to what is meant by the word *authority*. It refers to the kind of influence a president has over a first-line supervisor and is more restricted than the other power bases. At first glance, status power might be thought of as similar to reward or coercive power. But it differs in significant ways. First, the major influence activity of those positions of corporate authority is persuasion, not punishment or reward. We jawbone rather than dangle carrots and taunt with sticks because others in the company also have significant power which they could invoke in retaliation.

Second, the high-status manager can exercise his or her status repeatedly only because subordinates allow it. In one heavy-manufacturing division, for example, the continual specification of favored suppliers by a plant manager (often at unfavorable prices) led to a "palace revolt" among other managers whose component cost evaluations were constantly made to look poor. Third, the power base of those in authority is very circumscribed since authority only tends to work in a downward direction on the organization chart and is restricted to specific work-related requests. Status power is one of the weaker power bases.

Buying centers and individual managers usually display one dominant power base in purchasing decisions. In one small company, an important factor is whether the manager arguing a position is a member of the founding family—a kind of status power and attraction power rolled into one. In a large high-technology defense contractor, almost all decisions are made on the basis of real or reputed expertise. This is true even when the issue under consideration has nothing to do with hardware or engineering science.

The key to improved selling effectiveness is in observation and investigation to understand prospects' corporate power culture. The sales team must also learn the type of power key managers in the buying company have or aspire to. Discounts or offers of price reductions may not be especially meaningful to a Young Turk in the buying company who is most concerned with status power; a visit by senior selling-company management may prove much more effective for flattering the ego and making the sale. Similarly, sales management may wish to make more technical selling appeals to engineers or other buying-company staff who base their power on expertise.

The last two columns of Exhibit 2 show that the type of power invoked may allow the manager to support or oppose a proposal, but not always both. I believe status and expert power are more often employed by their holders to veto decisions with which they do not agree. Because others are often sold on the contemplated purchase, vetoing it generally requires either the ability to perceive aspects not seen by the average manager because of special expertise or the broader view that high corporate status is said to provide. Reward and coercive power are more frequently used to push through purchases and the choice of favored vendors. Attraction power seems useful and is used by both champions and vetoers. The central point here is that for many buying-center members, power tends to be unidirectional.

### Six Behavioral Clues

Based on the preceding analysis of power centers, I have distilled six clues for identifying the powerful:

1. Though power and formal authority often go together, the correlation between the two is not perfect. The selling company must take into account other clues about where the true buying power lies.

2. One way to identify buying-center powerholders is to observe communications in the buying company. Of course, the powerful are not threatened by others, nor are they often promised rewards. Still, even the most powerful managers are likely to be influenced by others, especially by those whose power is based on attraction or expertise. Those with less power use persuasion and rational argument to try to influence the more powerful. Managers to whom others direct much attention but who receive few offers of rewards or threats of punishment usually possess substantial decision-making power.

3. Buying-center decision makers may be disliked by those with less power. Thus, when others express concern about one buying-center member's opinions along with their feelings of dislike or ambivalence, sellers have strong clues as to who the powerful buyer is.

4. High-power buyers tend to be one-way information centers, serving as focal points for information from others. The vice president who doesn't come to meetings but who receives copies of all correspondence about a buying matter is probably a central influencer or decider.

5. The most powerful buying-center members are probably not the most easily identified or the most talkative members of their groups. Indeed, the really powerful buying group members often send others to critical negotiations becase they are confident that little of substance will be made final without their approval.

6. No correlation exists between the functional area of a manager and his or her power within a company. It is not possible to approach the data processing department blindly to find decision makers for a new computer system, as many sellers of mainframes have learned. Nor can one simply look to the CEO to find a decision maker for a corporate plane. There is no substitute for working hard to understand the dynamics of the buying company.

## 3. What Do They Want?

Diagnosing motivation accurately is one of the easiest management tasks to do poorly and one of the most difficult to do well. Most managers have lots of experience at diagnosing another's wants, but though the admission comes hard, most are just not very accurate when trying to figure out what another person wants and will do. A basic rule of motivation is as follows: all buyers (indeed, all people) act selfishly or try to be selfish but sometimes miscalculate and don't serve their own interests. Thus, buyers attempt to maximize their gains and minimize their losses from purchase situations. How do buyers choose their own self-interest? The following are insights into that decision-making process from research.

First, buyers act as if a complex product or service were decomposable into various benefits. Examples of benefits might include product features, price, reliability, and so on.

Second, buyers segment the potential benefits into various categories. The most common of these are financial, product-service, social-political, and personal. For some buyers, the financial benefits are paramount, while for others, the social-political ones—how others in the company will view the purchase—rank highest. Of course, the dimensions may be related, as when getting the lowest-cost product (financial) results in good performance evaluations and a promotion (social-political).

Finally, buyers ordinarily are not certain that purchasing the product will actually bring the desired benefit. For example, a control computer sold on its reliability and industrial-strength construction may or may not fulfill its promise. Because benefits have value only if they actually are delivered, the buyer must be confident that the selling company will keep its promises. Well-known vendors, like IBM or Xerox, may have some advantage over lesser-known companies in this respect.

As marketers know, not all promised benefits will be equally desired by all customers. All buyers have top-priority benefit classes, or "hot buttons." For example, a telecommunications manager weighing a choice between Bell and non-Bell equipment will find some benefits, like ownership, available only from non-Bell vendors. Other desired benefits, such as reputation for service and reliability, may be available to a much greater degree from Bell. The buyer who has financial priorities as a hot button may decide to risk possible service-reliability problems for the cost-reduction benefits available through ownership. Another manager—one primarily concerned with reducing the social-political risks as a result of service problems—may reach a different decision. Exhibit 3 schematically shows the four classes into which buyers divide benefits; the telecommunications example illustrates each class.

Outlining the buyer's motivation suggests several possible selling approaches. The vendor can try to focus the buyer's attention on benefits not a part of his or her thinking. A magazine sales representative, for instance, devised a questionnaire to help convince an uncertain client to buy advertising space. The questionnaire sought information about the preferred benefits—in terms of reach, audience composition, and cost per thousand readers. When the prospective buyer "played this silly game" and filled out the questionnaire, he convinced himself of the superior worth of the vendor's magazine on the very grounds he was seeking to devalue it.

Conversely, sellers can de-emphasize the buyer's desire for benefits on which the vendor's offering stacks up poorly. For example, if a competing vendor's jet offers better fuel economy, the selling company might attempt to refocus the buyer's attention toward greater speed or lower maintenance costs.

---
**EXHIBIT 3    Dominant Motives for Buying a Telecommunications System**

---

The benefits in bold type are more highly valued than the others and represent the company's "hot button."

| | Benefit Class | | |
|---|---|---|---|
| *Financial* | *Product or Service* | *Social or Political* | *Personal* |
| Absolute cost savings | **Pre- and post-sales service** | Will purchase enhance the buyer's standing with the buying team or top management? | Will purchase increase others' liking or respect for the buyer? |
| Cheaper than competitive offerings | **Specific features** | | How does purchase fit with the buyers' self-concept? |
| Will provide operating-cost reductions | **Space occupied by unit** | | |
| Economics of leasing versus buying | **Availability** | | |

---

The vendor can also try to increase the buyer's confidence that promised benefits will be realized. One software company selling legal administrative systems, for example, provides a consulting service that remote users can phone if they are having problems, backup copies of its main programs in case users destroy the original, a complete set of input forms to encourage full data entry, and regular conferences to keep users current on system revisions. These services are designed to bolster the confidence of extremely conservative administrators and lawyers who are shopping for a system.

Finally, vendors often try to change what the buyer wants, or which class of benefits he or she responds to most strongly. My view of motivation suggests that such an approach is almost always unsuccessful. Selling strategy needs to work with the buyer's motivations, not around them.

---

# 4. How Do They Perceive Us?

How buyers perceive the selling company, its products, and its personnel is very important to efficient selling. Powerful buyers invariably have a wide range of perceptions about a vending company. One buyer will have a friend at another company who has used a similar product and claims that "it very nearly ruined us." Another may have talked to someone with a similar product who claimed that the vending company "even sent a guy out on a plane to Hawaii to fix the unit there quickly. These people really care."

One drug company representative relates the story of how the company was excluded from all the major metropolitan hospitals in one city because a single

influential physician believed that one of the company's new offerings was impli-
cated in a patient's death. This doctor not only generalized his impressions to include all the company's products but encouraged his friends to boycott the
company.

A simple scheme for keeping tabs on how buyers perceive sellers is to ask
sales officials to estimate how the important buyers judge the vending company
and its actions. This judgment can be recorded on a continuum ranging from negative to positive. If a more detailed judgment is desired, the selling company can
place its products and its people on two axes perpendicular to each other, like
this:

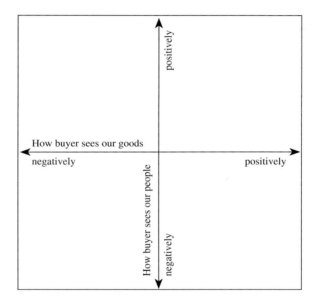

The scarcity of marketing dollars and the effectiveness of champions in the
buying process argue strongly for focusing resources where they are likely to do the
most good. Marketing efforts should aim at those in the buying company who like
the selling company, since they are partially presold. While there is no denying the
adage, "It's important to sell everybody," those who diffuse their efforts this way
often sell no one.

## Gathering Psychological Intelligence

While I would like to claim that some new technique will put sound psychological
analyses magically in your sales staff's hands, no such formula exists. But I have
used the human-side approach in several companies to increase sales effectiveness,
and there are only three guidelines needed to make it work well.

### *Make Productive Sales Calls a Norm, Not an Oddity*

Because of concern about the rapidly rising cost of a sales call, managers are seeking alternative approaches to selling. Sales personnel often do not have a good idea of why they are going on most calls, what they hope to find out, and which questions will give them the needed answers. Sales-call planning is not only a matter of minimizing miles traveled or courtesy calls on unimportant prospects but of determining what intelligence is needed about key buyers and what questions or requests are likely to produce that information.

I recently traveled with a major account representative of a duplication equipment company, accompanying him on the five calls he made during the day. None of the visits yielded even 10 percent of the potential psychological or other information that the representative could use on future calls, despite the fact that prospects made such information available repeatedly.

At one company, for example, we learned from a talkative administrator that the chairman was a semirecluse who insisted on approving equipment requests himself; that one of the divisional managers had (without the agreement of the executive who was our host) brought in a competitor's equipment to test; and that a new duplicator the vendor had sold to the company was more out of service than in. The salesperson pursued none of this freely offered information, nor did he think any of it important enough to write down or pass on to the sales manager. The call was wasted because the salesperson didn't know what he was looking for or how to use what was offered him.

Exhibit 4 shows a matrix that can be used to capture on a single sheet of paper essential psychological data about a customer. I gave some clues for filling in the matrix earlier in the article, but how sales representatives go about gathering the information depends on the industry, the product, and especially the customer. In all cases, however, key selling assessments involve (1) isolating the powerful buying-center members, (2) identifying what they want in terms of both their hot buttons and specific needs, and (3) assessing their perceptions of the situation. Additionally, gathering psychological information is more often a matter of listening carefully than of asking clever questions during the sales interview.

### *Listen to the Sales Force*

Nothing discourages intelligence gathering as much as the sales force's conviction that management doesn't really want to hear what salespeople know about an account. Many companies require the sales force to file voluminous call reports and furnish other data, which vanish, never to be seen or even referred to again unless a sales representative is to be punished for one reason or another.

To counter this potentially fatal impediment, I recommend a sales audit. Evaluate all sales force control forms and call reports and discard any that have not been used by management for planning or control purposes in the last year. This approach has a marvelously uplifting effect all around; it frees the sales force from filling in forms it knows nobody uses, sales management from gathering forms it doesn't

**EXHIBIT 4     Matrix for Gathering Psychological Information**

| Who's in the buying center, and what is the base of their power? | Who are the powerful buyers, and what are their priorities? | What specific benefits does each important buyer want? | How do the important buyers see us? | Selling strategy |
|---|---|---|---|---|
| _____ | _____ | _____ | _____ | _____ |
| _____ | _____ | _____ | _____ | _____ |
| _____ | _____ | _____ | _____ | _____ |
| _____ | _____ | _____ | _____ | _____ |

know what to do with, and data processing from processing reports no one ever requests. Instead, use a simple, clear, and accurate sales control form of the sort suggested in Exhibit 4—preferably on a single sheet of paper for a particular sales period. These recommendations may sound drastic, but where management credibility in gathering and using sales force intelligence is absent, drastic measures may be appropriate.

### *Emphasize Homework and Details*

Having techniques for acquiring sales intelligence and attending to reports is not enough. Sales management must stress that yours is a company that rewards careful fact gathering, tight analysis, and impeccable execution. This message is most meaningful when it comes from the top.

## Cautionary Notes

The group that influences a purchase doesn't call itself a buying center. Nor do decision makers and influencers think of themselves in those terms. Managers must be careful not to mistake the analysis and ordering process for the buyers' actions themselves. In addition, gathering data such as I have recommended is a sensitive issue. For whatever reasons, it is considered less acceptable to make psychological estimates of buyers than economic ones. Computing the numbers without understanding the psychology, however, leads to lost sales. Finally, the notion implicit throughout this article has been that sellers must understand buying, just as buyers must understand selling. When that happens, psychology and marketing begin to come together usefully. Closed sales follow almost as an afterthought.

**FIGURE 2**

*Matching
development
process to
product type*

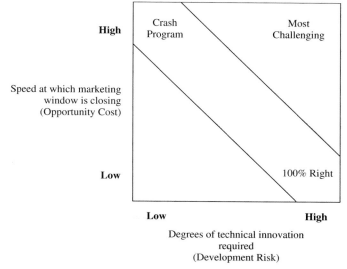

SOURCE: Edward G. Krubasik, "Customize Your Product Development," *Harvard Business Review,* November–December 1988.

different product contexts.[6] While they all have to systematically navigate the 13 stages of a new product's development and launch, different levels of formal management sign-offs and checkpoints are appropriate for the different new product contexts. When the development risks are high and the opportunity costs are low, it is not particularly advantageous to accelerate product development. Such a process could boost project expense and jeopardize product performance and cost. A carefully controlled transition across each stage may make sense. Popularly called the stage-gate system, such a process involves staging the development over several "gates."[7] The project may proceed to the next gate only and only if it clears certain well-specified hurdles. At the other extreme, when the development risk is low and opportunity costs are high, it is absolutely important to speed up the process. Several steps may have to run concurrently. Fortunately, the risks of development failure are also low. The hardest process to manage is when the risks as well as the opportunity costs are high. While technology and cost considerations will necessitate a carefully staged process, market considerations demand speed. The process has to carefully blend caution and aggression.

In summary, the new product literature offers us a wealth of guidelines on how to better manage the development and commercialization process, when to accelerate the steps, and how to effectively manage the teamwork. In this article, we focus on some common product-development and launch mistakes committed by firms that are fully cognizant of, and firmly committed to, the various

[7]Robert G. Cooper, *Winning at New Products* (Reading, Mass.: Addison-Wesley, 1993), pp. 95–120.

prescriptions referred to above. Even though the problems we describe here are executional, several of them are driven by a poor understanding of the development concept to start with.

# Marketing Mistakes

### A Framework

As shown in Exhibit 1, over the years many new product taxonomies have been offered. Products have been classified along various dimensions, such as newness of product/technology, newness to market, newness to company, extent of product change, extent of process change, and so forth. But curiously enough every one of these definitions assumes that the originator of the innovation and the customer are in complete agreement on the newness of the product or its breakthrough nature. But anecdotal evidence suggests that a significant number of new products fail precisely because suppliers and customers do not see eye-to-eye on what the product is supposed to do. There is a disjunction between the seller and the buyer. Consider the case of NeXT, a desktop computer developed by Steve Jobs, the legendary founder of Apple Computer.[8] Customers did not want the optical drive instead of the usual floppy drive. The new feature made it tough for them to switch work from a PC to NeXT. Even though the machine had other nifty features, such as hi-fi sound, customers never overcame their initial resistance. Students found it too expensive, while engineers thought that workstations delivered better performance and value. Thus, after spending $200 million to develop the product, Steve Jobs was forced to drop the product. Yet if he had listened to customers and gone with more standard technology earlier on, some analysts say he might have succeeded. The moral of the story is simple: The new product development process has to start with the voice of the customer, and in this case the customers were seeking an incremental rather than a radical innovation.[9] They were not prepared for the "next generation" product. They did not see the need for it, nor were they willing to pay for it.

In order to understand such supplier–customer misperceptions, we offer a framework to diagnose the problem. See Figure 3. On one axis we map the supplier's perception of the new product, and the customer's on the other. For simplicity, we divide the world into "breakthrough" inventions and "incremental" innovations, knowing full well that many intermediate positions are feasible. Breakthrough is an idea that is so different that it cannot be compared to any existing practices or perceptions. It employs a new technology and creates a new market. Breakthroughs are conceptual shifts that make history.[10] Incremental innovations, on the other hand, are

---

[8]Adapted from "Flops: Too Many New Products Fail."

[9]Vincent P. Barabba and Gerald Zaltman, *Hearing the Voice of the Market,* (Harvard Business School Press, 1991), pp. 19–35.

[10]Nayak and Ketteringham, *Breakthroughs,* p. 1.

---

**EXHIBIT 1    New Product Taxonomies**

---

| | Existing Products | New Products |
|---|---|---|
| **New Markets** | Market Development | Diversification |
| **Existing Markets** | Market Penetration | Product Development |

**Existing Products**        **New Products**

SOURCE: Ansoff H. Igor, "Market Strategy Given Newness of Markets and Products," *Harvard Business Review,* September–October 1957.

<br>

**Newness to Market**

| | Low | High | |
|---|---|---|---|
| **High** | | New Product Lines (20%) | New-to-World Products (10%) |
| **Newness to Company** | Improvements/ Revisions to Existing Products (26%) | Additions to Existing Product Lines (26%) | |
| **Low** | Cost Reductions (11%) | Repositionings (7%) | |

*(Left axis label: Newness to Company)*

SOURCE: Booz Allen & Hamilton, *New Products Management for the 1980s* (New York: Booz Allen & Hamilton, 1982).

<br>

continuations of existing methods or practices. Both suppliers and customers have a clear conceptualization of the product and what it can do. Existing products are sufficiently close substitutes.

When both the supplier and the customer view the new product context as a breakthrough, or as incremental, we then have the perfect match running from east to west in Figure 3. The mismatch is represented by the north–south axis.

## *Breakthroughs and Incrementals*

Breakthrough products require intensive technology and/or applications development. Customers are awed by the new product's potential. It is often doubtful at this stage if a large number of customers really understand how the product usage

**EXHIBIT 1**     *(concluded)*

**Process Changes**

| Product Changes | New Core Process | Next Generation | Upgrade | Tuning/ Incremental |
|---|---|---|---|---|
| **New Core Product** | Breakthrough | | | |
| **Next Generation Product** | | Platform | | |
| **Addition to Product Family** | | | | |
| **Add-ons and Enhancements** | | | | Derivative |

SOURCE: Steven C. Wheelwright and Kim B. Clark, "Creating Project Plans to Focus Product Development," *Harvard Business Review,* March–April 1992.

characteristics will evolve and what usage patterns it will involve. It is important to have a technology vision at this stage in anticipation of market development. While a few "opinion-leader" customers may share that vision, most customers may not have a clue. It would be futile, for example, to seek extensive customer opinion on product attributes and features because the product concept may appear too distant to be of immediate use. A bulk of the product development work, therefore, has to

**FIGURE 3**

*New product types*

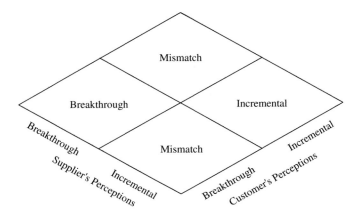

be undertaken with input from only a handful of customers. The effort is typically an "inside out" process, with the technology people playing an important role. A projective vision and a keen sense of market anticipation, which are known as empathic design, are required in the product development process.[11]

In contrast, customers will be able to play a major role in providing input for incremental products. These are, typically, evolutionary development from their viewpoint. Based on their own product-usage history, customers usually will have a precise definition of what improvements they need in the product. Because of their experiences in making the previous-generation product, manufacturers will be able to fairly accurately estimate the technological and manufacturing changes required to serve the customers' needs. In short, the customer's voice becomes the dominant impetus for new product design. Tools and techniques such as quality function deployment (QFD) and conjoint analysis are useful for such new product development activity.[12] Because customers know what they want, and because alternative solutions are usually available in the market, incremental innovations are often designed to meet narrow cost targets. Performance at a price, rather than performance alone, becomes an important design criterion. Even if it did not apply to the whole product, certainly component parts could benefit from reverse engineering key competitors' products. The voice of the distribution channel has to be factored into the product launch. The product design and pricing have to be sensitive to channels' profit considerations. The key differences are captured in Figure 4.

Wrongly interpreted, Figure 4 could misdirect managers into believing that minimal marketing input is required of breakthrough new products. Nothing could be further from the truth. Even though only a few customers may be able to connect with the company's technology visions, it is important to remember that the success of the new product depends on the crucial element of the manufacturer's being able to envision and build a market for its products. This often requires careful marketing thought up-front. One has to identify potential markets and customers; a program to educate them on the benefits of the new technology must be mounted to coincide with the new product's launch. At times a radically new sales and distribution system may be necessary. All this means that even though only a few customers may lend their voice to technology development, the new product introduction process must recognize and incorporate the market building and development activity.

In contrast, sales and manufacturing functions have a crucial role to play in developing and marketing incremental new products. That is because the sales/distribution channel is often the one that is closest to the customer and in the best position to read customer feedback. Many of the customer requirements may not necessitate fundamental technological innovation as much as feature and function improvements. Engineering/manufacturing could often be in a position to build these

---

[11]Dorothy Leonard-Barton, Edith Wilson, and John Doyle, "Commercializing Technology: Imaginative Understanding of User Needs," Harvard Business School Working Paper 93-053.

[12]Robert J. Dolan, *Managing the New Product Development Process* (Reading, Mass.: Addison-Wesley, 1993).

**FIGURE 4**

*Nature of the
marketing tasks*

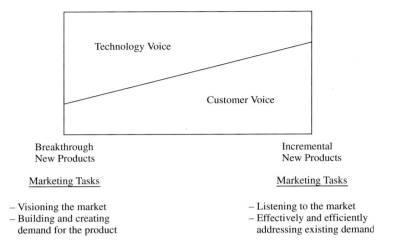

Breakthrough
New Products

Incremental
New Products

Marketing Tasks

Marketing Tasks

– Visioning the market
– Building and creating
  demand for the product

– Listening to the market
– Effectively and efficiently
  addressing existing demand

upgrades without resorting to an intense research/technology effort. Thus while R&D and marketing may play the lead role in breakthrough new product development, usually sales and manufacturing/engineering have a larger role to play in incremental new product development.

**Mistake No. 1.**   The most common mistake is the utter lack of sensitivity to the differences in the management tasks required of incremental versus breakthrough projects. There is an overwhelming tendency to treat them all alike. It is important to realize that cross-functional involvement is not a panacea to all new product development problems; what matters is the nature of the cross-functional involvement (such as those shown in Figure 4). Time and again we found short-term-results-oriented line people assigned to breakthrough development teams. Not only were they unable to envision how the market would develop, their pessimistic forecasts dampened the teams' enthusiasm. They in turn were extremely frustrated because the teams were unable to meet their request for hard customer-data or precise product-cost estimates. The solution is not to leave the line functions (like production and sales) out, but instead to incorporate the right kind of marketing and manufacturing thinking into the team. But it certainly would be dangerous to leave it all to the inventors. Technical people who are thrilled with the breakthrough idea may be short-sighted with respect to its commercial feasibility. Their market forecasts may have a higher correlation to their aspirations for the product than to market realities. At the other extreme, incremental product teams may find themselves saddled with thinkers and visionaries who question the value of the new product concept, who often ask for a thorough systemwide evaluation of every product or process change. "What's so new about this new product?" they often ask. Yet the field-level salespeople or the operations people on the team will vouch for its viability and urge a quick clearance to the next stage. They know the product will work and their customers will buy if only the new product is brought speedily into the market. They are shocked by the project's snail's pace. The moral of the story is simple: Cross-functional teams require people of appropriate cross-functional abilities.

**Mistake No. 2.**    Though not as common as No. 1, Mistake No. 2 is a tendency to assume that breakthrough projects equate with high-profile activities needing resources and top-management support, and that incremental projects are less important and need only back-pocket support.

This is untrue. The resource allocation decision has to be based on the long-term financial attractiveness of the project. Some breakthrough innovations may not have a large market potential to start with. The market will have to develop and grow with the adoption of the innovation. This being the case, it may be prudent to stage the allocation of resources on such projects. On the other hand, many incremental innovations may absolutely require a major investment up front. This is usually the case when the firm's existing product is hopelessly out-of-date in a very large market. Reengineering the product may require heavy manufacturing investments. The point is simple: Do not confuse the nature of the project with potential payoffs. While it is almost inevitable that top management would have to get involved in high-investment projects, it is not entirely desirable to delegate all low-investment projects. Some of them may involve technologies or anticipated market niches that could be of great strategic importance to the company, and without top management's support in the early stages, such projects may flounder. Thus, top management's involvement has to be selective and on a case-by-case basis, but certainly independent of the nature of the product.

In Figure 3, we referred to the north–south direction as the axis of mismatch. In this instance, the manufacturer's and customer's perception of the product's newness are divergent. In one case, the supplier of the technology may see the product as an incremental innovation, whereas the customer may perceive it as a breakthrough—we call this the shadowed new product (because the supplier may not see its true potential). In the other case, the supplier may see the product as an incredible breakthrough, whereas the customers may be lukewarm toward it—we call this the delusionary new product. See Figure 5.

## *Shadowed New Products*[13]

By *shadowed,* we do not mean that the product's technical merit or the customer's potential benefit is negligible, but that the product's contribution in economic terms to the company's portfolio is relatively minor in the short run. These are products that the company's engineers and R&D scientists discovered while pursuing other, more central projects. Alternatively, these are products that the company's sales force thought would serve some of the unmet needs of its existing customers. Either way, these products are not the central thrust of a company's

---

[13]A large part of this discussion is drawn from V. Kasturi Rangan, Rajiv Lal, and Ernie P. Maier, "Managing Marginal New Products," *Business Horizons* 35, no. 5, pp. 35–42.

**FIGURE 5**

*Seller–customer
mismatch*

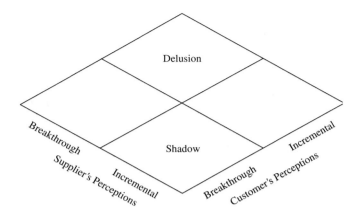

R&D or sales strategy. These are products discovered in the shadow of more important activity. Consequently, such products are not intended to account for a significant chunk of the company's revenues or profits. An example is the Post-It note at 3M Company.

The story goes that the original Post-It application came out of division manager Arthur Fry's desire to keep the bookmark from falling out of his hymn book. There is a similar story regarding 3M's Scotch brand transparent tape. It was apparently invented for an industrial customer who used it to seal insulation in an airtight package. When first developed, both of these products had limited application, and in fact the company was not even sure where the market was for such products. The products were invented for a specific use, rather than to serve a whole market. But today Post-It and Scotch brand tape are in the top five office supply items in the United States, and represent a multimillion-dollar business for 3M company. When initially launched, many such innovations appear marginal. All are small contributors individually, but down the road they can well turn out to have significant impact on a company's bottom line. However, very few companies pay attention to proactively marketing such products.

What reasons underlie the failed launches of so many shadowed new products? The fundamental reason is that these products do not generate the same sense of urgency or focus that accompanies "central" new products. Even though the product idea may have clear champions, because the product was invented relatively cheaply, the new product development team usually will not subject it to the same taxing commercial feasibility and test-marketing standards as the other central products in its pipeline. Many times such products bypass established processes to fall right into the hands of day-to-day line management. Commercialization usually follows organizational routines. And therein lies the crux of the problem.

**Mistake No. 3.**   Because managers already handle a portfolio of other products through existing manufacturing/sales systems, it makes sense to adopt the same for the new product. But the true appreciation for the new product comes in many cases from new customers in new segments, and even if they come from current customers, a different buying unit with different buying criteria may be responsible for its adoption. Using existing organizational systems often means completely missing the boat on the real customer's real needs. This is the customer who values the product as a breakthrough.

A frequent practice is to "make a little, sell a little" until the opportunity is crystal clear. Since the product is not central to the company's short-term financial well-being, there is a tendency to look for some signs of success toward which further attention and resources may be directed. Taking advantage of the existing organizational routines is certainly the cost-minimizing approach; sharing product management, sales management, and distribution is one outcome. Using common marketing and sales resources makes the most economic sense at the outset, with the intention of ultimately tailoring a program for the new product. But the product must show some initial signs of success, so managers wait and see. Meanwhile, a huge opportunity is being missed. It is sold as an incremental innovation to existing customers, when with a little imagination and creativity, an entirely new problem for an entirely new customer may be addressed. Market segmentation and channel selection are usually wrong, and because the product is anchored to existing solutions, it is usually underpriced. A higher price can be obtained, but that requires active customer education for the right customers.

Marketing is as much about creating and shaping customer needs as it is about serving well-identified customer requirements. Good marketers learn about and shape customer needs, even as they implement their marketing programs. The business-as-usual approach completely violates the interactive nature of this market development process.

While the wait-and-see and business-as-usual attitudes may be interpreted as a failing of management execution, top management must take its share of the blame, too. It is responsible for providing a corporate environment/culture that encourages entrepreneurship with rewards for success that outweigh the risks of failure. With a strategic new product, top management involvement is easily obtained. Decisions involving development, introduction, marketing, and sales occur at the top level. This allows senior management to make far-reaching choices and motivate the organization to reflect its priorities. In the case of shadowed new products, the decision to launch has neither strategic urgency nor the routine expediency of a product enhancement. Under these circumstances, lower level management has no incentive to take initiative either, because success may not get the attention of the top brass, whereas a failure will only unnecessarily diminish an existing reputation. The end result is a vicious cycle of wait-and-see and business-as-usual which accelerates the death of the product, followed by a quiet burial. This is a pity because these products cost very little to invent and make, but with imaginative marketing they could add significant new customer segments and new products for the company. Each new product by itself may not immediately be a significant contribution to the bottom line, but put together, they certainly can bring about significant new sales.

### *Delusionary New Products*

We take up these products last because they represent the largest proportion of new product failures. These are innovations where the suppliers of the technology have grandiose visions for the product, but their customers often do not share the same euphoria. We already outlined the predicament of NeXT, but there are literally hundreds more examples like that.[14] Vincent Barabba and Gerald Zaltman describe the VideoDisc fiasco:[15]

> Another example of how technology cannot stand on its own, no matter how advanced, is provided by RCA's $580 million VideoDisc venture. R&D made a major technological breakthrough that had many technological merits, such as a higher-quality (relative to VCR technology) means for watching movies at home; yet, because of improper analysis of the desires of the market, the venture failed. . . .
>
> . . . RCA's VideoDisc strategy had been heavily dependent on a few key assumptions: that the traditional mass-market customer would prefer a low price to more features, that dealers could clear up any consumer confusion about multiple formats, that VCR producers could not substantially reduce the price gap between their players and disc players, that dealers would welcome disc systems as they had VCRs, and that consumers would want to own video programming just as they owned LP records and audio tapes. . . .
>
> . . . In fact, the outcome quickly revealed that most of the key assumptions on which RCA had based its VideoDisc strategy were no longer valid. . . . Had the plan been for a stable product in a familiar business, it would have been well-conceived and well-executed, but for an innovative product in a marketplace destabilized by changing technologies, it was an approach that allowed little room for adjustment.

Why are there so many products with more "show" than "tell"? Don't these firms understand the discipline of knowing the customer? Don't they collect market research? Many do, but the disconnect, unfortunately, comes because of an inside-out process rather than a lack of customer information. As a result, the data interpretation is faulty, not necessarily the data collection. Because of the newness of the product, the technology, or the manufacturing process, to the company there's a justifiable air of expectation and excitement within. But the real question is whether the potential customer is equally excited. To customers, this product may be just one more additional line for consideration among the various available alternatives. They would perhaps like to know why the said offering is superior to competitive products—as far as they know they are viewing an incremental innovation rather than a breakthrough invention.

**Mistake No. 4.**    Such supplier misperceptions lead to faulty product positioning. There is an attempt to break new ground with the product, when in fact a "new and improved" positioning would be more palatable to the customer. The Sony Walkman product launch process is a nice illustration of how to do it right.[16] The product

---

[14]Donald W. Hendon, *Classic Failures in Product Marketing* (New York: Quorum Books, 1989).

[15]Barabba and Zaltman, *Hearing the Voice of the Market*, pp. 31–32.

[16]Nayak and Ketteringham, *Breakthroughs,* pp. 94–111.

development effort required tricky coordination between its tape recorder and headphone divisions. The whole idea of making a cassette player without a speaker or a recorder, but instead with a headphone, seemed quite at odds with Sony's product traditions. The concept itself would not have been commercially viable without the amazing speed of its product development team. The scale-up required innovative manufacturing techniques. Yet when the product was launched, it was priced at a modest $165, with a clear goal to bring it down to less than $100 within three years. The product was sold through broad-line electronic distribution channels. In short, the product was positioned, priced, and sold as through it was an additional offering in the mass distributed, modestly priced consumer electronic category of tape recorders, radios, and cameras.

Of course, we are not suggesting that all potential delusionary products should be priced and marketed through mass-market channels. Our argument is that they should be positioned and priced appropriately with respect to existing solutions in the marketplace. If such an effort in fact requires the company to go upmarket for a specific customer niche where the product outperforms existing solutions, by all means it should be marketed and channeled to reflect its premium status. Our point is that the positioning strategy be driven by the market, rather than by the ambitions of the product champions. The outcome of such an exercise could lead to the conclusion that there are no equivalent customer solutions in the market, and that in fact the product is a radical new idea. The inventors then have a clear breakthrough on their hands, and marketing resources would be needed to develop and create a market.

# Conclusions

The mismatches, that is, the shadows and delusions, could be corrected by aligning them with breakthroughs or incrementals. But it is important to drive the analysis at all times from the customers' viewpoint. A proper alignment will not automatically lead to new product success. It requires a careful piloting through the 13 steps indicated in Figure 1. The nature of the new product development process and the composition of the teams and the nature of their tasks will have to carefully reflect the nature of the new product. All this is hard work and creative work. But at least if the ideas are right, and when accompanied by good execution, the chances of success are maximized. On the other hand, if the alignment is mismatched, no amount of creativity and executional excellence can remedy a guaranteed failure.

# Creating Project Plans to Focus Product Development

*The long-term competitiveness of most manufacturers depends on their product development capabilities. Yet few companies approach the development process systematically or strategically. They end up with an unruly collection of projects that do not match long-term business objectives and that consume far more development resources than are available. The aggregate project plan methodology attempts to address this problem. It helps managers to allocate resources, sequence projects, and build critical development capabilities.*

The long-term competitiveness of any manufacturing company depends ultimately on the success of its product development capabilities. New-product development holds hope for improving market position and financial performance, creating new industry standards and new niche markets, and even renewing the organization. Yet few development projects fully deliver on their early promises. The fact is, much can and does go wrong during development. In some instances, poor leadership or the absence of essential skills is to blame. But often problems arise from the way companies approach the development process. They lack what we call an aggregate project plan.

Consider the case of a large scientific instruments company we will call PreQuip. In mid-1989, senior management became alarmed about a rash of late product development projects. For some months, the development budget had been rising even as the number of completed projects declined. And many of the projects in the development pipeline no longer seemed to reflect the needs of the market. Management was especially troubled because it had believed its annual business plan provided the guidance that the marketing and engineering departments needed to generate and schedule projects.

Steven C. Wheelwright and Kim B. Clark prepared this article.

To get to the root of the problem, the chief executive first asked senior managers to compile a list of all the current development projects. They discovered that 30 projects were under way—far more than anticipated and, they suspected, far more than the organization could support. Further analysis revealed that the company had two to three times more development work than it was capable of completing over its three-year development planning horizon. (See the chart "PreQuip's Development Predicament: Overcommitted Resources.")

With such a strain on resources, delays were inevitable. When a project ran into trouble, engineers from other projects were reassigned or, more commonly, asked to add the crisis project to their already long list of active projects. The more projects they added, the more their productivity dropped. The reshuffling caused delays in other projects, and the effects cascaded. Furthermore, as deadlines slipped and development costs rose, project managers faced pressure to cut corners and compromise quality just to keep their projects moving forward.

The senior management team also discovered that the majority of PreQuip's development resources—primarily engineers and support staff—was not focused on the projects most critical to the business. When questioned, project leaders admitted

## PreQuip's Development Predicament: Overcommitted Resources

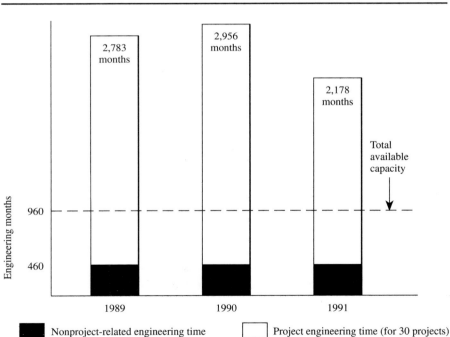

PreQuip had 960 engineering months each year to allocate to development work. But combining the time it would take to keep its current 30 projects on schedule with the time engineers spent doing nonproject development work, the company found it had overcommitted its development resources for the next three years by a factor of three.

that the strategic objectives outlined in the annual business plan had little bearing on project selection. Instead, they chose projects because engineers found the technical problems challenging or because customers or the marketing department requested them. PreQuip had no formal process for choosing among development projects. As long as there was money in the budget or the person making the request had sufficient clout, the head of the development department had no option but to accept additional project requests.

Many engineers were not only working on noncritical projects but also spending as much as 50 percent of their time on nonproject-related work. They responded to requests from manufacturing for help with problems on previous products, from field sales for help with customer problems, from quality assurance for help with reliability problems, and from purchasing for help with qualifying vendors. In addition to spending considerable time fixing problems on previously introduced products, engineers spent many hours in information and update meetings. In short, they spent too little time developing the right new products, experimenting with new technologies, or addressing new markets.

PreQuip's story is hardly unique. Most organizations we are familiar with spend their time putting out fires and pursuing projects aimed at catching up to their competitors. They have far too many projects going at once and all too often seriously overcommit their development resources. They spend too much time dealing with short-term pressures and not enough time on the strategic mission of product development.

Indeed, in most organizations, management directs all its attention to individual projects—it micromanages project development. But no single project defines a company's future or its market growth over time; the set of projects does. Companies need to devote more attention to managing the set and mix of projects. In particular, they should focus on how resources are allocated between projects. Management must plan how the project set evolves over time, which new projects get added when, and what role each project should play in the overall development effort.

The aggregate project plan addresses all of these issues. To create a plan, management categorizes projects based on the amount of resources they consume and on how they will contribute to the company's product line. Then, by mapping the project types, management can see where gaps exist in the development strategy and make more informed decisions about what types of projects to add and when to add them. Sequencing projects carefully, in turn, gives management greater control of resource allocation and utilization. The project map also reveals where development capabilities need to be strong. Over time, companies can focus on adding critical resources and on developing the skills of individual contributors, project leaders, and teams.

Finally, an aggregate plan will enable management to improve the way it manages the development function. Simply adding projects to the active list—a common practice at many companies—endangers the long-term health of the development process. Management needs to create a set of projects that is consistent with the company's development strategies rather than selecting individual projects from a long list of ad hoc proposals. And management must become involved in the development process *before* projects get started, even before they are fully defined. It is not appropriate to give one department—say, engineering or marketing—sole responsibility for initiating all projects because it is usually not in a position to determine every project's strategic worth.

Indeed, most companies, including PreQuip, should start the reformation process by eliminating or postponing the lion's share of their existing projects, eventually supplanting them with a new set of projects that fits the business strategy and the capacity constraints. The aggregate project plan provides a framework for addressing this difficult task.

# How to Map Projects

The first step in creating an aggregate project plan is to define and map the different types of development projects; defining projects by type provides useful information about how resources should be allocated. The two dimensions we have found most useful for classifying are the degree of change in the product and the degree of change in the manufacturing process. The greater the change along either dimension, the more resources are needed.

Using this construct, we have divided projects into five types. The first three—derivative, breakthrough, and platform—are commercial development projects. The remaining two categories are research and development (R&D), which is the precursor to commercial development, and alliances and partnerships, which can be either commercial or basic research. (See the chart "Mapping the Five Types of Development Projects.")

Each of the five project types requires a unique combination of development resources and management styles. Understanding how the categories differ helps managers predict the distribution of resources accurately and allows for better planning and sequencing of projects over time. Here is a brief description of each category:

*Derivative projects* range from cost-reduced versions of existing products to add-ons or enhancements for an existing production process. For example, Kodak's wide-angle, single-use 35mm camera, the Stretch, was derived from the no-frills Fun Saver introduced in 1990. Designing the Stretch was primarily a matter of changing the lens.

Development work on derivative projects typically falls into three categories: incremental product changes, say, new packaging or a new feature, with little or no manufacturing process change; incremental process changes, like a lower-cost manufacturing process, improved reliability, or a minor change in materials used, with little or no product change; and incremental changes on both dimensions. Because design changes are usually minor, incremental projects typically are more clearly bounded and require substantially fewer development resources than the other categories. And because derivative projects are completed in a few months, ongoing management involvement is minimal.

## Mapping the Five Types of Development Projects

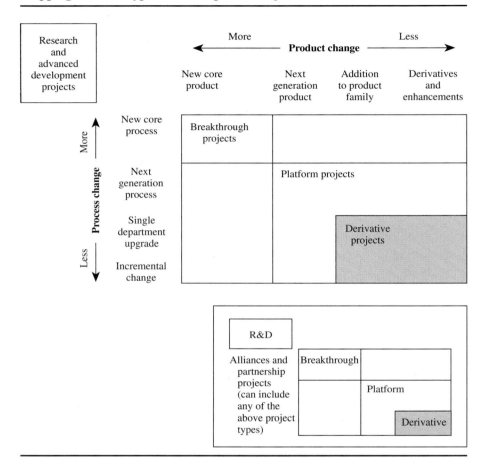

*Breakthrough projects* are at the other end of the development spectrum because they involve significant changes to existing products and processes. Successful breakthrough projects establish core products and processes that differ fundamentally from previous generations. Like compact disks and fiber-optics cable, they create a whole new product category that can define a new market.

Because breakthrough products often incorporate revolutionary new technologies or materials, they usually require revolutionary manufacturing processes. Management should give development teams considerable latitude in designing new processes, rather than force them to work with existing plants and equipment, operating techniques, or supplier networks.

*Platform projects* are in the middle of the development spectrum and are thus harder to define. They entail more product and/or process changes than derivatives do, but they don't introduce the untried new technologies or materials that break-

could easily create derivatives, all of which could be assembled and tested on a single production line. In one case, a variant of the C-101 was planned for the high-end laboratory market. By strengthening the casing and eliminating some features, PreQuip also created a product for the industrial market.

Mapping out the new mass spectrometer line and the three other product lines was not painless. It took a number of months and involved a reconceptualization of the product lines, close management, and considerable customer involvement. To provide additional focus, PreQuip separated the engineering resources into three categories: basic R&D projects; existing products and customers, now a part of the manufacturing organization; and commercial product development.

To determine the number of breakthrough, platform, derivative, and partnered projects that could be sustained at any time, the company first estimated the average number of engineering months for each type of project based on past experience. It then allocated available engineering resources according to its desired mix of projects; about 50 percent to platform projects, 20 percent to derivative projects, and 10 percent each to breakthrough projects and partnerships. PreQuip then selected specific projects, confident that it would not overallocate its resources.

In the end, PreQuip canceled more than two-thirds of its development projects, including some high-profile pet projects of senior managers. When the dust had settled in mid-1990, PreQuip had just 11 projects: 3 platforms, 1 breakthrough, 3 derivatives, 1 partnership, and 3 projects in basic R&D. (See the chart ". . . After: PreQuip's Development Process Was Manageable.")

The changes led to some impressive gains: Between 1989 and 1991, PreQuip's commercial development productivity improved by a factor of three. Fewer projects meant more actual work got done, and more work meant more products. To avoid overcommitting resources and to improve productivity further, the company built a "capacity cushion" into its plan. It assigned only 75 full-time-equivalent engineers out of a possible 80 to the eight commercial development projects. By leaving a small percent of development capacity uncommitted, PreQuip was better prepared to take advantage of unexpected opportunities and to deal with crises when they arose.

## Focus on the Platform

PreQuip's development map served as a basis for reallocating resources and for rethinking the mix of projects. Just as important, however, PreQuip no longer thought about projects in isolation; breakthrough projects shaped the new platforms, which defined the derivatives. In all four product lines, platforms played a particularly important role in the development strategy. This was not surprising considering the maturity of PreQuip's industry. For many companies, the more mature the industry, the more important it is to focus on platform projects.

Consider the typical industry life cycle. In the early stages of growth, innovative, dynamic companies gain market position with products that have dramatically superior performance along one or two dimensions. Whether they know it or not, these companies employ a breakthrough-platform strategy. But as the industry develops and the opportunity for breakthrough products decreases—often because the technology is shared more broadly—competitors try to satisfy increasingly sophisticated customers by rapidly making incremental improvements to existing products. Consciously or not, they adopt a strategy based on derivative projects. As happened with PreQuip, this approach ultimately leads to a proliferation of product lines and overcommitment of development resources. The solution lies in developing a few well-designed platform products, on each of which a generation of products can be built.

In the hospital bed industry, for example, companies that design, manufacture, sell, and service electric beds have faced a mature market for years. They are constantly under pressure to help their customers constrain capital expenditures and operating costs. Technologies are stable and many design changes are minor. Each generation of product typically lasts 8 to 12 years, and companies spend most of their time and energy developing derivative products. As a result, companies find themselves with large and unwieldy product lines.

In the 1980s, Hill-Rom, a leading electric-bed manufacturer, sought a new product strategy to help contain costs and maintain market share. Like other bed makers, its product development process was reactive and mired in too many low-payoff derivative projects. The company would design whatever the customer—a single hospital or nursing home—wanted, even if it meant significant commitments of development resources.

The new strategy involved a dramatic shift toward leveraging development and manufacturing resources. Hill-Rom decided to focus on hospitals and largely withdraw from the nursing home segment, as well as limit the product line by developing two new platform products—the Centra and the Century. The Centra was a high-priced product with built-in electronic controls, including communications capabilities. The Century was a simpler, less-complex design with fewer features. The products built off each platform shared common parts and manufacturing processes and provided the customer with a number of add-on options. By focusing development efforts on two platforms, Hill-Rom was able to introduce new technologies and new product features into the market faster and more systematically, directly affecting patient recovery and hospital staff productivity. This strategy led to a less chaotic development cycle as well as lower unit cost, higher product quality, and more satisfied customers.

For companies that must react to constant changes in fashion and consumer tastes, a different relationship between platform and derivative projects makes sense. For example, Sony has pioneered its "hyper-variety" strategy in developing the Walkman: it directs the bulk of its Walkman development efforts at creating derivatives, enhancements, hybrids, and line extensions that offer something tailored to every niche, distribution channel, and competitor's product. As a result, in 1990, Sony dominated the personal audio system market with over 200 models based on just three platforms.

Platforms are critical to any product development effort, but there is no one ideal mix of projects that fits all companies. Every company must pursue the projects that match its opportunities, business strategy, and available resources. Of course, the mix evolves over time as projects move out of development into production, as business strategies change, as new markets emerge, and as resources are enhanced. Management needs to revisit the project mix on a regular basis—in some cases every six months, in others, every year or so.

# Steady Stream Sequencing: PreQuip Plans Future Development

Periodically evaluating the product mix keeps development activities on the right track. Companies must decide how to sequence projects over time, how the set of projects should evolve with the business strategy, and how to build development capabilities through such projects. The decisions about changing the mix are neither easy nor straightforward. Without an aggregate project plan, most companies cannot even begin to formulate a strategy for making those decisions.

PreQuip was no different. Before adopting an aggregate project plan, the company had no concept of project mix and no understanding of sequencing. Whenever someone with authority had an idea worth pursuing, the development department added the project to its active list. With the evolution of a project plan, PreQuip developed an initial mix and elevated the sequencing decision to a strategic responsibility of senior management. Management scheduled projects at evenly spaced intervals to ensure a "steady stream" of development projects. (See the chart "PreQuip's Project Sequence.")

## PreQuip's Project Sequence

| Project Type | Development Resources Committed at Mid-1990 (% of Total Engineering Time) | Project Description | Project Number | Sequencing 1990 — 1991 |
|---|---|---|---|---|
| R&D | (Separate) | Advanced pump | RD-1 | |
| | | Electronic sensors | RD-2 | |
| | | Software | RD-3 | |
| Breakthrough | 12.5% | Fully automated self-diagnostic system for gas chromatograph | BX-3 | |
| Platform | 52.5 | Liquid chromatograph | A series | A-502 |
| | | Gas chromatograph | B series | B-502 |
| | | Mass spectrometer | C series | C-101 ... C-201 |
| | | Data processing and handling equipment | D series | DX-52 ... DX-82 |
| Derivative | 18.75 | Liquid chromatograph | A series | A-311, A-321, A-502X |
| | | Gas chromatograph | B series | B-22, B-32 |
| | | Mass spectrometer | C series | C-1/X, C-1/Z, C-101X |
| | | Data processing and handling equipment | D series | D-333, D-433 |
| Partnership | 10.0 | Medical/chemical diagnostic system | VMH | |

A representative example of PreQuip's new strategy for sequencing projects is its new mass spectrometer, or C series. Introduced into the development cycle in late-1989, the C-101 was the first platform conceived as a system built around the new modular design. Aimed at the middle to upper end of the market, it was a versatile, modular unit for the laboratory that incorporated many of the existing electromechanical features into the new software. The C-101 was scheduled to enter manufacturing prototyping in the third quarter of 1990.

PreQuip positioned the C-1/X, the first derivative of the C-101, for the industrial market. It had a rugged casing designed for extreme environments and fewer software features than the C-101. It entered the development process about the time the C-101 moved into manufacturing prototyping and was staffed initially with two designers whose activities on the C-101 were drawing to a close.

Very similar to the C-1/X was the C-1/Z, a unit designed for the European market; the C-1/X team was expanded to work on both the C-1/X and the C-1/Z. The C-1/Z had some unique software and a different display and packaging but the same modular design. PreQuip's marketing department scheduled the C-101 to be introduced about six months before the C-1/X and the C-1/Z, thus permitting the company to reach a number of markets quickly with new products.

To leverage accumulated knowledge and experience, senior management assigned the team that worked on the C-1/X and the C-1/Z to the C-201 project, the next-generation spectrometer scheduled to replace the C-101. It too was of a modular design but with more computer power and greater software functionality. The C-201 also incorporated a number of manufacturing process improvements gleaned from manufacturing the C-101.

To provide a smooth market transition from the C-101 to the C-201, management assigned the remainder of the C-101 team to develop the C-101X, a follow-on derivative project. The C-101X was positioned as an improvement over the C-101 to attract customers who were in the market for a low-end mass spectrometer but were unwilling to settle for the aging technology of the C-101. Just as important, the project was an ideal way to gather market data that could be used to develop the C-201.

PreQuip applied this same strategy across the other three product categories. Every other year it planned a new platform, followed by two or three derivatives spaced at appropriate intervals. Typically, when a team finished work on a platform, management assigned part of the team to derivative projects and part to other projects. A year or so later, a new team would form to work on the next platform, with some members having worked on the preceding generation and others not. This steady-stream sequencing strategy worked to improve the company's overall market position while encouraging knowledge transfer and more rapid, systematic resource development.

# An Alternative: Secondary Wave Planning

While the steady-stream approach served PreQuip well, companies in different industries might consider alternative strategies. For instance, a "secondary wave" strategy may be more appropriate for companies that, like Hill-Rom, have multiple

product lines, each with its own base platforms but with more time between suc-
ceeding generations of a particular platform.

The strategy works like this. A development team begins work on a next-generation platform. Once the company completes that project, the key people from the
team start work on another platform for a different product family. Management
leaves the recently introduced platform on the market for a couple of years with few
derivatives introduced. As that platform begins to age and competitors' newer platforms challenge it, the company refocuses development resources on a set of derivatives in order to strengthen and extend the viability of the product line's existing
platform. The wave of derivative projects extends the platform life and upgrades
product offerings, but it also provides experience and feedback to the people working on the product line and prepares them for the next-generation platform development. They receive feedback from the market on the previous platform, information
on competitors' platform offerings, and information on emerging market needs. Key
people then bring that information together to define the next platform and the cycle
begins again, built around a team, many of whose members have just completed the
wave of derivative products.

A variation on the secondary wave strategy, one used with considerable success
by Kodak, involves compressing the time between market introduction of major
platforms. Rather than going off to work on another product family's platform following one platform's introduction, the majority of the development team goes to
work immediately on a set of derivative products. This requires a more compressed
and careful assessment of the market's response to the just-introduced platform and
much shorter feedback loops regarding competitors' products. If done right, however, companies can build momentum and capture significant incremental market
share. Once the flurry of derivative products has passed, the team goes to work on
the next-generation platform project for the same product family.

Before 1987, Kodak conducted a series of advanced development projects to
explore alternative single-use 35mm cameras—a roll of film packaged in an inexpensive camera. Once used, the film is processed and the camera discarded or recycled. During 1987, a group of Kodak development engineers worked on the first
platform project which resulted in the market introduction and volume production of
the Fling 35mm camera in January 1988. (The product was later renamed the Funsaver.) As the platform neared completion, management reassigned the front-end
development staff to two derivative projects: the Stretch, a panoramic, double-wide
image version of the Fling, and the Weekend, a waterproof version.

By the end of 1988, Kodak had introduced both derivative cameras and was
shipping them in volume. True to the definition of a derivative, both the Stretch and
the Weekend took far fewer development resources and far less time than the Fling.
They also required less new tooling and process engineering since they leveraged the
existing automation and manufacturing process. The development team then went to
work on the next-generation platform product—a Funsaver with a built-in flash.

No matter which strategy a company uses to plan its platform-derivative mix—
steady stream or secondary wave—it must have well-defined platforms. The most
advanced companies further improve their competitive position by speeding up the

rate at which they introduce new platforms. Indeed, in a number of industries we've studied, the companies that introduced new platforms at the fastest rate were usually able to capture the greatest market share over time.

In the auto industry, for example, different companies follow quite different sequencing schedules, with markedly different results. According to data collected in the late 1980s, European car companies changed the platform for a given product, on average, every 12 years, U.S. companies every 8 years, and Japanese companies every 4 years. A number of factors explain the differences in platform development cycles—historical and cultural differences, longer development lead times, and differences in development productivity.[1]

In both Europe and the United States, the engineering hours and tooling costs of new products were much higher than in Japan. This translated into lower development costs for Japanese car makers, which allowed faster payback and shorter economic lives for all models. As a consequence, the Japanese could profitably conduct more projects and make more frequent and more extensive changes than both their European and U.S. competitors and thus were better positioned to satisfy customers' needs and capture market share.

# The Long-Term Goal: Building Critical Capabilities

Possibly the greatest value of an aggregate project plan over the long term is its ability to shape and build development capabilities, both individual and organizational. (See chart for eight steps of an aggregate project plan.) It provides a vehicle for training development engineers, marketers, and manufacturing people in the different skill sets needed by the company. For instance, some less-experienced engineers initially may be better suited to work on derivative projects, while others might have technical skills more suited for breakthrough projects. The aggregate project plan lets companies play to employees' strengths and broaden their careers and abilities over time.

Thinking about skill development in terms of the aggregate project plan is most important for developing competent team leaders. Take, for instance, an engineer

---

[1]Based on research by Kim B. Clark and Takahiro Fujimoto. See their article, "The Power of Product Integrity," *Harvard Business Review,* November–December 1990, p. 107.

## Eight Steps of an Aggregate Project Plan

1. Define project types as either breakthrough, platform, derivative, R&D, or partnered projects.
2. Identify existing projects and classify by project type.
3. Estimate the average time and resources needed for each project type based on past experience.
4. Identify existing resource capacity.
5. Determine the desired mix of projects.
6. Estimate the number of projects that existing resources can support.
7. Decide which specific projects to pursue.
8. Work to improve development capabilities.

with five years of experience moving to become a project leader. Management might assign her to lead a derivative project first. It is an ideal training ground because derivative projects are the best defined, the least complex, and usually the shortest in duration of all project types. After the project is completed successfully, she might get promoted to lead a larger derivative project and then a platform project. And if she distinguishes herself there and has the other required skills, she might be given the opportunity to work on a breakthrough project.

In addition to creating a formal career path within the sphere of development activities, companies should also focus on moving key engineers and other development participants between advanced research and commercial development. This is necessary to keep the transfer of technology fresh and creative and to reward engineers who keep their R&D efforts focused on commercial developments.

Honda is one company that delineates clearly between advanced research and product development—the two kinds of projects are managed and organized differently and are approached with very different expectations. Development engineers tend to have broader skills, while researchers' are usually more specialized. However, Honda encourages its engineers to move from one type of project to another if they demonstrate an idea that management believes may result in a commercially viable innovation. For example, Honda's new lean-burning engine, introduced in the 1992 Civic, began as an advanced research project headed by Hideyo Miyano. As the project moved from research to commercial development, Miyano moved too, playing the role of project champion throughout the entire development process.

Besides improving people's skills, the aggregate project plan can be used to identify weaknesses in capabilities, improve development processes, and incorporate new tools and techniques into the development environment. The project plan helps identify where companies need to make changes and how those changes are connected to product and process development.

As PreQuip developed an aggregate project plan, for example, it identified a number of gaps in its capabilities. In the case of the mass spectrometer, the demand for more software functionality meant PreQuip had to develop an expertise in software development. And with an emphasis on cost, modularity, and reliability, PreQuip also had to focus on improving its industrial design skills.

As part of its strategy to improve design skills, the company introduced a new computer-aided design system into its engineering department, using the aggregate project plan as its guide. Management knew that one of the platform project teams was particularly adept with computer applications, so it chose that project as the pilot for the new CAD system. Over the life of the project, the team's proficiency with the new system grew. When the project ended, management dispersed team members to other projects so they could train other engineers in using the new CAD system.

As PreQuip discovered, developing an aggregate project plan involves a relatively simple and straightforward procedure. But carrying it out—moving from a poorly managed collection of ad hoc projects to a robust set that matches and reinforces the business strategy—requires hard choices and discipline.

At all the companies we have studied, the difficulty of those choices makes imperative strong leadership and early involvement from senior management. Without management's active participation and direction, organizations find it next to impossible to kill or postpone projects and to resist the short-term pressures that drive them to spend most of their time and resources fighting fires.

Getting to an aggregate project plan is not easy, but working through the process is a crucial part of creating a sustainable development strategy. Indeed, while the specific plan is extremely important, the planning process itself is even more so. The plan will change as events unfold and managers make adjustments. But choosing the mix, determining the number of projects the resources can support, defining the sequence, and picking the right projects raise crucial questions about how product and process development ought to be linked to the company's competitive opportunities. Creating an aggregate project plan gives direction and clarity to the overall development effort and helps lay the foundation for outstanding performance.

READING

# 6 Commercializing Technology: Understanding User Needs

*Research managers in the 1990s are challenged to produce more relevant, potentially profitable knowledge and to produce it faster. This reading argues that imaginative understanding of user needs is a primary key to success. The chapter draws upon evidence from studies of new product development by Hewlett-Packard and others to substantiate that assertion and to explore its implications. A typology of technology commercialization situations is suggested, ranging from those in which technological potential aligns well with current markets to those requiring the creation of whole new businesses. Varying degrees of uncertainty and risk are associated with these commercialization situations and therefore each situation requires different tools for eliciting user needs.*

## Introduction

### Statistics

The statistics on technology commercialization in the United States are fairly grim. On average, as much as 46 percent of all resources devoted to product development and commercialization are spent on products that are canceled or fail to yield adequate financial returns.[1] A Booz Allen report estimates that for every 100 projects that enter development, 63 are canceled, 25 become commercial successes, and 12 are commercial failures.[2] However, some companies boast a success rate of 70 to 80 percent in new product launches; clearly it is possible to beat the averages through a superior product development process.[3]

---

This reading was prepared by Dorothy Leonard-Barton, Edith Wilson, and John Doyle.
Copyright © 1993 by the President and Fellows of Harvard College
Harvard Business School working paper 93-053.

[1]See Robert G. Cooper, *Winning at New Products* (Reading, Mass.: Addison-Wesley Publishing, 1986), p. 16.

[2]Booz Allen & Hamilton, "New Product Management for the 1980s," Booz Allen & Hamilton report, New York, 1982.

[3]Cooper, *Winning at New Products,* p. 17.

### Shorter Market Windows

The development process must be more efficient as well as more effective. One of the major forces driving an increasing focus on improving development practices is the ever shortening product life cycles in many industries.[4] Hewlett-Packard documented this tendency among their own products, as Figures 1 and 2 demonstrate. In Figure 1, each line on the graph represents the sales history over time for all HP products that were launched in the year where the line originates. Thus, for example, the cohort of products launched in 1979 brought in about $250 million worth of orders that first year, and increased to $600 million in 1980, which was their highest year; thereafter, sales very gradually dwindled off throughout the 1980s and into 1990. In contrast, the cohort of products introduced into the market in 1987 and in 1988 produced a very steep rise in sales the following year, but also dropped off dramatically thereafter.

Bringing their expertise in measuring waveforms to the analysis, Hewlett-Packard managers translated the data in Figure 1 into sales windows for Figure 2. In Figure 2, each point in the graph indicates the number of years that fall between two points: (1) the year that the sales of a particular cohort of products first reached one-half their eventual sales peak and (2) the year that sales again fell to that level after peaking. As the graph in Figure 2 indicates, that "sales window" has been narrowing over time as the curve describing the rise and fall of sales orders for a given cohort of products has become both shorter and steeper.

**FIGURE 1**

*Product sales history**

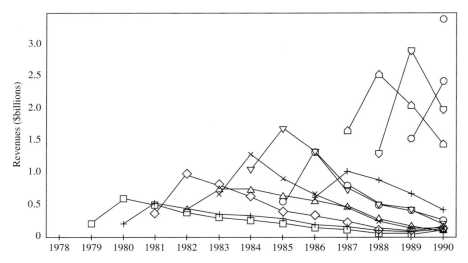

*Each line on the graph represents the sales history over time of all those products launched the year at which the line originates.

SOURCE: Courtesy of Hewlett-Packard.

---

[4]See Christoph-Friedrich von Braun, "The Acceleration Trap," *Sloan Management Review* 32, no. 1 (1990), pp. 49–50.

**FIGURE 2**

*Sales windows for product cohorts**

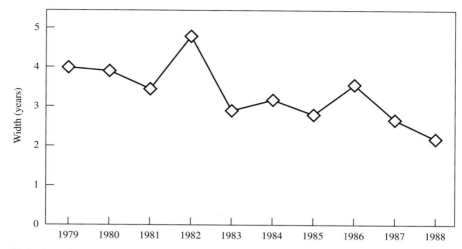

*Each point on the graph indicates the number of years between: (1) the year that sales of a particular cohort of products first reached one-half their subsequent sales peak, and (2) the year when sales again fell to that one-half peak level.
SOURCE: Courtesy of Hewlett-Packard.

### Time-Based Competition

Such shorter product life cycles have led companies to emphasize time as the basis of competition,[5] vying with each other to publicize bringing product to market in record time. However, in recounting such successes, managers sometimes conveniently overlook the reservoir of knowledge tapped for the final push to commercialization. That is, the publicized project time lines do not include the time spent developing support tools or conducting laboratory experiments. Nor are abortive prior attempts to build similar products acknowledged, although such projects may have yielded critical knowledge. For example, Digital Equipment brought their first engineering workstation, the 3100, to market in an unheard-of eight months. Besides departing from tradition to buy a MIPS company semiconductor chip, DEC also utilized UNIX-based computer-aided design tools available only in their research laboratories and mined graphical interface designs developed for prior, canceled projects. Developers candidly admitted they could not have made their frenetic dash to the market without the information garnered in these prior projects.[6] Similarly, Kodak brought out their Funsaver, single-use camera in only nine months

---

[5]For example, see Joseph Bower and Thomas M. Hout, "Last-Cycle Capability for Competitive Power," *Harvard Business Review* 66 (November–December 1988), pp. 110–18; Brian Dumaine, "How Managers Can Succeed through Speed," *Fortune* 119 (February 13, 1989), pp. 54–74; George Stalk, Jr., "Time—The Next Source of Competitive Advantage," *Harvard Business Review* 66 (July–August 1988), pp. 41–51.

[6]Kent Bowen, Kim Clark, Charles Holloway, and Steven Wheelwright, eds., *Visions and Capability: High Performance Product Development in the 1990s* (New York: Oxford University Press, forthcoming).

when they were challenged by Fuji. However, they were able to do so principally because an engineer had been working on the camera for two years with no official encouragement or even sanction.[7]

### Distinctive Competencies of the Corporation

As these examples suggest, speed to market often depends upon the development team's ability to pull from the knowledge warehouses of their corporation unutilized but technically developed concepts, designs, and tools. Such reservoirs of knowledge build up over time, shaped by the norms and values of the corporation, the skills of personnel, and the particular incentive systems in place; they can constitute unique technological competencies.[8] The notion that companies possess distinctive competencies that can be systematically deployed for competitive advantage has existed for decades.[9] However, it has received renewed attention lately because of disenchantment with strategies based on accumulating unrelated businesses, because of the recognition that Japanese competitors have exploited their capabilities very shrewdly,[10] and because successful new products often build on those competencies.[11]

### From Basic Research Toward Applied

At least superficially, this renewed interest in the accumulation of unique knowledge seems to conflict with another trend: the move by many corporations away from investments in central laboratories. Multiple arguments for this move are cited; principally, the inability of corporations to turn knowledge into practical applications and profit. Laboratories are therefore under increasing pressure to demonstrate their utility. Moreover, managers are increasingly aware that the distinctive competencies of a firm depend upon knowledge diffused throughout the organization—not just in the research laboratory. Some even denounce the idea of a special research facility. Chaparral Steel, one of the most successful United States–based minimills, is acknowledged as extremely innovative and has patented a number of inventions, yet they do not separate research and development from production.[12] Their CEO, an

---

[7]Ibid.

[8]Dorothy Leonard-Barton, "The Case for Integrative Innovation: An Expert System at Digital," *Sloan Management Review* 29, no. 1 (1987), pp. 7–19.

[9]Richard Rumelt, *Strategy, Structure, and Economic Performance* (Boston: Harvard Business School Press, 1974, 1986); Robert Hayes, "Strategic Planning—Forward in Reverse," *Harvard Business Review,* November–December 1985, pp. 111–19; Michael Hitt and R. Duane Ireland, "Corporate Distinctive Competence, Strategy, Industry, and Performance," *Strategic Management Journal* 6 (1985), pp. 273–93.

[10]C. K. Prahalad and Gary Hamel, "The Core Competence of the Corporation," *Harvard Business Review* 68 (May–June 1990), pp. 79–91.

[11]Modesto A. Maidique and Billie Jo Zirger, "The New Product Learning Cycle," *Research Policy* 14, no. 6 (December 1985), pp. 229–313.

[12]Dorothy Leonard-Barton, "The Factory as a Learning Laboratory," *Sloan Management Review* 34, no. 1 (1992), pp. 23–36.

outspoken former R&D director and a PhD metallurgist from MIT, maintains that research laboratories are idea graveyards—"not because there are no good ideas there, but because the good ideas are dying there all the time."[13]

### *Organization of the Chapter*

The research manager in the 1990s is thus challenged to produce more relevant, potentially profitable knowledge—faster. In this chapter, we focus on an activity critical to successfully meeting that challenge: understanding user needs. We first examine the evidence from Hewlett-Packard's investigation of their development practices and from academic studies that link imaginative understanding of user needs to successful technology commercialization. We next explore what it means to understand user needs, including the management dilemmas inherent in that process. The fourth section of the chapter proposes a typology of technology commercialization situations and associated mechanisms for understanding user needs when the products are developed in advance of the current market. These situations and sources range from aligning new products with a known market through traditional market research to creating whole new businesses through market intuition or applications identification.

## Hewlett-Packard's Product Definition Project

In the late 1980s, Hewlett-Packard (HP) faced a major shift in market focus from test and measurement to computers. This change necessitated a concomitant emphasis on increasing productivity and shareholder value. The corporation issued a challenge to each of the businesses: Halve the time to break-even (when cumulative product profits equal development costs) by simultaneously reducing product development time, increasing revenue streams, and controlling expenses. The challenge initiated much thought about the sources of overly long break-even times. Senior managers could identify a number of problems that recurred across multiple projects: "creeping elegance" of product definitions as enthusiasm for technical potential overwhelmed simplicity, "poor positioning because of poor feature sets," "user needs being incompletely understood," "competitive knowledge being inadequate," and "falling short of targeted performance." All such problems pointed, these managers believed, to an underlying weakness in the product definition phase of new product development. Product definitions were unstable during the course of the development projects, wasting resources and time when they shifted. Corporate engineering at HP therefore decided to develop a product definition process that would address these issues (see Figure 3).

---

[13]Cited in Alan Kantrow, "Wide-open Management at Chaparral Steel: An Interview with Gordon E. Forward," *Harvard Business Review* 29, no. 1 (1987), pp. 7–19.

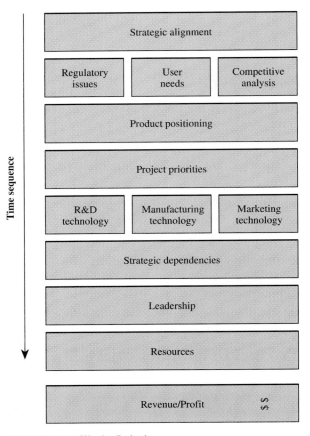

SOURCE: Courtesy of Hewlett-Packard.

Research into studies of new product development quickly revealed that problems with product definition were endemic to development.[14] One study particularly intrigued the Hewlett-Packard staffers. The University of Sussex had conducted a study to determine the factors leading to marketplace success of new products. Project SAPPHO[15] identified 29 product pairs in the first phase of their study, and 43 in a second phase; each pair consisted of one product that succeeded in the marketplace and one that did not. The key findings of the Project SAPPHO team were that:

1. Successful innovators have a much better understanding of user needs.
2. Successful innovators pay more attention to marketing and publicity.

---

[14]Ashok Gupta and David Wilemon, "Accelerating the Development of Technology-based New Products," *California Management Review,* Winter 1990, pp. 24–44; Cooper, *Winning at New Products;* Roy Rothwell et al., "SAPPHO Updated—Project SAPPHO Phase II," *Research Policy* 3 (1974), pp. 258–91.

[15]"Project SAPPHO—A Comparative Study of Success and Failure in Industrial Innovation," report on Project SAPPHO by the Science Policy Research Unit, University of Sussex, Brighton (London: Centre for the Study of Industrial Innovation, 1974).

**FIGURE 4**

*Product definitions in unsuccessful projects*

| | Project Number | | | | | | Percent Failing |
|---|---|---|---|---|---|---|---|
| Unsuccessful Products | 180 | 150 | 120 | 110 | 100 | 210 | |
| Users' needs understanding | O | X | O | O | O | X | 66.7 |
| Strategic alignment and charter consistency | X | O | O | X | O | X | 66.7 |
| Competitive analysis | O | O | X | X | O | X | 50 |
| Product positioning | O | O | X | O | X | X | 50 |
| Technical risk assessment | X | O | X | O | X | O | 50 |
| Priority decision criteria list | X | X | X | O | O | O | 50 |
| Regulation compliance | O | O | X | X | X | X | 33.3 |
| Product channel issues | O | O | X | X | X | X | 33.3 |
| Project endorsement by upper management | X | X | O | X | X | X | 16.7 |
| Total organizational support | X | X | O | X | X | X | 16.7 |

Legend:

X = Successfully completed.

O = Inadequately completed.

SOURCE: Courtesy of Hewlett-Packard.

3. Successful innovators perform their development work more efficiently than failed ones, but not necessarily more quickly.

4. Successful innovators use outside technology and scientific advice, not necessarily in general, but in the specific area targeted.

5. In successful development projects, the responsible individuals are usually more senior, with greater authority than their counterparts on failed projects.

Since the probability that these five factors distinguished between successful and unsuccessful projects by chance was less than 0.1 percent, the Project SAPPHO authors assert that the five factors significantly differentiate project success from failure. The SAPPHO project offered hope that a systematic investigation of successes and failures could enable Hewlett-Packard to construct a roadmap for better product definition. Therefore, in 1989, one of the authors, Edith Wilson, undertook case studies of 19 successful and unsuccessful projects in 9 of HP's 14 business groups. All the projects had been completed and the products introduced to the marketplace. Information was gathered through a combination of interviews and questionnaires directed toward engineers, middle-level managers, managers from the functions of R&D, marketing and manufacturing, and the division's general manager. Three major questions were asked: (1) What steps were taken to develop the product definition? (2) In hindsight, what went right and what wrong in the development and use of the product definition? (3) How was the product definition used during the development phase?

From the answers to these questions, Wilson documented the process used by successful project teams to define their products (Figure 4) and noted what differentiated the practices of successful teams from unsuccessful ones (Figure 5). Team performance

**FIGURE 5**

*Product definition
in successful
projects*

| Successful Products | Project Number | | | | | |
|---|---|---|---|---|---|---|
| | *190* | *170* | *160* | *140* | *130* | *200* |
| Users' needs understanding | X | X | X | X | X | X |
| Strategic alignment and charter consistency | X | O | X | X | X | X |
| Competitive analysis | X | X | X | X | X | X |
| Product positioning | X | X | X | X | X | X |
| Technical risk assessment | X | X | X | X | X | X |
| Priority decision criteria list | X | X | X | X | X | X |
| Regulation compliance | X | X | X | X | X | X |
| Product channel issues | X | X | X | X | X | X |
| Project endorsement by upper management | X | X | X | X | X | X |
| Total organizational support | X | X | X | X | X | X |

Legend:
X = Successfully completed.
O = Inadequately completed.
SOURCE: Courtesy of Hewlett-Packard.

on 11 product definition factors appeared to account for the difference.[16] (See Table 1.) The primary cause of difficulties in the marketplace identified in both the original study and the follow-up research conducted by Bacon, Beckman, Mowery, and Wilson in other companies was a failure to understand user needs.[17] This failure was not always, or even usually, attributable to a lack of effort. Some teams spent months and millions of dollars in a vain attempt to answer some fundamental questions about their customers. They faced problems in identifying the target user, the actual buyer who controlled the financial decision, and other stakeholders who affected the buying decision. The less-successful teams were unable to determine exactly what problems had to be solved to satisfy each link in the set of customers, from the factory to the end users. They could not translate user needs into product.

# Understanding User Needs

## Research on Product Success and Failure

The important elements of the process identified in the Hewlett-Packard study (and the SAPPHO project that inspired it) have also been remarked by a number of other new product development studies. A Conference Board study found inadequate market analysis most commonly cited as a cause of new product failure.[18] In a number of

---

[16]Only 10 factors were originally identified. The 11th was added in a follow-up study funded by the Sloan Foundation at five other companies (IBM, GE, GM-Delco, Motorola, and Xerox).

[17]Glenn Bacon, Sara Beckman, David Mowery, and Edith Wilson, "Managing Product Definition in High-Technology Industries: A Pilot Study," in press.

[18]D. S. Hopkins and E. L. Bailey, "New Product Pressures," *Conference Board Record* 8 (1971), pp. 16–24.

**TABLE 1   Factors in New Product Development**

*Factors*

| | |
|---|---|
| 1. Strategic alignment | How does the project contribute to the business unit's strategic objectives? |
| 2. Users' and customer needs | Is there a specific market segment targeted for the product? Can the team articulate the problems that the product must solve for it to be successful? |
| 3. Compliance issues | Has the team identified all the relevant compliance issues that the product must adhere to, including the manufacturing and recycling issues? |
| 4. Competitive analysis | Has the team identified the product's top three competitors (by market share) and thoroughly identified what their business and product strengths and weaknesses will be at the time of market release? |
| 5. Product positioning | Is the product defined to solve your customers' problems better than the competitors can and at greater value to the customers? |
| 6. Project priorities | What is the hierarchy of priorities for the project? Prioritize cost, date of market release, and features to identify what you would trade off for what. |
| 7. Risk management | Is the team taking the appropriate level of risk in R&D, marketing, and manufacturing? |
| 8. Market channels | Will the market channel required to be successful in this business be established by the time of market release? |
| 9. Management leadership | Does upper management know about this project, support the efforts, and provide the team guidance in making decisions? |
| 10. Resource availability | Do you have the staffing and funding needed to meet the goals of the project within the allotted amount of time? |
| 11. Dependency management | Are all internal and external strategic dependencies established and functioning well enough to assure yourselves that there will be no integration or schedule problems? |

studies conducted over the past two decades, Robert Cooper and his colleagues have identified inadequate attention to market as a primary factor leading to failure.[19] In a study of 235 new product development projects, William Souder similarly noted that a primary condition for technical success was the clarity of problem definition, which he equates with clarity of understanding user requirements.[20]

There is, therefore, a very strong consensus that understanding user needs is one of the key factors leading to commercialization success. However, opinions vary widely as to how that understanding may be achieved. In their study of 252 product development projects in 123 firms, Robert Cooper and Elko Kleinschmidt found that preliminary market assessments were conducted in the successful product development projects.[21] However, formal market studies, done in only a quarter of the projects, were usually rated as "poorly handled." Moreover, the studies tended to take the form of reactive competitive comparisons in over a fourth of those projects.

---

[19]Robert G. Cooper, "Why Industrial New Products Fail," *Industrial Marketing Management* 4 (1975), pp. 315–26; R. Canlantone and Robert G. Cooper, "A Discriminant Model for Identifying Scenarios of Industrial New Product Failure," *Journal of the Academy of Marketing Science* 7 (1979), pp. 163–83; Robert G. Cooper and Elko J. Kleinschmidt, "An Investigation into the New Product Process: Steps, Deficiencies, and Impact," *Journal of Product Innovation Management* 3 (1986), pp. 71–85; and Cooper, *Winning at New Products.*

[20]William Souder, *Managing New Product Innovations* (Lexington, Mass.: Lexington Books, 1987, p. 68).

[21]Cooper and Kleinschmidt, "An Investigation into the New Product Process."

There were almost no concept tests, that is, studying customer reactions to a proposed new product in concept form. Less than a fifth of the project teams studied what customers actually wanted or needed in order to generate product specifications. Moreover, there was at least as much detailed market research done for the failed projects as for the successful ones. Therefore, merely increasing emphasis on market research may not lead to better understanding of user needs and a higher probability of product success.

There are at least three major barriers to successfully introducing market-derived information into a new product development project: corporate core rigidities, the tyranny of the current market, and user myopia.

### Core Rigidities

As suggested above, the core competencies of a firm often aid the commercialization of technologies. However, the very same core technical capabilities that have made a company great, can also constitute core rigidities and hinder new product development.[22] New product ideas built on familiar technologies, using traditional, comfortable sources of information are more easily commercialized. In fact, synergy with the firm's capabilities (technological resources and skills) has been identified as one of the factors "fundamental" to new product success.[23] However, new product ideas built on unfamiliar technologies are more likely to be seen as "illegitimate"[24] and therefore see a more difficult birthing. In recognition of that fact, such ventures are often isolated from the rest of the organization.[25]

The core capabilities of a firm can constitute a core rigidity to technology commercialization in very subtle ways. Well-entrenched routines and ingrained culture favor certain technologies and information sources. In "technology-driven" companies, information about user needs often goes unheeded unless it comes from a source with status in the organization. The same characteristics and practices that constantly reinforce the ability of engineers to influence product design simultaneously undermine the ability of marketing (or manufacturing) people on the team to be heard.

Companies such as Kodak, Digital Equipment, and Hewlett-Packard owed their original marketplace success to technological innovation, and the primary sources of that innovation were the technologists. In such companies, the product design intuition of founders and other technical gurus early in corporate history is legendary. Some researchers in Hewlett-Packard Laboratories can still recall their skepticism

---

[22]Leonard-Barton, "The Factory as a Learning Experience."

[23]Cooper and Kleinschmidt, "An Investigation into the New Product Process"; also see Robert G. Cooper and Elko J. Kleinschmidt, "New Product Success Factors: A Comparison of 'Kills' versus Successes and Failures," *R&D Management* 20, no. 1 (1990), pp. 47–63; and Souder, *Managing New Product Innovations.*

[24]Deborah Dougherty and Trudy Heller, "The Illegitimacy of Successful Product Innovation in Established Firms," *Organization Science,* in press.

[25]Rosabeth Moss Kanter, "When a Thousand Flowers Bloom: Structural Collective, and Social Conditions for Innovation in Organizations," in *Research in Organizational Behavior,* vol. 10, ed. Barry M. Staw and L. L. Cummings (Greenwich, Conn.: JAI Press, 1988).

that the handheld calculator vigorously championed by Hewlett could ever function better than their slide rules; Gordon Bell at Digital Equipment is credited with the "one architecture" strategy that made their VAX line of minicomputers so popular. The success of such products came from anticipating what the market would buy, and the engineering function dominated.

Over time, these companies grew a strong technological capability that included not only skilled engineers but proprietary physical equipment—simulation systems, process equipment—that embodied years of accumulated, specialized knowledge. Hiring practices, incentive systems, and the values and norms of the company strengthened that capability by enabling the corporation to attract and hold the best technical minds—in certain fields. For instance, skilled chemical engineers migrated to Kodak, where they could aspire to the pinnacle of success represented by the top 5 percent of engineers who became film designers. Electrical and mechanical engineers headed for Digital or Hewlett-Packard. In contrast, for years (some would say still), software engineers entered any of these companies at a disadvantage, knowing their profession was not highly regarded. And in all of these companies, marketing people entered the company at their own peril. Their salaries, their status, their ability to influence key product design decisions were all subordinate to researchers and design engineers. Marketing skills were not part of the original distinctive competencies of these firms.

An initial lack of information from the market often causes unnecessary delays when it is uncovered and assimilated late in the project. For instance, during the design of the Deskjet printer at Hewlett-Packard, marketers tested early prototypes in shopping malls to determine user response. They returned from their studies with a list of 21 changes they believed essential to the success of the product; the engineers accepted 5. Unwilling to give up, the marketers persuaded the engineers to join them in the mall tests. After hearing the same feedback from the lips of the users that they had previously rejected, the product designers returned to their benches and incorporated the other 16 requested changes. Similarly at DEC, early in the development of a local area network switch, marketing personnel suggested a number of features that were rejected by engineers as unnecessary. Just one month before expected release of the product, a respected senior engineer visited several customers and discovered the rejected features were absolutely essential. The schedule was slipped several months to allow the design to be retrofitted. In both these cases, information about user needs was available, but the marketing people lacked the experience and status to influence product design. As a consequence, the product definition was altered late in the development process and the products reached the market later than necessary.[26]

### The Tyranny of Current Markets

On the other hand, listening too closely to current markets can also constitute a barrier to commercializing technology. Responding to a flood of marketplace demands for improvement along current product performance curves can leave too

---

[26]Dorothy Leonard-Barton, "Core Capabililties and Core Rigidities: A Paradox in Managing New Product Development," *Strategic Management Journal* 13 (1992), pp. 111–25.

few resources to assess the possibility that those curves are being fundamentally altered by new technologies. Therefore, traditional sources of market information and influence on new product development can constitute as substantial a core rigidity for a company as the traditional dominance of the engineering function or proprietary technological knowledge bases. Clayton Christensen observed this type of core rigidity in an extensive study of the computer disk drive industry.[27] He researched four architectural transitions represented by the reduction in disk diameter from 14 to 8, 5.25, 3.5 and 2.5 inches. Each reduction entailed not only "shrinking" individual components, but rearchitecting the relationships of components within the system.

Noting the tendency for these architectural changes to be introduced by new firms entering the market rather than by established firms, Christensen found a primary reason to be the disinterest of existing firms' customers in the smaller disks.

> The sluggishness or failure of established disk drive manufacturers faced with architectural change seems rooted . . . in the inability of their marketing and administrative organizations to find customers who valued the attributes of the new-architecture drives . . . not . . . because their architecture-related engineering knowledge was rendered obsolete. . . . Rather, the changes in product architecture seem to have rendered obsolete the established firms' knowledge of market.[28]

In the very few cases in which the new technological architectures did appeal to a firm's current customers, existing rather than entrant firms dominated. For example, Conner Corporation was able to make a "very smooth transition into 2.5-inch drives [from 3.5 inch]" because the smaller disks appealed to current customers.[29] The situation studied by Christensen exemplifies a common problem in many companies: "Outbound" marketing efforts (i.e., selling) tend to supersede "inbound" marketing efforts (i.e., market research and development). The impact on the bottom line of the outbound selling is much more visible and immediate than that of inbound. Managers very rationally emphasize those activities for which they are most directly rewarded. Moreover, more training is devoted to outbound promotion and selling activities, both in academia and within corporations, than is devoted to gathering and translating market information into feasible commercialization steps.

### Users' Natural Myopia

As the example of the computer disk industry suggests, the greatest challenges to understanding user needs are to select the right users as informants and to recognize when their suggestions may limit product design. Users are often myopic in a number of logical and natural ways. First, they see the potential to apply technology within their own bounded context and will naturally influence the design of the new

[27]Clayton Christensen, "The Innovator's Challenge: Understanding the Influence of Market Environment on Processes of Technology Development in the Rigid Disk Drive Industry," unpublished PhD thesis, Harvard Business School, 1992.
[28]Ibid., pp. 114–15.
[29]Ibid., p. 150.

product or process to meet needs within that particular environment. Software designers habitually face this problem. For example, a vendor designing a purchasing module for a manufacturing resource planning (MRPII) system to order and monitor purchased parts for a multiplant corporation solicited the help of users in a certain plant in the Northeast, assuming it was representative of all corporate plants. The vendor spotted the flaw in this assumption only after managers of shipping docks in a dozen other plants angrily reported being so buried every four months with thousands of long-lead-time purchased parts that they had to hire extra help. At the plant that served as the model of usage, only 15 percent of the parts ordered were long-lead-time items; a regularly scheduled delivery point of every four months was adequate. For all the other plants in the system, such parts represented over 40 percent of their purchased parts; they required that the flow be spaced out over time.[30]

Second, users are not all equally proximate to the latest trends in usage patterns. Designers of a system to monitor the progress of work-in-process inventory within a factory worked hard to make sure their software could accommodate the variety and volume of components moving down the line. Within weeks of installation, their system was obsoleted because the factory moved to a just-in-time system for which any buildup of inventory was anathema. When the factory workers pared the stream of components down to a thin, steady flow, they no longer needed a complex system to monitor voluminous work-in-process; a simple visual system sufficed.[31]

Finally, and most difficult, users cannot see their world through the eyes of the technologist and therefore cannot know what solutions, functions, enhanced features, or capabilities a technology may offer. Technology always offers more possibilities than can be recognized and commercialized. Examples range from establishing paternity through DNA tests of blood samples (not the most obvious application of the discovery of DNA) to holographic greeting cards (not the most profound application of holography). Therefore, technologists often cannot simply ask users what they want. However, ignoring user needs is clearly not the answer. Rather, developers need a whole range of identification, listening, and translation skills to translate user needs into commercialization opportunities. We turn now to a discussion of a proposed typology of technology commercialization situations.

## Design in Advance of the Market: From Alignment to Creation

Technology commercialization situations range from those in which technological potential aligns well with current markets (far left in Figure 6) to those which require the creation of new markets—sometimes even the creation of whole new businesses, with new infrastructure, standards, procedures (far right in Figure 6). In

---

[30]Dorothy Leonard-Barton, "Implementing New Production Technologies: Exercises in Corporate Learning," in *Managing Complexity in High Technology Industries: Systems and People,* ed. Mary Von Glinow and Susan Mohrman (New York: Oxford University Press, 1989).

[31]Dorothy Leonard-Barton and Deepak Sinha, "Dependency, Involvement, and User Satisfaction: The Case of Internal Software Development," Harvard Business School Working Paper 91-008, 1990.

**FIGURE 6**

*Typology of
technology
commercialization
situations*

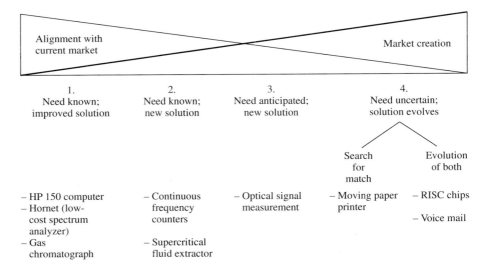

| 1. Need known; improved solution | 2. Need known; new solution | 3. Need anticipated; new solution | 4. Need uncertain; solution evolves |
|---|---|---|---|

Search for match    Evolution of both

| – HP 150 computer<br>– Hornet (low-cost spectrum analyzer)<br>– Gas chromatograph | – Continuous frequency counters<br>– Supercritical fluid extractor | – Optical signal measurement | – Moving paper printer | – RISC chips<br><br>– Voice mail |

those situations at the left, product definition and development follow quite well known paths; in contrast, in those situations represented by the far right side of Figure 6, commercialization is realized only through a combination of trial, perseverance, and serendipity. In the following pages, we describe each of the four commercialization situations and illustrate them with examples, many from Hewlett-Packard's experience. Thereafter, we will discuss some of the commercialization risks associated with designing in advance of the market and then briefly describe some methods of ascertaining user needs all along the spectrum from alignment with current markets to creation of new markets.

## An Improved Solution for a Known Need

Competition or explicit customer demands often drive technological improvements along known performance parameters for current products. In such cases, with or without extensive market research, developers often know that lower costs, more features, or better quality are likely to win in the marketplace. HP's Signal Analysis Division, which produces spectrum analysis devices used for testing and analyzing radio-frequency and microwave signals, had traditionally competed on product quality and performance rather than price. However, in the mid-1980s, the commercial market expanded, particularly at the low end, where Japanese offerings threatened HP products. Although a low cost spectrum analyzer existed in the laboratory (the Hornet), there was little interest in commercializing it until an R&D manager returned from a plant visit with a customer in Italy who pointed out that the Japanese had produced a low cost product with features comparable to HP's high-priced spectrum analyzer. Intent on bringing the Hornet to market within 18 months, the team nonetheless took time to conduct a totally unprecedented price study. Moreover, marketing personnel accompanied engineers on customer visits to assess user needs, although R&D maintained responsibility for product definition. The Hornet met both cost and schedule goals and was a marketplace success.

Less successful was the Hewlett-Packard 150, an early attempt to produce a personal computer. The day after HP introduced the HP120, a terminal for use with the HP3000 minicomputer, IBM introduced its first PC. HP responded by changing the project charter for the HP150, a follow-on to the 120. Rather than simply being a terminal, the 150 was now expected to have enough computing power to stand alone and be capable of supporting MS-DOS, the operation system for the IBM PC. One of the problems faced by the development team was that the marketing plan for the HP150 as a terminal for the HP3000 was not altered to reflect the very different set of users now targeted. Therefore, the product development team continued to optimize on the performance characteristics suitable for the customers originally envisioned. As a terminal, the HP150 was quite successful. However, as a personal computer, it was never profitable.[32]

In both of these cases, the developers established user needs in reactive mode. That is, the competition defined the meaningful parameters, on which the development team then attempted to achieve parity if not superiority. There were clear benchmarks against which to design. The challenge lay in identifying the right set of users to interview. Once correctly identified, those users could readily communicate their needs so as to guide design trade-offs.

A current need in the marketplace can be obvious to developers, even in the absence of direct competition or customer demand, just from knowing current cost or functionality barriers to usage. In such cases, developers proactively decide to "delight" their customers with leaps in performance that no competitors have attempted and no users directly requested. The challenges of pushing beyond current technical barriers can be very significant. In the early 1980s, HP was market leader in gas chromatographs, which was an old, mature market. In about 1983, managers in the analytical business decided on a bold target: a chromatograph with one-third the components of the current model and three times the quality—for one-third the price. Such a product was not just a logical enhancement of the current chromatograph. The design required a tremendous leap in performance. In fact, it "wasn't even on the same price/performance curve," yet the developers believed strongly that the customers would want it.[33] Customer forums and site visits to observe user practices helped developers identify critical features. As expected, the product was highly successful, not only in its traditional market, but also in new application areas because of its lower cost.

### New Solution to a Known Need

Users may have a need for which they would be incapable of imagining a solution without knowing about a particular technological advance. They could not ask for the solution because they do not know the technological potential exists.

---

[32]Bowen et al., *Visions and Capability.*

[33]Quotes from interview with Dr. James Serum, group R&D manager, Analytic Group, Hewlett-Packard, November 1992.

For instance, HP researchers took the initiative to develop a supercritical fluid extractor for the environmental testing market, knowing that current techniques for analyzing toxic residues in soils involved dangerous solvents and unpleasant, labor-intensive techniques such as boiling the soil and reconcentrating it to analyze the residue. By passing carbon dioxide in a supercritical, near-liquid state through the soil, they could extract the pesticides from the dirt. Once the carbon dioxide was released from the pressure that rendered it supercritical, it returned to an easily vented gaseous state, leaving behind the extracted organic sample. The extractor will connect to other HP analytical instruments and its use will improve productivity significantly. Only researchers aware of the laboratory experimentation conducted under supercritical conditions could have imagined this application. After conducting market research to establish uses of the technique, the team built a prototype and had lead customers run their samples through it. Currently used in Environmental Protection Agency laboratories, the extractor is not as high volume and profitable as the gas chromatograph. However, it solved an array of real customer problems.

The HP continuous frequency counter first introduced in 1986 originated in a somewhat similar situation. Traditional frequency counters for monitoring various types of waves gradually became outdated as transmitters generating frequencies increased in accuracy. One HP engineer envisioned a counter analogous to an oscilloscope that could read frequencies continuously as a series of digits which could then be plotted on an X/Y display and could track drift in frequency signals. However, even this analogy did not help communicate with prospective users, who responded very unenthusiastically when marketing described the new concept. Convinced that a current (if nonobvious) need did in fact exist, the engineers constructed a functional prototype which they persuaded marketing to take to the field. Somewhat to everyone's amazement, the prototype was seized by users with such enthusiasm that marketing sometimes had a hard time retrieving the models. Users saw immediate applications—including many the engineers had not anticipated. One customer wanted to hook the counter up to his radar system to check its functioning. The product became a great commercial success, representing approximately 15 percent of the division's sales. Most important to HP, this product halted the decline of a product line and reinvigorated it.

### A New Solution to an Anticipated Need

If meeting nonobvious but current user needs is a challenge, peering into the future to identify as yet unarticulated future needs of a given market is even harder. By extrapolating societal, technological, environmental, economic, or political trends, developers attempt to foresee what users will need in the future when those trends mature. To someone who understands both industry and societal trends, the needs themselves may be fairly obvious. However, timing is often extremely unclear. When will there be enough users or complementary technology or adequate infrastructure to justify development? Moreover, of course, the trends interact. For instance, society's demand for faster, more proximate means of communication interacts with the technological trends that are driving computers to become commodities and communications to become wireless.

Researchers at HP track a number of trends that may be harbingers of future markets. Long before fiber optics was a reality, or optical signaling technologies were on the market, Hewlett-Packard was designing optical signal measurement equipment to be ready when their customers needed it.

Many companies are tracking environmental trends which have reemerged in the 1990s as a likely potent influence on new product design. For instance, legislation in Europe mandating that companies accept back their products for recycling may foretell similar moves in U.S. markets. Yet currently, the supply of recycled materials outstrips both our capacity to process them and also the demand for their reuse. Industry is thus caught in a catch-22: Companies cannot recycle materials economically until they can process them on a large scale and consumers do not want to buy recycled goods because they are still too expensive. Companies have multiple chores to create a market for recycled materials: Create collection processes, create new process technologies to accommodate recycled materials, and stimulate demand for products designed from recycled materials.

### *An Evolving Solution to an Uncertain Need*

At times, technologists run far ahead of consumers by developing an application for which they initially identify the wrong market. When HP Laboratories first recognized their ability to develop a printer that moved not only the pen across a plotter, but also the paper underneath in the other direction, they were enthusiastic. The opportunity for small-scale, high-resolution printers seemed obvious to them. However, they were dismayed to find no interest from the division producing large printers. Only when they were able to engage the interest of the medical division for use in plotting electrocardiographs was a market identified. That technology has, however, been very successful. It repaid the relatively modest costs of its development many times over when it was incorporated into HP's pen plotters.

Such cases are often called—disparagingly—"technology push," because the technical possibility preceded any known user need. Laboratories and the basements of home inventors are full of failed solutions to unknown problems. However, the negative connotation of the phrase is misleading in two ways. First, many products on the market satisfy needs no user had felt or expressed and that embody no technology. The notorious pet rock, sold in the 1970s, perhaps best exemplifies "sellers push" product development. Second, of course, many extremely well known inventions initially had no user demand, although many people today would insist they need them—such as xerography or Post-it pads. Sometimes need and solution evolve together. For example, two widely used technologies that started life in quite different forms at IBM were shaped by trial and error and through the brutal help of internal corporate selection processes and the marketplace. The voice mail systems that are so ubiquitous today originated at IBM when a remote dictation system was designed so that traveling managers could relay their correspondence back over telephone lines to a pool of specially skilled typists in a manuscript center. The so-called Advanced Dictation System was not used as expected. Both managers and documentation preparation people disliked it. However, people started sending messages back to their secretaries using the system, which was consequently retitled the Audio Distribution System. In the very early 1970s, this system became a Speech Filing System—the prototype of current voice mail.[34]

The Reduced Instruction Set Chip (RISC) so widely used today similarly started life in a form very different from today's. In the early 1970s, when the eventual intersection of telephones and computers was foreseen, researchers at IBM saw a clear need to apply digital computing technology to digital switching for telephones. Since such switches have extremely long lives, the computer software that underlay their design needed to be structured to be able to evolve. Moreover, the hardware needed to be scalable. The computer architecture invented to meet this need was not used for this original purpose because of IBM business decisions, but was generalized and extended for less-specialized uses. It became the basis in the mid-1970s for what is known today as RISC architecture. Thus, a project originally aimed at helping IBM get into the telephony business was the origin for the architecture that evolved into RISC.[35]

At this right side of the spectrum pictured in Figure 6 is a strong element of serendipity. Technological potential and market need have to coincide in both time and place for the necessary synergy to occur.

## Challenges in Designing in Advance of the Market

The challenges in commercialization become increasingly more acute from left to right in Figure 6, that is, from alignment with current markets to the definition and creation of totally new markets (see Figure 7).

**FIGURE 7**

*Challenges of designing in advance of the market*

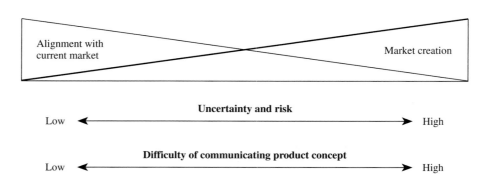

[34]Interview with Dr. Joel Birnbaum, vice president and director, Hewlett-Packard Laboratories, November 1992.
[35]Ibid.

## Uncertainty and Risk

Even alignment situations are not without risk. There is always the possibility that the competition will design a better product or get to market faster. Another risk is that the nature of the market segment will change. When HP first sold test and measurement equipment, each piece was a stand-alone "box," with independent functionality. However, today's customers want an integrated, total measurement system. Voltmeters or spectrum analyzers are regarded as components in total testing systems. As this example illustrates, alignment with a current market is far from a static process; the target is continually moving. However, commercialization of technology when no known market exists is obviously riskier and more costly. The fact that many corporations are scaling back on basic research suggests that they do not believe they can afford this type of wandering toward markets. The question then emerges: Who will fund the discovery process and where will it take place? The usual answers—universities, small companies, and national laboratories—all are somewhat facile. However, it is beyond the scope of this chapter to explore that issue.

## Communicating Product Concept

Communication of the product concept and elicitation of user reactions become progressively difficult and potentially more expensive as the commercialization situation departs from market alignment and moves toward market creation. Therefore, much more attention and many more resources must be invested in creatively interacting with potential users.

HP researchers could ask their current customers about a vastly cheaper and better gas chromatograph (Situation 1) because customers had a very clear concept of this instrument—what it looks like, what it does, and the like. A simple description of the proposed new chromatograph, combined with a two-dimensional sketch, conveyed enough information to the users, who could extrapolate mentally to a three-dimensional, functioning instrument.

However, customers could not imagine the continuous frequency counter (Situation 2) from mere description. Even analogy with a familiar tool (the voltage oscilloscope) was not enough. A two-dimensional sketch would not help, because it was the new functionality that they failed to grasp—not the physical shape of the invention. Only when they saw a three-dimensional, fully functioning prototype did they grasp the instrument's potential to meet their current needs.

Obviously, when the needs are not yet even felt, as in Situation 3, users may have an even more difficult time thinking ahead to assess whether they will want the technology and, if so, in what form. Like the technologists, they are uncertain about when and if necessary supporting infrastructure may be developed and they are often unsure how much they would pay for certain future products. General Electric Plastics (GEP) faces such a situation in stimulating interest in recycled plastics. GEP built a "house of the future" in Pittsfield, Massachusetts, using recycled plastics in such applications as countertops and faux slate shingles on the roof. Although the investment is considerable, such three-dimensional, functioning demonstrations of technologies in situ, as they would actually be used, are necessary to help customers understand the commercial potential. GEP has also worked on designing products for disassembly so that the component parts can be easily separated at the end of the product life in preparation for recycling. For example, in a joint venture with the design house Fitch RichardsonSmith, GEP designed an electric tea kettle explicitly for disassembly.[36]

In Situation 4, the problem is not only communicating a potential product concept, but also eliciting enough information through demonstration and use of a functioning prototype for developers to identify users and adapt their proposed solution to need. Obviously, this is a very-high-cost effort in terms of both time and money. Increasingly, technological tools such as virtual reality software may help developers present alternative potential futures without actually building products. Currently, prospective clients can walk through simulated buildings of the future; advanced computer-aided design tools allow viewers to revolve a three-dimensional object on the screen and view it from different perspectives; stereolithography enables immediate transformation of design specifications into three-dimensional (but, of course, nonfunctioning) solid models. However, none of these tools yet allow prospective users to actually experience the object being developed. Moreover, it is to everyone's benefit to develop better methods for anticipating market need rather than matching solution to need after the fact.

### Tools and Mechanisms for Understanding User Needs

When the product is well aligned with current markets, traditional market research can help track customers' needs quite well, for the needs are clear, current, and communicable. At the opposite end of the spectrum, when the uncertainty of investing in technology for an unknown market is so great, market intuition and serendipity play a large role, and it is not clear the process can be as systematized and structured. Situations 2 and 3, falling in the middle of Figures 6 and 7, are candidates for considerably more managerial attention. Here lie largely unexplored opportunities to considerably improve the process of technology commercialization through empathic design.[37]

*Empathic design,* as the term implies, means understanding user needs through empathy with the user world rather than from user articulation of needs. The significance of empathic design is lower at the two extremes of the technology commercialization situations—but still important to understand (see Figure 8). Even when the product being designed is aligned with current markets and the users are well known (far left of Figure 8), there are desirable product attributes that the user is often unable to articulate—or even imagine. Users are often totally unaware of their

---

[36]See Karen Freeze and Dorothy Leonard-Barton, *GE Plastics: Selecting a Partner* (Boston, Mass.: Design Management Institute, 1991).

[37]Dorothy Leonard-Barton, "Inanimate Integrators: A Block of Wood Speaks," *Design Management Journal* 2, no. 3 (1992), pp. 61–67.

**FIGURE 8**

*Tools and mechanisms for understanding user needs*

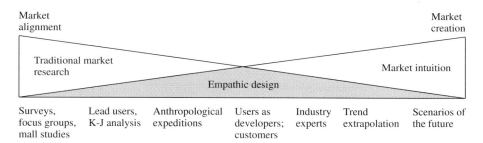

own psychological and cultural responses to symbols and forms and are unable to describe what they want until they see it. Therefore, so-called intangibles such as shape, appearance, and feel are usually determined by expert designers through empathic design. At the market creation end of the spectrum (far right of Figure 8), the ability of developers to imagine a future user environment in which their technology could usefully function requires some degree of empathic design. The ability of industrial designers to embody their imagination in sketches or models is particularly useful in envisioning potential futures. However, since the market is still being created, no real users have been reliably identified.

Empathic design is most powerful when developers are proposing new solutions, either to known or anticipated user needs (middle of Figure 8). In such situations, when product designers develop a deep understanding of the current user environment, they can then extrapolate about the way that environment may evolve in the future and imagine the future need their technology can satisfy. However, as discussed below, the mechanisms for creating an empathic design capability are less well known than those employed in traditional market research.

Tools to help explore user reactions to products at the market alignment end of the spectrum are widely researched and taught. Marketing departments in the western hemisphere are expert at conducting surveys and focus group interviews. So-called mall studies, mentioned earlier in the description of the changes made to the HP deskjet, exemplify more ambitious but still widely used techniques. Less widely employed are interviews with so-called lead users,[38] who are already at the cutting edge of current products. By anticipating their own immediate needs, they foretell the more distant needs of less-advanced users and guide the design of radically improved solutions. Other techniques are most helpful when users can identify a product concept, but important dimensions are unclear. An example is the "K-J" analysis, a highly structured process for gathering and analyzing qualitative data first developed by a noted Japanese anthropologist, Jiro Kawakita. It has been applied to quality improvement programs in Japan and the United States with the help of Professor Shoji Shiba of Tsukuba University[39] and to "concept engineering" at the Center for Quality Management in Cambridge, Massachusetts. Another example of

---

[38]Eric von Hippel, "Novel Product Concepts from Lead Users: Segmenting Users by Experience," M.I.T. Sloan School of Management Working Paper 1476-83, 1983.

[39]Shoji Shiba, Richard Lynch, Ira Moskowitz, and John Sheridan, "Step by Step KJ Method," CQM Document No. 2, Wilmington, Mass.: The Center for Quality Management, Analog Devices, 1991.

systematic need elicitation is the proprietary Value Matrix used by a group of design houses, the Design Consortium, to uncover the often latent desires of a wide spectrum of user/stakeholders in a client firm.[40]

The most powerful aid to empathic design is an anthropological expedition of some kind. Technologists immerse themselves in the user world, much as anthropologists do when they inhabit native villages in unfamiliar parts of the world. Designers or developers with a thorough knowledge of technological potential live in the user environment long enough and absorb enough understanding of that environment to empathize with user needs. They see how users cope with unnecessarily inconvenient, uncomfortable, inefficient, or inaccurate tools and consider how to solve the unspoken problems. Products designed through this process present users with functionality, ease of use, and other benefits they would not have thought to ask for themselves. One of the most famous designers in U.S. history, Henry Dreyfuss, used to require his designers to live with whatever tool they were designing. They rode corn pickers and prowled factories. Similarly, today, Hewlett-Packard product developers in the medical division spend time in intensive care units and hospital clinics. It was on such a visit recently that a product developer noticed the way that nurses, in the course of their duties, inadvertently blocked the surgeon's view of the television screen which the physicians used to guide their intricate work. To solve this problem, the product designer conceived of a tiny screen mounted on a surgeon's helmet, to keep the image directly and constantly in view. In a different type of anthropological expedition, Xerox has employed trained anthropologists and other behaviorists to investigate exactly how people actually interact with sophisticated copier machines, and to report their findings to the corporation as a whole. These explorations resulted in knowledge about users' assumptions and mental models that was very pertinent to machine design, but had never before been systematically gathered.[41]

One very obvious way to commercialize technology is for those who have experienced a problem to apply technology in its solution, that is, for users to become developers. Eric von Hippel has documented hundreds of cases in which users were the primary inventors of a new tool or process.[42] In order to bring user innovation inhouse, companies employ in their development organizations customers or individuals who have extensive experience in the user world. At HP, for example, the product line manager for mass spectrometry and infrared spectroscopy systems has a PhD in organic chemistry with a specialty in mass spectrometry. "Most of our senior managers have been born and raised in the [analytical chemistry] business . . . when we speak with customers, the full implications of every word are immediately relevant to us; . . . we can feel the pulse of the customer."[43]

---

[40]See John R. Hauser and Don Clausing, "The House of Quality," *Harvard Business Review* 66, no. 3 (May–June 1988), pp. 63–73. Such techniques are often used as the "front end" for Quality Function Deployment processes that translate user requirements into engineering specifications.

[41]John Seely Brown and Susan E. Newman, "Issues in Cognitive and Social Ergonomics: From Our House to Bauhaus," *Human-Computer Interaction* 1 (1985), pp. 359–91.

[42]Eric von Hippel, *The Sources of Innovation* (New York: Oxford University Press, 1988).

[43]Interview with Dr. James Serum, Hewlett-Packard, November 1992.

Rather than bringing customers in-house to represent the user world, some companies have pursued a policy of commercializing their basic technologies through partnering with customers. ALZA Corporation is noted for its nontraditional drug-delivery systems, that is, ways to deliver drugs into the bloodstream over time at a continuous rate. They partner with specific customers to design customized delivery systems for a particular drug. For example, Janssen Pharmaceutica sells transdermal patches for which ALZA tailored their membranes to deliver a painkiller, Duragesic, for cancer patients. Similarly, ALZA partnered with Pfizer to deliver medicine for the treatment of angina that may be taken just once, instead of three times, a day.

Another lens into the user world can be provided by industry experts. Allegheny Ludlum, a highly profitable specialty steel producer, set up a market development group almost 30 years ago. While the mandate for group members has changed somewhat over the years, their basic task is to entrench themselves in the personal networks of the customer base they serve. Each member of the group is a walking compendium of several vital kinds of information: intense technical knowledge about certain alloys and their application; widespread personal contacts among industry experts and customer companies; deep knowledge about standard-setting and regulation in their industry. This understanding of the user world is mostly tacit (i.e., in their heads).

When the user world lies in the future, developers need to extrapolate current trends and anticipate a world none can confidently predict. While technology commercialization in this situation usually depends upon the market intuition of well-informed gurus, techniques exist for formal scenario-construction.[44] The intent of such scenarios is less to predict exactly a future state than to stimulate consideration of nonobvious futures, to force "out-of-the-box" thinking (i.e., to divorce thought from a straight, unwavering trend line).

All of these tools and mechanisms have limits and costs. The inability of even very sophisticated market research to reliably predict actual user behavior on occasion is well known. There are many explanations, including the basic facts that attitudes do not predict behavior and that, as mentioned before, people are unable to articulate some of their aesthetic and even functional needs. Anthropological expeditions are time-consuming and require special skills. Experts hired in from the user world can become so enmeshed in daily business activities that they can eventually lose touch with the cutting edge.[45] The major limitation to creating industry experts

[44]Peter Schwartz, *The Art of the Long View: Planning for the Future in an Uncertain World* (New York: Doubleday Currency, 1991).

[45]This possible danger is exacerbated if high-level senior officials try to micromanage technical project details. In one company studied by Dorothy Leonard-Barton, project teams frequently complained that senior management "swooped down" midway through projects to tinker with technical details which they were no longer in a position to judge. Senior managers can also remain personally invested in an obsolete technology. In another company, a major move from glass to plastic materials was delayed at huge cost to the corporation. The principal reason, according to company informants, was that a critical senior official could not bear to desert his primary skill base and expertise in glassmaking. Only when he left the company was the switch finally made—some years after competition had already proven the profitability of the move.

is that their expertise is held in their heads. Such tacit knowledge is difficult to evaluate financially since commercialization ideas planted in a certain year may not yield sales for 5 or 10; moreover, tacit knowledge is not easily codified or transferred. Industry experts can also become too narrowly focused and adopt the same myopic view of the world that their users have. In short, they may go "native." Customer partners may engender similar risks, in that they can direct technology commercialization into narrow, self-serving niches. And, finally, market scenarios are only intended to provoke possibilities—not predict the future with any assurance.

Corporations are therefore well advised to pursue a wide range of these techniques to understand user needs. The wider the range available to guide technology commercialization, the more opportunity there is to apply the most appropriate technique to a given situation.

# Conclusions

Not all new products and processes are alike. They may arise either through a process of invention or innovation.[46] While innovation has the characteristics of "being both demandable and predictable within a finite time," invention does not.[47] If one represents the life of a particular technology through the useful oversimplification of an S-shaped curve (see Figure 9), it is clear that products and processes arising through invention potentially have a much longer life span than those arising through the more derivative process of innovation.[48] Therefore, inventive products are very desirable (albeit not to the exclusion of innovative ones). The dilemma addressed in this paper is that understanding user needs is absolutely critical to successful technology commercialization of both invention and innovation. Since innovative products and processes are derivative, users can directly help shape their design. Extensive tools and methods exist for eliciting user needs—even uncommunicated ones—for such products. Usefully channeling user input into the design of inventive products and processes is much more difficult, and we have far fewer tools and methods to apply to the process.

Our current ability to imaginatively understand user needs (i.e., to commercialize technology through empathic design and market intuition) is constrained by the limited number of people in our organizations who are capable of this art. The observations in this chapter suggest that the next managerial frontier for technology commercialization is to explore methods for better understanding uncommunicated, nonobvious but current user needs and unarticulated, nonobvious future needs. If

---

[46]Either of these may be preceded, of course, by a process of discovery. However, technological discoveries only provide opportunities; they must be shaped into useful products and processes.

[47]John Doyle, "Commentary: Managing New Product Development: How Japanese Companies Learn and Unlearn," in *The Uneasy Alliance: Managing the Product-Technology Dilemma,* ed. Kim Clark, Robert Hayes, and Christopher Lorenz (Boston, Mass.: Harvard Business School Press, 1985).

[48]Brian Dumaine, "How Managers Can Succeed through Speed," *Fortune* 119 (February 13, 1989), pp. 54–74.

**FIGURE 9**

*The S-curve of technology maturation*

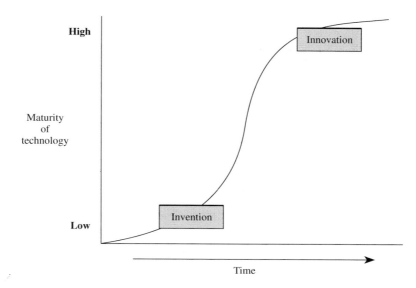

one primary method for creating this understanding is harnessing the creative imagination of individual gurus, then we need to consider how we identify such individuals and develop their skills to the highest degree possible. Another challenge is figuring out how to design various kinds of anthropological expeditions into user territory. Finally, we need better understanding of the limits and possibilities of market scenarios.

In this decade, companies globally confront the need to wring unnecessary buffers of time out of their development processes, but without destroying creativity. The capability to develop new products and processes quickly and effectively will distinguish industry leaders. Truly understanding user needs—not just their demands—enables speed without sacrificing inventiveness.

# Industrial Pricing to Meet Customer Needs

*When a customer buys a product, he or she goes through a complex process of balancing the price of the product against the perceived benefits, costs, risks, and value in use of the product. If the customer thinks this way when analyzing a purchase, it makes great sense for marketers to set prices with the same items in mind. To do this, marketers need to understand the use to which their customers put the products, the performance benefits, both physical and service, that are most important, and the different cost variables that the customer perceives, such as risk of product failure. To help marketers apply a customer approach in determining a price, the authors have provided a list of important concepts.*

Even back in "the good old days" of the very early 1970s, industrial marketers found pricing to be a great challenge. Then both customers and competitors were applying pressure, and since that time government price controls, double-digit inflation, a sudden recession, and finally an economic malaise combining some amount of inflation and recession have simply caused the situation to get worse. A cover article in *Business Week* stressed these changes:

> The chief characteristics of the new price strategy are flexibility and a willingness to cut prices aggressively to hold market shares. On the way out the window are many of the pricing traditions of the U.S. industrial giants.[1]

Our purpose in this chapter is *not* to explore the reasons behind these changes in pricing practice, nor is it to provide a set of pet solutions and perfect techniques managers can use to respond to the situation. Instead, we present a philosophy to help managers approach pricing situations, a coherent, rational framework in which

This reading was prepared by Benson P. Shapiro and Barbara B. Jackson.
Reprinted from *Harvard Business Review* 56, no. 6, November–December 1978, pp. 119–27.
Copyright © 1978 by the President and Fellows of Harvard College. All rights reserved.
[1]"Flexible Pricing," *Business Week,* December 12, 1977, p. 78.

managers can make pricing decisions, and finally some tools and constructs that will facilitate the application of the framework.

Although the general approach we suggest can be applied to pricing consumer goods, especially the more complex ones such as appliances and furniture, managers in companies making industrial products—that is, products not resold in their existing form directly to consumers—will find it most useful. These products include items sold to institutional markets such as hospitals and universities, as well as the more typical components, capital goods, supplies, and raw materials sold to manufacturers.

# Pricing Strategies

Managers normally set prices one of three ways. The first is for management to maintain a strong internal orientation, basing prices on its own costs, and, usually, adding some standard industry markup to average costs. Cost-plus is a simple system, but it fails to consider competitors, customers, or the volume, price, and profit relationships among costs. A well-known sophisticated version of this approach, target rate-of-return pricing, was developed at General Motors during the 1920s and 1930s. While it included consideration of volume fluctuations through the business cycle and the cost of the capital involved in the business, target rate-of-return prices were still based totally on internal costs, not on the market.

The second approach is to let competitors set prices, and then to meet them head-on. This strategy assumes that a marketer's company, its products, its image and position in the marketplace, and its cost structure are exactly like the competition's. A slightly more sophisticated version of this approach involves maintaining a set dollar or percentage differential between one's prices and the competitor's. A manager might, for instance, maintain a price of 5 percent below the market "leader" to allow for the leader's stronger reputation. However, this approach is mechanistic and does not allow managers either to build on their products' and company's unique strengths or to adjust for their unique weaknesses.

The third approach, which is more difficult than the other two, focuses on the customer. It requires marketers to assess carefully the value customers place on the product. Typically, industrial marketers have shied away from this approach, but now, given the difficult market conditions we have described, the need for such a thorough, customer-based approach seems clear. Fortunately, the opportunity for its application has been advanced by the emergence of new concepts and techniques. In what follows we will go into the customer-based approach and these concepts in more detail.

# How Customers Evaluate Products

The basic idea behind our customer-based approach may appear quite simple: Customers balance the benefits of a purchase against its costs. When the benefits outweigh the costs and when the particular product under consideration has the best relationship of benefit to cost, the customer purchases the product. Though the concept is simple, it is difficult to make operational; in particular, it is difficult to define product benefits and costs in terms of the customer's perspective.

In the industrial marketplace, the benefits can be functional (utilitarian aspects that might be attractive to engineers), operational (a product's reliability and durability would be important to manufacturing and operating managers), or financial (aspects attractive to purchasing agents and controllers). Benefits for individuals can also be personal; for example, the ego satisfaction of doing a job well or protection from the risk of termination.

The costs a customer perceives are just as diverse. They include clearly defined acquisition costs: seller's price, incoming freight, installation, and order handling costs. They also include less clearly defined costs such as the risk to the customer of a product failure (which can include the personal risk of making a poor decision, as well as the risk to the company of shutting down a production line or repairing a piece of equipment), fear of late or inaccurate delivery, custom modification after receipt of the item, and so forth.

The important point here is that the benefits are more complex and subtle than marketers often realize and the costs for the prospective customer are a great deal more than just the seller's price. A customer's decision to purchase a product is an exceedingly complex process involving perceptions and not merely hard and fast realities. Price is only a part of this process.

Simply, then, the marketer must determine the highest price that the customer would be willing to pay for the product. One could view that as:

*Benefits − Costs other than price = Highest price the customer will pay.*

To determine that price, the marketer needs to understand the customer's perception of benefits as well as his or her perception of the costs other than price. The marketer also needs to remember that his or her cost is unimportant in determining the customer's perceptions. The customer cares about the marketer's price, not cost. In fact, to make the statement even more accurate, the customer cares about his or her own costs, much more than about the marketer's price.

Furthermore, marketers need to be aware of the choices their competitors are offering the customer. Those options help determine the environment in which customers perceive benefits and costs, and, of course, they are possible substitute purchases.

This customer-based orientation has been called *utility* or *value* pricing. With this approach, a marketer looks at the utility or value of the product to the customer and compares that with the utility or value offered by competitors. A particular example, which involves a published case study on E. I. duPont de Nemours & Co.,[2] illustrates how important value pricing is.

In July 1954, DuPont introduced Alathon 25, a new polyethylene resin used in pipe manufacture. Until that time, all polyethylene pipe had been made from a by-product off-grade resin. While pipe produced from Alathon 25 looked exactly like

---

[2]E. Raymond Corey, "E. I. duPont de Nemours & Co.," in *Industrial Marketing: Case and Concepts,* 2nd ed. (Englewood Cliffs, N.J.: Prentice Hall, 1976), p. 179.

pipe made from off-grade resin, it had a longer life than competitive pipe and could withstand greater pressure.

After the product's shaky entry into the market, DuPont developed a strong promotional program for Alathon 25 which communicated its notable benefits to a careful selection of the extruders who made the resin into pipe. Alathon 25 sales grew strongly despite the fact that extruders sold the pipe to distributors for between $9.50 and $13.00 per 100 feet versus the $5.00 to $7.00 price for pipe made from off-grade resin. This price ratio, almost 1.9, is greater than the relative lives of the pipes would suggest.

An advertisement reproduced in the case study shows the secret of this strategy's success. It shows a farm application, a typical use of the pipe, where the pipe goes underground. It is clear that if the pipe bursts, it would have to be dug up—a time-consuming, expensive chore. The value or utility of the pipe is great because it is part of a complex system.

We can, then, restate our simple concept in marketer's terms: With a complete understanding of the end use, set a price based on the product's utility or value in use.

Obviously, such an approach requires that a marketer have considerable knowledge of his or her customers to completely understand their applications, including their subtle operational and organizational relationships. A marketer can get that knowledge by analyzing the customers' cost–benefit trade-offs.

## Analyzing the Customer's Perceptions

In setting prices, marketers of industrial products need to do the following:

1. Understand the total use of the product.
2. Analyze the benefit variables.
3. Analyze the cost variables.
4. Make cost–benefit trade-offs.

Although the first area is perhaps the most important, it is the least easy to generalize about because each application is so different. The marketer will simply have to study each end use. If the product is a raw material or component, it will be part of both the ultimate product and the process by which the product is made. If it is a piece of capital equipment, it is often only a part of a larger production system. The polyethylene pipe just mentioned is a good example. It was part of two important larger systems; the complex and tedious installation process and the completed system for transporting water.

### *Focusing on Benefit Variables*

A marketer can begin to develop a more complex sense of a product's utility as he or she analyzes the benefits to customers. In doing this analysis, the marketer will find it useful to regard the product as a set of physical attributes and as a set of "soft" service

---

EXHIBIT 1    **Product Space for Electric Motors**

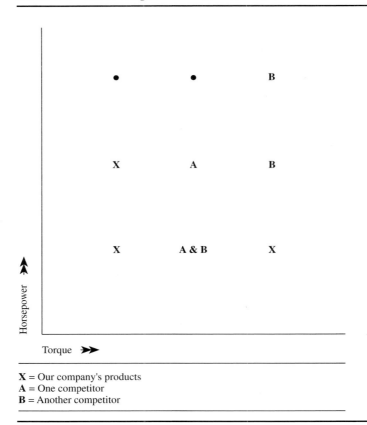

X = Our company's products
A = One competitor
B = Another competitor

---

attributes. Theodore Levitt has referred to this latter bundle of characteristics as the "augmented product."[3] Let us first consider the product's physical attributes.

One of the best ways to analyze a set of competitive products is to put them in a performance space (or map or graph) where the axes represent different performance variables.[4] Even though at the first cut one may think of many different dimensions along which to describe product offerings in a marketplace, on further analysis a marketer will usually find that two carefully selected variables tell most of the story.

In the case of electric motors, for example, the variables might be horsepower and torque. Exhibit 1 shows such a space. Each item in the competitive product lines

---

[3]*The Marketing Mode: Pathways to Corporate Growth* (New York: McGraw-Hill, 1969), chap. 1.

[4]The basic concept of placing products in a product or performance space was suggested by Wroe Alderson in 1957 in *Marketing Behavior and Executive Action* (Homewood, Ill.: Richard D. Irwin). Part of his thinking was apparently the result of earlier work by Hans Brems ("The Interdependence of Quality Variations, Selling Effort, and Price," *Quarterly Journal of Economics,* May 1948, pp. 418–40).

could be placed on a point in the space. Construction of such a space has three advantages. First, it forces the marketing manager to define explicitly the product's primary attributes. Second, it provides a visual way to compare competing lines. And third, and perhaps most important, it encourages the manager to develop an explicit product policy based on the main product characteristics.

As Exhibit 1 shows, products usually do not appear at all points in the product space. Instead, they appear at points that have particular technical significance or historical tradition. Thus, motors might be offered at 5 hp and 10 hp but not at 8.273 hp; printing presses would always be sized to match paper dimensions. This fact makes the product space much easier to work with. The space in Exhibit 1, for example, has nine feasible products, seven of which are being produced. Sometimes, of course, managers might choose to break with the established traditions of product positioning, but such situations are rare.

The product space is a particularly powerful tool when it is used as a visual technique for segmenting a market. Returning to our electric motor example, we can map different market segments in the space. Exhibit 2 shows how such a map might look. In some industries, where a small number of specific accounts make up the

---

**EXHIBIT 2   Product Space for Motor Pumps Showing Two Market Segments**

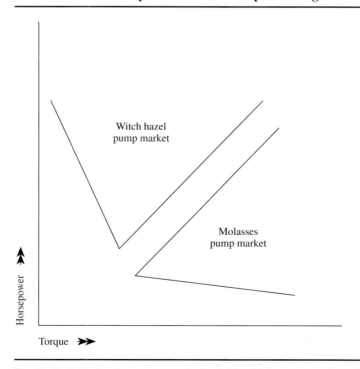

NOTE: In this idealized product space, motors for the witch hazel industry pump market would be of high horsepower and low torque because witch hazel is not viscous. Molasses, on the other hand, is gooier, has more viscosity, and companies making it need pumps of high torque (or turning power) relative to horsepower.

market, or a large share of it, the needs of individual accounts can even be mapped in the space.

But so far we have discussed only the physical attributes of competitive products, which in many industrial markets are identical or almost identical. The products are often purchased to specification. In those situations, the products are not differentiated, but the companies can be by the services they offer. One company might stress reliability of delivery and another quality of technical support. These service attributes can be mapped in much the same way that the physical characteristics are mapped in the product space. For example, in the copier marketplace the variables might be total price per copy and repair service responsiveness.

With most industrial products, the customer is purchasing an exceedingly complex system with many variables. While it is possible to study the trade-off explicitly[5] by conducting surveys, as would certainly be justified in large markets, it is often possible for a marketer to identify the important purchase criteria just by knowing intimately his or her customers' needs.

Focusing merely on product attributes and company services can, however, lead marketers into a very dangerous trap—that of marketing features and not benefits. Even though every good sales manager stresses to his or her salespeople that the customer buys benefits, most salespeople and many marketing managers stress features and forget benefits. To quote a familiar phrase, "The person who buys the ¼-inch drill bit does not want the drill bit but wants the ability to drill ¼-inch holes."

Thus, to the customer, "durability" refers to the ability to drill more holes before the bit must be replaced, not the hardness of the bit. Many marketing managers (and salespeople), however, would mistakenly stress the newer, harder alloy the bit is made of rather than the benefit of more holes between bit changes.

A very clever way to avoid the trap is to develop the performance space dimensions based on customer needs (i.e., number of holes drilled by the bit) instead of physical or service attributes. This procedure carries the customer orientation one important step forward.

### Calculating Cost Variables

Just as benefits are a complex group of physical and service attributes, perceived in different ways by different people, costs are much more than just the "price" the customer pays. In trying to calculate costs, it is useful to begin with the purchase price, and then add on the clear, explicit acquisition and use costs such as inbound transportation, installation, repair, labor, power, and so forth. Employing the concept of life cycle costing, the manager can consider all of the costs associated with a piece of equipment or a manufacturing process over the life of a product.

While life cycle costing has typically been used for capital equipment, it can be applied to almost any purchase, including that of a service or supply item. Most

---

[5]Paul E. Green and Yoram Wind, "New Ways to Measure Consumers' Judgments," *Harvard Business Review,* July–August 1975, p. 107; and Brian T. Ratchford and Gary Ford, "A Study of Prices and Market Shares in the Computer Main Frame Industry," *The Journal of Business,* April 1976, p. 194.

major make-or-buy analyses have the elements of life cycle costing in them if they are performed correctly. Applying the concept, a manager can trade off his or her customer's operating costs, power, or labor against capital investment.

But doing an effective cost analysis includes looking at less-obvious costs. For instance, if a product failure or an interruption in a manufacturing process presents a great risk to the customer, he or she is much more likely to pay a high price to ensure reliability than someone who does not perceive the same risk. Some companies, for example, purchase good components for their products because they know that their customers are very sensitive about performance. If the product fails, the customer has lost more than the monetary value of the component, and the company's relationship with the customer is lessened by that amount as well.

Creative ways of looking at the customer's perception of cost can lead to powerful, yet sometimes simple, marketing approaches. One manufacturer of laboratory instruments was plagued by a high number of very small orders for a limited variety of repair parts for one particular product line. On analysis, the product manager found that customers were annoyed at having to order small parts because the ordering cost was greater than the parts prices. Furthermore, the company was losing money on the parts for the same reason.

Even more costly, customers were upset at the downtime caused by not having the correct parts in stock. A few customers with many instruments seemed capable of keeping the right mix of parts in stock but others with limited experience could not develop good inventory rules. To alleviate the problem, the product manager developed repair kits with several different assortments of parts and offered them to customers using a large variety of instruments. The company's costs went down, customer costs decreased, and customer satisfaction increased because instruments were available more of the time.

### Making Cost–Benefit Trade-Offs

If the customer makes cost–benefit trade-offs in analyzing a purchase, then it seems sensible for the marketer to do the same in analyzing how to approach the customer. The simplest way to begin to understand the trade-off is first to look at only physical product attributes and at price. Leave for later a consideration of the service variables and the other factors that make up the customer's cost.

In many industrial markets, it is possible to define and examine a general price–performance ratio. A major performance variable in crawler tractors, for example, is horsepower. The price–performance ratio here thus becomes dollars per horsepower. A low ratio (1:0) indicates greater horsepower per dollar than does a higher ratio (2:0).

A marketer can use the performance space described earlier to do this kind of analysis by replacing one variable of the product's performance with price. On the graph in Exhibit 3, each item in a product line can be represented by a point. Any particular product line can be represented by joining together the points for each item in the line to form a curve. Price performance curves have been used in the computer industry with some success to show the development of the industry over

---

**EXHIBIT 3    Price–Performance Curves**

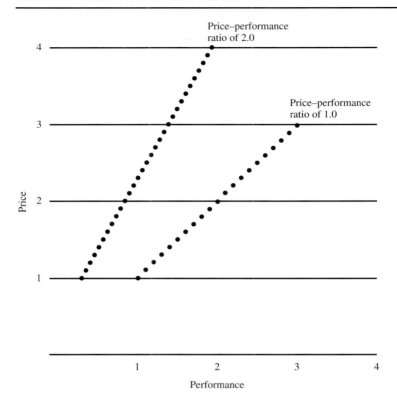

time. There, for example, one can see the greater performance per dollar (or productivity) resulting from each successive generation of computers.

Theoretically, it would be possible to build a three dimensional (or more) price–performance space, with several dimensions of product performance plotted against one price dimension. But as it is impossible for managers to visualize the three dimensional space, let alone more dimensions, it is more practical for them to select one primary performance characteristic.

The most clear-cut price–performance curve, however, leads one into the features versus benefits trap again. The performance attribute graphed in price–performance curves is usually a feature, not a benefit. The crawler tractor buyer, for example, is not really interested in horsepower, but in amounts of earth moved per hour. Here again, the space can be defined in customer-oriented terms such as yards of earth moved per hour.

---

**TABLE 1   A Customer Approach to Pricing**

1. A commitment to the philosophy that the customer chooses products by measuring benefits against costs.
2. An understanding that benefits involve a great deal more than physical attributes and that in many industrial situations it is the "soft" services which differentiate products.
3. A realization that cost involves more negative aspects of the purchase than price alone.
4. The perspective of benefits and costs in terms of a complete usage system, not in terms of an isolated part of that system.
5. Cognizance of the fact that different customers view benefits and costs in different ways, thus necessitating careful market segmentation.
6. The application of graphic techniques to understanding the position of products and product lines in terms of customer needs and competitive offerings.

---

Thus, instead of contrasting price with features or performance, the marketer should remember the end use of the product and look at price together with benefits and costs. To assess meaningfully the benefits and costs of a complex system requires a great deal of creativity and meticulous calculation. Throughout, the marketer should keep his or her eye on customers and their perceptions.

Furthermore, the marketer may have to consider as possible costs customer concerns which one usually does not even consider quantifying. For instance, if one is marketing a piece of capital equipment critical to a total manufacturing system, in considering the benefits of reliability a marketer might very well have to assess the cost to his or her customer of shutting down the whole production system if that risk is important to the customer. Different customers clearly will have different concerns and will use the product in different systems. As a result, they will likely perceive the same product as having different benefits and costs. For a summary of the important concepts of an analysis of cost-benefit trade-offs see Table 1.

# How Marketers Should Determine Price

To the industrial marketer, the price-determining process is much more complicated than just selecting a price. As the customer looks at price as an integral aspect of the product, so must the manufacturer. Thus, price should be seen as a design variable in planning the product, as one of several critical performance attributes. The intimate relationship between price and product policy makes a great impact on the whole product planning-pricing process.

For a particular example, let us look again at the crawler tractor business.[6] In the U.S. market, Caterpillar had traditionally dominated the market for large tractors

---

[6]For more on this particular situation, see the case study entitled "Deere & Company: Industrial Equipment Operations," Intercollegiate Case Clearing House, Boston, Mass. 02163, Order no. 9-577-112.

over 100 horsepower. On the other hand, Deere & Company had dominated the market for small utility machines under 100 horsepower. Then, at about the same time, Deere and Caterpillar entered each other's market domains. The new Deere large tractor unit had a hydrostatic transmission which, according to Deere management, provided about 15 percent better productivity per horsepower than the comparable existing units. Deere, however, was unfamiliar with the large tractor market and somewhat of an unknown to the customer in this marketplace.

In designing its new tractors, Deere had four courses of action open to it:[7]

1. It could introduce units slightly larger in horsepower than the competitive Caterpillar unit.
2. It could introduce units with the same horsepower as the Caterpillar units.
3. It could introduce units slightly smaller than the Caterpillar units.
4. It could place its entries between existing Caterpillar units.

The last option would require reeducating the marketplace, an ambitious undertaking in the face of such competent, well-entrenched competition.

Because this product was so complex, involving several years of design time and millions of dollars in engineering and tooling costs, Deere's decision was difficult and important. It was clearly both a product policy and a pricing decision. In the crawler tractor industry, part of price is determined by manufacturing cost. Cost, in turn, is determined by the size of the product as well as by other variables such as unit volume. Another important point is that the price can be changed, especially lowered, much more easily and quickly than the product can be changed.

(The general inflationary tenor of the economy has made it much easier to raise prices than it was previously, however. A price increase is not the shock it once was. In addition, if price is raised too high at one point, it can be readjusted by skipping a future industry price increase.)

The basic product design itself is the most difficult thing to change in any material way.

In considering these options, it is important to note the role of the customer's perception of performance. The appropriate pricing strategy might be different in a situation where the customers view horsepower as the primary variable than in one where they view productivity (yards moved per hour) as the key variable.

According to the case study (in which some data are disguised), Deere apparently introduced its tractor at about equal price and at slightly greater horsepower than Caterpillar's competing unit. To encourage rapid trial and adoption of its product, Deere management apparently passed on to the customer all of the benefit of higher productivity resulting from new technology. In addition, it seemingly did not want to stray far from industry-established tractor sizes.

---

[7]We very much appreciate the help of Ken Kessler of the Deere engineering staff for explaining these options to us.

## Pricing and Product Planning

If one accepts the basic importance of the customer's view in setting price, and the concept of the customer balancing benefits and costs, then it becomes clear that product planning and pricing become one process. In fact, in industrial marketing, it is almost impossible to separate them. To a great extent, price defines a product's market, competition, and potential application. It is influenced strongly by cost, which, in turn, is related to unit volume and performance. In the other direction, price affects unit volume.

Once a product is in a price–performance space, it is not fixed there forever; it can be moved either by changing its price, or by changing its physical or service performance attributes. Regardless, product planning and pricing must be managed simultaneously.

Perhaps two examples would be useful here. In one, a manufacturer of an expensive engineered plastic developed a new version of the product that provided some clear performance advantages over the existing version. Furthermore, on a direct cost basis, the new version was cheaper than the older one. However, when amortization of the development expenditure was added to the direct cost, the total was greater than the fully allocated cost of the older version.

The company had several clear choices involving the pricing of both items as well as the timing of the new product's introduction. It was possible, for instance, to introduce the new product at a premium price compared with the older one while holding the older one at its current price. Or management could reduce the older one's price. That option seemed especially interesting because company engineers expected to cut the processing costs of the old product through a new manufacturing process not applicable to the new version. If the price were to be cut, management had to decide whether to do so before the introduction of the new version or concurrent with it.

Finally, the company could simply replace the older version with the newer one. In approaching this situation, the managers involved had to consider benefits, customer costs, the usage systems, and customer perceptions, not just the company's own costs.

In another situation, a manufacturer of a specialized type of electric motor was under pressure from a new competitor who offered a lower-priced, lower-quality unit designed for the needs of a rapidly growing segment of the market. In this case, management could either develop a specialized motor for the same segment or could meet its competitor head-on by reducing the prices of its whole line. Management chose to develop a new motor for this segment rather than cut the price and sacrifice margin on its whole line. Fortuitously, the manufacturer then discovered other market segments, where its penetration had been low, which had applications for the new, cheaper, lower-quality motor.

As a competitive tool, pricing has a particularly strong advantage over product planning—as has been said, it is almost always quicker and easier to change the price than to change the product or the service. Changes in the "soft" service part of the product take a great deal of time to implement. One cannot easily develop a

EXHIBIT 4    **Planning Factors to Consider When Changing Prices
on Product Lines**

| | Action | | |
|---|---|---|---|
| *Planning Factors* | *Price Change* | *Reengineering of Existing Product or Processes* | *New Product Development or Major Process Change* |
| Longer-term impact | Low* | Moderate | High |
| Investment necessary | Low | Moderate | High |
| Risk | Low? | Moderate? | High? |
| Ease of competitive response | High | Moderate | Low |

NOTE: It is important to note that the term risk as used here may not be true risk. We have focused on short- and moderate-term risk. The true long-term risks may be quite different. In situations of rapid change, especially technological, it may be far riskier to make small product and process changes than to make substantial ones.

*To be read, the longer-term impact of a price change is low.

better applications engineering capability, upgrade a sales force, or implement a rapid order processing and delivery program. Thus, in the electric motor situation just described, if the problem were urgent and development of a new line a lengthy process, the manufacturer would almost have been forced to respond with price cutting.

Pricing changes are, however, easy for competitors to copy. Unless a company has an underlying cost advantage over another company, it is hard to develop a strong position solely on the basis of price. Exhibit 4 shows the impact, cost, risk, and ease of competitive response for various kinds of product line and price changes.

## *Relating Price to Cost Structure*

Up to this point our focus has been almost totally on the customer. But a company's own structure also plays an important part in the pricing-planning process.

A pricing policy should be structured in such a way that it takes maximum advantage of the company's cost structure and, wherever possible, builds on the company's distinctive competitive competence. It should be noted, however, that in most situations price can be used to shape demand, but not to change it radically. There are, after all, other elements of the customer's costs, as well as the benefits, to be considered.

A company that has a highly automated manufacturing plant, for instance, and an expensive sales force might want to generate large orders, giving substantial volume discounts to help do so.[8] Large orders, which make good use of the equipment's

---

[8]The Robinson-Patman Act makes it illegal for a company to favor one customer over another competing customer. But it does allow pricing which reflects costs savings. For more on this exceedingly complex law, see Richard A. Posner, *The Robinson-Patman Act: Federal Regulation of Price Difference* (Washington, D.C.: American Enterprise Institute for Public Policy Research, 1976).

economical long runs, justify the high cost of the sales call. On the other hand, another company with a broad product line, a more labor-intensive manufacturing operation, and a large distribution network with its attendant high fixed cost, might have a much more gentle slope to its volume-discount curve.

Managers cannot assume, however, that the large company–large order, small company–small order relationship always applies. In many situations, a small company can carve out a specialized niche around large orders and long runs. With top-level managers acting as account managers, a small company can service customers capable of placing large orders on a direct basis. The large manufacturer, on the other hand, can cover all segments of the market with a broad product line and intensive distribution. In doing so, it serves the small user as well as the large user.

The manager should base his other product policy, view of market segmentation, and price on the use (as measured by the size of a single-line entry on the order form) the customer is going to make of the product, rather than on the customer's size or total business it gives the manager's company.

There are many other situations where managers build a pricing policy around an existing cost structure. For example, managers can design a cost structure and its underlying manufacturing, marketing, sales, and distribution strategies to complement a particular product policy and pricing strategy. It seems to us that if a product policy and pricing strategy are indeed responsive to customer needs, the best long-term approach is to build the cost structure to fit them. While perhaps appropriate in the short term, market strategies that sacrifice customer benefits to protect the company's interests, such as an existing cost structure, are doomed in the long term.

## Concluding Note

We began this chapter discussing a basic philosophy built around customers and their perceptions of benefits and costs. That concept is the truly important one. Pricing must be done on the basis of customers' perceptions of the value of the product, which depend on their total usage systems.

Techniques such as the performance space and price–performance curves help to implement the concept of customer primacy. But they are techniques, not ends in themselves. Industrial marketers win or lose in the customer's mind.

# 8 Industrial Market Research: Beta Test Site Management

*The purpose of this reading is to set out guidelines for maximizing the value of a beta test program. The authors identify a variety of uses and purposes of such a testing program. They then set out the major benefits and costs to both vendors and test sites, based on an analysis of over 20 beta test programs. Finally, they provide management guidelines for effective implementation.*

## Introduction

The new product development process for a 50-cent candy bar and that for a $500,000 piece of computer hardware are the same—or so the textbooks say. In each situation, the manufacturer is advised to proceed through a number of sequential steps: idea generation → initial screening → concept testing → product use testing → market testing → introduction. In practice, however, the processes are quite different. Somewhat ironically, the process for the candy bar entry would likely follow the suggested model more closely and have a more scientific, rigorous appearance.[1] This is because candy bar buyers:

- Are numerous and easy to identify.
- All use the candy bar for the same basic purpose.
- Follow a short decision-making process in purchasing.
- Likely decide whether or not to buy a bar on their own.

Robert J. Dolan prepared this note.
Copyright © 1991 by the President and Fellows of Harvard College.
Harvard Business School note 592-010.

[1]See, for example, a description of the likely processes to be followed in "Note on Concept Testing" (HBS case no. 590-063) and "Note on Pre-Test Markets" (HBS case no. 588-052).

- Can easily articulate whether they like the bar or not after use.
- Need only a short time to use up the bar and become a candidate for a repeat purchase.

In contrast, possible adopters of the $500,000 computer system may be few in number and hard to find, vary in the intended application of the system, have a decision-making process characterized by broad participation by individuals across the company and long gestation time, and take a long time in deciding how well the product fits their needs.

These contrasts in buyer behavior cause significant differences in the effective implementation of the steps of the development process. The product use and market test phases for a candy bar would commonly involve large samples, rigorous statistical analysis, and carefully designed market experiments. The same phases for computers will usually find a handful of "respondents"—not selected with statistical analysis in mind. This handful is the vendor's beta test sites.[2]

R. G. Cooper's survey shows that money invested in the beta test phase of the new product development process is one of the key differentiators between industrial product successes and failures.[3] The frequent use of beta programs suggests their importance. However, there are no well-articulated guidelines for management of such tests. In practice, beta site selection and management seem ad hoc at many firms—driven by convenience rather than recognition of the trade-offs involved. This lack of effective management leads J. B. Elmer to refer to beta site testing as "an informal method that's really not research" and to suggest prototype-testing research as a way to avoid the "significant potential marketing hazards" of beta testing.[4]

The purpose of this chapter is to set out guidelines for maximizing the value of a beta test program. We begin by identifying the variety of relationships between vendors and sites. We then set out the major benefits and costs to both vendors and test sites, based on an analysis of over 20 beta test programs. Having established potential costs and benefits, we then provide management guidelines for effective practice. The small sample sizes inherent in beta test programs and the multiplicity of purposes possibly served to preclude reducing beta site management to a simple formula. However, specific prescriptions of value can be made.

Briefly stated, our guidance on effective beta management is this:

1. Carefully define the purpose of the program. In the next section, we set out and illustrate five major purposes of beta testing. Clarity in purpose aids in determining the number of sites required, the desired characteristics of sites, the length of the test, and data collection methods.
2. Design the testing program to guard against the significant threats to validity of a program. Central here is that beta sites are usually few in number and

---

[2]Alpha testing refers to the prior usage of in-house product testing.

[3]R. G. Cooper, "Identifying Industrial New Product Success: Project Newprod," *Industrial Marketing Management* 8 (1979), pp. 124–35.

[4]J. B. Elmer, "Software Developers Can Benefit from Prototype-Testing Research," *Marketing News,* January 1989, pp. 5–6.

selected purposively by the firm rather than randomly. The section called "Threats to Test Value" provides the major issues to be considered in this.

3. Understand and manage the sites' motivation for participating in the test. This can help in recruiting sites and designing the program to be implemented. This is the subject of the section named "Threats to Test Value."

The final section provides a summary and conclusions.

# Beta Test Purposes

By definition, a beta test is "a real world test of a system after it has passed all its laboratory tests."[5] Implicit in this definition is the fact that this test precedes the general availability of the product. An example of a basic function check of a system is Accu-Chek's testing of its electronic shelf pricing system for grocery stores.[6] The 90-day test provided Accu-Chek:

1. Validation of the basic concept of half-inch electronic labels changed by handheld computers replacing manual systems.
2. Diagnostic information on specific aspects of the program. Specifically, Accu-Chek obtained information pertaining to four constituent groups:
   a. Its *own field force* found that the labels were not easily installed.
   b. The size and position of the labels were not appealing to *consumers.*
   c. *Shelf-stockers* found the labels hung over too far, making item placement difficult.
   d. *Store management's* experience with the test system raised accuracy and security concerns which had to be overcome before large-scale adoption would be achieved.

Figure 1 shows this function and diagnostic check at the center of a beta site purpose diagram. While this purpose is at the heart of most test programs, important supplementary purposes are also served as indicated. As shown, the three major purposes served are:

1. Product.
   a. Basic function check.
   b. Refinement of core product design.
   c. Added features desired in core product.
2. Augmented product design.
   a. Support features.
      (1) Training required.

---

[5]J. G. Sweetland, "Beta Tests and End-User Surveys: Are They Valid?" *Database,* February 1988, pp. 27–32.

[6]"Technology Hits Shelf Pricing," *Discount Merchandising* (September 1989), pp. 72–74.

**FIGURE 1**

*Beta test purposes*

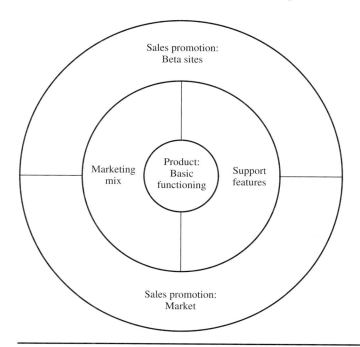

(2) Documentation adequacy.

(3) Other features.

   *b.* Marketing mix to support product introduction, especially:

     (1) Positioning.

     (2) Pricing.

3. Sales promotion.

   *a.* To beta sites:

     (1) Develop account relationship.

     (2) Trial path to purchase.

   *b.* To general market:

     (1) Publicity/credibility from passing test.

     (2) Reference accounts/demo sites.

     (3) Equivalent to preannouncement.

In addition to the data on the core product, a beta program can test and refine augmentation of the core. For example, in the software industry the core product becomes commoditylike after a short time and hence support programs are key. For example, Lotus's "agreements on support, connectivity, communication between vendor and user" were arrived at after "extensive beta testing of various arrangements."[7]

———

[7]E. Bender, "Software Hits, Lower Profits," *Computerworld,* May 12, 1986, pp. 35, 44.

Beta programs can also provide input to determining the appropriate marketing mix to support the product. Especially useful is testing to permit the calculation of the economic value to the customer, a key input to product pricing.[8] For example, the Cumberland Metals Industries case reports the field testing of a new type of pile driver pads.[9] Via collection of data on pile-driving efficiency in the two test sites, the company was able to calculate precisely the value of the pads to the customer. This would be the upper bound on what any individual would pay. Systematic analysis of the variance in the value can be the key to market segmentation, product positioning, and target market selection.

Finally, the outer ring of Figure 1 shows beta's use as a sales promotion device—to beta sites themselves and the market more generally. Xerox recently used 26 sites as betas for its $220,000 Docutech Production Publisher.[10] While Xerox's usual practice was to beta at five or six sites, the quintupling of the number of sites was due to the fact that "the company used the new product as a tool for building closer relationships with key customers." These closer relationships achieved through beta testing can result in sales as effectively as the beta test is a trial run for the test site. For example, the first four U.S.–based purchasers of Elran Technologies' ACE artificial intelligence software—AT&T, Pennwalt, General Dynamics, and Unisys—were all beta sites originally.[11]

Betas can have a market impact for the system more generally as a successful beta program reduces the uncertainty about the product in the eyes of potential adopters. For example, Data Communications (1987) labeled AT&T the "League Leader" as it "moved to nail down a significant piece of business by passing initial beta tests . . . at General Electric Corp."[12] Beta test results are news in the high technology area and can generate invaluable publicity as in a *Computerworld* article headlined "First Beta Test User Lauds Kontact for 'Smarts.' "[13] The first paragraph of the article read: "The first beta test use of Mitel Corp.'s $4,000 executive workstation said it has more 'smarts' than the Northern Telecom Inc. Displayphone and is more 'truly' an executive workstation than the more expensive Xerox Corp. 8010 Star."[14]

Beta test sites can be useful to the general market as reference accounts or demo sites for potential adopters. For example, Feredata sold their data base machine to National Resource Management, an oil and gas company in Dallas, based on a demo at Wells Fargo Bank. NRM Management commented: "We are impressed that Feredata took us to see the system at Wells Fargo. They [the bank] have different appli-

[8]For details, see J. L. Forbis and N. T. Mehta, "Value-Based Strategies for Industrial Products," *Business Horizons* 3 (May–June 1981), pp. 32–42.

[9]"Cumberland Metal Industries," Harvard Business School case 9-580-104, Boston, Mass., 1980.

[10]B. J. Feder, "A Copier That Does a Lot More," *The New York Times,* October 3, 1990, pp. 1, D8.

[11]J. Stein, "An Author's ACE in the Hole?" *Computerworld,* June 5, 1989, p. 104.

[12]"Timeplex's Link/100 Draws Mixed Industry Response," *Data Communications,* August 1987, pp. 85–86, 88–90.

[13]B. Hoard, "First Beta Test User Lauds Kontact for 'Smarts,' " *Computerworld,* January 24, 1983, p. 13.

[14]Ibid.

cations but the same type of thing, high-level inquiry."[15] The Apparel Technology Center was set up in Raleigh, North Carolina, to act as a beta test site for advanced apparel technology and to document performance of systems for reference by member companies.[16] Easingwood and Beard suggest that using a prestigious firm as a beta is a good way to "legitimize" a product, which is important for very new/complex products.[17]

Beta testing with Morgan Guaranty and Manufacturers Hanover has led to the establishment of Light Signatures as the standard of the industry in stock certificate fraud detection.[18] Light Signatures' system takes a fiber fingerprint of a stock certificate. Testing with Morgan and Manufacturers (and improving the system based on that test) facilitated obtaining the commitment of 25 major securities processors, getting banknote companies to design their documents in a way compatible with the system, and gaining the endorsement of the Securities Transfer Association.

Finally, Rabino and Moore not only position beta programs as serving the above purposes but also note their signaling properties—they "serve the important function of alerting selected customers to an imminent product launch."[19] Later, this "plays a critical role in enhancing product awareness as information about technical aspects begins to leak out and rumors are generated by the press."[20]

In summary, beta site testing serves a multiplicity of purposes, not just as a "checking-out" of the functioning of the product, as many propose. It is important, however, to give explicit priority to the desired purposes. The purpose to be served determines the type of site desired (e.g., "representative" for purpose 1, "large account" for purpose 3a, and "prestigious" for purpose 3b), number of sites (e.g., "few" for purpose 1's basic function check, "many" for purpose 2b, due to segmentation, and for purpose 3), the data collected from the site, and the agreement about confidentiality of results. Since different purposes lead to vastly different optimal designs, it is crucial to have these set prior to the start of the test.

## Threats to Test Value

There are four major issues to consider in designing a valid test:

1. Selecting the proper sites.
2. Timing the test at the right stage of the product development cycle.
3. Managing account relationships.
4. Managing the information flow from the sites.

---

[15]E. Myers, "Database Machines Take Off," *Datamation,* May 15, 1985, pp. 53–54, 58, 63.

[16]F. Fortess, "Squaring Off with the Competition," *Bobbin,* May 1988, pp. 104–6, 108, 110.

[17]C. Easingwood and C. Beard, "High Technology Launch Strategies in the U.K.," *Industrial Marketing Management* 18 (1989), pp. 125–38.

[18]T. C. Crane, "Shedding Light on Certificate Fraud," *ABA Banking Journal,* May 1988, pp. 22, 25.

[19]S. Rabino and T. E. Moore, "Managing New Product Announcements in the Computer Industry," *Industrial Marketing Management* 18 (1989), pp. 35–43.

[20]Ibid.

Due to the cost of managing a beta site, it is typical that few are chosen. The danger in using a small sample is well illustrated by Jaben's discussion of banks as beta sites: "One software development company, for example, chose only one beta site to test a new product. To please that bank, the developer made several changes. The only problem was, that particular bank was not representative of the industry, and the product became so customized that it could not be marketed to other financial institutions."[21]

While most firms do protect against this type of situation by using more than one site, it is crucial in segmented markets to understand (through other research) the variation in customers' requirements and evaluation criteria. Beta sites should be representative of the product's key target markets and be firms which will push the product to its useful limit in the test.

The second major issue is properly trading off the issues involved in timing of the beta test. One argument is to push the test toward the early stages of the new product development process where the results of the test are most easily incorporated into the design of the product. On the other hand, the argument is not to jeopardize an account relationship by sending out a product with lots of bugs in it as a beta. The need to make this decision reinforces the major point of the last section (i.e., be explicit about the goals of the beta test). When Westinghouse was offered a chance to beta IBM's 3090 scientific processing capability, its computer center director assessed the likely impact of a Westinghouse test on product design to be "about zero."[22] IBM was testing late in the process, apparently after much in-house testing, and the design was reasonably fixed. On the other hand, Jenkins reports that "performance issues they discovered in beta test" led Lotus to delay shipping Release 3.0 of 1-2-3.[23] One software industry consultant lays some of the blame for "vaporware" on the lateness of actual customer contact in the development process.

Third, there are account relationship issues not directly related to product performance. In the course of a beta test, a customer relationship may be built or it may be destroyed. The vendor has information needs which the tester can find intrusive. For example, if the vendor is using the beta for the purpose of doing an economic-value-to-the-customer calculation, the vendor must understand the economics of the tester's business to translate product performance into dollar returns. Similarly, assessing product performance may require more than unobtrusive measures (e.g., it may involve survey work with a wide variety of people within the tester's organization).

Account relationship considerations extend to nonsites as well. Frequently (for reasons to be detailed in the next section), potential testers view being a beta site as a great advantage. Hence, not being considered or selected can upset potential customers.

Finally, one must manage the information flow from a beta site. Nondisclosure agreements have grown increasingly difficult to work out and thus general publicity and information to competitors can flow from beta sites. For example, the head-

---

[21]J. Jaben, "Banks as Beta Sites," *United States Banker,* December 1987, pp. 31, 33–34.

[22]D. Stamps, "Beta Site Politics," *Datamation,* April 1, 1986, pp. 62–63, 66, 70.

[23]A. Jenkins, "Long Overdue—The Reasons behind Vaporware," *Computerworld,* October 5, 1988, pp. 11–13.

line on *Computerworld*'s article on CIGNA's beta testing of Lotus's Symphony was "Symphony gets mixed reviews from beta test site" and included CIGNA's judgment that "it is difficult to master, does not easily integrate data, and lacks the versatility of stand-alone packages."[24] Similarly, the *Computerworld* article on Chase Manhattan, "the first U.S. beta test site to go public with its Wangnet experience," had Chase's vice president of telecommunications strategy describing Wang as having been pushed "into a future for which it was not entirely prepared," noting "there have been a series of delays. . . . In the overall, Wang never even could have made the original dates," and "Wang has a lot of work to do with its operating system."[25] Whatever Wang learned from the test, one has to wonder how it could be enough to net out positively over this kind of publicity.

While nondisclosure agreements have historically functioned reasonably well in non-technology-laden environments, now the number of interconnects with a multiplicity of vendors makes this unworkable generally. Consequently, one must be aware that the fact that one is testing, and the general nature of the results of those tests, are not secret for long.

## The Test Site Interests

An effective beta test requires close cooperation from the test sites. Gaining this participation and cooperation requires understanding a site's motive for being part of a test. Firms consider and sometimes even compete to be part of a beta test program in order to do the following:

1. Get experience with the newest technology ahead of competitors.
2. Have the opportunity to influence product design to yield a product which better fits the firm's particular needs.
3. Have the added attention of vendor personnel in learning how to use the new technology.
4. Develop a relationship with the vendor in anticipation of preferential treatment such as price breaks.
5. Enhance their reputation as a pioneer on the forefront of technology.

The most common reason to seek experience as a beta site is to be first with new technology. The University of Pennsylvania Library was a beta site for a do-it-yourself online search system from Telebase Systems because previous experience with similar systems indicated a latent constituent need which could be satisfied with an upgraded system.[26] Gillette approached Digital Equipment to become a beta

---

[24]P. Korzeniowski, "Symphony Gets Mixed Reviews from Beta Test Site," *Computerworld,* August 13, 1984, p. 6.

[25]B. Hoard, ". . . But Beta Test Site Encounters Rough Seas," *Computerworld,* May 16, 1983, p. 7.

[26]E. G. Fayen, "The Answer Machine and Direct Connect: Do-It-Yourself Searching in Libraries," *Online,* September 1988, pp. 13–16, 19–21.

site for an office automation and communications software package. Gillette's director of MIS commented: "We begged them [to allow Gillette to be a beta site]. They had a system that no one else had that solved our particular need at the time."[27] Alper also reports that General Electric approached Coefficient Systems to beta their product. In this situation, General Electric did achieve the second benefit noted above. It explained its later adoption of the Coefficient Systems' product by saying: "We had tested their software. . . . As a matter of fact, they took most of the suggestions we gave them and incorporated them into the next version of the product."[28]

It is clear from these first two benefits sought by test sites that vendor and test site interests do not always perfectly align themselves with one another. A site may wish a long test period to keep the product from general availability to competitors. More important, though, the sites want customization. This places a heavy burden on the vendor to make sure that these benefits are widely sought by the market.

Important secondary benefits 3, 4, and 5 provided added impetus. Stamps reports that some firms try to develop a reputation as a beta tester in order to attract the top technical personnel in the computer industry.[29]

Understanding these inducements is necessary if the firm is to overcome the perceived barriers to being a test site. The president of Remington Shavers and Knives is not atypical in his view: "I don't like being a beta site."[30] The most common concerns are these:

1. The benefits to the test site are all uncertain. The product may never come to market or the test may reveal that it is not very well suited to the purpose of the tester.
2. If the function being performed by the beta system is a critical one for the tester's operation, a parallel system may have to be run because the beta system cannot be relied upon to do the job with the required accuracy.
3. The participation does involve a time commitment in learning how to use the system and provide the desired information to the vendor.

Explicit awareness of these potential barriers and attractions to being part of a beta program is very useful in terms of constructing a test so that the desired type of site is willing to be part of the program.

## Summary

Beta tests are a staple of industrial new product development. Their effective execution can be crucial to the proper design and ultimate market success of product. This chapter has set out explicitly the vendor and test site perspectives on beta programs.

[27]A. Alper, "Beta Sites: Pioneer Users Take Risks to Grab Technical Edge," *Computerworld,* August 25, 1986, pp. 1, 15.

[28]Ibid.

[29]"Beta Site Politics."

[30]"POS Flexibility Keep Remington Sharp," *Chain Store Age Executive* (July 1990), pp. 49–50.

The purpose of the test—which can vary markedly from one situation to the next—drives the optimal program design and thus must be set clearly. The incentives presented by the vendor yield certain participation and cooperation levels from potential sites programs. The relationship of the elements is as follows:

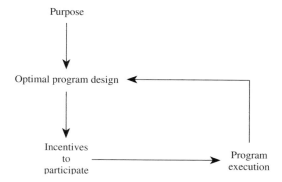

Many beta programs yield substantially less benefit (and in some cases have a negative net impact) to vendors than could be obtained. This chapter argues for more systematically setting priorities on purposes, guarding against threats to validity, and better understanding test site motivations as a path to greater contribution from this stage of the new product development process.

# Designing Channels of Distribution

*We present a framework and a method for addressing the new product channel choice decision. We offer a six-step method that involves:*

- *Disaggregating and prioritizing a distribution channel by customers' channel function requirements.*
- *Obtaining and combining customers' (and key informants') evaluations of the channel functions.*
- *Benchmarking existing channels (one's own as well as competitors').*
- *Identifying and constructing effective channel alternatives.*
- *Quantifying the short-term and long-term benefits and costs of each alternative.*
- *Selecting the appropriate channel by trading off the opportunities versus constraints posed by existing channel networks (if applicable).*

*The method requires extensive management participation to facilitate its implementation. We provide an illustrative application to demonstrate its managerial usefulness.*

For many businesses, the successful launch of new products is critical to maintaining market leadership. Unfortunately, empirical data indicate that one-third to one-half of all new products fail to meet a firm's financial and marketing goals.[1] A survey of 183 Fortune 1,000 firms indicated that nearly half of them had new product failures exceeding 40 percent.[2] This result is indeed surprising because these

---

V. Kasturi Rangan prepared this note.

[1] Booz Allen & Hamilton, *New Product Management for the 1980s* (New York: Booz Allen & Hamilton, 1982).

[2] G. Dean Kortge (1989), "Simultaneous New Product Development: Reducing the New Product Failure Rate," *Industrial Marketing Management* 18, no. 4 (1989), pp. 301–6.

failed products had been screened for technical soundness and commercial feasibility. Various explanations have been offered for these failures: insufficient attention to the commercialization process, lack of management support, and poor marketing planning and execution. In this chapter, we focus on one aspect of the launch decision: the choice of distribution channels. We offer a method to systematically evaluate, plan, and execute the channel choice decision for new industrial products.

The primary question is about channel structure; that is, which intermediary, or intermediary combination, is best suited to take the new product to market? There is an equally important corollary question: How should the intermediary network be managed once it is up and running? This and related management issues are dealt with in greater detail in Chapter 34, "Reorienting Channels of Distribution."

Fundamentally, the approach that we offer is similar to that suggested by Stern and Sturdivant[3] and Rangan, Menezes, and Maier.[4] The starting point is the customer and the building block is the channel function. In our experience the method has worked best when implemented by a cross-functional task force headed by a senior executive reporting directly to the CEO. The new product development team in many cases could double up as the channels task force. It is important for the task force, however, to commission appropriate teams to participate in the various steps, rather than assume all the expertise themselves. We first present a schematic overview of the design method, highlighting its six important steps, followed by an illustrative application.

# The Channel Design Framework

Step 1 consists of identifying homogeneous customer segments. Obviously, customers with similar requirements will need similar channel sources. It is important to keep in mind, however, that a customer is usually an end user and rarely a channel intermediary. For example, producers of agricultural chemicals should target the farmer and not the dealer. But producers of plastic pellets for making milk bottles should probably focus on the "dairy," not the "consumer," because that is where the product has value in the eyes of the end user. A dairy, especially a large one, will certainly need to worry about the cost and quality of the milk bottles. In some cases (e.g., a small dairy), the molder who manufactures the bottle might be the more appropriate end user. In any case, there should be a thoughtful end user, rather than intermediary, focus.

While advocating an emphasis on the end user may appear rather obvious, in our experience this has been a hotly debated issue in several business applications of this approach. Many industrial marketers have long looked upon their distribution channels as "customers" and rarely bothered to look beyond. Yet the primary

[3]Louis W. Stern and Frederick D. Sturdivant, "Customer-Driven Distribution Systems," *Harvard Business Review* (July–August 1987).
[4]V. Kasturi Rangan, A.J. Menezes, and Ernie Maier (1992), "Channel Selection for New Industrial Products: A Framework, Method, and Application," *Journal of Marketing* 56 (July 1992), pp. 69–82.

TABLE 1   **Eight Generic Channel Functions**

1. **Product information.** Customers seek more information on certain kinds of products, particularly products that are new and/or technically complex and those that have a rapidly changing technological component.

2. **Product customization.** Some products inherently need technical modification; they require customization to fit the customer's production requirements (e.g., special steel for a maker of surgical instruments). Many times, however, even a standard product may need to fulfill specific customer requirements or factors such as size or grade.

3. **Product quality assurance.** A customer emphasizes product integrity and reliability because of product consequences for the customer's own operations; for instance, a standard chemical may be of utmost importance to pharmaceutical manufacturers, given the liability associated with a defective final product. This is a measure of the application's importance to the customer.

4. **Lot size.** This function reflects the customer's dollar outlay for the product. If it has a high unit value or is used extensively, it is likely to represent a significant financial decision for the customer and is likely to lead to a concentrated purchasing effort.

5. **Assortment.** A customer may need a broad range of products and may require one-stop shopping. For example, an electrical contractor may need products that satisfy different electrical codes, depending on the nature of the project. At other times, assortment needs may simply be related to the breadth of the product line (e.g., size) and availability of complementary products (e.g., wires with electrical switches).

6. **Availability.** Some customer environments require the channel to support a high degree of product availability. These are usually customers whose product-usage rate is difficult to predict (e.g., spare parts, because they are required only when a machine breaks down), or customers who will switch to competition rather than wait when the product is unavailable. Notions of demand uncertainty and requirements of buffer inventory are related to this function.

7. **After-sales service.** Customers need services such as installation, repair, maintenance, and warranty. Often the quality and availability of such postsales services will influence the initial sale. The nature of this service will obviously differ by industry. For example, in the computer industry the compatibility and availability of hardware and software upgrades may serve as a key purchasing influence.

8. **Logistics.** Transporting, storing, and supplying products to the end user involve levels of complexity. For example, transshipping and transporting hazardous chemicals may require special investments likely to increase handling costs. Moreover, once such investments are in place, governing their effective use will involve additional transaction costs.

purpose of the distribution channel is to satisfy customer/end user needs, and intermediaries are conduits to effect this goal. The recommended method here is not intended to undermine the role of the intermediary, only to view them as a means to an end and not an end in itself.

Step 2 consists of identifying and prioritizing the customer's channel function requirements. A generic list appears in Table 1, but it should be treated only as a starting point. Each product-market context is unique, and channel function requirements that best represent customers' reality are most likely to lead to effective channel solutions. This information should be elicited from customers in as fine-grained detail as possible. For instance, it would be useful to know how keen customers are for the three-year warranty instead of the one-year, and how much they would be willing to pay for it; how sensitive they are for a two-hour versus a six-hour service response time; and so on. Table 2 provides an example.

---

**TABLE 2    Example: Channel Function Priorities and Operational Detail**

---

**Most Important**

1. **Product information.** Customers would like complete technical knowledge of product construction. They would prefer the availability of an expert to supervise installation as well as initial use. After the initialization, customers would be satisfied to exchange performance characteristics via computer, seeking assistance only when necessary.

2. **Product warranty.** Customers would prefer a 3-year warranty and are not willing to pay more than a 5% price premium to receive the same. In case of a product breakdown, they would like it repaired within 4 hours, and in any case not beyond 24 hours. Customers are willing to pay for the labor charges if repaired within 4 hours.

**Somewhat Important but Not Critical**

3. **Application engineering.** Customers would like application engineers to visit installations every month to assist in optimizing the system in operation.

4. **Availability of complementary products.** Customers would like to source complementary products simultaneously from the same channel source if possible.

5. **Credit terms.** Customers would like a 90-day credit term, if possible, but they can live with 30-day credit terms.

---

In our experience, the data for this step are most effectively gathered simultaneously with Step 1 (segmentation data). This way, segmentation and channeling strategies are consistent with each other and reflective of customers' needs.

Data gathering in Step 2 has to be based on customer input. For new products, this equates to potential customers, but depending on the nature of the innovation, these potential users may or may not be able to provide reliable feedback. In these cases, we suggest using a team of experts who have special knowledge of the products and how customers are likely to buy and use them. There are two such groups of experts. First are customer lead users. Eric von Hippel[5] identifies them as "users whose present strong needs will become general in a marketplace months or years in the future. Since lead users are familiar with conditions that lie in the future for most others, they can serve as a need-forecasting laboratory for marketing research." A second group of experts is often found in-house.[6] In the new-product channel context, judgmental projections of experienced salespeople, product managers, sales managers, and product development engineers can compensate for the absence of extensive customer data on purchases and usage behaviors.

Step 3 consists of benchmarking the seller's existing channel capabilities as well as competitors' channels with respect to customers' channel function requirements. Data from Step 2 will serve to prioritize and anchor customers' desired (or ideal) level of channel functions. A supplier executing at that level can therefore be assured of the lion's share of the business. But the supplier's channel capabilities may not match this functional profile. The larger the deviation on the important

---

[5]E. Von Hippel, "Lead Users: A Source of Novel Product Concepts," *Management Science* 32, no. 7 (1986), pp. 791–805.

[6]Jean-Claude Larreche and Reza Moinpour, "Managerial Judgement in Marketing: The Concept of Expertise," *Journal of Marketing Research* 20 (May 1983), pp. 110–21.

---
**TABLE 3    Channel Benchmarking**

A. Large Customer Segment

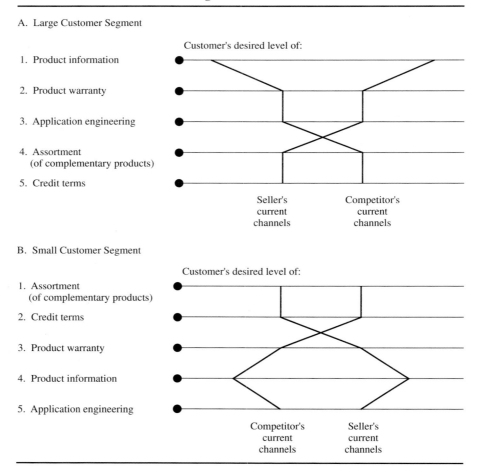

Customer's desired level of:

1. Product information
2. Product warranty
3. Application engineering
4. Assortment
   (of complementary products)
5. Credit terms

Seller's current channels    Competitor's current channels

B. Small Customer Segment

Customer's desired level of:

1. Assortment
   (of complementary products)
2. Credit terms
3. Product warranty
4. Product information
5. Application engineering

Competitor's current channels    Seller's current channels

---

functions, the less the chances of attracting customers. It is a good idea at this stage to also benchmark the channel capabilities of leading competitors. This will provide a comprehensive map of the company's relative channel strengths and weaknesses.

In the example in Table 3, the leading competitor uses a direct salesforce channel and is therefore able to provide a relatively high level of customer intimacy with respect to product information, product warranty, and application engineering functions, whereas the target firm uses a distributor channel and is therefore able to provide a better level of service with respect to availability of complementary products and credit terms. The firm's relative channel profile for two customer segments is shown. But because the large customers and small customers prioritize channel functions differently, the target company is likely to do poorly with the large customers if it were to sell the new product through its existing channels. On the other hand, it has a stronger profile with small customers because its distributors provide superior "assortment" and "credit terms."

When the various product options in the market are comparable in product functions, features, and price, Step 3 serves as a direct calibration of channel effectiveness. If there are product differences, however, the relative deviations from the customers' channel function requirements will not neatly map onto projected sales/market share. This is why some companies prefer to have product development people on the channels task force. Having the benchmarking and calibration step executed by the same team that identified, clarified, and prioritized customers' channel function requirements ensures measurement consistency and reliability.

Step 4 consists of creatively interpreting the output from Steps 2 and 3 to arrive at the feasible channel options that would satisfy customers' requirements. For example, large customers' needs from Table 3 could be potentially served by a direct salesforce, and small customers by a distributor channel. But it is also possible to serve large customers with a combination of direct salesforce and distributors, whereby the direct salesforce would handle the product information, product warranty, and application engineering functions, and the distributors would handle the product assortment and credit terms. Usually, various channel alternatives will be available to take a product to market (e.g., agents, brokers, manufacturers' reps, value-added resellers). The role of the channels task force here is to creatively identify channel alternatives with the potential of getting closer to customers' ideal requirements. For the example, in Table 4, Option 1 (seller → sales force → distributor → customer) is the current capability. Options 2 and 3 are hybrid combinations whereby the salesforce/agents perform a set of channel functions, and the

---

TABLE 4   **Generating Alternatives**

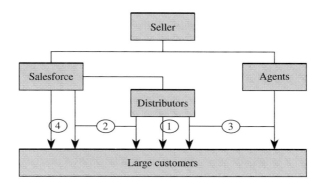

Option 1   Current method of going to market.
Option 2   Salesforce and distributors sharing channel functions among them.
Option 3   Agents and distributors sharing channel functions among them.
Option 4   Salesforce performing all channel functions.

distributors supplement the rest. It would be ideal for the salesforce/agents to deliver the product information, product warranty, and application engineering functions, and for the distributors to deliver the product assortment and credit function. This way both the large and small customers would be happy. Finally, Option 4 is a pure direct salesforce alternative, which would please the large customers.

It is important at this stage not to be restricted by real or imagined constraints. Issues of channel cost or conflict should be strictly deferred to Step 5. For example, one may conclude that under Option 1, the seller's existing distributors would be unable to adequately satisfy customers' product information, product warranty, and application engineering needs. But that should be no reason to rule out the option. If feasible, one should assume that with appropriate investments and training, distributors could rise to the desired level. Such an option should then be considered in the choice set at this stage.

Step 5 consists of systematically evaluating the benefits and costs associated with each option. Revenues, market share, market penetration, transaction costs, start-up costs, and opportunity costs must all be considered. Channel costs are not only influenced by the depth and extent of channel functions to be performed, but also by competitive behavior that influences the availability of channels. Varying investment strategies for each option from Step 4 will lead to differing customer satisfaction levels and consequently varying levels of outputs (revenue, profits, share, etc.). Investment options that push the profile in Table 3 closest to the customer's ideal will lead to the best outcomes, but that may come at a huge cost. Thus the options being considered here will have to be a multiple of those from Step 4—varying investment levels for each option. This analysis should be as quantitative and as specific as possible. An estimate of intensity (and number) of distributors, for example, is useful information. Qualitative factors such as channel motivation and level of conflict/cooperation may be considered as well. The appropriate channel, of course, is a sensible trade-off between output (e.g., revenues) and input (e.g., transaction costs). Companies with multiple product-market segments may draw up a short list of appropriate strategies for each segment rather than prematurely locking in on one. The reason for this becomes clear in Step 6.

Step 6 consists of elaborating the channel overlaps for multiproduct, multimarket businesses by aggregating the output from Step 5. Channel synergies and dysfunctionalities across product-market segments should be discussed, and trade-offs made within the pool of appropriate strategies. This discussion is likely to be productive and objective if Step 5 data are largely quantitative. Channel designers then have an estimate of the systemwide cost for trading each best option from Step 5. Benefit–cost analysis then becomes more meaningful, and if necessary the company might be better off investing in conflict resolution mechanisms rather than skipping customer-oriented optimal channels. Strategic long-run factors become very important at this stage of the evaluation. The key question is, "Do the channels provide a market advantage? Does it reflect strategy?"

Table 5 shows three different optimal channels for the three different target segments of a company. There are likely to be practical difficulties in the coexistence of these three channels. First, Segments 1 and 2 may be somewhat hard to demar-

**TABLE 5    Optimal Channels for Three Segments**

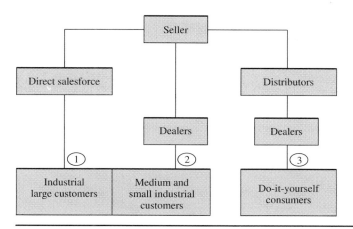

cate, especially with respect to the medium-sized accounts. Second, "dealers" for the industrial and consumer markets may overlap in some cases. But if the company's strategic focus was on the industrial market and, say, this accounted for 80 percent of the market potential, it may make a lot of sense to serve Segment 3 through industrial dealers (Channel 2) as well. Again, knowing the potential conflicts between the direct salesforce and dealers for the medium-sized accounts, it may be wise to negotiate dealer agreements carefully up front. Alternatively, as shown in Table 6, if a hybrid approach was second best for both of the industrial segments, and if the projected decrease in revenues and profits is less than the anticipated conflict costs of the ideal channel, it may simply make sense to go with the second best solution.

**TABLE 6    The Second Best Option: Hybrid Channel for Industrial Customers**

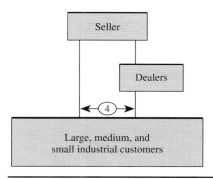

The key to effectively implementing this step is totally dependent on the care used and detail undertaken in the previous steps. In the absence of well-calibrated channel maps and concrete financial data, this crucial final step could deteriorate into a slugfest of personal hunches, which is exactly what this systematic procedure tries to overcome.

## Application: A Description of the Process[7]

What follows is a brief description of how the channel design method was implemented in a division of a large industrial company.

Manufacturing process changes had enabled this company to develop a new product, Scotchfiber (disguised name). Customers used Scotchfiber-type products for a variety of applications such as deburring metal parts; deflashing plastic and paper utensils; cleaning golf balls, tiles, and rubber articles; gripping fabric in textile mills; and containing components for assembly. Management was convinced of Scotchfiber's superiority, especially in the $100 million industrial cleaning and finishing market, which consisted of many specialty applications. The new product was to be directed originally only at large industrial users in various industries. Independent market research confirmed that these customers uniformly sought a high level of technical benefits. The product launch team headed by the director for marketing operations served as the channels task force.

Scotchfiber was a new product line for this company. Potential customers currently used alternative solutions to address their needs, and Scotchfiber applications had little overlap with the company's existing product lines. About 95 percent of the company's current products were sold to end users through a network of more than 500 independent distributors with the help of the company's 100 salespeople. Because of the new product's numerous potential applications and the strength of its distribution channels, management was inclined to route Scotchfiber through existing channels, which consisted of general-line finishing distributors.

With the help of the marketing manager, product manager, and two sales representatives, we worked out operational definitions for each of the eight channel functions identified in Table 1 to reflect the Scotchfiber marketing context. The function "product information," for example, was characterized by the degree of information a customer sought on (1) roll fiber length, fiber property, and construction density, and (2) usage properties, such as the ability to finish irregularly shaped pieces and interiors. The operational definitions for each function were typed on separate cards to be used as the basic interview guide.

We chose as key respondents 10 potential "customer experts" who were at the leading edge of adopting and using the new product. These lead users were considered the trendsetters in their industry and either had already started to use Scotch-

---

[7]A large part of this section is extracted from V. Kasturi Rangan, A. J. Menezes, and Ernie Maier, "Channel Selection for New Industrial Products: A Framework, Method, and Application," *Journal of Marketing* 56 (July 1992). Printed with permission of the American Marketing Association.

fiber in production trials or were in the process of placing the trial order. In addition, we selected 11 individuals from the company who had special knowledge about the product and/or its customer applications. Some of these "producer experts" were intensely involved in Scotchfiber product and application development, and the rest were involved in marketing the product to lead users.

Experts were interviewed individually to obtain their evaluations of customers' anticipated channel function requirements and priorities as they saw them. We chose three years as the time horizon for the new product channel study because the company's top management estimated this to be the time frame in which Scotchfiber, if successful, could establish itself in the market.

Combining the experts' evaluations is essential to making a good channel decision because knowledge is generally dispersed in the early stages of the product life cycle. Two broad approaches are used for combining experts' opinions: (*a*) group-oriented, where experts interact, inform, and build consensus, such as the Delphi method,[8] and (*b*) analytical (statistical), when interaction among the experts is impossible because of physical separation or confidentiality. Because some of the lead-use customers were considering proprietary applications of the Scotchfiber technology, we did not use the interactive Delphi method, but instead chose a mathematical "consensus" method developed by Robert Winkler.[9]

The new product channel profiles were presented to the new product launch team, which was made up of six members of the division's marketing and sales staff who were responsible for drafting an initial Scotchfiber marketing plan. None had participated as experts in the earlier evaluations. The launch team also benchmarked the capabilities of its existing channels as well as Scotchfiber's indirect competitors. This was done by a subcommittee of the task force aided by a market research firm. Armed with these data, the launch team met several times to reach the following conclusions:

- The anticipated customer requirements on product information, product customization, and product quality assurance for the new product considerably exceeded the current capabilities of the division's general-line finishing distributors.

- The anticipated channel function profile after the product was established (i.e., 3 years) matched that of the division's other products currently being routed through general-line finishing distributors.

- A new class of distributors, fiber specialists, which the company did not currently use, would also be able to satisfy the functional requirement for the established product. However, they would have difficulties fulfilling the first three functional requirements for the new product, but to a lesser degree than the current distributors.

---

[8]H. A. Linstone and M. A. Turoff, *The Delphi Method: Techniques and Applications* (Boston: Addison-Wesley, 1975).

[9]Robert L. Winkler, "Combining Probability Distributions from Dependent Information Sources," *Management Science* 27 (April 1981), pp. 479–88.

**TABLE 7    Feasible Channel Options**

|  | *Now (when product is new)* | *Three Years Later (when product is established)* |
|---|---|---|
| Option 1 | Salesforce | • General-line finishing distributors |
| Option 2 | Salesforce | • Fiber specialist |
| Option 3 | Salesforce and general-line finishing distributors | • General-line finishing distributors |
| Option 4 | Salesforce and fiber specialists | • Fiber specialists |
| Option 5 | Salesforce and general-line finishing distributors | • Fiber specialists |
| Option 6 | Salesforce and fiber specialists | • General-line finishing distributors |

Six channel paths were initially identified as feasible options for taking the product to market (see Table 7): two of these were pure options, while the other four were hybrid combinations of salesforce and distributors sharing channel tasks for the new product. Options 5 and 6, however, were eliminated as the group thought both of these options would entail very high switching costs and channel conflicts given the required change from one class of distributor to the other. It just didn't make sense to start with fiber specialists and switch to general-line distributors and vice versa. The costs of taking back inventory and any legal fees for rewriting and defending new contracts would far surpass the benefits. Thus, the choices for the optimal channel were reduced to four.

At this company, new products were assigned sales and profit targets: Line managers were expected to achieve or surpass both. The division's area sales managers and their key sales representatives were contacted for revenue and cost estimates of going to market using each of the four channel options. Instead of estimating variations in sales revenues through each option, area sales managers felt more confident in estimating the intensity of channel coverage each option required for achieving the fixed sales target. Knowing this, managers could estimate the cost of each channel option. Distribution costs were disaggregated into seven elements: demand generation (salesforce time, marketing, and advertising), distributor technical training, distributor administrative training, sales support (inventory carrying and customer credit), logistics (order processing, transportation, and warehousing), distribution margin, and opportunity costs (of salesforce time taken away from selling existing products).

Many cost elements, such as logistics, sales support, and distribution margin, can be computed once the channel options and the details of its implementation are known. But others, such as distributor training costs and opportunity costs, are essentially judgments for new products and channels that were obtained from area sales managers and subsequently refined by headquarters' accounting staff. We aggregated the costs for each channel option. Because the sales target was identical for all four options, the optimal channel in this case was the cost-minimizing option. The relative cost numbers are shown in Table 8. Option 3 was the optimal choice.

**TABLE 8    Relative Costs of Feasible Channel Options**

| | Demand Generation Costs | Distributor Training and Maintenance Costs | | Sales Support Costs | Logistics Costs | Distribution Margin | Opportunity Costs | Total Cost Index |
|---|---|---|---|---|---|---|---|---|
| | | *Technical* | *Administrative* | | | | | |
| Option 1 | High | Low | Low | High | Medium | Low | Medium | 102 |
| Option 2 | High | Medium | High | Medium | Medium | Medium | High | 110 |
| Option 3 | Medium | Medium | Low | Medium | Low | High | Low | 100 |
| Option 4 | Medium | Medium | High | Medium | Medium | High | High | 111 |

In Option 3, the salesforce and the general-line finishing distributors together called on end users to establish the product and effect sales. In three years, these same distributors would be expected to take on full responsibility for the product line; by then, it was assumed that the distributors would be sufficiently trained to service and maintain the several applications for the product.

# Conclusion

To evaluate the usefulness of the proposed method, we went back to the company a year after the new product launch to obtain information on how Scotchfiber was performing. We interviewed several members of the original launch team and a cross section of the field sales management and sales reps directly involved in the Scotchfiber marketing effort. A full year after launch, Scotchfiber sales were running 25 percent ahead of sales targets and profits were running 34 percent above expected levels.

Although these results pertain to evaluations at the end of the first year of a three-year planning horizon model, management believed the suggested method helped them make a good decision. Without the aid of this method, the company would have distributed the product through its 500 distributors, which, managers thought on hindsight, would have been a mistake. The company's decision makers initially underestimated the channel support required for the new product's launch. Formally incorporating customer judgments, an essential part of the method, helped remedy management misperception.

Our interviews also identified factors such as effective communication between headquarters and field sales as key reasons for Scotchfiber's success. But two of the top three reasons were "involvement of the direct sales force" and "the channel selection process." A key contribution of this research was the process itself. Other than bringing a conceptual framework to the new product channel decision, the research process integrated judgments from three important constituencies:

- Lead-use customers (the potential early adapters of the product).
- In-house experts (such as the product manager and distribution development manager).
- Line managers (sales reps and sales managers).

The process combined channel concepts with experts' judgments and managers' inputs to arrive at an appropriate channel for the new product. The managers' active participation generated substantial commitment to the method and facilitated its implementation. The very process of systematically focusing on the new product channel problem led to the discovery and improvement of several related (but not central to the method) tasks, all of which magnified the impact. There is a valuable lesson in this: The process of method development and implementation is perhaps as important as the underlying conceptual framework. While the method outlined here may be immediately more applicable to new product markets, the same principles have been used in several channel audits of mature product markets as well. Steps 1 to 3 are particularly useful. Knowing the capability of existing channels with respect to customers' channel function requirements and benchmarking them with competitors' channels provide useful diagnostics. While a structural change may not be feasible in some cases given long-established channel relationships, distribution managers can at least infer specific guidelines on how to manage existing channel networks to enhance their profile to be more in tune with customer needs.

SECTION III  # Managing Mature Products

# 10 Beating the Commodity Magnet

*All markets follow a cycle of growth and maturity, then commoditization and decline. In this reading we argue that while commoditization of an industry may seem inevitable, the better-managed firms find a way to make money in the commodity cycle. These firms know how and when to differentiate their products through innovation, service, and customer partnerships, and how and when to offer a no-frills product and seek cost leadership. Four such strategic options are detailed and discussed.*

## Introduction[1]

According to conventional wisdom, all markets follow a cycle of growth and maturity, then commoditization and decline. Profits are to be found in the specialty industries—electronics, scientific equipment, and aerospace—while more mature industries beset by declining demand and overcapacity cannot sustain comparable profitability. Hence, many corporations throughout the 1980s had sought to divest their mature or commodity-type businesses, while redeploying resources into something more promising. Our research refutes this conventional wisdom. Many companies in commodity businesses perform as well as or better than their counterparts in specialty businesses because they have learned how to demonstrate value for their customers. They have mastered the art of beating the commodity magnet.

These firms in an increasing number of commodity businesses—blood collection products, replacement motors, and steel strapping, among others—are

---

V. Kasturi Rangan and George T. Bowman prepared this reading.

Copyright © 1994 by the President and Fellows of Harvard College.

Harvard Business School note 594-122.

[1]Parts of this reading have been extracted from V. Kasturi Rangan and George T. Bowman, "Beating the Commodity Magnet," *Industrial Marketing Management* 21 (1992), pp. 215–24. They are reproduced here with permission from the authors.

becoming consistently profitable by knowing how and when to differentiate their products through innovation, service, and customer partnerships, and how and when to offer a no-frills product and seek cost leadership. These companies understand that commoditization can be a self-fulfilling prophecy in which lower price, profits, service, and customer loyalty interlock in a cycle of decline. While commoditization of an industry may seem to be inevitable, the better-managed firms find a way to make money in the commodity cycle, as the following examples suggest.

**Blood Collection Products.[2]**   Becton Dickinson & Company (BD) has maintained a commanding market share with a price premium in the market for needles, collection tubes, and lancets, despite low-price competition from a Japanese competitor, Terumo, Sherwood Medical, and entry attempts by Abbott Labs, Johnson & Johnson, and Corning Glass. Key success factors include stress on quality and the direction of its selling efforts to the lab technicians who actually use their products. One BD sales representative noted several instances when hospital administrators attempted to purchase less-expensive products but were rebuffed by bench technicians, who insisted on BD's well-known VACUTAINER® and MICROTAINER® name.

**Replacement Motors.[3]**   The replacement motor market for consumer durables has few entry barriers, hundreds of competitors, and distributors who have introduced private-label brands. When industry-leader GE began losing market share in the mid-1980s, it sought to learn more about customer requirements and discovered that 30 percent of all customers left the point-of-sale without the motors they had come to buy. In response, GE increased stock levels and efficiency of order fulfillment; it also fought price erosion by providing training and unique product information for wholesale counter personnel, and by creating a computerized cross-reference system that enabled wholesalers to determine which GE motor could be used as a replacement.

**Steel Strapping.[4]**   Despite low-cost competition from numerous competitors and fluctuating steel prices, Signode Industries has long maintained profitable industry leadership by taking a partnership approach to customer strapping requirements. Key elements in Signode's strategy are the study of each industry's strapping needs, the design of specialized equipment to meet those needs, and the service and sales of strapping consumables. Because of this systems sales approach, the Signode sales force maintains multiple contacts with customer organizations, ranging from vice presidents of manufacturing to plant managers and purchasing agents. In this way, Signode has become the standard-bearer of steel strapping; its competition has to provide products that fit into Signode equipment.

---

[2]Frank V. Cespedes and V. Kasturi Rangan, "Becton Dickinson and Company: Vacutainer Systems Division," Harvard Business School case no. 592–037.

[3]E. Raymond Corey, "GE Component Motors," Harvard Business School case no. 586-059.

[4]Rowland T. Moriarty, "Signode Industries," Harvard Business School case no. 587-157.

# Commodity Magnet

The product life cycle concept is well known. It traces the evolution of new product markets from the product introduction stage through growth to maturity.[5] See Figure 1. The theory is that product adoption is slow at the beginning as early adopters try out the product. There is usually a need for customer education and close supplier assistance to tide over the early technical uncertainties. Over time, as these uncertainties are debugged, more customers adopt the product and the market begins to grow more rapidly. But wider market acceptance will often attract new competitors and the ensuing battle leads to price deterioration. Customers, who are by now quite knowledgeable about the product may not need the same hand-holding they required in the earlier stages. Consequently, they may seek price concessions, adding to the competitive price pressures in the market. In an attempt to seek and hold customers, some suppliers may attempt to differentiate their follow-on services such as quick shipment, product warranty, product availability, and so on. But provision of these services costs money, and not all customers may see the value in paying the higher price. Worse still, some customers, especially the large ones, may demand all these services at the lower price, and some suppliers will acquiesce to these demands to keep their factories running in an intensively competitive environment.

**FIGURE 1**

*Product life cycle: implications*

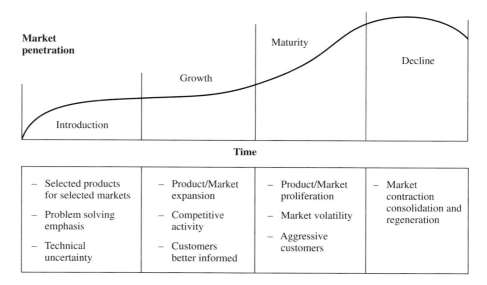

[5]See, for example, Philip Kotler, "Managing Products through Their Product Life Cycle," in *Marketing Management: Analysis, Planning, Implementation, and Control,* 7th ed. (Englewood Cliffs, N.J.: Prentice Hall, 1991), pp. 347–73.

**FIGURE 2**

*Market life cycle:
alternative
framework*

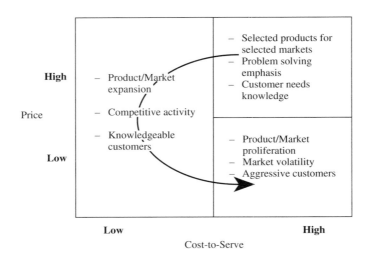

This description of the product life cycle sketched in Figure 1 has significant implications for managers when viewed along the two dimensions of price and cost-to-serve.[6] See Figure 2. The price dimension reflects the relative price of the product offering in comparison to other similar competing solutions. For a new product, the comparison is with existing, often inferior ways of solving the same problem. The cost-to-serve dimension again is a relative measure and reflects the marketing, sales, distribution, and customer service intensity needed to support the product during its life. It is easy to see from Figure 2 how the commodity trend could have grave implications for company profitability. As the market matures, relative prices tend to drop even as the cost-to-serve increases.

Figure 2 to some extent is a simplified explanation of the product life cycle dynamic. In some markets—for example, pharmaceuticals—there may be a significant pent-up demand for a new product, and if the product is protected by patents or technological advantages, the product may be able to command high prices at a relatively low cost-to-serve. Thus, the product could be launched as a "specialty" rather than an "augmented" offering. The offering may be augmented later when the pharmaceutical goes off patent. In other cases, the market evolution may proceed in other different ways, as indicated in Figure 3. In general, the commodity magnet has the tendency to pull the business from the northwest to the southeast quadrant, that is, from a specialty to a commodity.

But regardless of the nature of the product—grain or a computer—it is the market dynamics that distinguish a commodity. Most managers recognize the early warning signs of commoditization—increasing competition, availability of "me-too" products, customers' reluctance to pay for unnecessary features and services

---

[6]The matrix in Figure 2 is adapted from Benson P. Shapiro, V. Kasturi Rangan, Rowland T. Moriarty, and Elliot Ross, "Manage Customers for Profits (Not Just Sales)," *Harvard Business Review,* September–October 1987.

**FIGURE 3**

*Market types and
market evolution*

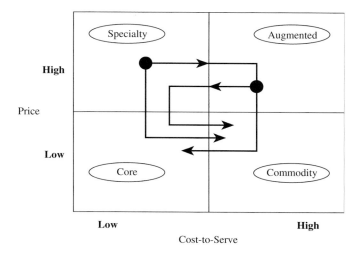

accompanying the product, and pressure on prices and margins in general.[7] Steadily
and deliberately as the market transitions to a commodity type, many buyers begin
to perceive the product and its suppliers to be homogeneous, and price becomes the
predominant buying criterion.

A few key points that are worth highlighting: The commodity trends described
above and sketched in Figures 1, 2, and 3 are inevitable in all product markets. The
pace of commoditization may vary—six months in semiconductors to nearly 15
years in certain specialty chemicals, but every product market will eventually face
the pull of the commodity magnet. It is important to note, however, that not every
firm in the said product market will necessarily follow in the market trend. Each
firm will take positions that are consistent with its capabilities and strategies. For
example, while the personal computer industry may be rapidly commoditizing, individual players such as Apple, IBM, Compaq, and Dell may all take different positions on the product map shown in Figure 3. Thus, in a commodity market, there
will coexist high-price–high-service players as well as low-price–low-service players. Different players will be offering augmented product, specialty products, and
core products all at the same time.

# Key Concepts

In order to formulate marketing strategies that are appropriate to avert the commodity magnet, it is important to understand a couple of key concepts that underlie the dynamic of the commodity trend. This is explained in Figure 4. The

---

[7]Benson P. Shapiro, "Specialties versus Commodities: The Battle for Profit Margins," Harvard Business School working paper no. 587-120.

**FIGURE 4**

*Key concepts*

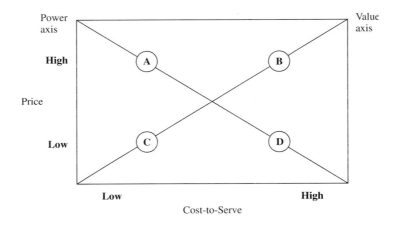

diagonal that runs from southwest to northeast represents an axis of value where a company charges a price that reflects the value of the service it provides. The southwest quadrant (C) represents a core, no-frills product that is not accompanied by highly augmented services. Correspondingly, the price paid by the customer is relatively low. On the other hand, the northeast quadrant (B) represents a product accompanied by intensive value-added services, for which the customer pays a higher price. All locations above the value diagonal signify that the company is able to extract a higher value than the services it renders, because customers perceive the firm's product as being superior to competitive offerings or substitutes. In short, all positions above the value diagonal reflect a product differentiation strategy. Positions below the value diagonal usually indicate that the firm is unable to extract the full value of the services it renders with its product. At the southeast corner (D), the company essentially gives away all its services free, perhaps in an effort to retain market share in a very competitive market environment. Thus, the cross diagonal represents an axis of power: the manufacturer is more powerful (differentiated) in the northwest and the customer in the southeast.

Clearly, strategy A would be the most advantageous for any firm, and will likely lead to the highest profits; the strategy is based on product feature/function superiority. Strategies B and C ensure an adequate and fair return to the firm, with B emphasizing differentiation through augmented services, and C emphasizing a low cost approach. Which strategy a firm should adopt, B or C, depends on its relative strengths and weaknesses with respect to other competitors in the field. Strategy D is rarely consciously adopted by any firm. Because of the customer and competitive environment, a firm reluctantly sinks to that quadrant. While a firm may be able to survive that environment in the short run, it is guaranteed to lead to losses in the long run because no business can afford to give away services without correspondingly increasing prices.

When a product is dragged down to a commodity status, the conventional marketing wisdom is to attempt to push it back up again by differentiating the physical product,[8] or adding value by innovating the product delivery system. There are several problems with that prescription. Some low-tech products may not have any further scope for product improvements. And even for high-tech products, not all firms have the resources to effect the necessary innovations. Moreover, investments in systems to add value are often costly (e.g., computerizing the order entry and inventory systems). Most of all, it is not entirely obvious that customers will place value on the improved product or service features—after all, it is a commodity market! Under such circumstances, what does a manager do to preserve the firm's profit position? How does one manage to beat the commodity cycle?

# Differentiation Strategies

Firms with differentiated products operating from quadrant A (in Figure 4) often cannot resist the temptation to charge high prices even as the market rapidly gravitates toward a commodity status. We believe that in a true commodity market, firms would be unable to sustain the A position without seriously undermining their market share. If a firm does not offer a real customer benefit or product differentiation, customers, as they become knowledgeable, are likely to switch to competition rather than stay with a firm that is apparently overpriced for the services it offers. It is much easier to move toward the value diagonal from A, before commoditization occurs. Once the market has already moved in that direction, to rise up from the D quadrant to the value diagonal is far more difficult for reasons we discuss later in this chapter. On the other hand, if the A position is sustainable because of true product advantages, it would be financially unwise to surrender the extra margins prematurely. One needs to keep a close eye on the market trend for signs of commoditization.

The key idea is to move toward a stable position along the value diagonal so that the manufacturer is firmly entrenched in quadrant B providing an augmented product, or in quadrant C providing a core product. In either case, both the firm and its customers are involved in a fair exchange. Although it may seem that there are unlimited directions to move toward the equilibrium axis, Figure 5 shows that a firm has only four really feasible options. Any other strategy would be difficult for either a firm or its customers to adopt. A firm in position A, for instance, attempting to move toward a position along the value diagonal, would find it impossible to pull off any movement in the AB to AC range, because that would require the company either to drop price or increase service, or both. This is likely to cause a strain on profits in what is already a tough market. Management is hardly likely to approve a plan that voluntarily surrenders profits when other potential options are available. Similarly, for a firm in position D, attempting to move its customers to the equilibrium axis along the DB to DC range would involve increasing price or decreasing service, or both. This is likely to lead to a steep loss in customers and market share.

---

[8]Theodore Levitt, "Differentiation of Anything," *Harvard Business Review,* January–February 1980. Also see Philip Kotler, *Marketing Management: Analysis, Planning, and Control,* 6th ed. (Englewood Cliffs, N.J.: Prentice Hall, 1988), p. 448.

**FIGURE 5**

*Strategies to beat
the commodity
magnet*

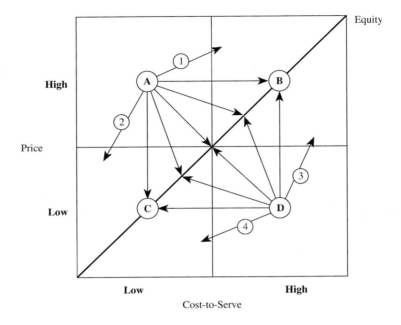

In the final analysis, there are only four feasible strategies, two that can be implemented before the onset of commoditization and two after. These are:

1. *Value-added strategy:* Moving to the value diagonal by increasing price as well as augmenting services.
2. *Process innovation strategy:* Moving to the value diagonal mainly by decreasing price and some cost-to-serve as well.
3. *Market focus strategy:* Moving to the value diagonal by focusing on customers who would pay the additional price for augmented services because they value them.
4. *Service innovation strategy:* Moving to the value diagonal mainly by decreasing cost-to-serve. Again, like the market focus, this strategy will lead to a reorientation of the customer base.

**Value-added Strategy.**     Value-added strategy allows a firm to forestall price erosion by providing value-added services to the product. Such services necessarily should go beyond those that a customer would normally expect (e.g., on-time order fulfillment). Installation, training, and technical support are among the many that are often used. Effective differentiators begin by asking what the buyer values. Learning may require formal research and should generate a comprehensive list of possible product and service offerings for each customer segment. Effective differentiators then critically evaluate the list of possible service offerings, choosing those with the greatest potential to leverage customer value over cost-to-serve. In any case, the strategy's purpose is to pamper the customer with a lot of services, enabling the supplier to earn a price premium over competition. The basic approach is one of bundling: The product and services when combined form a unique package that the customer values and is willing to pay extra money for.

The value-added strategy was central to the success of Becton Dickinson's VACUTAINER trademark systems division. Given the increasing competition and increasing customer sensitivity to price, the company consciously built its brand name and reputation. The wide assortment of needles and tubes, and their unique color-coded product identification schemes for the dozens of blood tests doctors performed, gave it a quality edge and image. The company complemented this strong product quality with an intense relationship effort at the bench level. That is, the company's sales force called on and cultivated hospital laboratory technicians who actually used the product. The combined effect of the value-added strategies has helped the company retain market leadership and profits even in a rapidly commoditizing market.

We should emphasize, however, that value-added strategies that do not provide real value to the customer are not likely to survive as the market deteriorates to a commodity status. Successful marketers like Becton Dickinson, by constantly enhancing the product and the delivery system, had so trained the customer to their standards and services that switching to a competitor's product would involve substantial retraining costs.

Customers' costs of possession and usage, in addition to acquisition, should be made an inherent part of the selling proposition. For instance, the benefit of providing just-in-time inventories may outweigh the price premium. Thus, the point here is not one of additional services alone, but value added, in such a way that the customer benefits are quantifiable. In short, value-added strategies that can clearly demonstrate added savings to the customer are likely to be sustainable in the long run.[9] Customers' costs of switching (to a competing product) are an important part of the cost calculation under this strategy. The seller attempts to minimize the buyers' costs of acquisition, possession, and switching. We call this value-in-use to distinguish it from the simple value-added strategy described earlier.

The value-in-use strategy was successfully employed in GE's replacement motors business. To improve customer service, GE helped its dealers to measure and improve fill rate (percentage of time customer orders are successfully filled in from stock) and average delivery time of in-stock and nonstock items (i.e., items that distributors get from GE after receipt of customer order). In addition, it installed a stocking and ordering information system for improving customer service. Contractors seeking GE motors could now obtain them easily, and the little extra they paid in price was more than offset by the near elimination of delay, costs of waiting, inconvenience, and uncertainty. The system helped customers routinize their procurement functions, enabling them to concentrate on their primary business-providing maintenance and repair services. The gain in alternative revenue far outweighed the extra price of motors.

[9]John L. Forbis and Nitin T. Mehta, "Value-Based Strategies for Industrial Products," *Business Horizons* 24, no. 3 (1981).

**Process Innovation Strategy.**    The crux of this strategy is to offer customers product at dramatically lower prices for the few services that are now stripped away. Usually such a steep drop in price is only feasible if the firm is able to innovate its design at considerably lower manufacturing costs, without significantly altering, and if possible enhancing, the features and performance of the current product. Such a strategy is often possible in new high-technology industries, where the component parts have rapidly improving performance-to-price ratios. The table below, for example, shows the significant jump in the performance/price ratios of successive generations of Intel's semiconductor chips for personal computers.

| *Intel Chip* | *Launch* | *MIPS* | *Price ($)* | *Performance/ Price Index* |
|---|---|---|---|---|
| 286 | 1982 | 1 | $   100 | 1.0 |
| 386 | 1985 | 5 | 200 | 2.5 |
| 486 | 1989 | 20 | 400 | 5.0 |
| (586) Pentium | 1993 | 100 | 1,000 | 10.0 |

Similar performance-to-price gains have been obtained in other key components like disk drives as well. The end result is a dramatic reduction in cost and increase in performance for each successive generation of personal computers. But even in traditional industries, such an improvement is possible because of innovative manufacturing technologies that firms are often able to develop. The dramatic gains made by innovative assembly line technology in the auto industry are a case in point.

The net effect of a process innovation strategy is usually an increase in market share and a rapid buildup of a loyal customer base. An example of the price innovation strategy was Digital Equipment Corporation's (DEC) VAX 11/780 minicomputer introduction. In the late 1970s, just before the proliferation of the minicomputer market and the invention of microcomputers, DEC came out with the VAX minicomputer. Instead of going head-to-head with market leader IBM's service offerings, DEC's managers reasoned that a segment of highly knowledgeable customers would be willing to take additional responsibilities for servicing the product and developing software applications. DEC's early insight enabled it to offer a highly desirable machine that had a much lower price, with fewer services, than IBM, but at a very attractive performance specification for the price. The company was quickly able to capture significant market share and profits as a result.

Sony's introduction of the 1270 superdata projector in 1989 is another example of the process innovation strategy.[10] Until then Barco Projection Systems, a Belgian company, and Electrohome, a Canadian company, shared worldwide leadership for overhead video projection equipment capable of reading and transmitting graphic signals. But unlike its competitors, Sony was not a niche player, but a mass-marketer with dominant share in the lower-end video and data markets. In addition,

---

[10]"Barco Projection Systems," Harvard Business School case no. 9-591-133.

the state of commoditization. In the early stages, a value-added strategy could serve as a defensive shield around the core product, whereas in the latter stages a firm would necessarily have to demonstrate to the customer savings from the added services that surround its core offerings. Similarly, a cost-leadership strategy in the early stages of market commoditization would have to focus on price/performance advantages and lower manufacturing costs, whereas in the latter stages an efficient deployment of marketing and sales resources is often an attractive option.

While some firms reconcile themselves to lower sales and profits with the onset of commoditization, many well-managed firms have learned to beat the commodity cycle. Our analysis and action strategies provide the framework for achieving such success.

# 11 Manage Customers for Profits (Not Just Sales)

*Many companies have found that high sales volume does not automatically mean high profits. Among the factors that do affect customer profitability are geography, order size, and extra attention to keep the account. Some customers simply cost more to serve. Other will pay any price to get a certain product. If companies want profits and not just sales, they should start by understanding the differences among their customers. Careful analysis of customers and products will steer sellers into more profitable markets. Sellers should know the exact amount and origin of costs: Understand their profitability dispersion and set prices according to the value customers place on each product, focus strategy according to their knowledge of customers and their own strengths, install information and other systems to support a chosen strategy, and analyze profit dispersion and rethink strategy continually.*

High sales volume does not necessarily mean high income, as many companies have found to their sorrow. In fact, profits (as a percentage of sales) are often much higher on some orders than on others, for reasons managers sometimes do not well understand. If prices are appropriate, why is there such striking variation? Let's look at two examples of selling and pricing anomalies:

• A plumbing fixtures manufacturer raised prices to discourage the "worthless" small custom orders that were disrupting the factory. But a series of price hikes failed to reduce unit sales volume. A study of operations two years later revealed that the most profitable orders were these custom orders. The new high prices more than compensated for costs, customers weren't changing suppliers because of high switching expenses, and competitors had shied from short runs because of the conventional wisdom in the industry.

---

This reading was prepared by Benson P. Shapiro, V. Kasturi Rangan, Rowland T. Moriarty, and Elliot B. Ross.

Reprinted from *Harvard Business Review* 65, no. 5, September–October 1987, pp. 101–8.

• A prominent producer of capital equipment, realizing it was losing big sales potential in its largest accounts, started a national account program. It included heavy sales support with experienced account managers; participation by high-level executives; special support like applications engineering, custom design services, unusual maintenance work, and expedited delivery; and a national purchase agreement with a hefty graduated volume discount.

Customers, however, viewed the program as merely a dog-and-pony show, having no substance. To convince the skeptics, top executives personally offered greater sales and service support and even more generous discounts.

Sales finally turned upward, and this "success" justified even higher levels of support. But profit margins soon began to erode; the big national accounts, the company discovered, were generating losses that were large enough to offset the rise in volume and the profitability of smaller, allegedly less attractive accounts.

Clearly these two companies discovered that it costs more to fill some orders than others. The plumbing fixtures executives raised prices precisely because they knew it was costing them more to fill small custom orders. The capital equipment company willingly took on extra costs in the hope of winning more sales. Management in both companies recognized that their price tags would vary, the first from boosted prices on custom orders, the other because of volume discounts. But executives in both companies failed to see that the cost and price variations would cause profound differences in the profitability of individual accounts and orders.

Many companies make this mistake. Managers pay little attention to account profitability, selection, and management. They seldom consider the magnitude, origins, and managerial implications of profit dispersion. In this article, we examine three central aspects of this important factor:

Costs to suppliers.

Customer behavior.

Management of customers.

# Costs to Suppliers

Profit, of course, is the difference between the net price and the actual cost-to-serve. In terms of individual accounts and orders, there can be dramatic differences in both price and cost.

Despite legal constraints that encourage uniformity in pricing, notably the Robinson-Patman Act, customers usually pay quite different prices in practice. Some buyers can negotiate or take advantage of differential discounts because of their size or the functions they can perform themselves, like in-house maintenance or technical support. And some customers exploit deals and promotions more than others. Moreover, the costs of serving customers and filling orders can vary significantly.

*Presale costs* vary greatly from order to order and account to account. Geography matters: Some customers and prospects are located far from the salesperson's home base or normal route. Some customers require seemingly endless sales calls, while others place their orders over the telephone. Some must be courted with top-level executives backed up by sophisticated account management techniques, while others need little special effort. Such variations in cost reflect differences in customers' buying processes or the nature of their buying teams. (Some teams are large and geographically and functionally dispersed; others are small and concentrated by location and/or function.) Finally, some customers demand intensive presale service, like applications engineering and custom design support, while others accept standard designs.

*Production costs* also vary by customer and by order. Order size influences cost, as do setup time, scrap rate, custom designs, special features and functions, unusual packaging, and even order timing. Off-peak orders cost less than those made when demand is heavy. Fast delivery costs more. Some orders call on more resources than others. A company that inventories products in anticipation of orders, however, will have difficulty tracing production costs to particular orders and customers. Accounting policies and conventions, furthermore, often cloud the distinctions in product costs.

*Distribution costs* naturally vary with the customer's location. It also costs more to ship via a preferred transportation mode, to drop ship to a separate receiving location, to find no back-haul opportunity, or to extend special logistics support like a field inventory.

*Postsale service costs* also differ. Sometimes customer training, installation, technical support, and repair and maintenance are profit-making operations, but businesses often bundle such services into the product price and the buyer pays "nothing extra" for them. For some items, including capital equipment, postsale costs are heavy.

Thus there are variations among customers in each of the four components of cost: before-the-sale expenses, production, distribution, and after-the-sale service. Moreover, if prices and costs do not correlate, the distribution of gross income will have a dispersion that is the sum of the individual price and cost dispersions, and thus much greater than either. Of course, prices and costs are often viewed as correlated, but our research suggests that they usually aren't—which produces a broad dispersion of account profitability.

With real cost-plus pricing, profitability could be uniform across customers despite wide variations in both costs and prices. But there is evidence that prices seldom reflect the actual costs in serving customers (though they may be somewhat related to production costs). In many businesses, the difference between the highest and lowest prices realized in similar transactions for the same product is as much as 30 percent, not including quantity discounts.[1] Look, for example, at the relationship between prices and total costs in one month's orders for a manufacturer of pipe resin (see Exhibit 1). The diagonal line indicates a price level equal to costs. If gross margin were the same on all orders, the orders would all lie along a line parallel to the

---

[1] See Elliot B. Ross, "Making Money with Proactive Pricing," *Harvard Business Review*, November–December 1984, p. 145.

**EXHIBIT 1   Wide Gross Margin Dispersion for a Pipe Resin Manufacturer for One Month**

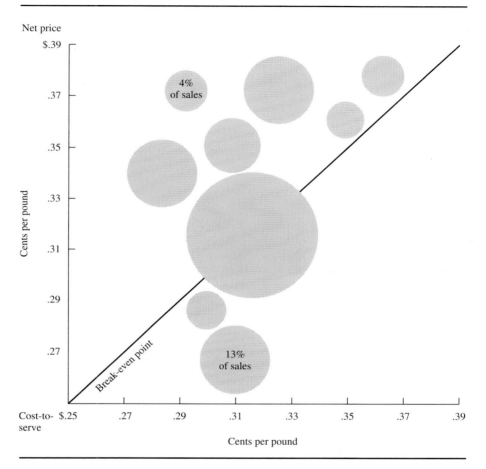

diagonal line. Instead, they are widely dispersed. Nearly 13 percent of sales volume resulted in losses of about a nickel a pound, while about 4 percent of volume generated an 8-cent profit. The rest fell somewhere between.

This pattern is not unusual. In a wide variety of situations, we have consistently observed a lack of correlation between price and the cost-to-serve. Some orders and customers generate losses, and in general the dispersion of profitability is wide.

# Customer Behavior

It is useful to think of customers in terms of two dimensions: net price realized and cost-to-serve. To show graphically the dynamics of the interplay between seller and buyer, we have devised a simple matrix (see Exhibit 2). The vertical axis is net

---

**EXHIBIT 2    Customer Classification Matrix**

---

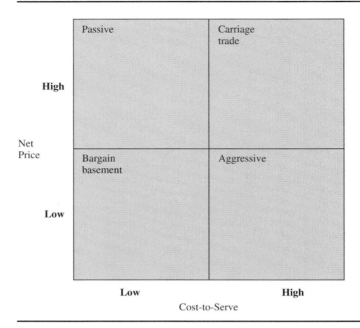

---

price, low to high, and the horizontal axis is cost-to-serve, low to high. This categorization is useful for any marketer. The *carriage trade* costs a great deal to serve but is willing to pay top dollar. (This category would include the customers of our introductory example, who placed small orders for high-cost custom plumbing fixtures.) At the opposite extreme are *bargain basement* customers—sensitive to price and relatively insensitive to service and quality. They can be served more cheaply than the carriage trade.

Serving *passive* customers costs less too, but they are willing to accept high prices. These accounts generate highly profitable orders. There are various reasons for their attitude. In some cases the product is too insignificant to warrant a tough negotiating stance over price. Other customers are insensitive to price because the product is crucial to their operation. Still others stay with their current supplier, more or less regardless of price, because of the prohibitive cost of switching. As an example from another industry, many major aircraft components cannot be changed without recertifying the entire aircraft. And in some cases vendor capability is so well matched to buyer needs that cost-to-serve is low though the customer is receiving (and paying for) fine service and quality.

*Aggressive* customers, on the other hand, demand (and often receive) the highest product quality, the best service, and low prices. Procter & Gamble, boasting an efficient procurement function, has a reputation among its suppliers for paying the least and getting the most. Aggressive buyers are usually powerful;

their practice of buying in large quantities gives them leverage with suppliers in seeking price deals and more service. The national accounts described in the second example at the beginning of this chapter drove hard bargains with the capital equipment supplier.

Marketing managers often assume a strong correlation between net price and cost to serve; they reason that price-sensitive customers will accept lower quality and service and demanding customers will pay more for better quality and service. Thinking in terms of service and quality demands unfortunately deflects attention from the critical issue of cost-to-serve. In addition, weak cost accounting practices that average costs over products, orders, and customers often support the high-cost, high-price myth. But as we have seen, costs and prices are not closely correlated.

A supplier of industrial packaging materials recently analyzed the profitability of its large national accounts. For each one it calculated approximate indicators of net price and cost-to-serve, based on averages of the aggregate values of a year's transactions. Top officers expected to find most of its customers in the carriage trade quadrant and the rest in the bargain basement. They were shocked when the results put about half of the 164 large customers in the passive and aggressive quadrants (see Exhibit 3).

We believe this pattern is more common than is generally recognized. Among the various factors influencing buying behavior, the most important are the customer's situation and migration patterns.

**Exhibit 3   Customer Matrix of an Industrial Packaging Materials Supplier**

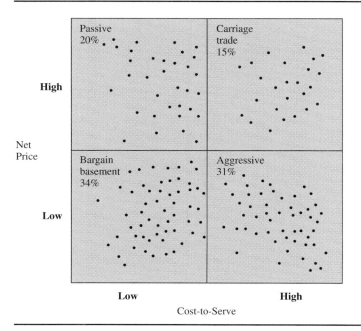

### Customer's Situation

Four aspects of the customer's nature and position affect profitability: customer economics, power, the nature of the decision-making unit, and the institutional relationship between the buyer and seller.

As we all know, fundamental economics helps determine a buyer's price and service sensitivity. Customers are more sensitive to price when the product is a big part of their purchases, more sensitive to service when it has a big impact on their operations. Independent of economics, buying power, of course, is a major determinant of the buyer's ability to extract price concessions and service support from vendors. The power of big customers shows in their ability to handle many aspects of service support in-house—like breaking bulk—for which they demand price adjustments. Sometimes small customers also wield considerable power. A technological innovator that influences industry standards commands the eyes and ears of suppliers. Thus, the relationship of cost-to-serve and customer size in this industry is not clear without careful measurement.

In respect to the decision-making unit, the purchase staff is generally sensitive to price, while engineering and production personnel are sensitive to service. These roles will affect decisions, depending on who most influences vendor choice and management.

Naturally, this element is bound up with any relationships that have built up between the buyer and seller. Long-standing friendships, long histories of satisfactory performance, and appreciation for any special help or favors all tend to make customers reluctant to pressure suppliers for price and service concessions. Procter & Gamble rotates the responsibilities of its purchasing department members to discourage the development of strong personal relationships with vendors.

### Migration Patterns

Changes in organizational buying behavior and competitive activity can produce predictable patterns of change in customer profitability. Often a relationship begins in the carriage trade category. Customers need extensive sales and service support, insist on high product quality, and do not worry much about price if the product is new to them. They need the functionality and will pay for it.

Over time, however, as the customers gain experience with the product, they grow confident in dealing with the vendor and operating with less sales and service support or even without any. The cost of serving them is likely to decline, and they are likely to become more price sensitive. In addition, the buying influence of the customer's procurement department often grows, while the role of engineering and operating personnel diminishes. This shift of course reinforces the tendency toward price sensitivity and away from service concerns. Finally, through rival product offerings (often at lower prices), customers gain knowledge that improves their competence with the product and thus their ability to demand price concessions and lessen their dependence on the vendor's support efforts.

If the customer perceives the product as trivial (as in the case of office supplies) and therefore does not seek it avidly, price sensitivity will not necessarily increase as service needs abate. In terms of the matrix of which Exhibit 2 is an example, migration will be toward the passive and bargain basement areas. If the buyer values the product and it is complex or service sensitive (like CAD/CAM equipment), the buyer may pressure the supplier for price reductions even while service requirements remain high. The migration tends to be downward from the carriage trade toward the aggressive quadrant, as in the case of electrical generation equipment for utilities. In commodities like pipe resin, a combination of customer experience, expanding influence of the purchasing staff, and increasing competitive imitation often leads customers into the bargain basement category.

## Management of Customers

The shifts toward the bargain basement and aggressive quadrants are part of the general tendency of products to evolve from high-margin specialties to low-margin commodities. The dispersion of customer profitability we have observed can be managed. We suggest a five-step action program: Pinpoint your costs, know your profitability dispersion, focus your strategy, provide support systems, and analyze repeatedly.

**Pinpoint Your Costs**.    Manufacturers can usually measure their factory costs better than costs incurred by the sales, applications engineering, logistics, and service functions. For instance, few companies have a sense of the cost of unscheduled executive effort to handle the demands of aggressive customers. So it seems likely that customer profitability varies more widely in businesses where a large percentage of the total expenditure is incurred outside the factory. This would be the case in many high-tech companies that have low manufacturing costs but spend a great deal on sales, design engineering, applications engineering, and systems integration.

Because many specialty products are custom designed and manufactured and carry heavy nonfactory costs, the cost dispersion for these products is greater than for commodities. But as we pointed out in our pipe resin example, profit dispersion can be high even in a commodity product.

Costs incurred at different times in the order cycle have different effects on the true cost to serve the customer or order. In major sales with long order cycles and long lead times, the presale effort may begin several years ahead, and service under warranty may extend several years after installation and billing. If the cost of capital is 15 percent, a dollar spent two years before the billing of the customer is worth $1.32, and a dollar spent three years after billing is worth only 61 cents at the time of delivery. Companies with long lead times and order cycles, such as sellers of power generation equipment and commercial airliners, with long-term, substantial service liabilities, evidently have cost dispersions much larger than average, except where progress payments balance out cost flows. These companies need particularly good control systems and management judgment to measure costs and act accordingly.

Companies with poor cost accounting systems have no way to determine order, customer, product, or market segment profitability. Consequently, their cost control and management systems will be weak, and the result is likely to be above-average dispersion of costs. The sales manager of a large office equipment supplier who lacked adequate cost information described his situation thus:

> It's management by anecdote. Salespeople regularly make passionate pleas for price relief on specific orders. When I press them for reasons, they say "threat of competitive entry." When I ask them if a cutback in service would be acceptable to make up for the price decrease, they give me a resounding no! What choice do you have in the absence of cost data, except to go by your judgment of the salesperson's credibility? I've wrongly accepted as many bad price relief requests as I've rejected.

An effective cost accounting system records data by product, order, and account, and records costs beyond the factory, including selling, transportation, applications or design engineering, and even unusual, unprogrammed activities like investments of blocks of corporate management time. Presale, production, distribution, and postsale service costs should all be recorded, analyzed, and related to orders and accounts.

Of course, there are enormous difficulties in creating and maintaining such a system. But even a system that estimates such costs only approximately can help a great deal. Twice a year, for example, one industrial company calculates the cost of serving three sizes of customers (large, medium, and small) and two sizes of orders (truckload and less-than-truckload) for a representative sample of accounts and orders. During the following six months, sales managers use these numbers to guide their decisions on price-relief requests.

**Know Your Profitability Dispersion.**    Once costs are known, the company can plot them against realized prices to show the dispersion of account profitability, as in Exhibit 2. Clearly the framework must be adapted to the characteristics of the business. Similarly, the price axis should be defined in a meaningful way. Since list prices are often misleading, use some sort of net price. However, discounts should not be double-counted under costs as well. The ultimate objective is a measure of net profit by customer and order. Tracking cost and price data by order is an essential first step in building an account profitability matrix.

Companies that know their costs and use cost-plus pricing schemes will find most of their accounts in the bargain basement or carriage trade quadrants of the matrix. Though this pattern is perfectly reasonable, sales management should try to develop accounts in the passive quadrant. Many such customers will accept higher prices because they like the product so much. The cost to them of negotiating a lower price (or better service) outweighs the extra benefits they would get. The passive quadrant represents a region of maximum value for both the seller and the buyer.

A dispersion of profits is no bad thing; only not knowing it exists is. The best managed companies know their costs well and set prices on the basis of product value to customers rather than cost-to-serve. So they have some accounts in the passive categories. In fact, their profit dispersion will be greater than that of companies pricing on a cost-plus basis. The worst managed companies, ignorant of their costs and setting prices mainly in response to customer demands, are likely to have a large number of accounts in the aggressive category, with, obviously, pessimistic implications for profitability.

**Focus Your Strategy.**   The next step is to use your knowledge of cost, price, and profit dispersion to define a strategy for managing your accounts. Here the company defines its personality. The low-cost, low-service, low-price provider would be in the lower left of a profitability matrix, while the company that offers differentiated and augmented products, intensive service, and customization—and, therefore, more value added—is in the upper right quadrant. Because any company's capability is necessarily limited, it cannot span the entire dimension. If it tries to, the poor focus will leave the company vulnerable to competition. This will allow rivals to jump into the aggressive quadrant with high service and low prices, drawing customers away from both the bargain basement and carriage trade quadrants. The result for the stretched-out company is reduced profitability.

The company has two strategy decisions to make. One is to locate the center of gravity or core of the company's business along the axis. The other is to define the range along the axis it will cover.

The fundamental choice to be made is the selection of customers, for companies that reside in a given quadrant will *generally* produce orders in that quadrant. Customers in each quadrant of the profitability matrix behave in a distinctive manner. The supplier has to decide which behavior is most consistent with its strengths. For instance, in an industry with high transport costs, like cement or sand, a customer located at the maximum practical distance from your plant is likely to be in one of the right-hand quadrants—for you. For a competitor whose plant is located near the customer, that account will probably be in a left-hand quadrant. Unless you can form a carriage-trade relationship with that customer—realizing high prices because of the value of your services—you would do better to concede the account to your competitor.

**Provide Support Systems.**   Unless it wants to follow a policy of cost-plus pricing, the company needs to develop processes and systems that will help it manage the profitability dispersion. The company's information system should produce reports based on order, customer, and segment profitability, not just on sales. Management must be oriented toward lateral cooperation among functions. A procedure that simply rewards salespeople for high unit sales and manufacturing personnel for low-cost production is unlikely to lead to the most profitable order mix.

Price-setting rates special attention. Companies that operate in the bargain basement and aggressive quadrants of the profitability matrix must often set up centralized offices to price large orders and screen customers' demands for services. A "special bids" group is often the only way to give the quick replies and careful analyses such orders require. Such a group can best balance financial implications, production and operating capacity, and customer needs, without giving away the store. Since carriage trade customers value the supplier's extra services, a cost-plus pricing policy may be appropriate for them. Finally, pricing for the trade in the passive quadrant has to be based on the value the customer places on the product.

The analysis, strategy, and customer negotiation functions must be kept separate. A men's and boys' coat manufacturer we know of is a good example of what happens when this rule is ignored. The owner's three sons headed divisions serving the department store, discount store, and export markets, while the owner himself managed the private-label business. He called on the three big general merchandise chains (Sears, Ward, and Penney), one of which gave him almost all of his business. The sons' divisions were very profitable, but the private-label unit was a big money loser.

Why was this so? Before a son went out to negotiate an order, the owner stressed the need to get high prices, keep costs reasonable, and secure orders that fit the company's abilities. The father analyzed large orders for profitability. But when the father went to talk to his biggest customer, no one pressured him to keep profits up. He consistently caved in to demands for lower prices, higher service, and better quality. His sons felt powerless to analyze his orders for profitability. The lesson: The same person should not set profit goals and negotiate with customers.

The more services a company provides, the more coordination is necessary among the engineers, field-service staff, and other functionaries in delivering the product and service. Likewise, the more a company increases its cost-to-serve, the more important interfunctional coordination becomes. Low-cost, low-price, low-service bargain basement operators don't need and can't afford elaborate logistics, field service, and other coordinating mechanisms. Carriage trade customers can't operate without them.

Deciding what strategic choices to make requires maintaining market research, pricing analysis, and cost-accounting functions. While these are high-leverage operations in which small investments can yield high returns, in hard times companies often view them as nonessential overhead expenses. This shortsighted attitude can be very damaging.

**Repeat Analysis Regularly.**    A one-shot profit dispersion and strategy analysis is of little use. Buying behavior and migration patterns, like markets and competitors, are dynamic. Migration patterns gradually dilute a company's account selection and management policies.

Cumberland Metals (a disguised name) made pollution control components for the Big Three auto companies in the mid-1970s. Margins were very good, reflecting the high value the auto companies placed on the product, their lack of experience with pollution control, and the absence of competition. The entry of competitors in the early 1980s and, on the customers' part, a shift in influence from engineering to procurement staff signaled a fundamental migration in their buying behavior, but Cumberland management ignored the warning signs. This inattention caused long-standing customer relations problems and a prolonged earnings slump.

Cumberland Metals is unusual because it had only three large accounts. The loss of accounts and orders from the carriage trade quadrant is normally a matter of erosion.

How often a company should analyze profit dispersion and strategy depends on the rate of change in the market and in technology. In many cases, a once-a-year analysis integrated with the annual marketing plan makes sense. In high technology or other rapidly changing industries, a more frequent review may be better. In any case, the main difficulty lies in setting up good systems to track costs, prices, and profits; once the supporting information is available, the analysis is not difficult to perform.

## Manage the Dispersion

A custom fabricator of industrial equipment, though operating at capacity, was losing money. The obvious problem was low price levels for the industry. Investigation, however, pointed to a mixture of poor pricing, poor cost estimating, and a lack of knowledge of profitability dispersion. Some bids were too aggressively priced: After winning contracts, the company then lost money on them. Executives had structured other bids to "make good money," basing them on inflated cost estimates. Astute competitors costed these bids better, handled the price negotiations more skillfully, and won the contracts. So the fabricator was winning only unprofitable bids.

The electrical products division of a large corporation, on the other hand, understood the importance of profitability analysis. It carefully analyzed its costs, developed a proactive pricing approach, and meticulously selected orders, products, and customers that fit its production competence and capacity. After a thorough before-and-after review, the financial analysis department at headquarters declared that the division had gone from a 5 percent loss to a 10 percent profit on sales in a glutted, static commodity market.

When meticulous analysis, a sensible strategy, and effective implementation are combined, a company can manage its profitability dispersion to generate profits, not just sales.

# 12 Close Encounters of the Four Kinds: Managing Customers in a Rapidly Changing Environment

*This reading describes four kinds of selling: (1) transaction, (2) systems, (3) major account management, and (4) strategic account relationships. It discusses the advantages, disadvantages, and risks of each kind of selling, with a special emphasis on how to construct strategic account relationships which embody importance, intimacy, and longevity for both the vendoring and the buying companies.*

"Get close to your customers and do what they want—be customer oriented!"

"Don't give away the store!"

"Selling is dead, there was respect, and courtship, and gratitude in it. Today it's all cut and dried, and there's no chance for bringing friendship to bear or personality."[1]

"Customer relationships are more important than they have ever before been!"

There are many different ways to think about the role of selling and customer relations in a very complex world. Perhaps the truest statement about relationships between buyers and sellers was in *Death of a Salesman,* by Arthur Miller. But, it wasn't made by Willy Loman, the salesman. It was made by his devoted wife, Linda: "It's changing, Willy, I can feel it changing."[2]

The management of account relationships, particularly those between organizations such as businesses or between businesses and major institutions such as governments, has grown more varied and more difficult. We need new ways to look at selling and serving customers.

There are four distinct ways to sell. We begin by examining these with an emphasis on the differences among them, and their relative strengths and weaknesses. The last half of this chapter focuses on the most complex form of selling—strategic account relationships.

Benson P. Shapiro prepared this note.
Copyright © 1988 by the President and Fellows of Harvard College.
Harvard Business School note 589-015.
[1]Statement by Willy Loman in Arthur Miller, *Death of a Salesman* (New York: Viking, 1949), p. 81.
[2]Ibid., p. 74.

Strategic account relationships receive this attention because they are new and very complex, replete with traps and expenses. They do not receive this attention because they are a panacea or even because they are appropriate for every vendor. They are not! The best way to understand their usefulness is to compare them with simpler, yet very serviceable approaches.

# Four Approaches to Selling

For many years—indeed, back to the days of open markets and caravan traders—personal selling was a fairly simple activity, consisting of a single exchange or a series of exchanges. This type of selling can be called transaction selling. During the last couple of decades we have seen the introduction and development of three more sophisticated forms of selling: systems, major accounts, and strategic account relationships. This section describes the three new approaches, and differentiates them from each other and the earlier transaction approach.

Transaction selling has evolved into an organized approach to making exchanges. The exchange is generally quite discrete, with a product moving from seller to buyer and money moving in the other direction after some period of negotiation and information exchange. This approach is still used for a wide variety of somewhat simple products ranging from office furniture to some standard electronic products to raw materials. The sale is either a one-time exchange or one transaction in a continuing series of exchanges; the product is often purchased on the basis of physical attributes, availability, convenience, or price. The seller views each sales transaction as the culmination of the immediately preceding activities. Any degree of relationship is viewed by the seller as a series of transactions separated by downtime for servicing the account.

## Systems Sales

The advent of complex systems required that the transaction approach be supplemented by more concern for customer benefits and the integration of system components. The system consisted of separate pieces, including individual capital equipment, parts, supplies, and services. Office and factory automation systems are typical examples, but petrochemical complexes and textile mills also fit the systems description. The systems sale necessitated the introduction and development of new sales techniques such as team selling, in which several different departments or functional areas (applications engineering, design, field service, etc.) of the vendor become involved in the sales process.[3]

Systems sales also appeared where the system was not in a physical form but was a program. In consumer package goods, for example, the system may be a pro-

---

[3]Benson P. Shapiro and Ronald S. Posner, "Making the Major Sale," *Harvard Business Review,* March–April 1979, pp. 68–79.

motional program involving several different product lines, national advertising, co-operative advertising, and in-store promotions. The system can also be a related set of services, such as a cash management or mobilization service sold to a company having many locations and bank accounts. The system involves more than "one piece" and is a major sale.

The systems sale differs in size and complexity from the transaction sale, and the ratio of service time between sales to actual selling time increases. But, the heart of the activity remains the sales transaction. There is still a tendency to view the time between sales as downtime. The sophistication of the approach has changed but the fundamental philosophy has not.

### Major Account Management

The increasing size and complexity of sales and the development of purchasing approaches like national contracts and master purchasing agreements led to more intimacy and permanence in buyer–seller relationships. Instead of buying a product or service, or even a set of products and services as in the systems purchase, the customer literally wanted to purchase a relationship with a vendor. The sales response was major account management, frequently called national account management because customers transcended regional sales boundaries. Major or national account management is becoming the crème de la crème of personal selling.[4] It is still evolving and its popularity is growing rapidly. At its core is an account manager who quarterbacks the vendor's approach to the customer and husbands the selling company's resources for the customer's benefit. Primary issues in national account programs include the organizational structure[5] and the quality of support provided by functional groups beyond the sales operation such as manufacturing and field service.[6] Its essence is a continuing relationship with a major vendor based on intense, well-coordinated service support.

Account management represents a change in sales philosophy. The actual sales transactions "are seen as the punctuation marks of a larger relationship. Sales are a 'natural fallout.'"[7] At this point in the development of sales approaches, the whole concept of selling changed. In essence, as shown in Exhibit 1, the shift was from a transaction orientation to a relationship orientation. The systems sale was simply a more important and more complex transaction. Major account management, however, was a change in fundamental philosophy. Exhibit 2, based on a chart by Thomas V. Bonoma, highlights the differences between transaction selling and relationship creation.

---

[4]See Benson P. Shapiro and John Wyman, "New Ways to Reach Your Customer," *Harvard Business Review,* July–August 1981, pp. 103–10; Benson P. Shapiro and Rowland T. Moriarty, Jr., "National Account Management," Marketing Science Institute, Cambridge, Mass., 1980, and "National Account Management: Emerging Insights," Marketing Science Institute, Cambridge, Mass., 1982.

[5]Benson P. Shapiro and Rowland T. Moriarty, Jr., "Organizing the National Account Force," Marketing Science Institute, Cambridge, Mass., 1983.

[6]Benson P. Shapiro and Rowland T. Moriarty, Jr., "Support Systems for National Account Management Programs," Marketing Science Institute, Cambridge, Mass., 1983.

[7]Quote from a speech by Thomas V. Bonoma, formerly of the Harvard Business School.

---
**EXHIBIT 1   Four Selling Approaches**
---

Transaction ⎫
System Sale ⎭                          Transaction Orientation

Major Account Management ⎫
Strategic Account Relationship ⎭        Relationship Orientation

---

Account management is expensive and difficult. It can only be used for major customers. And to be effective, it absolutely must be seen as a *philosophy of customer commitment,* not just a collection of advanced persuasion techniques. Its essence is superior customer responsiveness based on outstanding support systems. It goes beyond selling and has laid the foundation for strategic account relationships.

However, major or national account management, with all of its opportunities and rewards, as well as significant investments and costs, cannot satisfy the evolving needs for some closer, more permanent vendor–customer relationships. Joint product, service, and infrastructure developments have led to even more intimate buyer–seller relationships, which can be described as strategic account relationships. Such relationships are a subset of coalitions formed among companies that may be related as competitors, buyers and sellers, or sharers of jointly useful technology or resources.[8]

## *Strategic Account Relationships*

Strategic account relationships are a new and specialized approach so there are few publicly documented examples; furthermore, several with which I am familiar are proprietary and thus beyond discussion. It is instructive, however, to look at several examples.

---
**EXHIBIT 2   Transactions and Relationships**
---

| *Transaction Selling* | *Relationship Creation* |
| --- | --- |
| 1. Selling dominates learning | 1. Learning about the customer is intense and dominates selling |
| 2. Talking dominates listening | 2. Listening dominates talking |
| 3. Persuading the customer is product driven and benefits focused | 3. Teaching the customer is need driven and problem focused |
| 4. The goal is to build buyers and sales through persuasion, price, presence, and terms | 4. The goal is to build relationships through credibility, responsiveness, and trust |

---

[8] See for example Michael E. Porter, *Competitive Advantage,* (Free Press, New York, 1985), pp. 191–93 for a discussion of licensing and Joseph L. Bower and Eric A. Rhenman, "Benevolent Cartels," *Harvard Business Review,* July–August 1985.

The first is the Hartford Component Company, a disguised manufacturer of a somewhat specialized component for measuring instruments. Hartford competed directly with several other companies who used the same technology and with others whose components were based on competing technology. One of Hartford's primary customers, New Haven Instrument (NHI), made measuring instruments for chemical analysis and medical diagnosis. Some of its products were based upon the Hartford component. After several months of negotiation, based upon years of successful vendor–supplier relations, the companies agreed to a joint development effort. Hartford management understood that to develop its technology further it needed more product use knowledge, additional technical expertise in several related engineering disciplines, and an assured outlet for its new product, which would take substantial time and funds to develop. NHI faced intense worldwide competition and needed a "technological leg up" to improve its position. It lacked the ability to develop its component technology and wanted to leverage its strong customer relationships, applications knowledge, and skill in related technologies. Neither of the companies, each with sales of $50 million to $200 million, wished to merge, but each needed something more important, intimate, and permanent than their previous preferred vendor–major customer relationship.

Their strategic partnership involved a joint development effort, information exchange, and a carefully developed sales agreement which gave NHI a temporary exclusive purchase agreement for the components and Hartford an assured source of sales. Despite the high cost, substantial required level of cooperation and integration between vendor and customer organizations, and the requisite loss of autonomy for each, both organizations believed the arrangement was successful and worthwhile. Each, because they managed the relationship well and had carefully defined expectations, gained a great deal.

This example demonstrates the three attributes upon which strategic account relationships must always be based:

1. Importance.
2. Intimacy.
3. Longevity.

Importance usually involves three forms of interdependence: financial, technological and/or design, and strategic. Either the vendor or the customer must be exceedingly important to the other financially. Sometimes the companies, as in the Hartford–New Haven case, are mutually important to one another financially. Technological and/or design cooperation is at the heart of most strategic partnerships. Shared technological and/or design development is the element that *most* separates situations appropriate for strategic account relationships from those more appropriate for selling. Strategic importance is usually based on the technological/design relationship supplemented by the financial importance of one to the other.

Intimacy and longevity flow from the nature of the necessary relationship. Companies cannot do *joint* development without sharing intimate technological, design, and operating information. Trust is a critical ingredient in the relationship because it enables the intimacy.

Longevity is necessary to protect the intimacy, and to enable the partners to reap the financial rewards. The investments have long and hopefully high payouts. Longevity ensures a relationship during the payout period after the investment period.

Another strategic account relationship is that between the EDS (Electronic Data Systems) part of General Motors and what was the Information Systems (IS) portion of AT&T. EDS had substantial skills in integrating computers, telecommunications gear, and software to customer systems. AT&T IS sold telecommunications equipment, computers, and related equipment; it did not have sufficient systems integration skills to satisfy all its customers. EDS and AT&T IS signed a systems integrator agreement under which EDS was considerably more than a distributor because of the size and significance of the systems integrator role.

In another strategic account relationship, Fujitsu Fanuc Ltd., a Japanese robot vendor, established a joint venture with General Motors. The joint venture gave Fanuc a window on factory technology and robot application beyond what it could gain as a more traditional vendor. The joint venture, which sold robots and related factory automation equipment to GMC and other customers, enabled GMC to better understand and capitalize on rapidly evolving robot technology. It also gave GMC greater financial return from its factory automation development work because it gained returns on sales to other customers.

# Comparisons and Applications

Exhibit 3 describes the four types of sales approaches. On the left is the transaction approach, with systems selling, major account management, and strategic account relationships each representing evolutions in sophistication and horsepower. Most important are the differences in goal and essence. The transaction and systems approaches emphasize sales, while the major account and strategic relationship approaches emphasize the mutuality of a long marriage. As we move from left to right we see the impact of the sale and the approach increase for both buyer and seller. Thus, the organization level and size of the buying and selling teams increase, as does the length of the relationship.

However, the relative amount of vendor effort also increases. Integration and information flow within the vendor organization expand in response to the increased effort and because of the degree of customer responsiveness and service required. As we move from left to right on the chart, the relative amount of account work done by the sales force decreases and the amount done by supporting functional units such as manufacturing, field service, logistics, and so on, increases. *This means that more and more of the salesperson's time must be spent on internal coordination and service support and less in customer persuasion.* The best relationship managers have as much internal as external focus, a paradox to most old-time salespeople. The salespeople must have broad account-related goals instead of narrow sales-related goals.

Because of the effort involved, a vendor can support only a few strategic account relationships. Most customers will be systems or transaction customers. Some will be major accounts.

---

**EXHIBIT 3     The Four Types of Sales Approaches**

---

| | *Transaction* | *Systems* | *Major Account Management* | *Strategic Account Relationship* |
|---|---|---|---|---|
| 1. Goal | Sales and satisfied customers | Systems sales and satisfied customers | The position as preferred supplier | An enduring, intimate relationship |
| 2. Essence | Product sales because of performance, price, and effective selling | Integration benefits from good support and team selling | Intense service through account management | Company-to-company bonding with an institutional relationship leading to a shared destiny |
| 3. Impact on buyer | Lowest | | | Highest |
| 4. Impact on seller | Lowest | | | Highest |
| 5. Organizational level and size of buying team | Lowest | | | Highest |
| 6. Organizational level and size of selling team | Lowest | | | Highest |
| 7. Length of relationship | Shortest | | | Longest |
| 8. Relative amount of vendor effort | Lowest | | | Highest |
| 9. Information needs at all levels of vendor | Lowest | | | Highest |
| 10. Vendor management integration needs | Limited | | | Highest |
| 11. Sales force goals | Narrow—sell products | | | Broad—manage the partnership |
| 12. Number of customers appropriate for each approach | Most or some | Most or some | Not many | Very small |

---

NOTE: In some industries such as electronics the transaction sales are called box or piece part sales to contrast them from systems sales.

Exhibit 3 describes the most appropriate sales approach. Since transaction selling is the easiest and cheapest, it should be used wherever possible. When products become complex and sophisticated, shift to the systems approach. For many companies that is all that will be needed!

When the importance of individual customers grows, and the customers need intense service because of the nature of their buying process and dependencies, the seller must switch to major account management and relationship selling. The shift must be a philosophical one—a commitment to customer service and responsiveness. It is not just the use of improved techniques. Major account management is indeed a powerful tool, but it is expensive in terms of support and integration cost and effort. It is an efficient competitive weapon only when it is justified.

Finally, for the few situations where customer importance (financial, technological and/or design, and strategic), intimacy, and longevity are high, use the most potent weapon: strategic account relationships. It is the most expensive because of support and integration demands, and loss of autonomy, but it is justified where the relationship must be long and intimate, and where the rewards are strategic.

Simply put, the message is, use the cheapest tool (see the transaction column in Exhibit 3) wherever possible. Escalate [to the right] only when necessary and justified.

## Why Get Closer?

If transaction selling is so much cheaper and easier than the three other types, do we need systems selling, major account management, and strategic account relationships? When are they justified?

Systems selling evolved because of product changes and the resulting changes in the customer's buying process. Some products became more complex, with more separate parts and services, and the pieces had to fit together. The added complexity meant that other people and departments had to become involved in the purchase. When machine tools, for example, were relatively simple, the engineer at the customer company could give a clear specification to the purchasing agent, who could negotiate for a good price. While there might be a few conversations between the engineer and purchasing agent, the communication was generally simple and the coordination needs limited.

As machine tools were replaced by complex multipurpose machining centers, the whole buying process changed. What had been a simple stand-alone machine purchase became a complex systems purchase. Process engineers, product design engineers, manufacturing management, logistical personnel, procurement executives, and financial specialists had to get involved. The machining center changed the way various departments operated, the role of inventory and product variety (oops, the product and marketing managers need to be involved!), the whole concept of coordinated engineering, manufacturing, and logistics, and the risk of downtime. Service and support became complicated. New types of suppliers were needed.

Successful vendors developed better sales techniques to match the more complicated buying process and product configuration. Systems selling was the integration of these techniques into a new sales approach.

Additional, broader changes in the environment, however, forced the quantum change to major account management. Mergers, acquisitions, bankruptcies, and differential growth led to a smaller, more concentrated account base in many industries. In some, such as the market for commercial jet engines and aircraft, as few as a dozen customers control the market. These became do-or-die customers. They had to be approached well. Economic concentration brought added changes to the buying and selling organizations. There were more buying, receiving, using, producing, inventorying, shipping, and selling locations. Sales calls had to be made on more customer locations from more different sales locations. As well, the sales effort had to be coordinated with more support (manufacturing, inventorying, etc.) locations.

The communication and coordination needs entered another sphere. It was not about one or a few systems, or one or a few large, complex transactions—it was about a total vendor–customer *relationship.* And to make matters worse, the dispersion was not simply geographical. It involved many buying and selling organizational jurisdictions. The problems of internal coordination at the vendor became as important as vendor–customer coordination.

At the same time, the impact of *vendor,* not just product choice, increased substantially. Experience, good and bad, of computer buyers especially influenced views of vendor importance. Because computers of different manufacturers could not talk to one another in the 1960s, 1970s, and early 1980s, commitment to a product was a long-term commitment to a vendor and a technological approach. Thus, it was natural that a computer vendor, IBM, led the development of major and national account marketing.

Individual transactions and annual vendor-to-customer sales increased dramatically in size. Bonds between vendor and customer became more intimate. Coordination became difficult. The risk of a poor choice soared. Also, major and national account management became a fad. Those who thought it was a collection of advanced sales techniques failed. Those who saw it as a new philosophy of vendor–customer cooperation and internal vendor coordination, and who were able to make it work despite organizational inertia, complexity, and jurisdictional warfare succeeded. The difference between success and failure was clear and involved many functions. Better customer relationships enabled vendor engineers, for example, to do a better job of developing new products. The new products improved the relationship, and the better major account marketer grew further ahead of the disorganized, disoriented competitor. The better sales approach led to greater business success.

In some businesses, the vendor–customer relationship grew even closer. Joint technological work was the cause in many but not all situations. An interesting marketing-oriented situation developed at NutraSweet, where a patented sweetener made the company a primary supplier to Coca-Cola and Pepsi-Cola. NutraSweet's "branded ingredient strategy" linked its marketing strategy inextricably to its customers. The transactions were large and the dollars very great. More important, however, NutraSweet and Coke *and* NutraSweet and Pepsi had a long-term interest in promoting NutraSweet-branded diet soft drinks. Such joint marketing, operating, and/or technological dependencies led to strategic account relationships.

The evolution of the four sales approaches is really the history of more complex responses to more demanding customer purchase initiatives. Systems selling arose because of buyer demands beyond those which could be filled with the traditional transaction approach. Major account management represented a still more powerful approach to greater customer opportunity. The antecedents for the strategic account relationship approach lie in original equipment manufacturer (OEM) industrial marketing and in franchised distributor arrangements. Suppliers of complex, important components to OEMs have found it necessary to do joint development and engineering work together. The proprietary nature of the products and interfaces developed led to long-term relationships. A manufacturer of numerically controlled machine tools, for example, is typically locked in to a computer control vendor for a five-year or so generation of controls. Thus, the *minimum* commitment of the OEM machine tool maker to the control vendor is five years.

Franchised distributors in the industrial, commercial, and consumer sphere (e.g., McDonald's and Dunkin' Donuts) have intimate, long-term relationships with the franchiser who supplies a mixture of branded marketing and advertising, technical support, capital equipment, and merchandise. The long-term intimate relationship of the franchiser and franchisee is a strategic account relationship with a very specific legal definition.

Because the four different sales approaches offer such different rewards and involve such different costs, they must be applied to the right situations. Transaction selling will be ineffective where major account management is needed, and strategic account relationships will be wasted where major account management will do. Thus, accounts and prospects must be segmented for different approaches.

## Segmenting Accounts and Prospects

Given the differences among the four different sales approaches in cost and impact, it is appropriate to consider which accounts and prospects might be appropriate for each approach. Much has been written about market segmentation, but the approach here focuses primarily on segmenting an existing customer base.[9]

The easiest way to segment customers is by size: typically, there are more small customers than large ones. If they are ranked by size from largest at the top to smallest at the bottom and are visualized as a pyramid (see Exhibit 4), the increasing width of the base indicates the increasing number of smaller amounts. This simple approach is a useful beginning.

The account volume can often be visualized in a pyramid or triangle (see Exhibit 5) that is upside-down with a large base at the top. That is because the few large accounts typically comprise a disproportionate amount of volume. The point at the bottom comes from the many accounts that represent a small percentage of total volume.

The largest accounts also often demand and perhaps justify more service and customization per dollar or unit of volume. This is reflected in the right-hand triangle on Exhibit 5, which has a wider top than the middle triangle, which reflects sales volume.

A simple approach is to apply the transaction sales approach to the smallest accounts (labeled micro in Exhibit 4), the systems approach to the next, and so on up to the strategic account relationship approach at the very top for the few largest

---

[9]For more on commercial/industrial market segmentation see Thomas V. Bonoma and Benson P. Shapiro, *Segmenting the Industrial Market* (Lexington, Mass.: D. C. Heath and Company, 1983); Benson P. Shapiro and Thomas V. Bonoma, "How to Segment Industrial Markets," *Harvard Business Review,* July–August 1984; and Thomas V. Bonoma and Benson P. Shapiro, "Evaluating Market Segmentation Approaches," *Industrial Marketing Management,* October 1984.

**EXHIBIT 4     The Customer Pyramid**

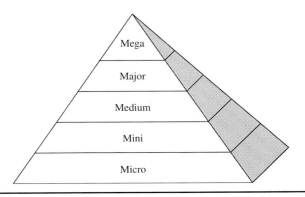

mega accounts. This method is mechanistic and heavy-handed but better than a random approach. However, it neglects sales potential, account profitability, customer needs, and vendor rewards beyond sales volume and profits.

### *Expanding beyond Size*

Potential is easy to add to the process. The simplest way is to use the pyramids and triangles to represent realizable potential instead of only current sales volume. The same general shape is likely to appear, but the approach is more future-oriented. Specifying potential requires some careful analysis of each account, a good place to begin effective account planning.

Account profitability can be added by using the account profitability matrix (Exhibit 6), which separates accounts (and orders) by realized price and cost-to-

**EXHIBIT 5     Customer Potential and Customer Demands**

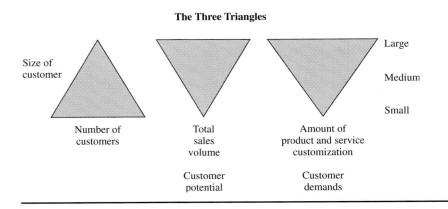

**EXHIBIT 6    The Customer/Order Profitability Matrix**

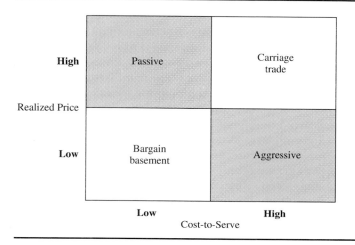

serve. "Passive" accounts, which pay high realized price and are inexpensive to serve, are more attractive than "aggressive" accounts, which pay low realized prices and are expensive to serve.[10] This approach requires an account profitability analysis system and fairly well-developed account plans to determine which accounts will provide incremental profitable business. Such pro forma analysis is important because the cost of serving an account with the strategic account relationship approach is much higher than with the transaction and systems sales approaches or even major account management.

There is no reason to use a more expensive approach when customer needs and prospective vendor rewards do not justify it. Wherever possible the least expensive, easiest approach (to the left on Exhibit 3) should be used. Only a few customers will justify the strategic account relationship approach, and a fairly small number relative to the account base will justify major account management in most vendors.

The accounts and prospects most likely to demand these advanced approaches are also usually the accounts most sensitive to *vendor* quality and performance as opposed to price, *product* quality and performance, rapid availability, and convenience. Commodity markets are characterized by buyers who emphasize price. Specialty markets are made up of buyers who want either rapid availability, convenience, *product* quality and performance, or *vendor* quality and performance.[11] The specialty buyers who are sensitive to vendor quality and performance are most appropriate for the advanced sales approaches.

---

[10]"Manage Customers for Profits (Not Just Sales)," Benson P. Shapiro, V. Kasturi Rangan, Rowland T. Moriarty, and Elliot B. Ross, *Harvard Business Review,* September–October 1987.

[11]For more on these distinctions, see Benson P. Shapiro, "Specialties versus Commodities: The Battle for Profit Margins," Harvard Business School case no. 587-120, Boston, 1987.

Finally, some accounts have special attributes that make them appropriate for special account relationships. An account providing an entry into a new marketplace, technology, or manufacturing process may be attractive far beyond its current sales volume and profitability or future potential for volume or profitability. A good example of such an account occurred in a high-technology material supplier. A midsized account was identified for strategic account relationship treatment because it was a consistent technological leader in the company's most important market. The materials supplier felt that being close to the technological cutting edge was in many ways more important than current volume. The account was viewed, because of its technical prowess, as the account of the future.

Some strategic accounts will help the vendor to manage product mix in a strategic sense. Such an account might, for example, take rejected product that is not up to specification for other customers but is much better than scrap. This can have a major impact on operations and profitability.

Finally, other attributes which make an account appropriate for strategic account relationship development include industry visibility and image and "ability to work with." When we confront implementation, we will give more consideration to ability to work with.

If we define *strategic accounts* as those appropriate for the development of strategic account relationships, we would include the following characteristics as criteria:

1. Current sales volume.
2. Future sales potential.
3. Current profitability.
4. Future profitability.
5. Strong customer service needs.
6. Strong customer interest in *vendor* quality and performance.
7. Entry into a new market, technology, or manufacturing process.
8. Impact on product mix.
9. Industry visibility and image.
10. Ability to work with.

Ideally, a strategic account will be high on all criteria. But often one or even several criteria will have to be sacrificed in some situations. The list indicates the need to go beyond current volume and even current profitability. Myopia is dangerous when planning for the long term. Perhaps the only more dangerous trap is to select too many strategic accounts so that none gets the amount of attention it needs.

## Special Services for the Few

The amount of special sales and service attention provided and the number of strategic accounts can be combined, as shown in Exhibit 7. The vertical dimension is the number or percentage of accounts receiving special effort and the horizontal

**EXHIBIT 7   Allocation of Customer Support**

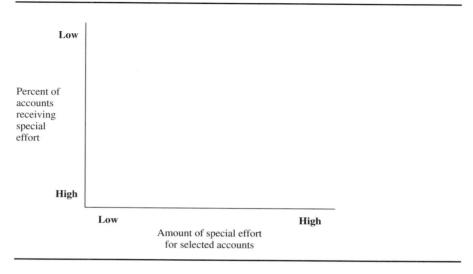

dimension is the amount of the special effort. On the upper right, a few customers get major special attention. In the lower left, many customers get little differentiation. The line between the two (lower left to upper right as shown in Exhibit 8) can be a constant cost line. The choice of giving a great deal of special effort to each of a few customers versus less-special effort each to a larger group is indeed strategic.

**EXHIBIT 8   Allocation of Customer Support**

Low
Few customers
get anything
special

Few customers
get major
attention

Percent of
accounts
receiving
special
effort

No differentiation
Low attention

No differentiation
High attention

High

Low                                                    High
Amount of special effort
for selected accounts

If the account base is concentrated (few customers and prospects comprise a large percentage of potential) and the accounts are interested in special services, then the upper right-hand corner of intensively nurturing a few accounts with the strategic account relationship approach will pay off. A more dispersed account and prospect potential and/or less responsiveness to special services suggests less differentiation for a larger group of accounts.

One problem with Exhibit 7 is that it is somewhat unidimensional. Perhaps a more complete way to look at the total account and prospect base is to ask what number should get each type of sales approach. Nonetheless, the issue is raised boldly by Exhibit 7.

Now that we have examined the four different sales approaches and seen that most vendors will have a mixture of the four, we turn to a deeper analysis of strategic account relationships. Before we do so, however, it is necessary to emphasize that these complex relationships are not appropriate to every vendor or to every customer of any vendor. They get special attention here because they are new and complex. Little is understood about strategic account relationships and even less has been written. We begin with the customer's view, the best place to begin.

# What Do Strategic Account Relationships Provide to Customers?

The essence of strategic account relationships is the provision of a special set of efforts by the vendor. These efforts must provide a long-term competitive advantage to the customer. The customer hopes to get some mixture of technological, operational, and strategic benefits from the approach.

Most strategic account relationships are fostered by intense and rapid technological development. The need for technological specialization and integration has forced customers to look beyond their boundaries for the skills and resources they need. Often the two partners must integrate their technologies and design their products with one another. Because the technology is so pervasive and the integration so complex, the level of sharing must be high. Design and development must often be performed jointly with a great deal of frequent cutting and fitting.

Many customers and prospects seek operational rewards from the strategic account relationship vendor. Sometimes these fall out from the technological integration, at other times they are the primary benefit.

Evolving approaches to manufacturing such as just-in-time force intimate operational coordination. And because components, equipment, and systems exchanged in a strategic partnership are often customized with no second source and no other prospective customers, the operational integration system has fewer safety valves and alternatives than more traditional approaches. Thus, sales forecasting and capacity planning must be joint. Higher levels of technological and design integration create the need for greater operational integration.

The relationship between NutraSweet and its primary customers is an example of operational benefits focused on joint marketing interests. Consumer franchiser-franchisee relationships such as McDonald's and Dunkin' Donuts are another example of marketing benefits to the relationship.

By their nature, strategic account relationships work only in situations where the relationship is at the heart of the strategy of both companies. This is because the cost and effort involved in making a strategic partnership can only be justified if there is a strategic need. The cost and effort are not justified and will not be provided unless the need is clear to the relevant and powerful managers on both sides of the relationship as well as to the lower level people who must actually do the work. General Motors needed Fanuc's factory automation skills to survive and prosper in a hostile competitive environment. Fanuc needed a large, worldwide base of leading edge, high-volume customers, advanced applications knowledge, and factory involvement to develop its leading position in robots. Both companies needed each other to prosper.

## How Are Strategic Account Relationships Nurtured?

Strategic account relationships require importance, intimacy, and longevity. The intimacy sets the tone for the very nature of the relationship. The technological, operational, and strategic integration lead naturally to the high level of organizational integration that must be present in strategic relationships. This is not the typical salesperson–purchasing agent relationship. It also goes far beyond the still evolving team and multilevel selling approaches that developed in the 1970s and early 1980s, to some extent, as parts of major account management. The organizational integration must extend to many parts of the vendor and customer organizations. Engineers must talk to engineers, production people must talk to one another, and top management must get together as well.

Sometimes employees of the seller must be located in the facilities of the customer to work together, or even to operate equipment. In the chemical industry, some vendors have found it advantageous or even necessary to operate leased equipment at a customer site. This raises a raft of issues about integration, including everything from union contracts to cafeteria and parking privileges.

Old-fashioned arm's-length organizational relationships are not enough; the relationships must be person to person. In many cases, the success of a person in the vendor or customer organization is more dependent on a personal relationship with someone in the partner organization than with anyone in his or her own. The designers must work at a high level of cooperation and intimacy, often melding different technologies and philosophies.

The organizational and personal integration can only take place between a vendor and a customer who have some common values and culture. That is unfortunate because sometimes the greatest strategic and technological rewards might come from working with a company quite disparate from your own. The likelihood of success, however, tends to go down in such a situation. Management support on both sides and unusual organizational arrangements might help, but there are disparities that cannot be bridged regardless of the amount of goodwill, effort, and potential reward.

Finally, there is financial integration. The strategic bond here is so great that a typical financial relationship is often too weak to reflect it. Some strategic account relationships work on a typical "I make it, I sell it, you buy it, and you pay for it" basis. But much more likely are arrangements that better reflect the relationship. Certainly outright acquisition is one approach. Formal joint ventures such as GM-Fanuc are much more likely. Other approaches include development contracts, supply contracts, licensing, and very strong informal relationships. Seldom does the buyer ask for bids for a specified product. Instead, the development is joint and the financial relationship attempts to reflect the sharing of risk, contribution, and reward. Roy Shapiro has captured a great deal about these new types of relationships in "Toward Effective Supplier Management: International Comparisons."[12]

### *Integration beyond the Vendor and Customer Relationship*

The integration in a strategic partnership must extend sometimes beyond the two partners to the vendor's suppliers and the customer's customers. The system is sometimes so complex that other levels in the supply chain or distribution channel must be involved to provide all the needed strategic, technological, operational, and financial horsepower.

Finally, integration within each of the partners must be stronger than in a normal company. Roy Shapiro argues that the purchasing, engineering, and production functions in the customer company must become more integrated to deal with suppliers in strategic account relationships. The vendor organization must also be well integrated. Everyone must sell and service the strategic partner. If the engineering and sales functions cannot operate well together, it is hard to believe that they will be able to work with customers in an intimate relationship.

All this integration must be justified by substantial rewards.

# The Rewards

Strategic account relationships offer the selling company the opportunity to leverage its skills and resources, develop long-term customers, and build strong competitive positions. Companies in a wide variety of industries have understood the rewards and opportunities. Some have reached them successfully, others have failed.

Strategic account relationships do not necessarily represent a way station between acquisition, which in a sense is the ultimate form of strategic partnership, and the more arm's-length forms of buyer–seller relationships. Instead, they can represent a continuing vendor–customer relationship which is very special because of the rewards it offers to both parties. The exchange of knowledge, including "soft" management skills and competence as well as "hard" technological capability, is at the

---

[12]Harvard Business School Working Paper 9-785-062.

core of many strategic account relationships. The seller can learn how its product is used and develop unique applications approaches. The customer is willing to share such knowledge with an outsider because it expects to gain knowledge and unique support for its new activities.

If the partnership is with a distributor, the supplier gets the commitment of resources to its product line, and the investment of the distributor's organization in unique capabilities useful only for the supplier's product line. For example, distributor salespeople may spend substantial amounts of time learning the benefits of the products, their competitive positioning, and the ways in which they can best be sold. Distributor engineers will learn the minutiae of interfacing the vendor's product with their customers' products and systems, and distributor service people will learn how to maintain and repair the equipment. The distributor is willing to make the commitments because of the permanence and intimacy of the relationship. In the distribution realm, the strategic account relationship is different more in degree than in nature from a solid, close, but typical major or national distributor–vendor relationship.

The permanence of the relationship leads naturally to a long-term customer commitment. The sales and the knowledge exchange lead to a stronger competitive position. Sometimes, for example, a vendor cannot afford to invest in a major new product without the long-term commitment of a customer to ensure the profitability, or at least to limit the financial risk, of the venture.

In some industries, the astute choice and effective management of strategic account relationships is a critical determinant of success. The choice and management of the partnerships presents some major traps, however.

# Traps

The traps can be divided into four groups:

1. Attempting to develop too many strategic account relationships.
2. Picking poor strategic account partners.
3. Allocating too few resources to the relationship.
4. Losing sight of the importance of cultural compatibility in the relationships.

Because the relationships are so intensive and extensive, it is possible for a company to maintain only a few strategic account relationships. Some companies have a very concentrated customer and prospect list with few existing and potential accounts and a high proportion of sales potential in an even smaller number of them. These companies often have little choice but to develop several, or at most a few, strategic account relationships. But even companies with very extensive prospect and customer lists cannot have more than a few strategic account relationships given their attendant high demands on resources and time.

One of the most subtle forms of strategic account demands is product and service customization. If the customization is major and, as is often the case, affects the whole vendor organization and product line, the vendor will be torn apart by too many strategic account relationships. Each account will pressure the vendor to emphasize its needs and approach. If the vendor has too many conflicting pulls, it will be able to satisfy none well and, perhaps more sadly, will lose its own internal organizational coherence and end up with a poorly integrated, incoherent product line.

If the vendor can only have a few relationships, and if the relationships are strategic, it is clear that the choice of the accounts is critical. A poor choice leads to wasted resources, but that is not the major cost of the poor choice. The highest cost of a poor choice is usually the opportunity lost to develop an effective strategic account relationship with another customer or prospect. Instead, a competitor may move in and reap long-term rewards. The choice of accounts is particularly hard when it is impossible to have strategic relationships with two accounts who compete intensively with one another.

The criteria for choice, and their priority, must be set very carefully indeed. They should include:

1. A leading-edge technical and/or operational capability.
2. A willingness to share in joint technical and/or operational development.
3. A willingness to make the vendor an important part of the customer's business activities, including frequent meetings with a wide variety of functional units within the customer organization.
4. Substantial sales potential.
5. Long-term profit potential.
6. An existing relationship as a basis for the partnership.
7. Good cultural fit.

The technical and/or operational capability and development in criteria one and two above must relate to activities of clear strategic importance to the vendor. The capability might be "hard" as relates to a scientific or engineering capability or "soft" as relates to a particular form of operational capability such as marketing, service, or manufacturing.

Some companies have attempted to develop strategic accounts without devoting enough resources to each relationship. Sometimes this is because they have tried to develop too many account relationships, or have chosen to use strategic account relationships where they are not justified and supportable. At other times, they underestimated the cost and commitment needed.

Four forms of resource starvation have been particularly typical:

1. Not assigning enough top management skill and power or enough technical and functional expertise to the relationships. The strategic accounts justify and require the best staffing and attention.
2. Using a sales-oriented approach when more skills in engineering, production, service, financial, and so on, are needed. This is not a standard sale; it is a long-term, intimate partnership.

3. An unwillingness to develop custom products and services for each strategic account. The custom nature of each partnership is one of the major limitations in the number that can be developed. If each relationship needs a separate product line, and the base business needs its own product line, the total diversity must still be supportable by the engineering, production, service, and logistics functions.

4. If personal relationships are to develop, people must spend time together. Travel and telephone budgets must be extensive enough to support relationship and trust development. And the managers and experts working on the accounts must have adequate time available to do the job. Some might have to move to the partner's location on an extended, but temporary, basis. The drain of international partnerships with the attendant travel (jet lag is a real cost!) is very high indeed.

Patience is an important part of nurturing strategic account relationships. One top-level executive complained to me, "We have been at this strategic account relationship thing for three whole months and sales at the account aren't up!" Major account management takes a long time and strategic account relationship development takes even longer. Many months are needed to build a good personal relationship and even longer to build the deep institutional bonds of the strategic account relationship approach. Patience is particularly important when the joint projects involve major technological development or when the customer is a mature, cyclical company. The down cycle is often the best time to build strategic relationships but the more visible benefits such as sales increases will often not accrue until the up cycle.

Another particularly good time to build strategic account relationships is when the supplier industry is oversold and the customer is in desperate need of support. Short-term optimization of profits by such maneuvers as price gouging or allocation of scarce products to new customers instead of established ones can cost dearly over the business cycle and make it absolutely impossible for a vendor to establish the deep trust needed for this type of relationship.

The life cycle of the relationship dictates that, as in most situations, the investment must be made before the rewards can be reaped.

Finally, some companies have neglected to understand the delicate mating of cultures which leads to successful relationships. Some pairs of cultures are hard to integrate and some impossible. Partnerships require compromise and constant joint nurturing to succeed.

# Implementation—Building Institutional Relationships

Although strategic account relationships are fairly new, it is possible to suggest some guidelines for success. Some are similar to those for acquisitions, an even more intimate and permanent relationship. The critical issue is the human management of the relationship, which must engender something closer than the typical buyer–seller relationship but cannot be internal management such as in an acquisition.

To avoid the traps:

1. Develop only a few strategic partnerships. Recognize that some customers will be transactional customers, some systems customers, a limited number major or national accounts, and a very small number strategic account relationships. If the number of such partnerships goes beyond being countable on one's fingers, the relationships won't be truly strategic!

2. Choose accounts who meet the explicit chosen criteria and who share a long-term vision of the future. If the relationships are to be strategic, they must be long term. If they are to be profitable, they must last long enough to generate revenue after the expensive, initial investment period. Look at them as long-term company-to-company relationships, not as related to one product, technology, or worst of all, one deal.

3. Allocate enough resources to the relationship. If the resource allocation is parsimonious, the relationship is doomed.

4. Understand that the relationships involve a substantial loss of autonomy. Decisions will no longer be made only on the basis of the needs and desires of one organization, but on the joint needs and desires of both partners. This loss of autonomy is one of the primary costs of strategic account relationship. The loss will be most severe in those activities which are closest to the heart of the relationship—often product design and technology choice.

5. Develop a financial relationship that reflects the long-term needs and interests of both parties, and which is flexible enough to adjust to changing conditions (if it is a long-term relationship, conditions will change), and explicit enough to avoid arguments about interpretation. It helps to identify, discuss, and clarify issues which are likely to create problems in the future. The relationship should be so intimate and pervasive that parts of it cannot be "swept under the carpet" in hopes they won't be noticed. Instead, the disagreements will fester until the infection destroys the relationships. There are a great many financial forms that the venture can take. All the relevant ones from supply contracts to joint ventures should be explored to find the optimum mix of flexibility and explicitness.

Finally, we turn to the management of the relationship. If the partnership is to succeed, the relationship must be institutional. That is, it must supersede the relationship between any two individuals and become a relationship between organizations.

Major account relationships depend upon an able account manager who can mobilize internal resources to support the account and who can call on many people at the account with confidence and competence. The account manager becomes the primary node in the communications network:

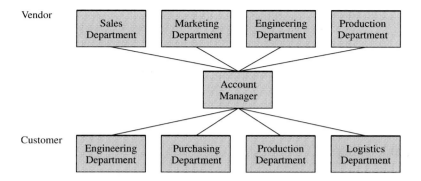

A true strategic account relationship cannot operate with one primary node. There must be intense communication among many vendor and customer functions:

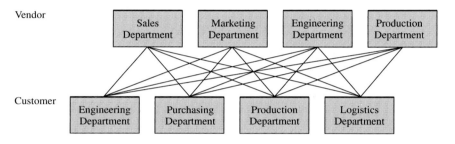

The problem with this scheme is that the communication can easily become unmanageable and uncoordinated as well as inefficient. One approach that appears to work well in many situations is to have a senior partnership team consisting of two top-level executives, one from the vendor and one from the customer, and a group of senior functional executives who manage and coordinate the partnership. In a way, this idea imitates the joint venture board of directors, but in a much more informal and day-to-day oriented way.

The senior partnership team should not replace or limit other direct communications. Instead, it should manage and coordinate the relationship, and nurture cross-company integration and communication at all levels in all functions. If the engineers do not talk to one another, for example, the benefits of the partnership will not accrue, but the costs will.

National account management has been described as a case of making and keeping promises to customers.[13] This view is appropriate in all four sales approaches, even transaction selling. But it is especially true in the relationship-building activities of major account management and strategic account relationships. Because of the long-term nature of the activities and results, yesterday's promises

---

[13]Benson P. Shapiro and Rowland T. Moriarty, Jr., "Support Systems for National Account Management Programs: Promises Made, Promises Kept," Marketing Science Institute, Cambridge, Mass., 1983.

must be kept tomorrow. When the promises are not kept, it hurts the present relationship which can have long-term impact because of the strategic nature of the relationship. The great upside opportunity of strategic account relationships puts emphasis on unmade promises as well. The unmade promise is, in essence, a lost opportunity. It sacrifices the long-term return from the relationship in the same way that unkept promises hurt the present situation.

## Concluding Note

Before we considered strategic account relationships we looked at all four kinds of selling. Transaction selling is inexpensive and very utilitarian where it is appropriate. Systems sales are useful for the larger, more complex transactions. When the philosophy moves from one of transactions to one of relationships we encounter major account management. Relationship selling is not just a better set of techniques for making sales: It is a different philosophy based upon continuity and trust. When the importance, intimacy, and longevity of the relationship warrant it, the vendor should move from major account management to a strategic account relationship.

Strategic account relationships are a response to the need to develop and manage more complex, and more permanent, partnerships between suppliers and customers. They are expensive and difficult but they can offer great benefits when used selectively and implemented well. Undoubtedly some companies will view them as a panacea. They are not. In fact, in most industries they will supplement and enhance only a small part of the company's sales and marketing effort. They differ in intensity and degree, but not truly in nature, from major and national account management; they differ in fundamental nature from transaction and systems selling, however. There are four kinds of close encounters in selling, but one is closer than the others.

# 13 Segmenting Customers in Mature Industrial Markets: An Application

*In mature industrial markets, segmenting customers on size, industry, or product benefits alone is rarely sufficient. Customer behavior regarding trade-offs between price and service also becomes an important criterion. In this reading, we offer a framework to enable such buying-behavior-oriented microsegmentation of industrial customers. We apply our framework to segment the national accounts of a large industrial company and show how the results of our segmentation study may be used to redirect the firm's resources and customer segments.*

Segmenting is the art of identifying distinctive customer groups that exhibit homogeneous needs. The point of segmentation is to be able to tailor the marketing mix to address the unique needs of the various segments. A number of bases for segmentation have been offered in the literature, including:

- Demographic descriptors such as geography, standard industrial classification code, and account size.
- Product end use or application.
- Buying situation.
- Customer decision-making style.
- Customer buying behavior.
- Customer benefits.

Market segmentation designs based on product benefits are widely recognized as the state of the art and superior to traditional segmentation schemes based on industry type or customer size. Coles and Culley,[1] for example, illustrate how DuPont segmented its market for Kevlar by three unique customer benefits:

---

V. Kasturi Rangan prepared this note.

This note is adapted from V. Kasturi Rangan, Rowland T. Moriarty, and Gordon Swartz, "Segmenting Customers in Mature Industrial Markets," *Journal of Marketing* 56 (October 1992), pp. 72–82. Reprinted with permission of the American Marketing Association.

[1]Gary J. Coles and James D. Culley (1986), "Not All Prospects Are Created Equal," *Business Marketing* 71 (May 1986), pp. 52–58.

- For potential fishing boat owners: Kevlar's lightness promised fuel savings, increased speed, and the ability to carry fish weight.
- For aircraft designers: Kevlar had a high strength-to-weight ratio.
- For industrial plant managers: Kevlar could replace the asbestos used for packing pumps.

Such segmentation schemes, though very useful for new products, are too broad to leverage marketing-mix resources as the product-market matures. By then, competitors are able to offer equivalent products, and many buyers may therefore be unwilling to pay a price premium. This is especially true of industrial raw materials and supplies that are hard to differentiate by functions and features alone. Steadily and deliberately, as the market becomes a commodity, price and service become important buying criteria for some customers. Only by further segmenting each macro segment (be it demographic, end-use applications, or benefit) can a marketer really begin to understand the heterogeneity in buying behavior.

Product life cycle (PLC) theory contends that prices tend to drop as the product market matures.[2] Two underlying forces cause that trend. The first is customer learning during the PLC. As the product matures, many customers who by now are totally familiar with the product's characteristics, functions, and features no longer require the same intensity of product information that was once provided by its supplier. As a result, they are unwilling to pay the cost of such services. The second force is the result of competitive action that in a mature market makes equivalent products at similar or lower prices available to customers.

Given this market dynamic, customers in mature markets may be aligned along the two dimensions of price and cost-to-serve[3] (see Figure 1). Customers who demand a low price will be offered a no-frills product accompanied by minimal service, and customers who value an augmented product will pay a higher price and receive the full complement of services. Price differentials due to product quality differences are small because competitors, by then, are able to offer more or less equivalent products. Thus, any major price variations stem from differences among services provided. Customers who receive the core product pay less because it costs less to serve them than those who demand and value the full service.

In keeping with this rationale, firms operating in mature environments expect to align their customers along the value axis in Figure 1. The southwest quadrant (C) represents a core, no-frills product without much service, and the northeast quadrant (B) represents an augmented product accompanied by intensive value-added services. In both cases, the price-service offering is equitable to the seller and the buyer. The core-product customer pays a lower price and the value-added customer pays a higher price. This rationale, however, is based on the seller's expectations of how customers would behave in a mature market.

---

[2]George S. Day, "The Product Life Cycle: Analysis and Applications Issues," *Journal of Marketing* 45 (Fall 1981), pp. 60–70.

[3]B. P. Shapiro, V. K. Rangan, R. T. Moriarty, and E. Ross, "Manage Customers for Profits (Not Just Sales)," *Harvard Business Review* 65 (September–October 1987), pp. 101–8.

**FIGURE 1**

*Potential buying
behavior segments*

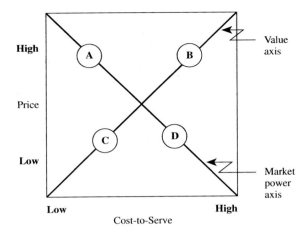

There is an alternative, which is given by the market power axis in Figure 1. Customers see only the price dimension of the matrix; they do not know the seller's cost-to-serve. Because of market maturity, however, there are usually several sellers that can offer similar products, and many customers may therefore attempt to shop around for price. Guaranteed purchase volumes and large order sizes are usually offered as the bait. As a result, customers may not necessarily align themselves along the value axis as sellers expect, but prefer to operate in quadrants C and D, depending on their knowledge of competitive offerings and their own market power.

In the northwest quadrant (A), the supplier is able to extract a relatively high price without providing the necessary services to go along with it. This is usually the result of a truly superior product offering that competitors are unable to match because of technological or other reasons (such as patent protection). Sometimes it is possible for ill-informed customers to overpay, but such a situation is unlikely to persist in the long run.

In sum, all locations above the value axis indicate that the seller is able to extract a higher value than the services it renders because customers perceive the firm's product offering as superior to competitive offerings or substitutes. Positions below the value axis usually indicate that the firm is unable to extract the full value of the services it renders with its product. Along the value axis itself, the exchange is fair. We will now describe how this framework may be used to further analyze a company's customer segments in mature industrial markets.

## Database

The main purpose of this study was to validate the buying behavior framework depicted in Figure 1 and demonstrate its use for managerial action. We therefore sought a research site where the product-market environment was in the mature phase of its PLC, characterized by price pressures and the availability of equivalent

sales calls were measured as calls per year, unbilled work was estimated in dollars, and applications engineering in hours. These individual components were linearly converted to a 1-to-10 scale and the three rescaled measures then averaged to yield a composite score.

3. *Account size.* While various aspects of account size have been identified as influencing buying behavior, we measured account size simply as the total purchase volume of all Signode products in the most recent 12 months.

4. *Market share.* A different measure of dependency is a single supplier's proportion of business in the buyer's total purchases of a product category. We measured this as Signode's share of dollar sales volume for each account. As part of their routine sales reporting, Signode's salespeople estimated the total dollar volume of each account's steel-strapping purchases. Knowing Signode's actual sales to the account, we computed Signode's market share—an indicator of the buyer's preference for, as well as reliance on, Signode's products.

## Buying Behavior Variables from National Account Reps and NAMs

We considered customer sensitivity to price and service changes to be two important aspects of buying behavior. Sales reps were asked the following question for each of their accounts: "If you were able to drop (increase) prices by 7 percent, what is your best estimate of the percentage of increase (decrease) in sales volume that would result?"[5] The 7 percent represented a level of price discounting that the management had selectively used in the past to retain certain large volume accounts in the face of competitive activity. Service elasticity was measured in the same way, except that the unit of change was broken down by its individual components for better comprehension. We thus generated four customer demand elasticities:

5. For decrease in price.
6. For increase in price.
7. For decrease in service.
8. For increase in service.

In addition to these demand elasticities, estimated the national account sales reps, four more buying behavior indicators—product importance, switching potential, market knowledge, and decision-making process complexity—were using the data collection process described above.

9. *Product importance.* Depending on the application and extent of usage, the importance of steel strapping varied over Signode's national accounts. Customers that perceived the product line to be critical were thought to devote more energy and consideration to the buying process.

---

[5]This is a widely used approach by researchers to generate quantitative judgments. The original idea was proposed by J. D. C. Little, "Models and Managers: The Concept of a Decision Calculus," *Management Science* 16, 1970, pp. B466–85.

10. *Switching potential.* Over the years, several customers had built a trusting relationship with Signode because of the product or the service or both. These customers were expected to deviate less from normal purchasing patterns, while other customers might be more likely to switch at lower levels of dissatisfaction.

11. *Market knowledge.* Regardless of the stage of market maturity, customers vary substantially in their knowledge of competitive products and prices; they search for information in varying degrees. Naturally, customers with a detailed knowledge of alternative suppliers' steel-strapping offerings were expected to use somewhat more aggressive negotiation strategies.

12. *Decision-making process (DMP).* The complexity of the buying decision-making process is a reflection not only of product and vendor characteristics but also of the buying organization's priorities and purchasing strategies. At Signode, national account reps suggested that customers with considerable leverage usually required several sales presentations and often contract-by-contract negotiation before an agreement could be reached.

## Analysis and Results

To identify buying behavior microsegments, we performed a hierarchical cluster analysis based on the 12 variables of Table 1.[6] Mean values of the buying behavior variables are shown for each microsegment in Table 2.

### Buying Behavior Microsegments

**Segment 1: Programmed Buyers.**   Customers in this microsegment were small and viewed the product as a routine purchase item. They had the lowest average sales of any group and were not particularly price or service sensitive. The product was not very important or central to their operations. Compared to those in the other three microsegments, these customers had the lowest market share of Signode products.

We subsequently learned that many of these accounts used rules of thumb to allocate their purchases. They split orders among two or three vendors in fixed proportions. Signode, because of its market-leader reputation, received a major share of these purchases—on average, about 54 percent. Perhaps because of their routinized procedures, these accounts invested little effort in the buying process, either in negotiating purchases or in investigating alternative sources. In return, Signode charged them the full list price and provided below-average service. Because cus-

---

[6]In comparisons of 30 methods for estimating the number of clusters, Glen Milligan and Martha Cooper  recommend the use of three statistics for determining the number of clusters: the cubic clustering criterion, the pseudo F statistic, and the pseudo $t^2$ statistic. We used these to arrive at the four segments shown in Table 2. See Milligan and Cooper, "An Examination of the Procedures for Determining the Number of Clusters in a Data Set," *Psychometrika* 50, no. 2 (1985), pp. 159–79.

TABLE 2    **Group Means**

| Behavioral Surrogates | Segment 1: No. of Accounts = 54 | Segment 2: No. of Accounts = 65 | Segment 3: No. of Accounts = 22 | Segment 4: No. of Accounts = 11 |
|---|---|---|---|---|
| 1. Relative price | 0.0% | −7.9% | −10.1% | −11.3% |
| 2. Relative service | 3.6 | 4.9 | 5.6 | 7.1 |
| 3. Account size (sales) | $122,000 | $472,000 | $1,100,000 | $2,100,000 |
| 4. Market share | 54.2% | 67.8% | 71.9% | 68.3% |
| 5. Percentage increase in sales for price drop | 5.6 | 8.9 | 8.7 | 11.8 |
| 6. Percentage decrease in sales for price raise | 15.5 | 27.9 | 24.5 | 22.7 |
| 7. Percentage decrease in sales for service drop | 5.1 | 9.2 | 12.5 | 12.3 |
| 8. Percentage increase in sales for service raise | 1.2 | 3.0 | 5.2 | 7.3 |
| 9. Product importance | 2.5 | 3.0 | 3.5 | 3.5 |
| 10. Switching potential | 3.8 | 4.4 | 4.5 | 4.6 |
| 11. Market knowledge | 4.0 | 4.5 | 4.6 | 4.7 |
| 12. DMP complexity | 3.2 | 3.6 | 3.3 | 3.4 |

NOTES: Of the 161 complete data records, the clustering algorithm omitted nine cases as outliers. Nos. 5 and 6 are percentage increase or decrease in sales for a 7% price change; Nos. 8 and 9 are percentage increase or decrease for a unit of service change.

tomers in this segment tended to systematically allocate market share rather than evaluate the price-volume trade-offs, we characterized the purchasing behavior of this microsegment as programmed buying.

**Segment 2: Relationship Buyers.**    Customers in this microsegment were also relatively small. The product itself was moderately important in their operations and, unlike the programmed buyers of segment 1, they were more knowledgeable about competitive offerings. While customers in this microsegment paid lower prices and received more service than programmed buyers, they also gave Signode a higher market share (67.8 percent).

Although customers in this microsegment had a propensity to switch, they were less prone to switching than their counterparts in the third and fourth segments. In addition, in comparison with their more aggressive counterparts in the third and fourth segments, these buyers did not push Signode for price and service concessions, and they paid higher prices for relatively less service. This difference in value received probably explains their extreme sensitivity to price increases. On average, a 7 percent price increase in this microsegment would decrease purchase volumes by as much as 28 percent. As these customers seemed to prefer Signode's partnership to a mere price exchange, we labeled the behavior of this segment as relationship buying.

**Segment 3: Transaction Buyers.**  Customers in this microsegment were, on average, twice as large as the relationship buyers. They received price discounts averaging about 10 percent and an above-average service level; they had the highest sensitivity to decreases in service. The product itself was very important to their operations. Customers in this group were very knowledgeable about competitive offerings, and while valuing Signode's service offerings, they would not hesitate to switch suppliers. Because the customers here actively considered the price-versus-service tradeoffs, but often favored price over service, we labeled them transaction buyers.

**Segment 4: Bargain Hunters.**  Customers in this microsegment were large-volume customers that received the largest price discounts (averaging 11.3 percent) as well as the highest level of service. They were sensitive to any changes in price or service; the product was very important to their operations. They were most knowledgeable about alternative suppliers and most likely to switch suppliers at the slightest dissatisfaction. Customers in this segment were the ultimate bargain hunters.

## Discussion

The purpose of this study was to identify buying behavior variations in macrosegments such as national accounts. We argued that such an analysis would be useful in redirecting a company's price versus service offerings in mature industrial markets. Figure 2 shows the alignment of the behavioral microsegments with respect to the relative price and relative service variables.

At the time of the study, Signode's management was under severe pressure from its national accounts to reduce prices. The buying behavior microsegmentation and the concurrent analysis of the judgmentally generated sales elasticities,

**FIGURE 2**

*Segment profile*

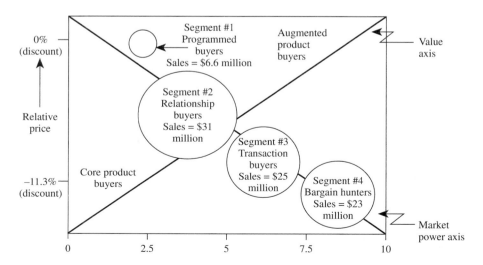

however, suggested that price and service changes would not be equally effective in all four segments. When sales variations were estimated for each microsegment, Signode found that breaking even on a 7 percent price change would require total sales volume to change by about 20 percent. Similar estimates for changes in service showed that breaking even on a one "unit" service change would require total sales volume to change by 8 percent. Although these numbers should be viewed with caution because the data were gathered from salespeople in a judgmental exercise, the estimates generally suggest that:

- Decreasing price is unprofitable for Signode because the estimated increase in sales is far below the required 20 percent for every microsegment in Table 2 (see row 5 in Table 2).
- Increasing price is profitable in the programmed buyer microsegment—sales decrease of only 15.5 percent compared with a break-even of 20 percent. It exceeds the break-even number for all other microsegments (see row 6 in Table 2).
- Decreasing service is profitable in the programmed buyer microsegment because the estimated sales drop is 5.1 percent. It exceeds the break-even of 8 percent in all other segments (see row 7 in Table 2).
- Increasing service is barely profitable in the bargain-hunter microsegment sales increase of 7.3 percent compared with a break-even of 8 percent. It is far below this number for all other microsegments (see row 8 in Table 2).

It is interesting to note that programmed buyers were willing to pay a relatively higher price without demanding additional service. In a sense, these accounts were willing to pay a premium to maintain their rule-of-thumb purchase allocations to have the flexibility of buying a high proportion (46 percent) of non-Signode products. Compared with other national accounts, programmed buyers were not as sensitive to price or service changes. Instead, to increase market share in these accounts, Signode's salespeople would need to influence their customers' underlying decision-making processes. Thus, Signode management directed the sales reps handling these accounts to focus their efforts on changing the buying decision-making strategies that limited Signode's share.

The bargain hunters posed a more immediate problem. These accounts were critical to the company because of their very large size—11 accounts contributed nearly 25 percent of national account revenues. These accounts, however, also demanded the lowest prices and the highest levels of service. Worse still, bargain hunters had the highest propensity to switch to competitive suppliers. Thus, managing the bargain hunters would require considerable tact and skill to keep them from switching while countering their discount requests. To protect company margins, Signode management decided that price cutting should be used only as a defense against price cuts of competitors. Instead, Signode offered additional service in hope that this would improve sales volume beyond the estimated 8 percent break-even point. In addition, the NAMs were directed to take an active role in handling these 11 accounts.

The relationship buyers and transaction buyers of the middle microsegments had somewhat similar profiles, except that the former were less likely to press

Signode for price and service concessions. Though the relationship- and transaction-oriented customers did not pose an immediate problem, both microsegments were sensitive to price and service trade-offs. Because Signode management was concerned about the potential migration of these accounts to the bargain hunter microsegment, a separate service management group was created to explore ways of adding service value for this group of customers.

# Conclusion

We believe the practice of industrial market segmentation has lagged behind the theoretical developments in the field. Although the concept of buying behavior–based segmentation was advanced two decades ago, virtually no application of the concept has been published to date. Of course, there are many important and valid reasons for this applications gap. Yet, as our research here demonstrates, considerable value can be gained by attempting to move toward buying behavior–based segmentation. A knowledge of segment behavior helped the Signode Company redirect marketing resources for profit gain.

Following the analyses at Signode, we believe that even a simple framework, such as the two-dimensional plot of price versus cost-to-serve in Figure 1, is capable of unearthing a rich subsegment of behaviors in industrial accounts. As can be seen from the figure, the diagonal equates the price to cost-to-serve for the seller. We hypothesize that the seller's profit would be roughly equal for accounts located on this axis—when customers want services (augmented product), they are willing to pay higher prices. The cross diagonal, however, represents an axis of product differentiation. Clearly, customers who demand and get high levels of services for low prices must have alternatives, just as those customers who pay high prices must find the product attractive even though they do not receive the full battery of services. Obviously, the seller's profits are likely to be higher in the northwest and lower in the southeast quadrant compared with the diagonal axis. Understandably, the segment descriptor variables and dimensions are likely to vary across applications; nevertheless, a few variables could provide rich diagnostics for management actions.

In addition, our research demonstrates a practical and implementable method for constructing buyer behavior–based segments from readily available data sources. The key, of course, is to identify variables that adequately capture the variance in buying behavior and that address a specific management problem. By selecting the segment descriptor variables to address management's concerns with price and service—two variables under Signode's control—the buying behavior microsegmentation was designed to provide useful guidance for Signode's account management policies.

We acknowledge that one application does not necessarily prove the rule, but at least it provides a benchmark for future studies. Our purpose here was to demonstrate the usefulness of our segmentation framework for managers.

# Once More: How Do You Improve Customer Service?

*The authors offer a broadened concept of customer service to include core product characteristics such as performance and quality, in addition to support factors like delivery and repair. They argue that critical elements of customer service vary by phase of the order cycle (preorder, order-to-shipment, and postshipment) as well as by the type of business (flow versus project business). They conclude by providing guidelines on how to implement a customer service program in a cross-functional context.*

The business community is presently flooded with articles, books, speeches, and workshops stressing the importance of keeping close to the customer as a means of achieving competitive advantage and market leadership. However, while customer service has become a dominant topic, experts repeatedly find that good service is more the exception than the rule. Is it an issue of attitudes, culture, and the lack of a "service obsession" at companies, or are other factors more relevant? What is customer service in a given situation, and how can managers diagnose internal activities that help or hinder external responsiveness?

One reason customer service workshops have not brought marked improvement is that they usually preach to the converted. Most managers realize that service is important, but often core organizational issues impede good service. Emphasizing "service culture" may momentarily galvanize the firm, but it ultimately will not help if management preaches service without addressing organizational factors.

A decade ago, *In Search of Excellence* (Peters & Waterman 1982) focused attention on the components of service, providing examples of companies and individuals that exhibited qualities of superior customer service. However, in many ways service now occupies the status of "motivation" as defined by Frederic

This article was prepared by Frank V. Cespedes.

Reprinted from *Business Horizons* 35, no. 2, March–April 1992, Indiana University Graduate School of Business.

Herzberg (1968) in his classic article, "One More Time: How Do You Motivate Employees?" Anxious for quick answers to a complex issue, many managers enthusiastically greet new quick fixes. Friendliness, responsiveness, and zeal become the fundamental attitudes associated with good service. Unfortunately, these attitudes are analogous to what Herzberg called hygiene factors—necessary but insufficient catalysts for obtaining the behavior and results desired.

## What Is Customer Service?

Many companies define customer service as product delivery and repair. As a result, they tend to focus on delivery time, order fill rates, and billing-error minimization to determine good or bad service.

However, other factors also help determine the value of a purchase to a prospective buyer. The most obvious of these involves the product's price/performance characteristics, quality ratings as determined by the industry or respected outside rating agencies (Underwriters Laboratories in electrical equipment or *Consumer Reports* for many consumer durables), and the specifications of the product relative to the purchaser's particular requirements. But various prepurchase and postpurchase elements that add value to the item also must be seen as components of customer service. These nonproduct components include any information and ordering costs, inbound logistical costs, operation and maintenance costs, and, in many cases, disposal or trade-up costs.

Having understood that customer service should encompass broader product and nonproduct components of customer satisfaction, two ideas must be kept in mind when evaluating service efforts and goals.

First we examine value-in-use. This idea is that "the product is what the product does" (Corey 1983); the product is the total package of benefits customers receive when they buy it. This includes the functional utility of the goods; any technical assistance in applications development provided before the sale; training or repair services provided after the sale; assurances of timely delivery through the supplier's distribution network; and any brand-name or reputation benefits that help the buyer promote its product or services to customers. Benefits might also include the buyer–seller relationship itself. Particularly in industrial markets, interpersonal relationships developed among people in buying and selling organizations have intangible but real value. Conversely, the package of benefits in some situations might not include personal contact because it is more efficient to reorder or conduct other aspects of the transaction via automated, online systems.

The point here is that customer service should include more than product-related functions or employee friendliness. Service must encompass an entire range of possibilities by which a vendor can contribute to the customer's business operations. The ultimate economic justification for providing such services is to shift purchase criteria away from sheer price toward other value elements that help differentiate a vendor in its market.

For example, consider marketing developments in the health care industry. Since 1983, when the government changed its reimbursement procedures for Medicare patients, hospitals have encountered intense cost pressures, making them more sensitive to price. One result of this new price sensitivity was the formation of more (and more powerful) group purchasing organizations (GPOs) in which a number of hospitals made volume purchases in return for substantial price discounts. Because of the volume they represented, these GPOs were typically designated major or national accounts by most suppliers. However, as one sales director noted, "Our national account program was really a national discount program, eroding our margins and often our contacts with end users at hospitals."

Nevertheless, in recent years some suppliers have altered their marketing strategies to redefine customer service and deliver a value to GPOs extending beyond price. For example, some drug companies now bundle products—offering discounts on sole-source items when purchased along with multisource products. Such services benefit hospitals by substantially lowering transaction costs in frequently purchased product categories. These services also enable vendors to better position their off-patent products. Additionally, bundling enables vendors to negotiate multiyear contracts with GPOs across product lines, further reducing costs while increasing the vendors' "share of mind" at end-user levels. Other suppliers have developed inventory management programs which have grown in perceived value as more hospitals adopt just-in-time inventory policies. Still others give client hospitals data on the total costs of patient care in a given diagnostic category and explain how product acquisition, training, and disposal procedures affect these costs. Furthermore, some suppliers now recognize their field sales force is part of the product they sell. End-user preference for many health care products is built on the individual sales representatives' detailing and follow-up activities, as well as on the technical strength of the vendor's product.

For example, Becton Dickinson negotiates corporate contracts with GPOs, but focuses its field sales efforts on the hospital "bench people"—lab technicians and doctors who actually use the products, care intensely about the quality and reliability of what they use, and complain loudly to hospital administrators if they do not get the product they want. As one Becton Dickinson manager notes, "In recent years, I've seen a number of instances where purchasing wanted to standardize acquisition around a less-expensive product, but the labs complained and insisted on our product." The common theme in these examples is that the suppliers provided and promoted services affecting the value-in-use of their products.

In consumer packaged goods, the concentration of retail trade, availability of point-of-sale data, and direct product profit information make such services crucial in maintaining retailers' shelf space. In many industrial-product markets, strategic partnerships—and a company's position as preferred supplier—often depend on the vendor's ability to manage customer service in the broader sense. More generally, the evolving nature of production makes it increasingly difficult to distinguish between manufacturing and service businesses. As Gershuny and Miles (1983) have shown, the standard criteria used to distinguish between these two sectors are so problematic that calculating economic activity on this basis requires making many subjective or arbitrary choices. Moreover, firms' product offerings to customers now typically consist of tightly interrelated mixtures of tangible goods, real-time services, and ongoing information exchange (Norman and Ramirez, 1989), which in turn require an integrated view of production, marketing, and customer service.

One advantage of approaching service from this broader perspective is that it enables the company to develop value-based pricing policies reflecting the costs and benefits of the total product offering. In addition, this often enables the firm to differentiate a product or service traditionally viewed as a commodity. For example, L. E. Muran sells stationery, pencils, and other office supplies in a market made even more competitive in recent years by the entry of high-volume, low-priced office superstores. In response to this heightened competition, Muran and individual corporate clients jointly produce a catalog of regularly ordered items and then distribute the catalog to each of the client's secretaries. The secretaries check off what they need, and the Muran sales representative picks up the orders daily. Muran then delivers individual orders to each customer location within 48 hours and also delivers regular usage-by-department reports to customer headquarters. The director of worldwide purchasing at one such customer site notes: "We used to buy stationery, allocate space for a stockroom, and maintain four people and a supervisor to run it. Now we order all these supplies from Muran and call it our 'stockless stationery' policy."

Having understood the broader concepts of service, we recognize that customer service means different things to different customers. Many companies struggle with customer service because they treat service as a constant quality between buyer and seller—a discrete set of characteristics buyers are looking for—rather than as a variable across market settings. As a result, companies often spend much time and money developing customer satisfaction indices that serve only as exercises in pseudospecificity and mock quantification. These indices typically average different characteristics into a single set of factors that at best satisfy few individual customer purchasing and service criteria. Additionally, when efforts are made to avoid averaging, these indices become mere checklists of characteristics that are oblivious to many trade-offs between services offered and relative costs.

Critical elements of service typically vary by type of customer, as well as different phases of the order cycle and account relationship with an individual customer. For example, applications engineering or other technical services may loom particularly important for companies having few R&D or in-house service organizations. However, they are valued less by large companies with extensive R&D and in-house service personnel, where there is higher value placed on ordering ease and prompt delivery.

Several years ago, General Electric conducted an extensive audit of service factors in its industrial business units. Its findings are applicable to companies that similarly sell a variety of products in diverse markets. GE managers distinguished between what they called flow goods (standardized products usually ordered from stock and sold through distributors) and project business (semicustomized orders with substantial engineering content, typically involving various products assembled as a system by different GE business units). GE's results indicated marked

**FIGURE 1**

*Critical elements of customer service: typically vary by phase of the order cycle and by type of business*

|  | Preorder | Order-to-Shipment | Postshipment |
|---|---|---|---|
| *Flow Business* | • Accurate, timely quotations<br><br>• Knowledgeable sales force | • On-time, complete, accurate shipments<br><br>• Accurate, timely order tracking/status reports | • Timely, responsive complaint resolution<br><br>• Quality, timely in-warranty and out-of-warranty service |
| *Project Business* | • Accessibility and responsiveness of personnel<br><br>• Quality, timely application support<br><br>• Product availability information | • Flexibility to react to customer changes to the order<br><br>• Experienced project managers<br><br>• Ownership/authority for multiproduct department orders | • Competent installation support<br><br>• Accurate, timely billing<br><br>• Effective spare parts support |

SOURCE: "General Electric: Customer Service," Harvard Business School case no. 588-059.

differences in the service expectations of customers across the flow goods and project business order cycles (see Figure 1).

Accurate and timely quotations, and field sales representatives knowledgeable in current pricing and delivery terms and conditions, are particularly important when generating flow business orders. These products are often sold by distributors as part of a larger package of goods (most not manufactured by GE); thus, accurate and timely quotations are key to both end-users and intermediaries. In contrast, project business lead times and selling cycles are longer. Technical staffs' accessibility and responsiveness to customers' often ill-defined and evolving specifications are primary service components.

In the order-to-shipment phase, punctual and accurate shipments, as well as shipment tracking reports, are valued flow business services. Whereas the products are often relatively inexpensive and standardized, their availability is usually crucial to throughput at the customer's manufacturing plant. Consequently, reliable order shipments and tracking are especially valued. Efficient, standardized, and predictable procedures are important elements of distribution for these products. However, in project businesses, more uncertainty inherently lies in the order-to-shipment phases. Thus, project business customers value a supplier's flexibility and willingness to react to changes in the order. Standardized terms and conditions can actually become impediments to the execution of required services for these businesses. Due to this fluctuating environment, experienced project or account managers are the most important and valued promoters of customer relations.

Quick response to complaints and warranty claims are key components of after-sale service for flow goods customers. In fact, providing out-of-warranty service for these products often serves to distinguish one vendor from the next in flow product categories. As a result, a close working relationship with distributors is often an important prerequisite for good service in this type of business. However, project business postshipment service involves a different range of supplier–customer activities, including installation, training, and the maintenance of spare parts for these semicustomized system sales.

These differences must be recognized and managed, for they influence the relevant time period used in measuring service levels and costs as well as the amount and type of services inherent in achieving customer satisfaction in each type of business. For example, FileNet, a leader in the growing image processing industry, places service emphasis on applications development, system configuration, customer training, installation, and postsale maintenance and repair. It offers two distinct service contracts that provide different maintenance and repair responsiveness, based upon the customer's relative sensitivity to downtime and the availability of in-house programmers able to assist in applications development.

Many other companies are simultaneously involved in flow and project transactions with customers. Rather than use homogeneous measures of customer satisfaction, these companies must develop a portfolio of service strategies. In addition, these differences influence the degree and type of internal coordination required to provide effective service.

## Customer Service and Internal Marketing

Customer service, as defined here, is inherently a multifunctional activity. This can be illustrated by considering the typical order cycle in most industrial businesses (see Figure 2). Within the selling company, as the order moves from the customer's

**FIGURE 2**

*Customer service involves most functions in an organization*

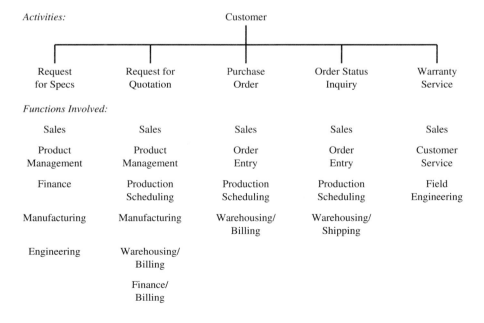

request for specifications and quotation to the purchase order and after-sale warranty service, the progress of an order typically involves numerous functions.

Two aspects of the order cycle are particularly noteworthy. First, field sales is typically involved in nearly all activities. Therefore, any service initiatives not recognizing field sales' role (and the implications of service changes for sales training, compensation, or performance evaluation) are likely to be short-lived or actively subverted by the company's primary customer-contact personnel. Second, though typically held responsible by the customer for any order processing problems, salespeople (or other front-line customer-contact personnel) usually have little direct authority or expertise concerning the many other areas involved in filling the order. Those most directly responsible for managing customer encounters face a series of internal marketing tasks to develop and maintain appropriate service levels. They must often persuade personnel in other functions, each of which has its own particular standard operating procedures, to help customize the order and attendant services for a particular customer.

One reason service problems persist at many companies, despite management's repeated chanting of the "keep close to the customer" mantra, is that those within the firm active in selling, marketing, manufacturing, and financing typically have different incentives and thus view the customer differently. For example, sales personnel often welcome, and argue for, product line extensions or customized solutions in an effort to cover different market segments and accounts with a variety of product configurations. However, what may seem only a minor modification to a salesperson often entails a major operating change in manufacturing, service, or product management. Product line extensions may require new processes, employee training, different production equipment or service expertise, and disrupting established (and seemingly proven) operating procedures in all areas.

Similarly, marketers usually do not need to be convinced about the importance of service; they often argue for substantial investments in same-day service, flexible terms and conditions, or no-fault/money-back service guarantees, all in an effort to "increase our share"—a typically salient goal of the marketing function in most firms. Meanwhile, finance people often evaluate a proposed investment of product design, capacity, and service in terms of quantifiable IRR, NPV, or short-term cash flow implications. And accounting affects the inputs of these calculations by allocating service overheads in ways that both sales and marketing (as well as individual product managers) often consider wrong or arbitrary (Anderson 1981; Barwise et al. 1989).

In each instance, the sources of potential conflict are clear. People in different areas of a firm typically have distinctive skills, resources, and short-term objectives. But external responsiveness requires internal coordination across these areas, placing customer service squarely in the middle of the crossfire between necessary cooperation and potential conflict. Moreover, this situation is further complicated because product-related elements receive the bulk of managerial time and attention, even though nonproduct elements of customer value are often crucial. Consider, for example, the following areas fundamental to completing tasks in any complex and time-constrained organization.

**Management Responsibility.**    In many companies, the product elements of customer service have focused management responsibility in the form of product or brand managers, but the various nonproduct elements do not. If good service can be likened to a performance (Shostack 1985), consider that in moviemaking there is one person who is responsible for continuity—making sure the scenery in one take is congruent with the scenery for next day's filming of the same scene.

However, in most business organizations, the different activities required to develop and process an order typically have no one function or manager responsible for overseeing all the required activities. The closest thing to an order overseer in many companies is the formal customer-service staff, which usually plays a reactive role to customer complaints and has little actual authority to expedite or alter the flow of an order. The result, as one manager describes it, is the "Florence Nightingale brigade: customer-service staff trying to patch up and soothe a customer wounded in an internal war neither of them started."

In the computer industry, nearly every major vendor has recently stressed some form of systems integration provision to accommodate large clients and influential data processing buyers, who have increasing needs for smooth network communications around the world. But many of these same vendors sell and service this offering through hardware, software, and peripherals organizations that are heritages of a previous stage of competition. The result is often uncoordinated service, for separate components arrive at different times and in different quantities. Another result, as one irate computer customer recently commented, is a "pass-the-buck situation, where several product divisions are involved but nobody has control over the complete system."

**Plans and Budgets.**    Management responsibility usually means developing formal business strategies and plans, complete with budgets and financial tracking of activities. Again, companies often have management controls in place for product-related elements, but nonproduct elements are managed on a more ad hoc basis, often without any planning process, financial controls, or method for making inevitable trade-offs among different customer groups. Indeed, the emphasis during the past decade on service culture has motivated many companies to consciously eschew plans and budgets for service activities. The tone of reasoning is: "We want our service people to be action-oriented zealots for the customer and not fettered by plans or budgets that put them in a short-term or bean-counting frame of mind."

But often the unintended result of these good intentions is that service initiatives tend to be driven by the most pressing needs at the time. The ongoing procedures of the firm do not reflect the continuing importance of service, resulting in a reactive, intermittent approach, characterized by periodic programs aimed at service excellence. In many instances, these programs actually damage the firm's service reputation: They raise customer expectations but do not deliver consistent levels of service quality, and the customer tends to focus on lapses from the promised threshold.

These programs can also damage management morale. At one large U.S. corporation, for example, the CEO had grown concerned about customer complaints, so a well-respected senior vice president was appointed to head a task force to fix service problems. However, the vice president soon found that

> customer service [is] not a new issue [here]. The Corporate Marketing files quickly coughed up numerous internal and outside reports on service dating back over 20 years. In fact, customer service has traditionally been the most studied, least engaged issue in [this] company, and even the recent top management attention [is] perceived by middle managers as just another fad.

How does the firm prevent service from becoming a fad? Because service components are typically dispersed throughout a company, planning and budgeting become important means for service realization. These seemingly bureaucratic and action-inhibiting mechanisms also make factors perceived as intangible (and therefore unimportant) more tangible to busy and resource-constrained functional areas.

**Measurements and Evaluations.**   One reason service programs are difficult to sustain is that few managerial measures actually relate customer support expenses to profit-and-loss criteria. The cost accounting systems in most companies are set up to allocate costs by product volumes; they in turn drive the salient financial and performance measurements at the firm (Kaplan 1984). Marketing managers can track activities by brand; marketing research staff can measure product sales by region, channel, or competitor; and manufacturing managers can track variances by product category. However, even as customer service receives more rhetorical emphasis, customer data are usually absent, leaving most managers with little knowledge of account profitability. Moreover, as one observer notes, when companies do track customer support expenses, rather than product-related profitability, they usually measure it in terms of sales volume or gross margin with no allocation of SG&A costs or assets (Myer 1989).

Further, this responsibility is often vested in the sales organization staff. Their compensation is generally tied to revenue goals, giving them every incentive to endorse any service program, regardless of its profitability impact. This situation has been exacerbated in recent years as sales-automation efforts, implemented at great cost and with great attention to user-friendly technology, have tended to freeze in place obsolete accounting systems that generate little actionable data about customer-maintenance costs. The frequent result is what one manager calls "the service boomerang: based on our accounting measures, we charge toward providing certain 'value-added' services to customers; but then charge right back when the actual ROA is disappointing."

Culture-building activities may be resoundingly successful, and everyone may well realize that service is important. However, in the absence of specific measures (and the presence of continuing pressures to make quarterly earnings), service expenditures become discretionary—allocated when budgets allow and dropped when cost pressures increase. This is analogous to the typical cycle of advertising expenditures in many firms: The level of spending is actually the result rather than the cause of historical sales volumes. That is, firms tend to cut advertising spending when sales are flat or when cost pressures are most intense. But one can argue that at this juncture, advertising and service are most important.

**Accountability.**    This is the scarcest resource in any complex organization, its dearth being particularly apparent in the area of customer service. In an effort to manage the multifunctional efforts required to provide good service, companies increasingly define service as the responsibility of all employees. But in any large organization, everybody's business tends in practice to be nobody's business. This unintentionally exacerbates the lack-of-accountability syndrome plaguing service efforts at many firms. At GE, for example, one of the first steps taken by corporate managers charged with improving service was simply to locate the people in each GE business unit primarily responsible for customer service. "We were surprised by what we didn't find," noted one executive. "There was no one person responsible for these matters in the businesses, and so no champion to raise awareness of the issues involved."

This situation can be debilitating in terms of actual service provided because, as another manager describes it, "Customer service is inherently an optics issue; it has to remain visible and a central part of someone's agenda. Otherwise, things don't happen, or they consistently happen after the fact." In most Western companies, de facto responsibility for service resides with the sales and marketing function: When dissatisfied, customers typically complain to the field salesperson, and different marketing managers are involved at nearly all points of the typical order cycle described in Figure 2. Indeed, most definitions of marketing in our business school textbooks cite customer service as central to marketing activities. When pressed for a description of their fundamental role in the organization, most marketing practitioners also cite customer service, or its fraternal twin, serving customer needs.

By contrast, responsibility for service is a less-specialized function in most Japanese firms, where engineering and manufacturing managers pursue more continuous contact with customers after the product is bought. When a Japanese company learns a customer is dissatisfied with the design of its product, it is not uncommon for the company to dispatch the design engineer, who then determines if the problem is significant enough to warrant redesign. By contrast, customer complaints in Western companies are handled much farther downstream in sales and marketing, and then brought upstream through manufacturing and product development.

Many factors account for these differences, including the now well-known differences in employment policies, manufacturing policies, and historical emphases on quality control (Aoki 1988; Mahon and Dyck 1982). But despite statements to the contrary by some Western observers, service is not everybody's business in the Japanese firm. The engineer (or manufacturing manager or product-development leader) is often held personally accountable for customer reaction. When customer service is an issue, the task facing Japanese managers is the same as for their Western counterparts: to expand and maintain their colleagues' understanding of customer needs, priorities, and preferences. It is the worst of both worlds, however, to remove product design and delivery from production and field sales—where palpable knowledge of customers and products ultimately resides—and then turn around and declare that customer satisfaction is everybody's business.

# Managing Customer Retention

Given the issues outlined here, it should not be surprising that good service seems more often the exception than the rule. Improving service can start by helping management be clear about both the product and nonproduct components of customer value in the business, and then by paying attention to structures and systems that aid in the coordination of service components dispersed in the company.

In many businesses, realigning internal activities to provide better service is ultimately justified by competitive pressures. However, in the short run, this holds true only if management understands the economic value of customer retention and the factors that build and extend the buyer–seller relationship.

This has always been a salient feature of high-fixed-cost service businesses, where up-front costs of property, plant, and equipment can only be justified if the customer "stays with us" beyond the initial transaction. As a result, banks, credit card companies, airlines, and other such businesses were among the first to stress customer retention and relationship marketing programs of different sorts (Reichheld and Sasser 1990).

This imperative is also increasingly true of traditional manufacturing businesses. In these firms, new production technologies and big buyers' needs mean that suppliers must sell a system of tangible goods and intangible services, the cost of which requires customer retention over time to be economically justified for the supplier.

The marketing dynamics of customer retention at cable television companies can help illustrate issues relevant to a variety of other product-market environments. Given the cost structure of a cable franchise, the variable costs of serving an installed customer are minimal. Ideally, such customers become "annuities," as they remain part of the subscriber base and generate monthly fee revenues. In this respect, the economic value of a cable customer is the discounted value of a series of payments associated with that customer over a relevant time period. Conversely, customers become profitable to a cable franchise only after they have stayed on the system for some time. For example, one franchise found that a basic cable customer had to remain a subscriber for at least six months before the franchise recouped its costs of installing and servicing that customer. Including the amortized costs of plant construction, a basic customer had to be a subscriber for 11 months before it returned a profit for the firm. As a result, "churn" (people disconnecting the cable service for some reason) has always been a prime concern, and cable-TV firms have developed a variety of marketing programs aimed at understanding churn and minimizing its potentially devastating effects on supplier profitability.

One method of understanding customer retention is to distinguish between two types of disconnects in the customer base: those related to the product (customers dissatisfied with the franchise's particular program offerings or the quality of its transmission service) and those related to the nonproduct elements of customer value (customers dissatisfied with any of the particular transaction services or customer-support aspects of the cable franchise). In addition, there are two time periods during which the cable company can influence the behavior of customers: before and after installation of the product (see Figure 3).

that the price a product can command is less a reflection of raw materials and labor than of marketing-related services like selecting appropriate product features, determining the product mix, and ensuring product availability and delivery.

In cases we have reviewed, sales increases arising from advanced marketing and sales information technology have ranged from 10 percent to more than 30 percent, and investment returns have often exceeded 100 percent. These returns may sound like the proverbial free lunch, but they are real.

Because of the complexity of their marketing organizations, large companies are good prospects for what we call marketing and sales productivity (MSP) systems. Tangles of national account management, direct sales, telemarketing, direct mail, literature fulfillment, advertising, customer service, dealers, and distributors all offer opportunities for efficiency improvements. But even small companies that adopt MSP systems can expect impressive results.

Marketing automation investments by a $7 billion electronics manufacturer and an $8 million custom printing company each produced a first-year return of more than 100 percent. The electronics concern installed a sales support system for more than 500 salespeople. Sales rose 33 percent, sales force productivity rose 31 percent, and sales force attrition dropped 40 percent. The reduced attrition alone produced savings in recruiting and training costs that paid for the company's $2.5 million investment in less than 12 months. At the custom printer, an $80,000 investment in a minicomputer and telemarketing software returned a 25 percent increase in sales and attained payback in less than six months.

Increasing marketing productivity even a small amount can have a great impact on the bottom line. MSP systems have a double punch because they can reduce fixed costs and variable costs. Lower fixed costs mean lower break-even points. So a given percentage increase in sales produces a correspondingly larger increase in operating profits, as the chart on the next page shows. Meanwhile, lower variable costs mean that every sale contributes more to the bottom line. Indeed, because lower variable costs make the slope of the new contribution curve steeper, the absolute size of the financial advantage continues to grow as sales rise.

Despite the proven worth of this technology, few companies have automated any part of their marketing and sales functions. Even fewer appear to understand the significant strategic benefits that can accrue from marketing and sales automation; most early adopters have automated as a matter of faith rather than as part of a strategy for gaining competitive advantage. A better approach begins with an understanding of what marketing and sales automation can do, how it works, and how it can be implemented.

# What the Systems Do

Distinct from general office automation systems, MSP networks are of course specific to marketing and sales. They support more intense product or service differentiation, improved customer service, reduced operating costs, and more streamlined operations. Here are some MSP systems and the tasks for which they are customarily used:

## An MSP System Creates a Financial Advantage

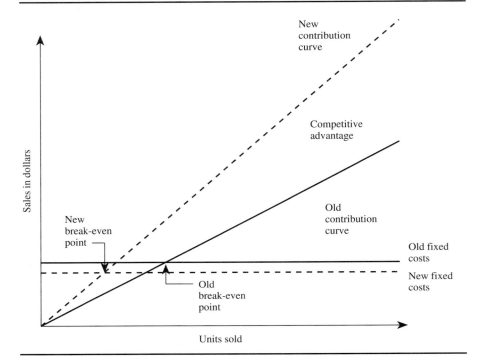

*Salesperson productivity tools*—Planning and reporting of sales calls, reporting of expenses, entering orders, checking inventory and order status, managing distributors, tracking leads, and managing accounts.

*Direct mail and fulfillment*—Merging, cleaning, and maintaining mailing lists; subsetting lists (or markets); tracking and forwarding leads; customizing letters, envelopes, and labels; generating "picking lists" for literature packages; and managing literature inventory.

*Telemarketing*—Merging, cleaning, and maintaining calling lists; subsetting lists (or markets); tracking and forwarding leads; ranking prospects; and prompting scripts (sales, customer service, and support).

*Sales and marketing management*—Providing automated sales management reports (sales forecasts, sales activity, forecasts versus actuals, and so on); designing and managing sales territories; and analyzing marketing and sales programs by such criteria as market, territory, product, customer type, price, and channel.

MSP systems can automate the work of a single salesperson, a single marketing activity like direct mail, or a company's entire marketing and sales operation. MSP systems also cut across every type of information technology from single-user PCs to networks of PCs, minicomputers, and mainframes serving thousands of users.

A simple system meets the needs of one fast-growing $25 million producer of data communications equipment that sells its products through 65 distributors. To cut down on paperwork in handling sales leads, the company adopted a PC-based MSP system. (See the flow chart showing its operation.) Compare this with the networks supporting the more than 5,000 direct salespeople of a major office automation vendor. (See the "map" showing its operation.) This vendor's system combines direct selling, distributor relationships, telemarketing, and direct mail to generate, qualify, rank-order, distribute, and track sales leads; fill prospects' requests for product and price information; update customer and prospect files; provide sales and technical product support by telephone; and automate order entry and sales reporting.

While the scales of these two networks are obviously vastly different, both of them collect, organize, and update information about every lead generated, every sales task performed, and every customer or prospect closed or terminated. What is less obvious, but no less important, is the basis both systems provide for improving marketing and sales executives' decision making.

Most MSP databases contain essential information on customers, prospects, products, marketing programs, and marketing channels. Some systems supplement the essentials with industry data (growth rates, entries, exits, and regulatory trends) and data on competitors (products, pricing, sales trends, and market shares). For most businesses, the information incorporates a subtle but important shift from other databases. Rather than focusing on products (What was the cost to produce each

## A Simple MSP Flow Chart for Handling Leads

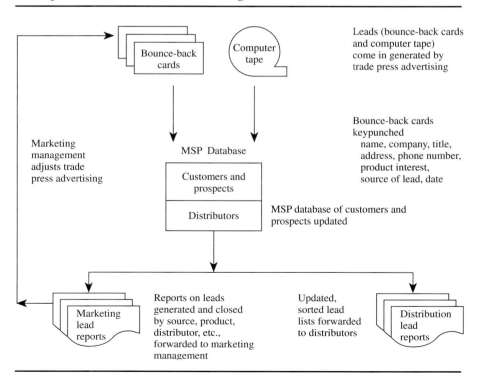

unit? How many units were made, sold, and shipped?), the MSP database is customer driven.

Whenever marketing or sales activities are performed, the database captures information that answers questions about customers and their needs. Who were the prospects? What were their interests? How were these interests generated? Which sales or marketing personnel performed which tasks? When were the tasks performed? Which follow-up tasks are required and when? Did any sales result? Gradually the database becomes a rich source of marketing and sales information, enabling management to track marketing activities and measure the results of marketing programs.

## How They Aid Productivity

MSP systems improve productivity in two ways. First, automation of selling and direct marketing support tasks boosts the efficiency of the sales and marketing staff. Second, automating the collection and analysis of marketing information improves the timeliness and quality of marketing and sales executives' decision making.

These networks make direct sales and direct marketing more efficient by automating highly repetitive support tasks, like answering requests for product literature and writing letters, and by reducing the time salespeople spend on nonselling tasks, like scheduling sales calls, compiling sales reports, generating proposals and bids, and entering orders. In 1985, Xerox installed an internally developed MSP system in its southern region. Xerox credits the system with a 10 to 20 percent gain in sales force productivity and with trimming $3 million off the company's 1987 marketing support and overhead budget. By automating sales administration and support tasks, Xerox has given its salespeople more time to sell.[2]

MSP systems for direct marketing also hone the efficiency of customer contacts. For example, a system for the telemarketing function can schedule and dial calls based on the prospect's priority, prompt the telemarketer with a sales script, and automatically update customer files. At Aratex Services, a $500 million uniform supply company based in Encino, California, telemarketers using the company's old manual system each made 35 to 40 calls per day and about one sale per month. Working with an automated system, each telemarketer now makes 50 or 60 calls daily and lands three or four sales per month.[3]

Automated networks also elevate the impact of each sales communication. Access to the central database gives salespeople and direct marketers information to improve the quality of the contact, whether it is by mail, by telephone, or in person. A large financial services concern uses a telemarketing system to handle account inquiries. While responding to a customer's request or query, the telemarketer is prompted by the system to update the customer's profile information and to cross-sell other financial products.

---

[2] Thayer C. Taylor, "Xerox: Who Says You Can't Be Big and Fast?" *Sales & Marketing Management,* November 1987, p. 63.

[3] Kate Bertrand, "Converting Leads with Computerized Telemarketing," *Business Marketing,* May 1988, p. 58.

At a division of Vanity Fair that makes women's and children's apparel, salespeople use laptop PCs to access the corporate database for up-to-date inventory and order status information on 2,000 stockkeeping units. This step has trimmed the company's order cycle from more than two weeks to just three days. It also has made ordering more accurate, resulting in greater customer satisfaction, reduced order cancellations, and a 10 percent increase in sales.

In companies with many channels, MSP systems upgrade efficiency by using the central database to track and coordinate all marketing activity. Without this coordination, independent marketing groups often unwittingly pursue conflicting goals. At one multibillion-dollar office automation company, a direct salesperson had just nailed down a big order by giving a key account the maximum price discount. Before the deal was signed, however, the telemarketing group reached this customer and undercut the salesperson's price by 10 percent. Aside from the damage to its reputation, this vendor lost much of its expected margin on the sale.

This company is now installing an MSP system that will collect and organize information on all marketing programs and activities, including: (1) all customer contacts, whether by mail, phone, direct salesperson, or national account manager; (2) the status of all sales efforts; (3) the origins of all leads; (4) all leads that are being qualified internally and by whom, and all leads that have been forwarded to distributors; (5) all customers who decided to buy; (6) what and when they purchased; and (7) any incentives or promotions that helped close the deal. Coordination of information through this system is expected to prevent further embarrassments.

## A Management Tool

Creation of an MSP database is an investment in astute management. The database chronicles every one of a company's marketing and sales activities, from advertising that generates leads to direct mail and telephone qualification of the leads to closing the first sale—all the way through the life of each account. It enables marketing and sales management to relate marketing actions with marketplace results.

At the $25 million data communications company whose lead-handling system we diagrammed, marketing managers use this system to evaluate media placements on the basis of sales closed. Before this procedure was in place, the company had no way to link information on leads to sales and evaluated media placements solely on the number of leads generated, not closed.

MSP systems also reduce marketing inertia because they streamline the implementation of marketing programs. For example, after designing an in-house system to organize and manage its customer/prospect files, one $2.5 million industrial manufacturer let 70 manufacturer's agents go and replaced them with in-house direct mail and telemarketing functions. The results? The company raised its accounts by 50 percent and cut marketing costs from 18 percent of sales to 13 percent.

Systems for sales force automation also drive the rapid implementation of less drastic changes in marketing programs. By using telecommunications software and laptop PCs, Du Pont's Remington Arms division has trimmed the time requirement for a national rollout of pricing and promotional programs from two weeks to less than two days.

As marketing managers become accustomed to these systems, they find new uses for them, like analyzing and modeling the buying behavior of prospects and customers. The database at Excelan, a $39 million marketer of circuit boards and software in San Jose, California, was essential in identifying a shift in customers' buying behavior from a very technical product focus to an office automation orientation. This discovery has influenced the marketing and sales managers' decisions about hiring and training employees as well as about selecting and developing new target markets.

Account histories also improve management's ability to devise and implement account management policies based on profits. By linking orders, services delivered, and prices paid with the actual costs of lead generation, preselling, closing, distribution, and postsale support, MSP systems furnish the tools for analyzing and adjusting the marketing mix. Grede Foundries, a Milwaukee producer of castings for original equipment manufacturers, has used the MSP system to develop a "perceived quality index" that yields a more complete and more accurate measure of customers' reactions than simply tracking returned goods. The system also provides pricing support. By tracking quoted prices and final selling prices, the system gives management a better idea of the price that will win a particular job.[4]

---

**Economies of Scale?**

Small businesses may gain an initial competitive edge from MSP systems because they often can adopt these systems much faster than their big counterparts. With fewer levels of management, small companies are faster on their feet in making decisions. They also tend to have simpler marketing organizations, usually relying on a single-method, single-channel selling system like a small direct sales force.

Large companies face two imposing barriers. First, they generally have both multiple layers of administration and cross-functional decision-making groups. When analyzing, evaluating, and adopting MSP systems, large companies draw in not only marketing and sales but also the accounting, finance, and MIS functions. Second—as a glance at the flow chart and map shows—their marketing organizations customarily rely on complex arrangements of communications methods and selling channels. Accordingly, their MSP systems require great sophistication and customization.

In large companies, marketing and sales automation is a high-stakes decision needing the support of many parties. In a major telecommunications company, the evaluation and selection of an MSP system called for: (1) initial screening presentations by three software vendors; (2) detailed presentations to 15 senior executives; (3) a visit by eight managers to a company with an operating MSP system; and (4) at least nine internal follow-up meetings, including presentations to the vice presidents of marketing and sales, the general managers of the ten operating companies, the directors of the MIS and MIS-procurement groups, several financial analysts, and several senior salespeople. More than 40 people had a hand in the decision. All this work occurred in a period of more than nine months after the corporate decision to automate marketing and sales.

But the story doesn't end there. Once the company had selected a $200,000 off-the-shelf system, it spent 18 months and $250,000 more installing and customizing the software. During the next two years, functional additions to the system and training of the end users added more than $1 million to the cost.

---

[4]Louis A. Wallis, *Computers and the Sales Effort* (New York: Conference Board, 1986).

Moreover, automated networks coordinate and direct sales resources—including salespeople, distributors and agents, direct mailers, telemarketers, and manufacturers' representatives—toward the highest priority prospects and customers. Hewlett-Packard's (H-P's) Qualified Lead Tracking System (QUILTS) electronically transmits inquiries to a telemarketing center, which qualifies and ranks them and electronically returns them to H-P headquarters. The company has trimmed the turnaround time for leads from as much as 14 weeks to as little as 48 hours. Hot leads are handled even faster; they are telephoned to the field sales force from the telemarketing center.[5] Similarly, field salespeople in Chevron Chemical's fertilizer division in San Francisco use laptop PCs to access rank-ordered prospect lists in the company's mainframe. At any time, the salespeople have access to leads that are only 24 hours old. Before automation, new prospect lists were printed at headquarters and mailed to the field reps, which took one to two weeks.

Finally, the MSP database is a management tool for making better use of marketing resources—that is, ensuring that they are employed to further corporate goals rather than the goals of individual marketing or sales groups. While this may sound like something management does without effort, our research shows that optimizing marketing resources is much more easily said than done. In several companies we've looked at, salespeople routinely discard hundreds or even thousands of sales leads, making little or no effort to evaluate or review them. In essence, they are dissipating the resources that generated these leads—budgets for advertising, trade shows, public relations, and other communications media.

In their defense, the salespeople complain that pursuing raw leads is a waste of time. And they are generally right. In one of these companies, salespeople who followed up the raw leads averaged only one or two sales per month, while those who followed their instincts averaged more than three. The cost of pursuing the raw leads was at least one lost sale per salesperson per month. To the salespeople, ignoring the leads was common sense. On the other hand, the advertising group, which was evaluated on the number of leads generated, was increasing its budgets to generate more and more leads. One company has solved this problem by implementing an MSP system that will use telemarketing to qualify leads before sending them to the salespeople. The system will also close the loop, allowing management to evaluate both the company's advertising placements and its sales efforts on the basis of their contributions to revenues and earnings.

Efficiencies gained through task automation and improved marketing management are interdependent and reinforcing. Task automation drives the collection of more complete customer and marketplace information, and more informed decision making targets marketing and sales activities where they are most effective. In this way, marketers get a bigger payoff from low-cost, low-impact selling methods, like direct mail and catalogs, as databases customize the timing and content of mass-marketing campaigns. At the same time, high-cost, high-impact selling methods,

[5]Karen Blue, "Closing the Loop: Hewlett-Packard's New Lead Management System," *Business Marketing,* October 1987, p. 74.

## Map of an Integrated MSP System for a Major Office Automation Company

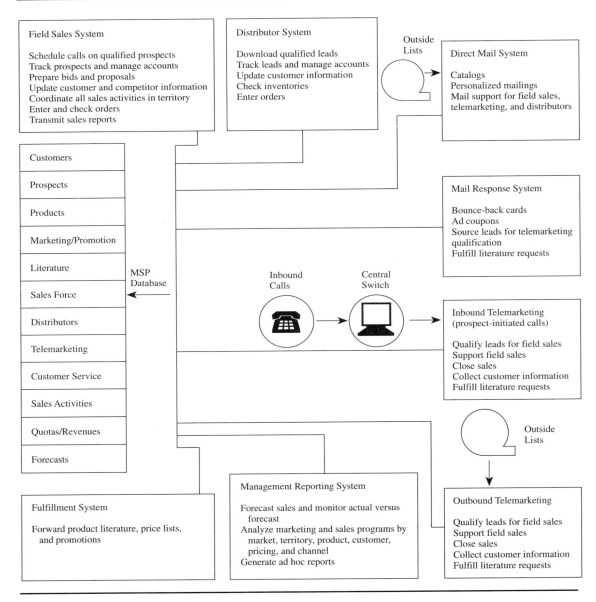

like personal selling and national account management, become more efficient as MSP systems perform routine sales support tasks, reduce nonselling time, and synchronize the use of these resources.

When you combine low-cost, low-impact methods with high-cost, high-impact approaches to gain just the right amount of stimulus at just the right time, you can obtain hefty impact at minimum cost. Hewlett-Packard, for one, has taken advantage of this synergy and has discovered the savings made possible by orchestrating direct mail, telemarketing, and personal selling.

# How to Get from Here to There

The cases we have reviewed show that companies implementing MSP systems encounter many of the same barriers they would confront adopting any new technology.[6] From our observation, the process can be streamlined by following six guiding principles.

1. *Clarify the scale of the project as well as potential additions.* An audit of the marketing and sales tasks will yield these categories: those that must be automated now, those that will or may be automated later, and those that will not be automated. This simple exercise will identify marketing and sales activities that must be coordinated and focus the automation effort on getting measurable results without sacrificing flexibility.

It is important to view the project not from the perspective of the marketing groups but from a corporate perspective. With a corporate view, the company can build a "battleship"—a system that takes advantage of information-sharing and task-coordination synergies. Without this strategic perspective, independent marketing groups are more likely to invest in a number of incompatible and wasteful "rowboats." And even a rowboat can cause problems. At a big high-tech manufacturer, eight salespeople had their own PC-based sales force automation system installed. By raising issues of compatibility, data entry, and "file structure definitions," they delayed the start-up of a companywide, 300-salesperson MSP system for more than a year.

2. Concentrate on tasks that can add value for the customer. As in other corporate activities, marketers can get competitive advantage in two ways: by lowering costs and by enhancing the differentiation of the product or service offering. At the custom printer we referred to, streamlined job-costing and order-entry processes enable customers to price and place orders with one phone call. The real-time order-entry and order-tracking capabilities of the Vanity Fair unit's salespeople have upgraded its customer service. In both cases, customers benefit from better service, and sellers benefit from lower costs.

Other companies add value by using automation to improve the exchange of information during sales calls. The 22 salespeople in Hercules's Fragrance and Food Ingredient Group use their laptop PCs and a computer program called Flavor Briefs to consult with prospects on applications. Otherwise, Hercules salespeople would be unable to provide such detailed advice on their product line's many applications. The system saves the customer and the salesperson time and also furnishes a valuable service.

---

[6]Dorothy Leonard-Barton and William A. Kraus, "Implementing New Technology," *Harvard Business Review,* November–December 1985, p. 102.

3. *In the budget process, account for hidden costs and intangible benefits.* Budgeting for an MSP system entails overcoming three principal obstacles: high perceived financial risk, poorly understood benefits, and biased capital budgeting systems.

First, automating marketing and sales is costly. A typical hardware and software outlay per salesperson ranges from $4,000 to $7,000—so automating the tasks of 100 field salespeople can cost between $400,000 and $700,000. In addition, if the MSP system must communicate with other corporate information systems, it is likely to require the development of specialized minicomputer, mainframe, or communications networking software.

Department-level telemarketing or direct mail systems range in price from $30,000 to more than $100,000. Sales or marketing management software may up the price another $30,000 to $100,000. Of course, the cost of tying all these pieces together depends on how many pieces there are, where they are located, and how they communicate. It would not be unusual for a company with 500 salespeople as well as telemarketing, fulfillment, and direct mail operations to spend between $3 million and $5 million on integrated MSP hardware and software.

But the budget process must anticipate and account for hidden costs too. In a number of cases we studied, in-house information was so scattered and communications equipment so incompatible that simply preparing a customer list required a major effort. Other hidden costs include system customization, expert consulting, and end user training. Depending on the circumstances, these services can double or even triple the overall cost.

Because malfunctioning of an automated marketing system can threaten a business's revenue stream, it's advisable to budget for the cost of two systems—automated and manual—until the network has proved out. Naturally, all these expenses ratchet up the perceived financial risk of MSP automation.

On the other side of the equation, estimating the full financial benefit of an MSP system is extremely difficult. Tangible productivity gains, like increases in selling time and cost reductions on telephone campaigns, can be gauged fairly accurately. But intangible productivity gains, like better marketing decision making, more responsive customer service, and deeper understanding of customers, are much more difficult to track.

Still, it would be a mistake to ignore them, especially since capital budgeting processes are often biased against intangible productivity investments. Furthermore, few marketing managers and even fewer sales managers know much about their companies' capital budgeting processes—especially when huge investments in information technology are at stake. Senior executives have to take care that the process remains flexible enough to give MSP automation a reasonable evaluation.

An MSP system is a strategic investment for the whole corporation. But unlike other assets that are consumed over time, the more it is used, the more valuable it becomes. So it should be viewed as a long-term asset, not as the expense of a functional group. And, needless to say, senior management must match the scale of the company's investment to the scale of the project. Otherwise, fragmented marketing budgets will foster fragmented automation. The result, as noted above, may be many MSP rowboats with little or no coordination or compatibility.

4. *Make any tests realistic.* Because launching a full-scale network can be tremendously risky, most companies hedge their bets first by piloting automation on small portions of their marketing operations. A single function, like telemarketing or personal selling, is usually the test site. If this pilot is successful, the company adds more functions.

This ramp-up strategy, however, has serious drawbacks. It permits no insight into the complexity of coordinating multiple marketing and sales activities. Though single-function solutions may yield gratifying returns, evidence of their true worth may also stay hidden until they are combined into a system that demonstrates synergy. Consequently, estimates of financial returns based on single-function pilots may be negatively biased.

Finally, critical performance limitations may remain hidden unless the complexity and scale of the test parallel the system's actual use. One big manufacturer's telemarketing pilot ran flawlessly, providing the telemarketers with a steady stream of calls and instant access to customer profiles and scripts. But eventual integration of telemarketing with other MSP networks seriously degraded the performance of the overall system. Every time the telemarketers asked for new information during a call, they were confronted by blank computer screens for more than 40 seconds. As the business manager put it, "That's a long time to talk about baseball."

A company with a multichannel, multimethod marketing system is better off with a pilot plan that automates a multifunctional subset of the marketing organization. In this type of pilot, an integrated system, encompassing all marketing and sales functions, is installed for a single division, region, product line, or customer group. This experience is likely to be more realistic than the single-function approach.

5. *Pinpoint the roles and responsibilities of those selecting, designing, and operating the system.* Even standard MSP systems, though they may be touted as off-the-shelf products, require extensive customization. This necessity complicates the selection or design process in a number of ways.

- The process requires expertise in technology (computers, data communications, and software) as well as in marketing and sales.
- Naturally, a company's existing MIS systems are likely to constrain the choice (or development) of an MSP system.
- Marketing professionals and MIS professionals rarely speak a common language, and they often approach marketing automation projects with different perspectives. While marketing thinks about functionality (e.g., Will the system help perform marketing and sales tasks?), MIS people often focus on technical considerations (e.g., Will the system interact with other corporate information systems? Who is responsible for ensuring the integrity of corporate databases?).

It's senior management's job to make sure that the MIS and marketing professionals talk to each other and work together. It's not easy. An MIS group may automate its conception of marketing and sales only to discover later that the automated system does not actually work. Everybody knows of cases in which the MIS department loads the sales force down with reams of report forms to complete and return to headquarters. Of course, much of the requested information is irrelevant from the salesperson's standpoint, and the report forms end up in the same round file as the old lead cards.

During the long, complex process of designing and implementing a major MSP system, responsibilities sometimes become diffuse and project accountability gets blurred. In one case we know of, poorly defined responsibilities for MIS and marketing have caused big headaches. Bickering over cost allocations and database controls has made the company's $1 million MSP system useless. The MIS group will not allow marketing to access the corporation's databases. But the marketing group's computer budget is too low to keep the marketing database up-to-date. (Not surprisingly, headquarters viewed the entire MSP development process as a marketing expense instead of a corporate investment.)

6. *Modify the technology and the organization to support the system.* As in every instance in which management implements new technology, it must pay close attention to the attitudes of people in the organization. In successful MSP implementations that we have seen, both the organization and the MSP system have gone through an interactive process of change—altering the technology to fit the marketing and sales environment, then altering the environment to fit the technology.

To be useful, for example, the MSP database obviously must contain accurate, up-to-date information. Because obtaining this information requires salespeople to use the system and to support the information collection process, they have to become adept at using the new technology. Problems can result, however, if the end-users lack computer skills or if they are uninterested in using the system.

Training can overcome skill problems (if enough money is budgeted and enough time set aside), but lack of interest is harder to deal with. Experience suggests that the best way to sell the sales staff on the network is to demonstrate that it can give every user something back. That is, by helping salespeople or telemarketers work more productively, MSP systems can boost not only the company's sales but also *their* sales and *their* compensation.

For many companies, postponement of automation of the marketing function may seem to be a good way of skirting a difficult decision, but this do-nothing posture condemns the organization to being a marketing laggard. It may also be a costly mistake. Early adopters of MSP systems have gained superior competitive advantage. Compared with their "manual" competitors, they perform selling tasks with greater economy and impact. They know their customers better and can tailor their sales communications to supply just the right amount of sales stimulus at just the right time. Overall, they craft and control their marketing programs more intelligently. In the long run, the competitive barriers they establish may change the nature of marketing in their industries.

In view of this impressive record, some marketers about to embark on automation may embrace unrealistically high expectations. But MSP systems cannot work miracles. They will not offset a poorly conceived or poorly executed marketing strategy. They will not compensate for an inferior sales force, and they will not sell inferior products. Complex MSP systems are difficult to implement, and the associated returns, like any other lasting accomplishment, have to be earned.

# Reorienting Channels of Distribution

*Traditionally, distribution channels have been viewed as vertical marketing systems where responsibility was transferred from one layer to the next, like passing a baton in a relay race. Distribution channels in the future are likely to look more like horizontal alliances of suppliers and intermediaries, all with the aim of efficiently and effectively addressing customers' real needs. These transitions, driven by an underlying change in the economics of production and distribution, are leading to distinct trends in the distribution industry. In this chapter, we focus on three primary trends: hybrid channels, multiple channels, and shorter channels. After exploring the challenges managers face as they reorient their distribution, we highlight the effects of such changes on supplier–intermediary relationships.*

Distribution channels of the future are likely to look distinctly different from their counterparts of the 1970s and even the 1980s. These transitions are being driven by changes currently sweeping the customer and competitive environment—proliferation of information technology, polarization of customers (consolidation on the one hand, and fragmentation on the other), manufacturing systems that can mass-customize, and quick shipment distribution logistics. As a result, many distribution questions that were once considered central are no longer so regarded. For example, the dilemma of direct versus indirect channels does not seem to be much of a puzzle to managers anymore. Instead, new priorities of a strategic nature are being raised as practitioners and researchers attempt to cope with the dynamics of a changing business environment.[1] Can channels serve to create competitive entry barriers? Can they enhance product differentiation? Can they enable customer intimacy? Can

V. Kasturi Rangan prepared this note.

Copyright © 1994 by the President and Fellows of Harvard College.

Harvard Business School note 594-118.

[1]V. Kasturi Rangan, Raymond E. Corey, and Frank Cespedes, "Transaction Cost Theory: Inferences from Field Research on Downstream Vertical Integration," *Organization Science* 4, no. 3 (August 1993), pp. 454–77.

**225**

**FIGURE 1**

*Channel options:
traditional view*

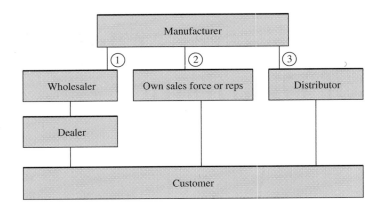

they cushion suppliers' exposure to uncertainty? Such questions seem to be of far more interest to managers building distribution channels today. It is useful to ask why this definitive shift in channel management emphasis is appearing. Fundamentally, it boils down to the nature of the distribution work. Environmental forces have changed its underlying economics and characteristics.

Traditionally, distribution channels have been viewed as vertical marketing systems where responsibility was transferred from one layer to the next, like passing the baton in a relay race. Thus in Figure 1, under option 1, the manufacturer would send a truckload shipment to the wholesaler, who then broke bulk and sold to the dealer, who in turn stocked the product and persuaded the end user to buy. If the product needed after-sales service, the end user took it back to the dealer, who also maintained and repaired the product in the field. Even though the product may have passed through several layers in the distribution system, the end user relied solely on the dealer for the fulfillment of a complete bundle of channel functions, such as information, inventory, and repair.[2] Others in the vertical system played a supporting, backstage role. The wholesaler, in this case, broke bulk and provided a wide assortment of products for the dealer's selection, but the customer fulfilled all its requirements—assortment, lot sizes, information, and repair—from the dealer and dealer alone. Manufacturers could access customers through alternative channel systems as well—directly (or through reps) or through one-step intermediaries such as distributors. These are shown as options 2 and 3 in Figure 1. But no matter which system was used, the end user fulfilled its channel function requirements mainly from one source. It was uneconomical to unbundle and allocate functional responsibility over several channel members.

A small customer that bought through the dealer channel, in Figure 1, might have actually preferred to get technical information directly from the supplier, but because of the small lot size of its purchases, it would have to seek product information as part of distribution support from the local dealer. It would be simply too

---

[2]See Louis W. Stern and Adel I. El-Ansary, *Marketing Channels,* 4th ed. (Englewood Cliffs, N.J.: Prentice Hall, 1992), pp. 1–41.

costly for the supplier to contact and provide this information directly, and costlier still for the end user to await product shipment from the factory. Even though the customer was not fully served in regard to the information function, overall it was still better to get the channel bundle from the dealer than not at all. By the same token, a large customer that bought directly from the sales force might have preferred not to pay cash and not to carry inventory, but that was the price of doing business directly with the supplier.

A small customer that bought through the dealer channel, in Figure 1, might have actually preferred to get technical information directly from the supplier, but because of the small lot size of its purchase, it would have to seek product information as part of distribution support from the local dealer. It would be simply too costly for the supplier to contact and provide this information directly, and costlier still for the end user to await product shipment from the factory. Even though the customer was not fully served with regard to the information function, overall it was still better to get the channel bundle from the dealer than not at all. By the same token, a large customer that bought directly from the sales force might have preferred not to pay cash and not to carry inventory, but that was the price of doing business directly with the supplier.

All this has changed with the information and technology revolution of the 1990s. Direct marketing and database marketing and its variations have enabled sellers to contact far-flung and often small customers for only a fraction of the cost of a direct sales call. Local distributors may no longer be the only cost-efficient alternative. Computer-aided quick shipment systems enable transporters to schedule and dispatch less-than-truckload orders with more or less the same speed and efficiency as full loads. The customer, therefore, does not suffer any inconvenience or product unavailability. Flexible manufacturing systems allow suppliers to produce small lots at only a marginally higher cost than scale-efficient large orders.[3] In short, the economics of manufacturing and distribution have changed. Traditional thinking suggests that transactions involving complex exchange of information and intensive investments would be best served direct, and those characterized by simple exchange and less-intensive investments would be best served indirect.[4] In the current environment, this conventional wisdom is under attack. The roles of the intermediary, the distributor, and the dealer are all evolving. New forms of direct channels are emerging, and indirect channels are getting shorter (fewer intermediary layers). The role of the distributor buffer between the manufacturer and the retail dealer is under threat in several business environments.[5] Firms will face unique opportunities and challenges as they adapt their channels to this changing environment.

However, what is sauce for the goose is sauce for the gander: Distributors have experienced the benefits of information technology too. In many cases, because of

---

[3]See "How to Bolster the Bottom Line," *Fortune,* Autumn 1993.

[4]Oliver E. Williamson, *The Economic Institutions of Capitalism* (New York: Free Press, 1985), pp. 85–102.

[5]As examples are too numerous to cite, we provide two illustrations: "GE Component Motors Operation," Harvard Business School case no. 587-157; and "Distributors' Links to Producers Grow More Fragile," *The Wall Street Journal,* October 28, 1992, sect. B, p. 2.

the assortment and variety of products they handle, they have been better able to exploit the economies of scope from information systems. Moreover, distributors in general have steadily updated their technical investments in channel systems. Chemical distributors, for instance, have innovated product safety systems, pharmaceutical distributors have innovated information systems, computer distributors have innovated customer support systems, and so on.[6] In all, distinctions between manufacturer and distribution channel capabilities in taking the product to market have blurred. This has put the customers and end users in the driver's seat. They have a wider channel choice and, in many cases, the option of unbundling channel functions and sourcing them from the most efficient member. It is not unusual for a customer, therefore, to seek information directly from the supplier as a prelude to negotiations on product specifications, quality, quantity, and prices, while retaining local distributors for effecting delivery and providing after-sales service.

To put it simply, the concept of channel strategy has been turned on its head. Instead of viewing the problem as one of choosing which intermediaries can reach the customer, the new approach is how customers' channel requirements can be efficiently addressed. It starts with the customer, not with the supplier, and the focus of the analysis is on channel functions, not intermediaries.[7] Channel selection is not an afterthought, but rather an integral part of the strategy of being customer oriented. In the following section we discuss three broad channel trends and their implications for channel managers.

# Hybrid Channels

This is a channel structure in which the supplier and its channel partners share in the execution of the channel functions. That is, the supplier may perform some of the channel functions (e.g., sales negotiation and order generation), while its channel partners may perform the rest (e.g., physical distribution and order fulfillment). Other channel members might specialize in yet more channel functions (e.g., after-sales service). In essence, in the channel system the parts work together, with certain members specializing in certain channel functions. See Figure 2. The key distinction between this hybrid channel and the conventional channel is the horizontal nature of the task allocation. The customer's total needs are satisfied by a team of channel partners (including the supplier), each specializing in a few tasks. In the conventional model, the hand-offs were vertical, with each member performing a full bundle of channel functions required of the next level.

As suggested earlier, the trend toward functional specialization (and therefore horizontal channels) is being driven by customers' desires to receive products and services in the most cost- and time-efficient manner. This means that channel

---

[6]See "Who's Winning the Information Revolution," *Fortune,* November 30, 1992.

[7]Louis W. Stern and Frederick D. Sturdivant, "Customer Driven Distribution Systems," *Harvard Business Review,* July–August 1987. Also see V. Kasturi Rangan, M. Menezes, and Ernie P. Maier, "Channel Selection for New Industrial Products: A Framework, Method and Application," *Journal of Marketing* 56 (July 1992), pp. 69–82.

**FIGURE 2**

*Hybrid channel*

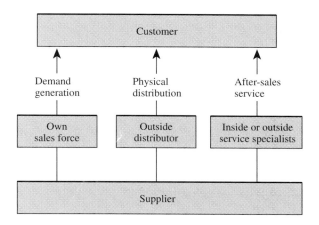

functions may have to be unbundled and offered separately, especially for the larger customers.

The health care industry abounds with hybrid examples. Becton Dickinson's Vacutainer Systems division negotiates directly with all large hospital buying groups for its blood collection needles, syringes, and accessories.[8] When the deal is finalized, Becton Dickinson signs a Z-contract with the concerned hospital buying group and provides a list of its authorized distributors. Becton Dickinson's distributors effect the physical distribution—ordering, storing, and supplying products to the appropriate hospital at the desired time in desired lots. They are able to do this at an efficient cost given the plethora of other products they already supply the hospitals. Thus, order entry and fulfillment costs are only incremental. At the same time, the cost-containment environment in the health care industry makes it attractive for buyers to negotiate directly on high-volume/high-value orders, and the competitive environment makes that necessary for suppliers as well. It gives them better control on sales, profits, and market shares.

The computer industry is also rich in hybrid channels. Witness the rise of value-added resellers (VARs) that tailor solutions for customers in niche markets—banking, retailing, CAD-CAM, and so on. While VARs provide the specific knowledge regarding the software, they have to work closely with computer vendors for hardware equipment and system configuration. Customers need hardware and software integrated in order to address their problems, but the channel expertise is such that it takes two members to put together the perfect solution.

But with new channel forms come new management challenges; the biggest one has do with channel compensation. Because the channel member interfacing with the customer is no longer responsible for performing the full bundle of channel functions, it cannot be expected to receive a margin or commission structure similar to the traditional system. Ideally, channel members under the new system should be compensated only for the functions they perform. But herein lies a catch. All members in the hybrid system must adequately perform their functional responsibilities

---

[8]"Becton Dickinson & Co.: Vacutainer Systems Division," Harvard Business School case no. 592-037.

**FIGURE 3**

*The free-riding
problem*

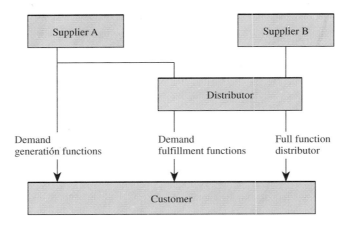

for the final sale to occur. If one member fails to do so, the whole team suffers un-less some other team member covers up for the errant colleague. Such a system is open to abuses of free-riding, and the most valuable player often ends up bearing the cost most. The reward, however, is shared by all. At least, in the traditional vertical system, poor performance correlated directly with lower sales and therefore lower margins. In the new system, poor performers could earn rewards for someone else's efforts.

Managing a hybrid system requires strong leadership. The team captain has to ensure an equitable allocation of work as well as reward. This is easier said than done because in reality an outside channel member will often be part of other competing channel systems as well. For instance, in Figure 3, a distributor who is a functional specialist in Supplier A's hybrid channel system and a full-function player in Supplier B's vertical channel system could end up overallocating its resources to Supplier B. That is because its commissions are likely to be higher from B because of the full-function support it provides. Moreover, without this distributor's efforts sales of Product B and the associated commissions would be at risk. Whereas for Product A, other channel members may be pulling in the demand anyway. A heavy-handed carrot-and-stick approach is hardly likely to motivate loyalty or dedicated effort, and higher distribution margins would only violate the economic premise of hybrid channels.

Hybrid channels are very costly to monitor and administer, and seem to work only in environments that can afford high channel margins. That way distributors can be motivated by the carrot of commissions. In low-margin industries, hybrid channels seem to work only for market leaders. Such suppliers usually bring their market clout to lead their hybrid channel partners. Free-riding, for instance, is punishable by loss of orders, and in this case by a big amount. A leading industrial supply company, for example, calls on many of its accounts directly, but routes all its orders through its distribution network—a classic hybrid system. A free-riding distributor, however, will not get the company's nod. The company has multiple distributors in the same market area. Those who don't play by the rules do not get mentioned warmly by the sales force when writing the order. Theoretically, the customer could still buy from the free-rider but they rarely do so because of the influence of the direct sales channel. Thus, a combination of carrot and stick does the trick. Unfortunately, for weaker suppliers, the hybrid channel coordination costs often exceed the benefits of functional effectiveness. Such firms then have to trade off effectiveness for the simplicity and functional aggregation of the vertical arrangement. They may have to rely on full-function distributors to compete with the specialized hybrid channels of the market leaders. Alternatively, if market segment coverage is not an issue, such firms might be able to offer hybrid support for certain selected market niches.

# Multiple Channels

Not to be confused with hybrid channels, multiple channels reflect the range of channels available to a customer. A buyer of personal computers, for example, could buy the same model (often the same brand) from a direct mail catalogue or a computer superstore or a computer specialty store, each at a different level of price and service. Ideally, these different service levels are meant to reflect the needs of the differing buying segments. So the expectation is that a consumer who is price sensitive but very knowledgeable about product features and specifications would order from a direct-mail catalogue. But the customer who seeks a lot of product information and education from the channel might prefer a computer specialty store. Additionally, this customer would need the reassurance, hand-holding, and local service of the specialty store. While sound in theory, unfortunately consumers do not come neatly segmented into such air-tight compartments. There is a lot of inter-segment movement across purchase occasions. Moreover, with accelerating product life cycles, proliferation of products, and fragmentation of customer segments, multiple-channel approaches are often the only way to provide market coverage. Different customers with different buying behaviors will seek out channels that best serve their needs.

So what is the problem? As shown in Figure 4, the real issue rests with the leaky gray area in the middle, which permits infiltration of customers from the adjoining segments. These are customers that patronize both the full-service channel as well as the low-price channel. As long as the higher price is a fair reflection of the higher service, they will be channel loyal, but if the service is unnecessary or can be obtained at a lower cost than what the price premium would justify, customers will cross over to the low-price channel. In a number of business environments, presales service is a public good which customers can experience without a purchase commitment. For example, nothing precludes a customer from getting a full-function demonstration from a computer specialty store, and then sourcing product from a low-cost mail order retailer. The customer takes the full-service channel for a free ride.

Another type of conflict occurs in multiple channels when a full-product-line distributor uses a loss-leader strategy to steal customers from competitors. Consider

**FIGURE 4**

*Multiple channels*

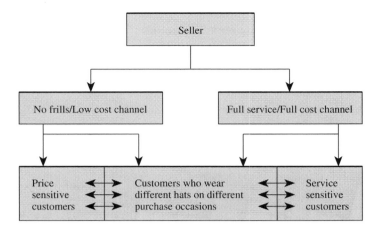

the channel illustrated in Figure 5. The company wishes to segment its market by large and small customers. The large customers buy high volume Z machines, and occasionally for their smaller plants a small number of X machines. Distributor A is set up to address this market exclusively. Distributor B, on the other hand, is set up to address the smaller customers who need X products.

Because of its technical complexity, if we assume that the distributor margin for product Z is substantially higher than that for X, it is easy to see how channel conflicts can occur. Distributor A could undersell product X because its overheads are already covered by the high-margin Z operation. This will certainly upset B's operations and lead to customer cross-overs. Of course, the opposite could happen if distributor margins for X are greater than for Z, and B undersells A. In this case, even though the large customer cannot cross over to Channel B (because the Z product is unavailable in that channel), the customer could nevertheless feel gouged and dissatisfied with its distributor (i.e., A), causing acrimonious debates and conflicts. In a

**FIGURE 5**

*Multiple channel conflicts*

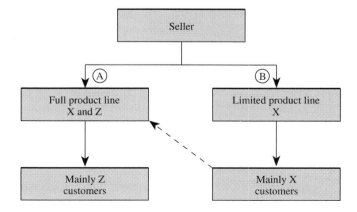

nutshell, the problem is caused by a lethal mixture of leaky market segmentation and price differentiation in the multiple channel network. What is the solution?

The common approach to managing multiple channels is to demarcate products and models by channels. Thus, direct comparisons are minimized. The demarcations, of course, work well when there are true feature differences between products. At times, in spite of product differences, competing channels will be able to offer similar problem-solving capabilities by patching/bundling products appropriately; for example, personal computers for workstations, and workstations for minicomputers. A potential solution, in such cases, is to render the patched product price uncompetitive. Such a measure restores legitimacy to the principal channel. Other channel coordination mechanisms to promote cooperation, such as joint incentives or customer partitioning, work only when one of the channel members happens to be a supplier-owned channel (e.g., own sales force or captive distribution). It rarely works when the multiple members are all independent. In our experience, the product demarcation approach is as effective as any other conflict-reduction mechanism we have seen. And when used in conjunction with other methods, it results in quite effective channel management. It has one other advantage: providing a seller the option of organizing sales and distribution channels by product line. There still has to be considerable coordination across products and channels in terms of customer segmentation, product demarcation, and pricing, but all of it is internal to the company. Once a product is priced and enters a sales channel for a particular customer segment, there is no confusion externally in front of the customer.

Multiple channels are more widely prevalent in fast-changing, as opposed to stable, market environments. When the product-market matures slowly, the channel profile usually evolves and stabilizes to reflect the needs of the new consumer buying pattern: The channel adapts to the customer buying pattern. Even if multiple channels are necessary to reflect market plurality, each channel is clearly specialized to serve a specific buying pattern. Crossovers are less common. Witness the rise of discount stores in the late 1970s and early 1980s. They were clearly targeted to the value conscious shopper, even while the service conscious shopper continued to patronize the specialty stores. The two channels often stock, display, and sell different brands, and attract a very different clientele. Another example comes from the power tool industry. Black & Decker sells its Quantum line through Wal-Mart, while its De-Walt line is routed through hardware specialty stores. While one goes for the DIY (do-it-yourself) customers, the other goes for the professional craftsman. But such is not the case in the more dynamic industries. Computer models that start their life in specialty stores gravitate to the catalog retailers in less than six months. The early buyers may not face channel dissonance, but the latecomers always do. While they may seek the service of the specialty outlet, the price of the discount outlet is too tempting to pass. Moreover, in dynamic environments customers' shopping and buying behaviors themselves are ever changing. Customers' buying criteria and customer segments are transient and dynamic as well. Multiple channels will be as common as are these environments in the 1990s.

# Shorter Channels

As the economics of distribution changes, the functions of certain distribution levels are being rendered superfluous. There is a trend toward shorter channels. Of all the various intermediary types, the role of the master distributor or the wholesaler is possibly the one most at risk. See Figure 6. With the advent of quick shipment distribution logistics, retailers do not lose much time anymore in ordering directly from the supplier. And again from the supplier's side, with the availability of modern information technology, tracking and responding to retail-level orders are vastly more manageable. Information technology and quick shipment logistics have vastly diminished the need for dual inventories in the pipeline. In an intensely competitive environment, the extra margin saved at the master-distributor level then becomes a price advantage at the customer level. Witness the rise of retail-distributors like W. W. Grainger in the electrical goods industry. With over 300 stores, selling about 40,000 SKUs (stock-keeping units), Grainger has forced a reorientation in the industry. Both the seller and the dealer view the master distributor as the unwanted fat in the system. The rise of Home Depot in the construction industry, and Terminix and Orkin in the pest-control industry, are further examples of the general trend.

Ironically, in many industries master distributors were set up by manufacturers that did not have the inventory carrying capacity, the geographic reach, or the capability to fulfill small orders. The master distributor served as the essential conduit to retail distribution. But retail dealers have become larger and more sophisticated in handling both suppliers and customers. For small retail dealers, which still need extra support in product assortment or credit, master distributors may be the only way to go. But only those master distributors will survive that proactively use the advances in information and logistics technology to their advantage and combine that with excellent service of small orders. Such opportunities for success are likely to be limited in the future.

From a supplier's point of view, then, a key task is to manage the transition. Those suppliers that have successfully used a master-distributor channel in the past

**FIGURE 6**

*The role of master distributors*

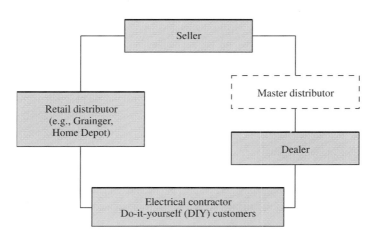

will find it hard to bypass this level. The upfront investment is daunting, and the risk of failure serious. After all, the master distributors performed the inventory-carrying and credit-advancing functions. They own all the relationships with the dealer accounts. Moreover, the potential order sizes may appear too small for effective fulfillment. Newer and more nimble competitors, however, will almost always choose the cost-efficient alternative of skipping the master-distributor level. As the supplier (with the master-distributor channel) loses revenue, share, and profits, the pressure to change may be tremendous, but the will to change is usually lukewarm, especially for the traditional leaders and large incumbents. Their entrenched relationships with these master distributors are high, and it is not as though these channel partners are unwilling to slice their margins or increase their channel efforts. In fact, they are not the cause, but rather the victim of changed economic circumstances.

Suppliers attempting to change in a half-baked, staged manner have inevitably failed. One cannot redress the situation by selectively shorting the channel for big dealer accounts, leaving master distributors to serve the smaller accounts. There is no way they can survive the subsequent intrabrand price competition that their customers—the small dealers—will face from large dealers who now have direct supplier access. One cannot have one's cake and eat it too. There are only two solutions. Either bite the bullet and shorten the channels once and for all, or do everything possible to bolster the master distributor's operations. The channel-shorting option is best implemented when the market is growing rather than shrinking. Another opportunity might be to implement the change simultaneously with the launch of a new range of very attractive products. Essentially, the timing should be such that the pull-through demand is strong enough to offset the lack of distributor push-through. This initial wave is necessary to realign and consolidate relationships with new channel partners. American Cyanamid, in 1985, overhauled its channels for Agricultural Chemicals simultaneously with the launch of a series of breakthrough new products. The new product success legitimized new channels, garnered dealer enthusiasm, and enabled a rapid implementation of the new margin structure.

Alternatively, suppliers could choose to work very closely with their master distributors and help them transform their distribution business. They should be trained to integrate the new economies offered by information and logistics technology to shape their business. If need be, suppliers should invest in such a transformation, treating the master distributors as their own master warehouse. Master distributors who are willing to throw their weight behind one or a few noncompeting suppliers will obviously enhance their chances of being selected for such special partnerships. Independent master distributors with multiple supplier affiliations have no choice but to constantly innovate their distribution operations merely to survive.

# Conclusion

Regardless of the structural form, distribution channels of the future will certainly be more interactive with the customer. In many cases, customers will be able to modify products to suit their unique needs. Even now, some environments provide that latitude. Computer customers, for example, can almost transform their entire hardware system by the choice of the software and accessories. But in the future, given the increasing speed of the feedback loop, suppliers will find it necessary to offer a menu of features and functions rather than prepackage them into set product configurations. The Frito-Lay story is well known. Its route salespeople enter in call data (by store) into a hand-held computer—shelf stock, shelf space, competitor stock, promotion activity, and other such field level data. This information is uploaded to the main computer every evening, and by dawn the next day such information from all markets is processed by the mother computer, and an optimal field-level call plan is worked out for every sales representative across the country—products, assortments, prices, promotions, and the like.

The auto industry is moving toward offering customers a wider array of customizing options (control panels, leg room, interior and exterior trim, etc.), all for delivery within two or three weeks. Future distribution channels will truly have to receive in addition to transmitting channel functions. Current channels are hopelessly inadequate in this regard. Customer complaints and returned goods are usually accepted through an auxiliary channel, which is often not a part of the core distribution system of a company. Channels will have to accept their new role as a two-way communications network gracefully if they are to be really customer responsive, not just customer oriented. This can be accomplished within the structure of hybrid channels, multiple channels, or even conventional vertical marketing systems, but clearly a lot more data and information have to be shared and exchanged among the channel partners to make the two-way network a reality. Traditionally, the supplier controlled product information and the channel controlled market information, and they each used their power bases to, at times gently and at times rudely, lean on each other. While the supplier usually expected channels to deliver sales output, the channel expected a return-on-investment. It was a sales versus margin battle that manifested itself in many interesting standoffs as illustrated in Table A.

---

**TABLE A    Contentions**

| *Manufacturer* | *Distributor* |
|---|---|
| • You must carry a full line of all the products we make. No cherry picking. | • We can try, but we can't sell "dogs." We should concentrate on our strong points. |
| • We need you to concentrate on our products. | • We need exclusive territories. |
| • We need your active involvement in selling new products and developing new markets. | • It is very costly to do so. How will you compensate us for the effort? |
| • We need to know about y(our) customers in greater detail. | • We don't keep such records. (". . . Not a chance—They'll start selling directly.") |
| • You need to improve your sales effort. | • You need to improve your sales promotion. |
| • Your channel margins are too high. | • Your prices are too high. |
| *We need to work together.* | *We agree.* |

But ultimately, as Table A concludes, sellers and distributors needed each other in order to reach the end customer. While the supplier and distributor battle each other, the real war is for customers, and often in the past this got translated into a desire for channel control. There was a confusion of the means for the end. In the future, channel alliances will have to energize and help each other win the competitive battle. They need to get the cake first, before they can quarrel about its allocation.

One should not, however, naively interpret this to mean that the future will see minimal channel conflicts. Quite to the contrary, as pointed out in our discussion of shorter channels, hybrid channels, and multiple channels, administering the new channels demands tremendous leadership. Issues of free-ridership, allocation of financial discounts, product and customer demarcation norms, and so on are all likely to occupy a full plate. There is one difference. These are conflicts all aimed at directly improving the system's effectiveness in addressing the customer's needs. The customer was forgotten in the old model (Table A) but will in fact be at the center in the new.

# Managing Hybrid Marketing Systems

*Companies are creating new hybrid marketing systems that promise to become the dominant marketing design. These systems offer greater coverage and reduced costs, but they are also harder to manage. Managers can make the task easier with a "hybrid grid," a map that illustrates the combination of channels and tasks that will optimize cost and coverage. Another tool, a marketing and sales productivity (MSP) system, can help managers create customized channels and service for specific customer segments.*

There was a time when most companies went to market only one way—through a direct sales force, for instance, or through distributors. But to defend their turf, expand market coverage, and control costs, companies today are increasingly adopting arsenals of new marketing weapons to use with different customer segments and under different circumstances. In recent years, as managers have sought to cut costs and increase market coverage, companies have added new channels to existing ones; they use direct sales as well as distributors, retail sales as well as direct mail, direct mail as well as direct sales. As they add channels and communications methods, companies create hybrid marketing systems.

Look at IBM. For years, IBM computers were available from only one supplier, the company's sales force. But when the market for small, low-cost computers exploded, IBM management realized that its single distribution channel was no longer sufficient. In the late 1970s, it started expanding into new channels, among them dealers, value-added resellers, catalog operations, direct mail, and telemarketing. IBM had built and maintained its vaunted 5,000-person sales force for 70 years. In less than 10 years, it nearly doubled that number and added 18 new channels to communicate with customers.

This article was prepared by Rowland T. Moriarty and Ursula Moran.
Copyright © 1990 by the President and Fellows of Harvard College.
*Harvard Business Review,* November–December 1990, pp. 146–55.

Apple Computer also started out with a clear and simple channel strategy. It distributed its inexpensive personal computers through an independent dealer network. But when the company began to sell more sophisticated systems to large companies, it had to change. Apple hired 70 national account managers as part of a new direct sales operation.

In adding these new channels and communications methods, IBM and Apple created hybrid marketing systems. Powerful forces lie behind the appearance of such hybrid systems; all signs indicate that they will be the dominant design of marketing systems in the 1990s. At the same time, smart managers recognize the high risks of operating hybrid systems. Whether the migration is from direct to indirect channels (such as IBM) or from indirect to direct (like Apple), the result is the same—a hybrid that can be hard to manage.

The appearance of new channels and methods inevitably raises problems of conflict and control-conflict because more marketing units compete for customers and revenues; control because indirect channels are less subject to management authority than direct are. As difficult as they are to manage, however, hybrid marketing systems can offer substantial rewards. A company that can capture the benefits of a hybrid system—increased coverage, lower costs, and customized approaches—will enjoy a significant competitive advantage over rivals that cling to traditional ways.

Examples of hybrid marketing systems extend beyond high-tech businesses such as computers to older industries such as textiles, metal fabrication, and office supplies and to service industries such as insurance. Many of the examples in this article are high-tech companies because the accelerated pace of high-tech industries foreshadows trends that tend to occur more slowly in other industries. The trend to hybrid systems, however, appears to be accelerating in many industries. According to one recent senior manager survey, 53 percent of the respondents indicated that their companies intend to use hybrid systems by 1992, a dramatic increase over the 33 percent that used those systems in 1987.

Two fundamental reasons explain this boost in the move to hybrids: the drive to increase market coverage and the need to contain costs. To sustain growth, a company generally must reach new customers or segments. Along the way, it usually supplements existing channels and methods with new ones designed to attract and develop new customers. This addition of new channels and methods creates a hybrid marketing system.

The need to contain costs is another powerful force behind the spread of hybrid systems, as companies look for ways to reach customers that are more efficient than direct selling. In 1990, the loaded cost of face-to-face selling time for national account managers can reach $500 per hour; for direct sales representatives, the average is about $300 per hour. Selling and administrative costs often represent 20 to 40 percent of a company's cost structure and thus have a direct effect on competitive advantage and profitability. For instance, Digital Equipment's selling and administrative costs in 1989 were 31 percent of revenues; for Sun Microsystems, the figure was only about 24 percent.

Given such economics, many companies are pursuing techniques such as telemarketing, which costs about $17 per hour, or direct mail, which runs about $1 per customer contact. A marketing strategy built on such low-cost communications methods can yield impressive results. Tessco, a distributor of supplies and equipment for cellular communications, emerged as one of the industry's fastest-growing competitors by relying on low-cost communications methods. Tessco generates leads through direct mail and catalog operations; it uses telemarketing to qualify sales leads, make its sales pitch, answer questions, and close the sale. It then follows up each sale with service telemarketing and maintains accounts through an automatic reordering process. The result: Tessco enjoys significantly lower costs than most of its competitors, which continue to rely on traditional methods such as direct sales.

# Wright Line's Problems

Despite the proliferation of marketing methods, few companies pay sufficient attention to the design of marketing systems or seek to manage them in ways that optimize coverage and costs. Indeed, most companies decide to add new channels and methods without a clear and realistic vision of an ultimate go-to-market architecture. These decisions are usually made separately and independently—and often swiftly as well. As a consequence, companies can find themselves stumbling over their hastily constructed, overlapping hybrid system.

Consider how an ill-conceived and mismanaged hybrid system contributed to the 1989 hostile takeover of Barry Wright Corporation. Many factors made the Massachusetts–based company vulnerable, but a principal cause of its troubles was the performance of a major subsidiary, Wright Line, Inc. A leading supplier of accessories used to store, protect, and provide access to computer tapes, diskettes, and other media, Wright Line was struggling vainly to halt the erosion of its market position.

Wright Line's troubles stemmed from a decision made in the early 1980s to reorganize its marketing and sales functions. Previously, the company had sold its products exclusively through a direct sales force. Although the company had been growing rapidly and adding new sales reps every year, Wright Line's management was alarmed by several trends: inability to increase market penetration, declining sales productivity, high turnover of sales reps, and what appeared to be a fundamental shift in the market away from the company's traditional stronghold in large, central computer installations.

After analyzing these trends, Wright Line supplemented its direct sales force with additional marketing channels and communications methods.[1] The company formed two new units: a direct marketing operation to handle midsize accounts through direct catalog and telephone sales, and a unit to serve small accounts and to

---

[1]Channels are either direct or indirect. Methods are the communications options companies can use to reach potential customers; they may also be direct or indirect. For example, through a direct channel, a company may use account managers, a sales force, or telemarketing. The same methods may also be used singly or in combination through indirect channels.

A simple graphic captures the elements of a hybrid marketing system. Along the top are the basic marketing tasks required to obtain and maintain customers: generation of leads; qualification of these leads; presales activities, such as sales calls to woo specific customers; closing the sale; provision of postsales service; and ongoing management of the account.

Along the side of the grid are the various marketing channels and methods used to reach customers, ranging from elaborate direct to elaborate indirect options. The shaded areas represent one possible approach through a direct channel: direct mail to generate leads, telemarketing to qualify leads and manage presales and postsales activities, and a direct sales force to close deals and manage the account on an ongoing basis.

The hybrid grid can be a useful diagnostic tool to identify points of overlap and conflict in a marketing system. It can also aid in the design of a new marketing system tailored to the needs of specific customers. As a marketing map, the grid depicts the situation at a particular moment and needs to be updated as changes occur.

## The Hybrid Grid: The Elements of a Hybrid Marketing System

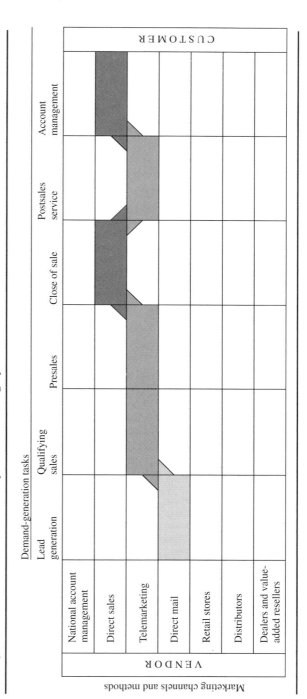

241

attract nonusers through indirect channels. Management's goals were to combine the advantages of high-quality personal selling to major accounts with lower-cost, increased coverage of smaller accounts.

Signs of trouble appeared almost immediately. By 1985, the reorganization had yielded declining growth rates, diminishing market share, and plummeting profits. Inside the company, strife over account ownership was rampant, and turnover among the direct sales reps reached an all-time high. Worst of all, Wright Line's customers grew confused and angry after encountering different sales offerings of the same products under widely disparate terms and conditions. Wright Line's best customers became alienated, and its margins shrank as major accounts ordered the company's products from discount suppliers.

By the time new leadership tried to untangle the mess, it was already too late. Its stock weakened by Wright Line's rapidly eroding market position and declining profitability, Barry Wright Corporation was taken over in 1989.

The Barry Wright story is an extreme example of an increasingly evident problem. Fewer and fewer major industrial or service companies go to market through a single channel or a "purebred" channel strategy that matches a specific product or service to an exclusive segment. Rather than designing an ideal distribution strategy, companies tend to add channels and methods incrementally in the quest to extend market coverage or cut selling costs. Unfortunately, such actions typically result in conflict and morale problems inside the marketing organization and confusion and anger among distributors, dealers, and customers on the outside.

## Mapping the Hybrid

At the heart of the problem of designing and managing hybrid systems is the fundamental question of what mix of channels or communication methods can best accomplish the assortment of tasks required to identify, sell, and manage customers. The trick of designing and managing hybrid systems is to disaggregate demand-generation tasks both within and across a marketing system—recognizing that channels are *not* the basic building blocks of a marketing system; marketing tasks are. This analysis of tasks and channels will identify the hybrid's basic components and permit managers to design and manage the system effectively.

A map of tasks and channels—what we call a hybrid grid—can help managers make sense of their hybrid system. (See "The Hybrid Grid" on page 602.) A hybrid grid, for example, can be used to illustrate graphically what happened at Wright Line and what might have happened differently.

Before its reorganization, Wright Line used direct sales for all demand-generation tasks and all customers (see the chart "Wright Line's Marketing System: What It Had"). When it reorganized in 1982, Wright Line wanted the direct sales force (unit 1) to perform all demand-generation tasks for big customers, the new direct response unit (unit 2) to concentrate exclusively on midsize customers (using catalogs and telemarketing), and the new third-party and resale unit (unit 3) to market to

# Wright Line's Marketing System: What It Had

| Marketing channels and methods | Demand-generation tasks | | | | | |
|---|---|---|---|---|---|---|
| | Lead generation | Qualifying sales | Presales | Close of sale | Postsales service | Account management |
| National account management | | | | | | |
| Direct sales | ALL CUSTOMERS | | | | | |
| Telemarketing | | | | | | |
| Direct mail | | | | | | |
| Retail stores | | | | | | |
| Distributors | | | | | | |
| Dealers and value-added resellers | | | | | | |

VENDOR — CUSTOMER

small customers and nonusers through indirect channels (see the chart "What It Wanted").

Instead, Wright Line wound up with a marketing system that was neither what it wanted nor what it needed (see the chart "What It Got"). The three marketing units were performing all of the demand-generation tasks for many different types of customers. Units 1 and 2 bickered constantly over account ownership. To avoid losing accounts, for example, some sales reps improperly classified accounts to hide them from the direct response marketing division. Those who complied were frustrated by guidelines that prohibited them from calling on smaller and midsize accounts in their territories and growing with them. The activities of unit 3 added fuel to the fire. Among major customers, purchasing managers who read catalogs and received visits from the sales reps of office supply vendors found that Wright Line products were available at a substantial discount off the direct sales price.

In many respects, Wright Line's experience was typical, both in terms of the problems the company faced and its approach to solving them. Management's effort focused on identifying new channels that could be added to or substituted for all of the marketing tasks performed by the existing direct sales force channel. But this approach incorrectly assumes that each channel must perform and control all demand-generation tasks. The hybrid grid forces managers to consider various combinations of channels and tasks that will optimize both cost and coverage.

In addition, the company assumed that certain channels could best serve all the needs of certain customer segments. Hence, units 1, 2, and 3 were aligned with big, midsize, and small customers. The process of aligning high-cost channels—that is, the direct sales force—with big customers and low-cost channels with small customers is very logical, if that is the way customers buy. In Wright Line's case, however, customers bought from multiple sales channels. The attempt to use a single channel to reach a single customer group resulted in severe channel conflicts, along with customer confusion.

The design of an effective hybrid system depends not only on a thorough understanding of channel costs but also on a thorough understanding of buying behavior. When a new channel is added to service a particular customer segment, the segmentation scheme must clearly reflect the customer's buying behavior—not just the channel costs of the company. The design of an effective hybrid system requires balancing the natural tension between minimizing costs and maximizing customer satisfaction. In Wright Line's situation, the hybrid design was driven by costs, without regard for buying behavior.

Wright Line's fatal flaw was basing its marketing strategy on what was best for the company, not what was best for its customers. In focusing its costliest marketing resources on the targets with the highest potential payoff and devoting less-expensive resources to less-promising accounts, it ignored the buying behavior of its customers. Too late, Wright Line discovered that its customers could not be segmented so neatly, nor would they conform docilely to the company's perception of its most efficient channel structure. Its hybrid system was intended to lower costs and increase coverage. Instead, Wright Line lost control of both its channels and its customers.

**Wright Line's Marketing System: What It Wanted**

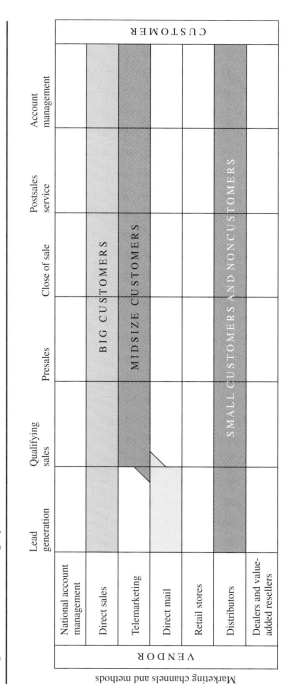

| Marketing channels and methods | Lead generation | Qualifying sales | Presales | Close of sale | Postsales service | Account management |
|---|---|---|---|---|---|---|
| National account management | | | | | | |
| Direct sales | BIG CUSTOMERS | | | | | |
| Telemarketing | MIDSIZE CUSTOMERS | | | | | |
| Direct mail | SMALL CUSTOMERS AND NONCUSTOMERS | | | | | |
| Retail stores | | | | | | |
| Distributors | | | | | | |
| Dealers and value-added resellers | | | | | | |

VENDOR / CUSTOMER

**Wright Line's Marketing System: What It Got**

Demand-generation tasks

| Marketing channels and methods (VENDOR) | Lead generation | Qualifying sales | Presales | Close of sale | Postsales service | Account management |
|---|---|---|---|---|---|---|
| National account management | | | | | | |
| Direct sales | BIG, MIDSIZE, AND SMALL CUSTOMERS | | | | | |
| Telemarketing | | BIG, MIDSIZE, AND SMALL CUSTOMERS | | | | |
| Direct mail | | | | | | |
| Retail stores | | | | | | |
| Distributors | BIG, MIDSIZE AND SMALL CUSTOMERS | | | | | |
| Dealers and value-added resellers | | | | | | |

CUSTOMER

246

The hybrid grid illustrates how Wright Line might have successfully designed and managed its hybrid system (see the chart "What It Needed" on page 609). The company could have used direct mail and response cards to generate leads among potential customers of all sizes and to perform most other tasks for small accounts. It could have used telemarketing to qualify leads among big and midsize prospects and determine approximate order size. It could have routed qualified prospects interested in buying a certain amount of equipment to direct sales reps. (Qualified prospects that turn out to be current national accounts would be turned over to the appropriate national account managers.) To midsize customers, it could have made phone calls to close sales and handle accounts; a direct sales rep or a national account manager could have performed these tasks for larger customers. For all customers, telemarketing could have been used for postsales tasks like reordering.

This version assigns demand-generation tasks to various channels, balancing both cost and customer buying behavior. Distributors were a principal part of Wright Line's setup. But this approach avoids using indirect channels, thereby allowing the company to maintain broad coverage without sacrificing control of pricing and product policy. (Of course, indirect channels are appropriate and necessary in many situations.) By establishing boundaries around genuine segments and building bridges across tasks, Wright Line might have gained the advantages of expanded market coverage and cost-effective marketing management without losing control of its marketing system and its customers.

# Managing Conflict in Hybrid Systems

Conflict is an inevitable part of every hybrid system. When a company adds a channel or substitutes a new communication method within a channel, existing stakeholders—sales reps, distributors, telemarketers—invariably resist. And why not: Each faces a potential loss of revenue as well as competition for ownership of customers. In seeking to build and manage a hybrid system, therefore, companies must recognize and communicate the existence of conflict as the first and most important step.

The next step is to assess the magnitude of the conflict, asking some simple but penetrating questions: How much revenue does the company have in conflict? (Revenue is in conflict whenever two or more channels simultaneously attempt to sell the same product to the same customer.) Where is this conflict? How do channels and customers react to it? How much management time is devoted to dealing with the conflict?

The answers to these questions will vary by industry and by company, but some generalizations are possible. Clearly, a company with no revenue in conflict may be sacrificing coverage, failing to attract new customers by focusing too narrowly on a particular segment. Indeed, a certain amount of conflict in a hybrid marketing system is not only inevitable but also healthy. On the other hand, as the Wright Line story illustrates, conflict that is pervasive across channels is debilitating and potentially destructive.

the company paid the direct sales reps their normal commission for every sale regardless of whether they were responsible. Once the new units became established, the company phased out this system of double pay.

# Orchestrating a Hybrid System

Once a hybrid system is up and running, its smooth functioning depends not only on management of conflict but also on coordination across the channels and across each selling task within the channels. Each unit involved in bridging the gap between the company and the customer must "hand off" all relevant information concerning the customer and the progress of the sale to the next appropriate unit.

A recent technical tool called a marketing and sales productivity (MSP) system can be an invaluable aid in coordinating customer handoffs.[2] Beyond this, an MSP system can help a company combine and manage distinct marketing approaches to produce customized hybrid channels. An MSP system helps serve customers by identifying and coordinating the marketing methods best suited to each customer's needs. In other words, it allows the development of customized channels and service for specific customer segments.

An MSP system consists of a central marketing database containing essential information on customers, prospects, products, marketing programs, and methods. All marketing units regularly update the database. At any point, it is possible to determine previous customer contacts, prices quoted, special customer characteristics or needs, and other information. These systems can significantly lower marketing costs and increase marketing effectiveness by acting as a central nervous system that coordinates the channels and marketing tasks within a hybrid system. With a fully integrated MSP system, it is now possible to know how much it costs to acquire and maintain a customer—essential data in understanding a company's marketing productivity.

Data Translation, a small manufacturer of computer peripherals, installed an in-house MSP system to manage its hybrid marketing organization. At the outset, the company could not afford to hire sales reps but instead generated leads through trade advertising that featured an 800 number. Interested prospects received the company's catalog; they were also encouraged to call and speak to an inside sales representative about products. All contacts with prospects were tracked by the MSP system. Inside sales reps were supported by a group of technical engineers who handled customer inquiries. When Data Translation later added a direct sales force, it continued to rely on its MSP system to coordinate various marketing tasks, including generating leads and dealing with customers who call.

Coordinating the handoffs within its hybrid system and knowing the cost of acquiring and maintaining its customers gives Data Translation significantly lower marketing costs than its competitors. These lower costs translate directly into competitive advantage and bigger margins.

---

[2]For an analysis of these systems, see Rowland T. Moriarty and Gordon S. Swartz, "Automation to Boost Sales and Marketing," *Harvard Business Review,* January–February 1989, p. 100.

# Capturing the Benefits

Staples, a Massachusetts–based office supplies company, is achieving outstanding growth through clever allocation of marketing tasks based on what it has learned about customer behavior. At its birth in the mid-1980s, Staples's founders decided to offer discounted office supplies in a retail superstore format, targeting white-collar companies with up to 100 employees. Staples encouraged customers to accept a free savings card that granted additional discounts and, more important, allowed the company to track purchases and to build up a customer database.

Armed with this information, management discovered that its penetration of businesses with 2 to 10 employees was good, those with 10 to 20 not so good, and those with more than 20 quite weak. Customers in the latter two segments wanted more service. In response, Staples started accepting phone orders and added a delivery service. It has also used direct mail, telemarketing, and catalogs and has considered adding a direct sales force to handle large accounts. An MSP system orchestrates and monitors the entire hybrid system and provides management with performance and productivity information on each marketing element. Staples credits much of its success to the design and implementation of its hybrid system.

Many signs indicate that hybrid systems will be the dominant design for going to market in the 1990s. How a company manages its system will help determine its fate in the marketplace. A company that designs and manages its system strategically will achieve a powerful advantage over rivals that add channels and methods in an opportunistic and incremental manner. A company that makes its hybrid system work will have achieved a balance between its customers' buying behavior and its own selling economics. A well-managed hybrid system enables a marketer to enjoy the benefits of increased coverage and lower costs without losing control of the marketing system. Further, it enables a company to customize its marketing system to meet the needs of specific customers and segments.

In sum, a company with a successful hybrid marketing system will accomplish the following:

- It will recognize that the design and management of its marketing system is a powerful weapon in an increasingly competitive and continually shifting battle for customers.
- It will construct its marketing system using marketing tasks, not entire marketing channels, as the fundamental building blocks.
- It will anticipate, recognize, communicate, and contain conflicts inherent in the marketing system.
- In designing boundaries between customer segments, it will strike a balance between too loose and too strict limits.
- It will form policies and an organizational structure that allow new channels to grow, minimize internal conflict, and reinforce segment boundaries.

- It will exploit information technology and other managerial tools to coordinate handoffs of customers and accounts from one channel or method to another and eventually develop customized marketing systems for each important customer or segment.

*"Do you ever get the feeling we're not the only global marketplace in the universe?"*

Cartoon by Nick Downes

# SECTION IV Managing Product Market Diversity

# 18 Managing Market Complexity: A Three-Ring Circus

*In this reading, we propose models of organization that address the various product-market environments posed by the product life cycle. We frame these changes along the two dimensions of uncertainty and diversity. We offer three sets of organizational characteristics to reflect the three stages of market development: entrepreneurship and innovation (Stage I), efficiency and dedication (Stage II), and expansion and co-ordination (Stage III). Contrary to current wisdom, we argue that form (or structure) is as important as process. We conclude with illustrative case examples.*

In Reading 10, "Beating the Commodity Magnet," we presented a framework for viewing the market life cycle that emphasized two important decision variables, price and cost-to-serve. We traced the price/cost dynamics as the market matured. The four strategies we discussed had implications, not only for price and service levels, but also for other aspects of the marketing mix, such as new products and distribution channels. The focus of that chapter was on marketing strategy. Here we pick up that theme and attempt to understand the underlying causes that drive the commodity cycle. Our attempt in this chapter is to take an overarching marketing organization viewpoint, rather than focusing primarily on marketing strategy.

A simple but effective way to characterize the market maturity process is along the two dimensions of uncertainty and diversity. Uncertainty stands for technological uncertainty, end-use uncertainty, manufacturing uncertainty, and all the other unpredictable events that accompany the birth and development of a brand new product-market, and diversity stands for variety and proliferation in products, applications, and customer segments.[1]

This note was prepared by V. Kasturi Rangan.

Copyright © 1994 by the President and Fellows of Harvard College.

Harvard Business School note 594-119.

[1]See Jeffrey Pfeffer and Gerald R. Salancik, *The External Control of Organizations* (New York: Harper and Row, 1978), for a detailed discussion of *uncertainty*. See Howard E. Aldrich, *Organizations and Environments* (Englewood Cliffs, N.J.: Prentice Hall, 1974), for *heterogeneity*. Our *diversity* construct is similar. Also see Gregory G. Dees and Donald W. Beard, "Dimensions of Organizational Task Environments," *Administrative Sciences Quarterly,* March 1984, for an update on measurement and operational indicators of the uncertainty and diversity constructs.

**FIGURE 1**

*Market life cycle:
Key drivers*

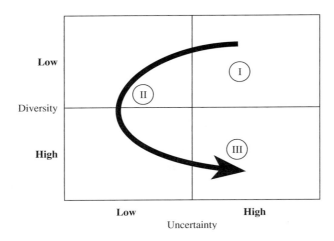

There is an inevitable, incessant rhythm to the market life cycle depicted in Figure 1. Usually, a focused group of customers will find applications for a new technology and adopt it; this is in Stage I. If the technology and its application are successful, a period of predictable growth follows, in Stage II; both suppliers and customers are knowledgeable, comfortable, and satisfied with the product-market exchange. As more customers seek the product, applications proliferate and competitors with the appropriate capabilities join the fray. This leads to a more diverse environment with a higher degree of uncertainty—Stage III. Such a market evolution has implications for how a business is organized and how the industrial marketing function is executed. If businesses are to be successful, different stages imply different organization systems.[2]

## Stage I: Entrepreneurship and Integration

An initial product introduction, when the technology is new to the world, usually involves a high level of risk for both the seller and the buyer. The seller may not have mastered the technology or the manufacture of it in commercial quantities. Doubts about its problem-solving capabilities linger, and the product or its application has to be proven in the field. The initial adopters face similar uncertainties. The new product must deliver the promised functionalities, which may involve changes in the buyer's manufacturing and marketing systems as well. Anything could go wrong. Under these circumstances, buyers need considerable technical support and hand-

---

[2]The arguments we present in this paper have been inspired by the seminal works of Paul R. Lawrence and Jay Lorsch, *Organizations and Environments* (Boston: Harvard Business School Press, 1967), and James D. Thompson, *Organizations in Action* (New York: McGraw Hill, 1967). Follow-on work by many authors, such as R. Miles and C. Snow, *Organizational Strategy, Structure, and Process* (New York: McGraw Hill, 1978), are all relevant but are too numerous to cite here.

holding—a close buyer–seller relationship. One way for buyers to absorb uncertainty in this early period is to target customers or customer segments that would potentially value the new technology highly enough to take the added risk accompanying it. A sensible product/market strategy is one of focus on a few key products in a few key markets. Only after the technical uncertainties and risks have been mastered does it make sense to broaden one's product line and application base.

In this "high uncertainty/low diversity" environment, sellers obviously need a good working relationship with their customers, and this can only come with close coordination among their engineering/R&D, manufacturing, marketing, and sales functions. In small organizations this is usually addressed by providing managers with broad cross-functional responsibilities. It is not unusual in some companies for manufacturing managers to do the selling and customer servicing, just as sales managers schedule the shop floor in others. And, of course, the CEO or the president often becomes involved in the day-to-day details of all the functions, from purchasing to customer service.

In large companies, given their sheer volume of activities, such a general management orientation may not be feasible. But the various functions will still have to work very closely to overcome the hurdles of bringing the new product to market in a timely, effective manner. Figure 2 illustrates the interfunctional dependencies in a typical new product development process. Regardless of how it is done—either having functions with cross-functional responsibility, or having them all specialized but tightly integrated and coordinated—an essential requirement of the early market life cycle is that organizations have a high degree of participation, involvement, and

**FIGURE 2**

*The new product development process*

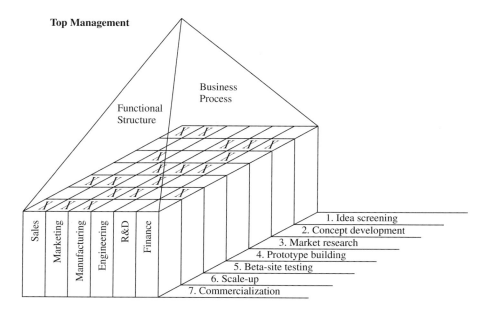

flexibility among the functions in developing, manufacturing, and marketing the product.[3]

# Stage II: Efficiency and Dedication

In Stage II, both the sellers and the buyers feel a lot more comfortable with the technology; uncertainty levels are much lower than they were at the product launch stage. The sellers by now have mastered production, giving customers with similar application needs—who were watching from the sidelines—the confidence to adopt the new product. In fact, competitive considerations in their end-use markets will force these buyers to accelerate the new product adoption. While the market segment may still be focused, the number of user customers in the few segments will rapidly increase.

The challenges of managing technological uncertainties are now replaced by the challenges of managing scale. Suppliers will need to design, make, and sell products in large numbers. This will require dedicated attention to the functions. For example, distributors will specialize in holding stock and providing customers ready availability, the marketing department will focus on setting prices and generating demand, and the production department will specialize in making and shipping product. Essentially, as the firm settles down into a more certain environment, efficiencies of marketing and manufacturing operations become an important determinant of profit. The demand patterns by now are well known and by effectively serving that demand at low cost, firms are likely to improve sales, share, and profits. As the market life cycle advances, therefore, a firm will usually attempt to specialize and aggregate responsibilities by function. At this point, flexibility and participation are replaced by specialization and centralization. Members or departments that specialize in particular functions will own authority as well as carry responsibility for effecting those tasks.

In order to succeed, organizations must adapt to this changing environment. An interfunctional organization, suitable for entrepreneurship, will now need to transform to a functional structure. But the complexity and challenge of a modern organization are such that even as one product line matures, another may be about to be launched. As such, the integration and flexibility required of new product-markets as well as the scale and efficiency required of predictable and growing product-markets must coexist within the same organization.

The point is simple: As the market life cycle in Figure 1 advances, both functional specialization plus business process integration and coordination are needed. In small companies this is much easier to achieve. In larger operations, the sheer size of the marketing, manufacturing, or R&D operations requires dedicated functional management. Even if managers started out as generalists, the intensity of the job is certainly bound to turn them into specialists. Hence the need for a structure

---

[3]For a more detailed explanation see Steven C. Wheelwright and Kim B. Clark, *Revolutionizing Product Development* (New York: Free Press, 1992), chap. 7.

**FIGURE 3**

*The order fulfillment process*

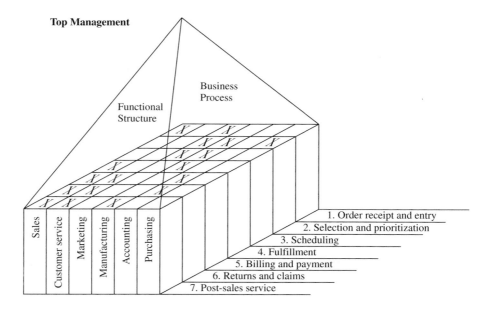

Top Management

Business Process

Functional Structure

Sales | Customer service | Marketing | Manufacturing | Accounting | Purchasing

1. Order receipt and entry
2. Selection and prioritization
3. Scheduling
4. Fulfillment
5. Billing and payment
6. Returns and claims
7. Post-sales service

that formally encourages integration and coordination among the functions. Many brilliant entrepreneurs have been burned at this transition. They have been either unwilling or unable to accommodate the winds of change.

It is not the new product development process alone that needs a cross-functional orientation; the customer acquisition and retention process can be just as cross-functionally demanding. The latter consists of all those activities that differentiate the product/service offering in the eyes of the customer leading up to the initial sale and then repeated sales of the product. Figure 3 illustrates the interfunctional dependencies in a typical order-fulfillment activity.[4] It should be obvious from a comparison of Figures 2 and 3 that the set of functions and also the nature of their coordinating tasks are different across the different processes. Unless an effective mechanism exists to coordinate these crucial processes, one could well end up with two powerful engines pulling in opposite directions.

Consider the "customer retention process." It requires a constant monitoring of customer sentiments with regard to various aspects of the business, for example, product reliability, order fulfillment, and service response. But one cannot unilaterally raise these services higher and higher to reach a perpetual state of customer delight. First, such an option may not be financially optimal. But more important, each external customer satisfaction measure also reflects an internal process such as quality enhancement, low-cost manufacturing, or just-in-time logistics. Until and unless the external customer satisfaction process is synchronized with the internal quality management process, uncoordinated enhancement efforts will not be

---

[4]Benson P. Shapiro, Kasturi V. Rangan, and John J. Sviokla, "Staple Yourself to an Order," *Harvard Business Review,* July–August 1992.

all that effective. Furthermore, while customer satisfaction might be a key process to ensure customer retention, the new product development process or the order generation process might be the key lever to acquiring new customers. What is needed is value enhancement, not only for the customer, but also for the company and its shareholders. One should not forget that while each of these processes is cross-functional, its center of gravity usually rests with one or a few functions. For example, few would deny the centrality of R&D in new product development, and that of marketing in its commercialization. Similarly, few would deny the importance of manufacturing and customer service in order fulfillment. Functional strength is required for effective leadership in process management and also to serve as the focal point for synchronizing activities across processes. Only in this way can value for the customer be translated to value for all.

While the bigger crime, in many companies, has been top management's myopic rush to reorganize structure without consideration to the underlying core processes, some senior managers have shown undue haste for business process reengineering. In their anxiety to be market-driven, they are quick to abandon functional structures in favor of process management by teams. While the latter is bound to deliver short-term results, its long-term sustainability is doubtful in the absence of functional nourishment and nurturing.[5] While the core processes provide the essential circulation system and the nervous system for a business, without the skeleton of the structure, it would be impossible for the processes to fulfill their goals effectively.

# Stage III: Expansion and Coordination

The evolution of the market life cycle to Stage III is usually accompanied by other related changes in the product/market environment. What previously was a relatively focused market with specific applications and known competition from a few key players has grown considerably more diverse. Market maturity is usually accompanied (even precipitated) by the appearance of competitors with similar product offerings. Customers, by now completely familiar with and knowledgeable about the product, demand special services to fulfill their unique requirements. Market growth slows in Stage III as most of the readily available potential has been exhausted. In addition, uncertainty has by now returned, this time in the form of demand volatility as firms battle for share in a mature market. As manufacturers scramble to differentiate their products in the different segments, product variety, customer segments, buying behavior, and channel arrangements begin to proliferate. Confronted by such diversity, firms have little choice but to coordinate across customers, customer segments, products, channels, and geographies. Product decisions have to be viewed in the context of the business unit's other products, sales

---

[5]The popular press is full of process reengineering examples. See, for example, "The Search for the Organization of Tomorrow," *Fortune,* May 18, 1992, and "The Horizontal Corporation," *Business Week,* December 10, 1993. For a detailed explanation of process reengineering concepts see Michael Hammer and James Champy, "Reengineering the Corporation," *Harper Business Press,* New York: (1993).

**FIGURE 4**

*Managing a complex business environment*

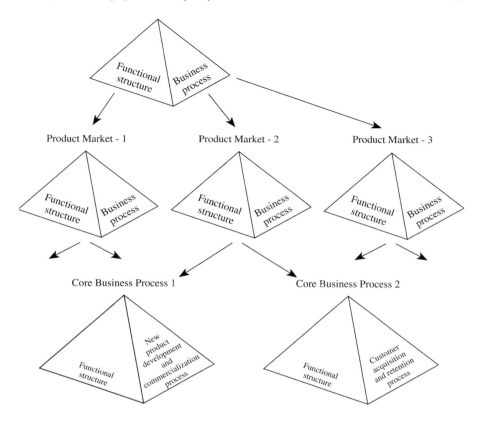

force decisions must be harmonized in the context of a firm's overall distribution channels, and marketing decisions have to be made in the context of a firm's corporate strategy.

The task of managing such a business environment is truly challenging. The complexity goes up exponentially. The different optimal functional structures and core business processes for the different product/market businesses all must be integrated into an overarching organizational system. See Figure 4. The company in that example operating in three product-markets will have to coordinate across a minimum of six core business processes and three functional structures. It is highly unlikely that these structures and processes will be consistent with one another given the company's conscious decision to participate in three different product-market segments. Yet, coordination will be necessary given an underlying common technology, shared operational resources, or overlapping customers across the three business segments. Thus, the organization will need interdepartmental, interfunctional, and interdivisional coordination. It will need flexibility, speed, efficiency, integration, and coordination all at once. "It is a three-ring circus," as the CEO of one such corporation proclaimed. "One has to manage new products, mature products, and product-market diversity, all simultaneously. When the bear has done its trick,

**FIGURE 5**

*Organizational
tasks over the
market life cycle*

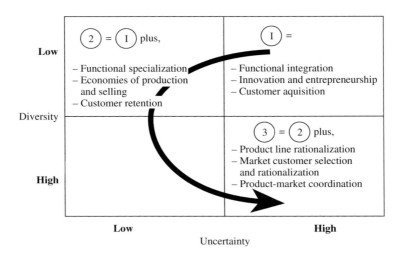

the ringmaster has to turn to the elephant. And when those two have been coaxed to deliver their act, the ringmaster has to sweat out the inclusion of the lion for the grand finale. The management style suited for one is most ill-suited for the other." Firms that are able to cope and manage the complexity are likely to receive high rewards because of product-market coverage; the risks are equally high for firms that cannot.

The dynamic of the market life cycle forces organizations into increasingly complex forms. It is not merely a question of changing from one form to the other. As shown in Figure 5, the Stage III organization is more complex than a Stage II organization, which in turn is more complex than a Stage I organization. At each stage the organization has to manage an additional level of complexity. Not every company in the market is doomed to escalating complexity, however. Firms, after all, can choose to play in whichever environment they wish. This, in fact, has been offered as a definition of strategy. A Stage II organization, for instance, can be considerably less complex if its managers decide to take a strategic focus on mature markets, a quite successful and sustainable approach under the right circumstances. It would then alleviate the necessity to organize for entrepreneurship and integration (new products), in addition to efficiency and dedication (mature products). Similarly, Stage III firms might choose to focus only on a few nonoverlapping product markets. Some of these might be new product ventures and other mature products, but as long as these businesses do not compete for the same customers, it should be possible to split the company into a Stage I and Stage II organization, focusing on different businesses.

In spite of a company's best efforts to reorganize, there is bound to be some amount of competition among its various divisions. Even so, it might be less costly for the corporation to allow some interdivisional rivalry, rather than attempting to coordinate heterogeneous divisions, because a shoddy transformation into a Stage III organization could stifle entrepreneurship and speed; teamwork degenerates into an activity wherein minutes of the meeting are kept and hours wasted. The result is a never-ending business decline to focused niche competitors in every niche. The only way to compete may be to cut the ties (real or imaginary) with the company's other business. IBM's move in 1992 to set up a PC company (separate from its mainframe and minicomputer businesses) may have been motivated by such arguments.

# Case Studies and Conclusions

Consider the case of General Electric's Engineering Plastics division (GE Plastics or GEP).[6] With sales of about $5 billion in 1990, it was the largest engineering plastics company in the world. In 1957 it began with a successful polycarbonate product trademarked Lexan, which could be used to replace glass. In 1964, GEP introduced yet another resin, trademarked Noryl, which could be molded and blended with other resins to produce items such as personal computers, TV cabinets, and automotive dashboards. In 1988, with the acquisition of Borg-Warner's chemical operations, it added a low-end plastic, ABS, with applications in a wide array of consumer products such as kitchen appliances.

In the 1970s, the engineering plastics market was in its early growth stage (exceeding 25 percent per year). Automobile, appliance, and computer companies were the early adapters. New applications had to be carefully developed. Price was not an issue because plastics were replacing metals, which were heavier, costlier, and more expensive to process or machine. GEP approached this market with a strong emphasis on market development. After 1985, however, this scene changed. GEP found itself competing against other plastics, and in particular the cheaper blends, as customers who had first entered the market with a highly engineered product began to selectively downgrade their requirements. While overengineering was the accepted rule when metal parts were replaced with plastic, as companies became more familiar with plastics and their abilities, they became more willing and able to achieve an acceptable end-product performance with a lower-end, lower-priced plastic. The buying decision, purely engineering-driven in the 1970s, began to migrate toward price, manufacturability, and product availability.

When GE Plastics first entered the market with its polycarbonate product, the only significant competitor was Bayer. As its product line grew, so did its competition. When GE Plastics introduced Noryl, it went head-to-head against Du Pont's Nylon. Likewise with the addition of ABS, it gained another formidable opponent in Dow. Thus, from a single, focused product market, the company moved slowly but steadily to a multiproduct market with many competitors and slow (single digit) growth in the 1980s.

Obviously, this situation required a change in organization structure. In the 1970s the company was organized along product divisions. That is, the polycarbonate product had its own dedicated manufacturing, technology, and marketing

---

[6]"GE Plastics," Harvard Business School case no. 591-029.

resources; other products were similarly organized. The product-based structure had served GEP very well for many years; indeed, it was credited with much of the company's explosive growth during the early 1980s. At that time, penetrating new markets—converting customers from steel or concrete—was critical. A bottom line of profit and loss was clear for each product, and product loyalty was strong. The optimal organization created a sense of ownership, team responsibility, and accountability. Employees were encouraged to view themselves as general managers and entrepreneurs. But in the 1980s such a structure caused problems. First, competition among product divisions confused customers. Plastics cannibalized its own product lines in front of customers. A senior GE Plastics manager put it this way: "The Lexan marketing rep told the customer that Lexan was best, then the Noryl rep said that Noryl was best. Customers asked us, 'Will the real GE Plastics please stand up?'"

Second, the product division duplicated many tasks. Each business unit tried to be independent, so each operated distinct groups for MIS, finance, customer service, and purchasing. Finally, every product champion was also a product defender. The product-based structure established and entrenched vested interests.

In 1985, the company changed to a functional structure. See Figure 6. Worldwide it had three geographies (Americas, Europe, and Pacific). Within each geogra-

**FIGURE 6**

*GE plastics:
Organizational
transition*

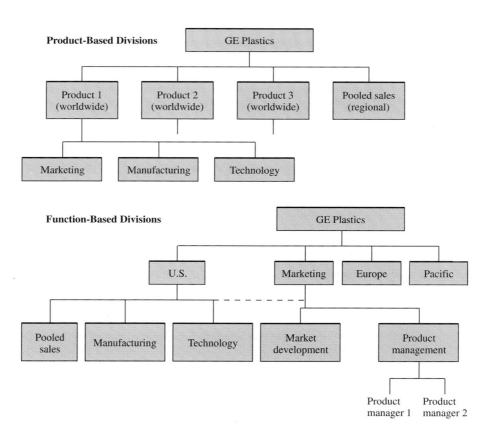

phy, marketing, sales, manufacturing, and technology were common functions for all products. The profit-and-loss responsibility now resided with the geography head. Product managers, who reported to the marketing director, served as the focal point for product-related decisions. In the new structure, the product manager was the critical link for coordination within GE Plastics. Marketing and product management became worldwide functions, with only a dotted line into the geographies.

Then in 1989, the U.S. auto industry entered a period of deep recession followed by the computer and appliance industries shortly thereafter. GE Plastics entered the classic Stage III—high-diversity, high-uncertainty environment. It was in multiple, overlapping product markets with intensive competition for a stagnant, if not mildly declining demand. But because GE Plastics' three products all competed with each other to a significant extent, and because all three products were often bought by the same customer, it had no choice but to play the "Three Ring Circus," an entrepreneurial, flexible organization for developing new products and applications, a cost-efficient and interfunctionally integrated organization for building customer loyalty and profits, and a well-coordinated organization across product divisions and geographies to ensure external consistency and uniformity.

Other conglomerates, such as Europe's ASEA Brown Boveri, with $25 billion sales in 1990, present a different kind of challenge.[7] The company participates in approximately 50 business areas (BA) worldwide, including power transmission, robotics, steam turbines, and metal casting. The company operates about 1,100 factories and employs 250,000. The BA leader for power transformers, for example, is responsible for 25 factories in 16 countries. Fortunately, however, in spite of its staggering business diversity, the company's complex task of organizing itself is aided by the lack of product-market overlaps among its various businesses. Unlike GE Plastics, the product divisions do not cannibalize each other's revenues but are stand-alone, independent businesses. It is possible, therefore, for ABB to organize itself with daring simplicity. See Figure 7. ABB's global matrix consists of two dimensions. Along one dimension is the classic global network consisting of the worldwide head of the business area, who is responsible for product-market strategy and performance without regard for national borders. On the other dimension is the traditionally organized national company. Thus, the head of ABB's robotics company in Norway is charged with manufacturing and marketing industrial robots in Norway and providing capacity for exports according to the business unit's worldwide production plan. But the various heads of their respective business companies in a country also report to the country head. In Germany, for example, ABB's national company, with over a dozen businesses, reports a revenue of $4 billion and acts like a national company employing nearly 36,000 people. The head reports to a board of directors and prepares financial statements comparable to other German companies.

The beauty of ABB's organization is that each cell in the matrix represents an independent stand-alone company. Cell X could be the industrial robotics business

---

[7]William Taylor, "The Logic of Global Business: An Interview with ABB's Percy Barnevik," *Harvard Business Review,* March–April 1991.

**FIGURE 7**

*ASEA Brown
Boveri's matrix
organization*

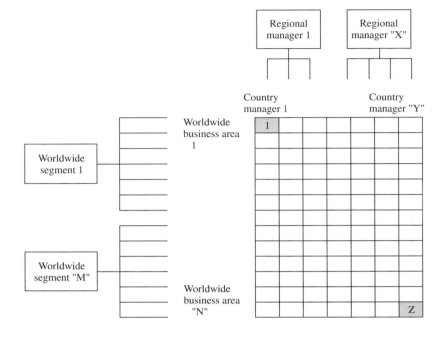

in Norway and Cell Z could be the power transformer business in Germany. The businesses within each country (i.e., column 1 or column Y) do not compete for customers and have dedicated manufacturing and engineering facilities. The only thing they compete for is resources. Across the countries, however, businesses could well compete with each other for the same customers. This is especially true of global businesses like locomotives. There is therefore a need for worldwide coordination, which is provided by the business area leader. Even predominantly local businesses need coordination, because it may be cheaper for ABB to produce all in one or a few countries for shipment to demand areas, rather than local production all over the world. Here is where the "geographies" could butt up against the "businesses," and such issues are coordinated at the top by the executive committee.

Not all companies, however, are at one extreme (GE Plastics) or the other (ABB). Often, it is a challenge to even figure out what the synergies and overlaps are. Millipore Corporation,[8] for instance, a $750 million company with an Analytical Instrumentation business and a Membrane Separation business, struggled with exactly that question. Both divisions often sold to the same customer. While the analytical instruments salespeople sold to the process control laboratory, the membrane sales force sold to the operations people. There were overlaps, but no cannibalization. They sold different products. But most important, one product was in a highly competitive mature market and the other was still a growing market with limited competition. The company's management had either to design a comprehen-

---

[8]"Millipore Corporate Strategy," Harvard Business School case no. 594-009.

sive Stage III organization or alternatively develop two: a Stage I (for new products) and a Stage II (for mature products) organization. Not an easy decision to make under any circumstances.

With increasing globalization in the 1990s, the coordination problem is demanding more attention. A large proportion of industrial customers are global, with worldwide manufacturing and sales. This introduces a different kind of market overlap—product and pricing decisions across geographies have to be coordinated, because the customer is the same! But at the same time it is important to recognize that the manufacturing and marketing environment in the geographic areas (e.g., Europe, the United States, and Japan) are considerably diverse, justifying an independent administration.

There are no easy solutions, and it is not our intention to pretend that there are. We strongly argue, however, that organizations should carefully evaluate their product-market environments before undertaking a reengineering effort. Clearly, different environments will necessitate a different process for focus. We also emphasize the need for structural anchors. It is fine to break the functional walls, but the interfunctional processes need to be coordinated in order to make a holistic and effective contribution. Without strong leadership at key links of the process chain, and a creative system to coordinate these links, managing a complex environment could be the equivalent of managing chaos.

Finally, an organization can effectively alter the environment in which it chooses to play by altering the portfolio of its product-markets. The bottom line: Strategy is all about product-market selection, and organization is all about the systems, processes, and structures necessary to effectively address customers' needs in the selected product-market.

# 19 Variety versus Value: Two Generic Approaches to Product Policy

*This reading follows the dynamics of product line evolution in an industry as a whole. It traces six phases starting with a custom design on to the coalescing of demand and supply around a dominant design. The cycle of proliferation then repeats itself as suppliers and customers attempt to find new ways to differentiate their offering and make profits. This reading discusses the underlying interactions between the suppliers and customers, as well as suppliers among themselves, that drive the tension between "diverse specification" and "universal benefits."*

The marketing executive exploded:

We are in the cosmetics business. We can't offer a lipstick line with fewer than 36 colors. Our customers buy color. We even call the industry "*color* cosmetics." If you can't make 36 colors in your factory, we should get someone who can!

The manufacturing manager stood up, looked away from the conference table and retorted:

You have never understood finance and profits! You only think about sales. You have no conception of inventory management, setup costs, and return problems. In fact, you don't know a damn thing about business. All of our product lines are too long! In each one a few items make up most of our volume. But, no, you need a "full line." We aren't going to introduce still another line with 36 colors because my people and I just won't do it.

He then stalked from the room.

This confrontation is one of many which occurs on a regular basis. The issue is product line length. The sides are generally drawn between marketing and sales managers on one side demanding "a full line" and manufacturing and logistics people on the other fighting for "a more rational approach to product line management."

This note was prepared by Benson P. Shapiro.
Copyright © 1987 by the President and Fellows of Harvard College.
Harvard Business School note 587-119.

The problem is important in many industries. The heat it generates is often overwhelming. The anger and frustration permeate management meetings and lead to deeper, broader interfunctional schisms.[1] And there is little light to be shed on the problem. It seems often to be a matter of bias and "professional dogma."

The purpose of this chapter is to shed light on the topic and to provide a general framework for analysis. It will not address the question of whether or not to add a particular item to a product line.[2] Instead, it provides a conceptual framework for understanding the different points of view and a process for making decisions about product line length. Perhaps most important it demonstrates the dynamic nature of product line length decisions. The appropriate length at one time is probably not going to be the appropriate length at another. Most of the focus here will be on industrial and commercial products instead of consumer products. The thinking can be applied to all product areas, however, perhaps even including services.

The best place to begin to understand product line management is with the customer and the way in which customers choose among competing products.

## Industrial Customer Trade-Offs

Customers want two substantially different sets of product attributes or characteristics: *universal benefits* and *diverse specifications.*[3] Universal benefits are those product attributes which every customer wants; for example, durability and reliability. Customers' willingness and ability to pay for these attributes differ, but all would prefer a more durable or more reliable product over a less-durable or less-reliable product at the same price.

Diverse specifications, however, are not attractive to all customers. Some actively want them and some actively do not. In the consumer goods market, most of the differences in desires for diverse specifications come primarily from differing tastes. One man prefers a paisley tie, while another actively dislikes such a tie. Other diverse specifications relate to size. The small-footed woman wants the size 5 shoe which would be of no use to the large-footed woman.

In the industrial marketplace, diverse specifications occur because of the fit between the product and other parts of the customer's usage system. The fit can be physical or can relate to the operating traditions of the user. A chemical plant that is piped in 10-inch stainless steel piping will not find 9- or 12-inch piping easy to fit into its system. The 32-bit computer manufacturer (the number of bits measures the size of the units processed) will not be able to use 16-bit memory units. Machine operators accustomed to working with a brand of equipment will generally prefer to

---

[1] For more on marketing/manufacturing frictions, see "Can Marketing and Manufacturing Coexist?" by Benson P. Shapiro, *Harvard Business Review,* September–October 1977, pp. 104–14.

[2] For more on a process to add or delete items see Barbara B. Jackson and Benson P. Shapiro, "New Way to Manage Product Line Decisions," *Harvard Business Review,* May–June 1979, pp. 139–49.

[3] These terms were coined by Peter Patch, a doctoral candidate at Harvard Business School, based upon the work of Kelvin Lancaster, a British economist.

stay with that brand unless there is some clear reason to change. Deere bulldozer operators will not, in all likelihood, welcome a change to International Harvester or Caterpillar.

Separation of attributes into universal benefits and diverse specifications makes it easier to discuss the customer's product choice decision: The decision comes down to trade-offs among various universal benefits and between universal benefits and diverse specifications. For example, one customer might prefer more durability at a higher price than a second customer who is more price sensitive. Both want durability and low price, but the second is relatively more interested in price and less in durability. Still another customer might accept the low level of durability and pay the higher price but only for a product that included a diverse specification of great interest. Our three customers thus have the following interests:

|            | Low Price | Long Durability | Diverse Specification |
|------------|-----------|-----------------|-----------------------|
| Customer 1 | Low       | High            | No                    |
| Customer 2 | High      | Low             | No                    |
| Customer 3 | Low       | Low             | Yes                   |

The marketer who looks at this situation has a series of decisions to make regarding product policy. The important assumptions underlying the decisions are:

1. At any given price, all customers prefer more durability.
2. At any given level of durability, all customers prefer a lower price.
3. Customers trade off price for durability.
4. Some customers want diverse specifications and are willing to pay more, accept lower durability, or both.

The decisions which the marketer has to make are:

1. What durability level to offer.
2. What to charge at each level.
3. What diverse specifications to offer.

The first and third of these decisions focus primarily on product policy. The second, also related to product policy, is primarily concerned with pricing. The second is also a much-less-permanent decision because price can be changed much more easily than product policy.

Underlying the two product policy decisions is another decision that is even more fundamental: the number of items in the product line. There seem to be two essentially different approaches, given this discussion of diverse specifications and universal benefits.

# Two Approaches to Product Policy

One product policy alternative is to develop a *variety*-oriented product line that stresses the fit of each item to divergent customer needs. The variety will include two kinds of diversity. One kind is in the trade-off of universal benefits against each other. In the example above, the items in the product line would vary in the durability and price of each item. The line might begin with a low-price/low-durability unit; each successive unit would have increasing durability at a higher price.

The second kind of diversity involves diverse specifications. Each item in the line would have a different mixture of diverse specifications in addition, perhaps, to the different mix of universal benefits deriving from the first form of diversity.

Returning to our simple example of one diverse specification and two universal benefits (price [or low price] and durability), we might picture the product line as follows:

|         | Price | Durability | Diverse Specification |
|---------|-------|------------|-----------------------|
| Item 1  | High  | High       | No                    |
| Item 2  | Low   | Low        | No                    |
| Item 3  | High  | Low        | Yes                   |

This line has three items and covers the feasible set of possibilities. A low-price, high-durability product would not be possible because it would not be profitable: Durability adds cost.

If one expands the example to multiple levels of durability and price, and several universal specifications, the product line increases in potential size and diversity:

| Durability | Diverse Specification A | Diverse Specification B | Diverse Specification C |
|------------|-------------------------|-------------------------|-------------------------|
| High       | Yes                     | Yes                     | Yes                     |
| •          |                         |                         |                         |
| •          |                         |                         |                         |
| •          |                         |                         |                         |
| High       | Yes                     | No                      | No                      |
| •          |                         |                         |                         |
| •          |                         |                         |                         |
| •          |                         |                         |                         |
| Low        | No                      | No                      | No                      |

If the number of universal benefits increases, the size and diversity of the potential product line increases further.

Because the variety approach to the product line views this diversity as an opportunity, the variety marketer attempts to offer many items. A variant of this approach is to offer a smaller number of items in a segment of the possible offerings. The theory is the same: Offer a product that best meets the customer's desire for both a unique set of diverse specifications and a unique mix of universal benefits. Each customer or perhaps each usage or purchase situation is approached as an opportunity to be met.

Developing an item for each unique mix of universal benefits trade-offs and diverse specifications is, however, expensive. The product line must consist of many items or an intense coverage of a limited area of the market, which implies an engineering function which can either custom design each item or design many different items efficiently. The manufacturing operation must cope with the production of many different lots with low unit sales. The logistics function must be able to process and monitor many small orders and to ship a diverse set of small individual orders. The applications engineers and repair people must be able to handle custom designs or a great diversity of designs. Finally, the salespeople and/or distributors must be able to help customers choose among the many options. All of this support is expensive and cannot be spread over many units per item.

The variety product line can be profitable only if the customer values the unique mix of product attributes (trade-offs among universal benefits and specific choices of diverse specifications) enough to pay for the intense service and a profit. (I will return to the issue of how to operate in a variety approach after I discuss the second product line approach.)

Some customers are willing to compromise their interest in a specific mix of universal benefits and diverse specifications in order to save money. They will trade off a particular mix of universal benefits and give up diverse specifications in return for more of another universal benefit—low price. The price can be lowered substantially because of the different operating logic behind this product line. The central concept to the customer is *value:* utility per dollar.

The value-oriented product line does not meet the needs of individual customers or usage or purchase situations. Instead, the opportunity to obtain more universal benefits per dollar, even if diverse specifications are sacrificed and even if the mix of universal benefits is not ideal for the customer or situation, causes the customer to purchase the product. While the variety product line attempts to *meet customer needs,* the value product line attempts to *pull customer demand to an alternative* item that provides better value or more utility per dollar.

The value approach works because the limited product line leads to economies in the engineering and design, manufacturing, logistics, applications engineering, field service, and sales functions. There are few designs, so engineering costs are amortized over many units. The short product line leads to long production runs with attendant opportunities for learning curve savings and the application of automated manufacturing technology. Setup time is amortized over the long runs. Logistics has a simpler job with fewer different items to order, inventory, and ship. Applications engineers and field service people can more efficiently support the short line. And salespeople have a faster, easier story to tell and less to learn.

<u>**EXHIBIT 1**</u>   **Value versus Variety**

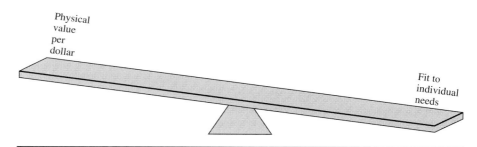

To the customer, the trade-off is between the *fit to his or her individual needs* of the variety approach or the *higher physical utility per dollar* of the value approach. Exhibit 1 shows the trade-off.

From the customer's point of view, the nature of the trade-off will be driven by three things:

1. The utility of diverse specifications and a unique mix of universal benefits.
2. The utility of price.
3. The price difference between the unique item that fits the customer's needs and the compromise item which offers more physical utility per dollar.

The price difference, item 3 above, in turn, is determined by the cost differences between providing the unique item and the compromise item, and the marketer's pricing approach.

### *Variations on the Variety Theme*

Before looking more deeply into the marketing implications and the dynamics of change between value and variety product lines, I would like to create a more detailed taxonomy of product policies by dividing the variety-oriented approach into two further approaches. (See Exhibit 2.)

At the exhibit's right-hand extreme is the custom-designed item. These items can be, within the limits of feasibility, designed and built to meet the precise trade-offs in universal benefits and the precise set of diverse specifications desired by a customer. If, for example, the customer wants a retail display case which is 19 feet, $3^{5}/_{32}$ inches long, the custom-design manufacturer can supply it if the tolerances can be met and if the size is not too great to be accommodated in its factory. If the manufacturer can operate to a tolerance of 1/32 of an inch and can accommodate cases up to 20 feet long, it can make any case between the minimum feasible, let us say 2 feet, in 1/32 inch increments up to 20 feet. Thus, it has a product line of 18 feet (20 − 2) times 12 inches per foot times 32 32nds per inch, or 6,912 variations. It is easy to see that if the manufacturer offers a range

**EXHIBIT 2    Variety—Special Purpose and Custom Design**

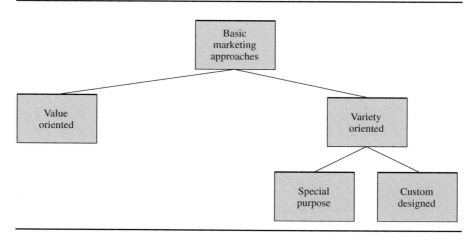

of custom heights and widths, materials, lighting options, cooling and heating options, and so on, the line for a product as simple as a retail display case can become long indeed. It will not be infinite because there are tolerance and size limits, but it can grow very fast because of the multiplicative nature of the combinations.

The custom-designed product line includes a great deal of service content in engineering and design, specification, applications engineering, field service, and sales. Custom-designed products can be mechanical, electronic or electrical, or chemical. One can, for example, purchase custom-compounded chemicals. Some custom products such as power plants are even built at the customer's site. It is difficult to differentiate between the marketing of a service and a truly custom on-site constructed product.

### *Special-Purpose Products*

Because the cost of true custom-designed products is so high, some marketers offer a more limited form of variety: special-purpose items. Often, these products are custom built from a standard set of basic units with accessories and options. A lathe, for example, may be offered in several basic sizes, but with a variety of options concerning motor size, feeds, speeds, control electronics, and the like.

We see the same distinction in the consumer goods area where homes and clothing (e.g., suits and dresses) can be purchased as custom designs and autos from some manufacturers can be specified with a wide range of options and accessories (special purpose).

In some situations, the special-purpose units are not custom built. Instead, the manufacturer has a broad product line designed to meet the precise needs of many customers, or purchase or usage situations. The difference between custom-designed and more standard special-purpose items is just like the distinction between the variety and the value orientations. Custom-designed products offer more fit to a specific need in terms of trade-offs among universal benefits and choice of diverse specifications than special purpose units, unless the special-purpose unit has the precise attributes the customer desires. As the number of relevant universal benefits and diverse specifications increases, the likelihood of a special-purpose unit offering the precise mix any given customer wants goes down. Thus, in the move from custom designed to special purpose, the process of compromise has begun. As one moves further to the left in Exhibit 2 from special-purpose variety to value, the amount of trade-off increases. The lure of a lower price for greater physical utility convinces the customers to trade off precise fit for more physical utility per dollar.

In the value-oriented product line a manufacturer can offer only a few items. The customer makes the compromise to obtain the greater physical value per dollar.

### Who Wants Variety?

To the industrial customer, the utility of the added variety will be a function of:

1. The utility of the diverse specification.
2. The utility of the unique trade-offs among universal benefits desired.
3. The customer's sensitivity to price.
4. The vendors' price policies as reflected in the price difference between the good-fit custom-designed products or special-purpose products and the more compromised value-oriented items.

While it is impossible to predict all situations, it is possible to generalize about the four factors above.

By and large, the utility of diverse specifications varies greatly by situation. In general, diverse specifications are more important than trade-offs among universal benefits. Interest in diverse specifications is probably the most powerful market segmentation variable, and does the most to define the limits of a product's applicability. A company, for example, with Apple Macintosh computers cannot use accessories, supplies, or software designed only for IBM and IBM-compatible personal computers. Many diverse specifications are binary; that is, they either exist or do not. Most of the remainder are discrete, such as the size of piping which, in large-process pipes, is in inches. Thus, diverse specifications are normally not an issue of "a bit more here" or "a bit less there." They either are or are not. Paper is either legal size (14 inches long) or it is not. Such variables are thus powerful determinants of buying behavior.

In addition, diverse specifications are analytically difficult to handle because they are discontinuous and their relationship to purchase intentions or purchase behavior is discontinuous and very bumpy. Hence, while an increase in durability may increase buying intentions—and thus sales—gradually, introducing a diverse specification will cause an abrupt change. The difference can be seen in the graphs on the next page:

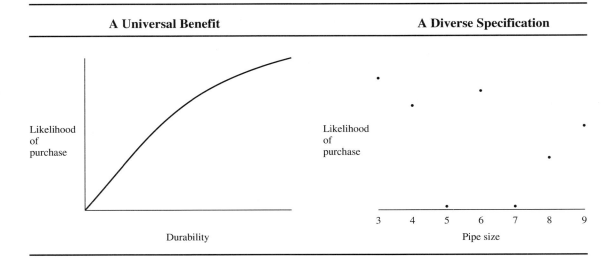

**A Universal Benefit**

**A Diverse Specification**

Likelihood
of
purchase

Durability

Likelihood
of
purchase

3     4     5     6     7     8     9

Pipe size

In the graph on the right, purchase is possible only at pipe sizes of 3, 4, 6, 8, and 9 inches. Sizes between the inches do not sell at all, and even 5- and 7-inch pipe does not sell.

Most buyers who want fit and are thus interested in the variety-oriented (special-purpose and custom-designed) product lines are interested more in diverse specifications than in universal benefits. It is easier to compromise among universal benefits because of their more continuous nature. Therefore, unique positions in the trade-off among universal benefits are less important and less powerful to the buyer, and thus to the seller, than unique collections of diverse specifications.

The trade-off between price, on the one hand, and the unique collection of universal benefit trade-offs and diverse specifications, on the other, tends to depend upon the impact of the product on the customer's performance system and on the customer's cost position. Products with high cost-impact and low performance-impact tend to be more amenable to the value approach because the customer is price sensitive and relatively attribute insensitive. This leads to the chart shown in Exhibit 3.

The diagonal going from lower right to upper left in Exhibit 3 also is a price sensitivity diagonal. Customers in the upper left will be more price sensitive. This means that the most appropriate pricing policy for a vendor is to obtain higher margins in the lower right and to decrease margins as the product moves toward the upper left.

The underlying driving force then becomes the customer's interest in product attributes compared to the customer's interest in price. The interest in product attributes breaks down into the interest in diverse specifications and the interest in a unique trade-off among universal benefits. The interest in diverse specifications, as argued earlier, is likely to be higher.

EXHIBIT 3   **Product Line Appropriateness as a Function of Customer Impact**

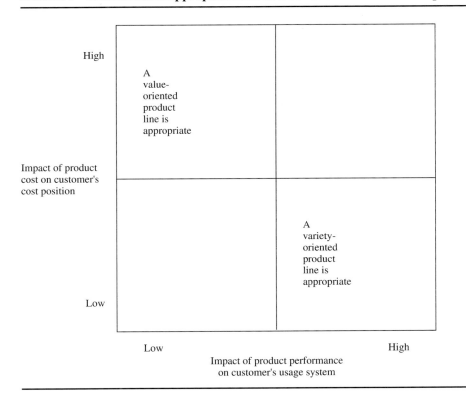

## The Dynamics: The Product Evolution Trajectory

Innovation and change in product lines can be related to the variety and value approaches by the product evolution trajectory. Almost every industrial market begins with a few customized units which are experimental attempts to mate a technology and a need. At this stage, neither the customer nor the supplier knows what is possible or what is needed except in the broadest terms. The potential benefits for the customer and potential profits for the vendor are great, so both devote substantial support to the project. Early computers and robots and most industrial markets have gone through this type of embryonic period. We now see it in integrated factory automation systems, robot vision systems, and local area networks to connect telecommunications and computer equipment.

As the industry develops, it evolves into a phase of special-purpose units to do things that would otherwise not be possible. Computer-controlled machine tools maintain tolerances and provide efficiency not previously possible, for example. Engineered plastics, offering new combinations of characteristics, is another example.

## *A Dominant Design Arises*

At some point in the development of the industry a dominant design arises that provides great universal benefits per dollar. This creates a value-oriented product line. Because the universal benefits per dollar are very high and in all likelihood fairly well positioned with regard to the trade-offs most customers want to make among universal benefits (otherwise it would not develop into a dominant design but would stay as a special-purpose product), growth comes fast. The rapid growth encourages increased production and greater marketing expenditures to spread the word. The production and marketing investments resonate with each other and grow with the market, encouraging competition and coalescing product lines around the new dominant design.

Often the market will develop with two subsets of the value-oriented dominant design. One will be oriented toward higher performance at a greater price and the other will be a stripped-down model offering lower universal benefits at a lower price. The market develops in this fashion because neither vendors nor customers can make fine or difficult distinctions in trade-offs among universal benefits. One group of customers, however, seems more interested in greater universal benefits and another in lower prices. The distinctions are coarse but further market segmentation is difficult. This is particularly true for products that are considerably more complex than the alternatives they replaced. Small business telecommunications equipment would be a good example.

The dominant design and its imitators lead to narrow product lines with few items. Competition tends to be on the basis of universal benefits. The market, both supply by vendors and demand by customers and prospects, coalesces around the dominant design and its close substitutes. Unit volume grows. Prices decrease because of greater manufacturing and marketing economies.

## *The Demise of the Dominant Design*

Over time, however, customers grow more sophisticated in the use of the product, and vendors attempt to gain relief from the intense competition around a limited number of fairly comparable items. Some try to differentiate themselves by service and relationship; others, however, begin to offer important product variations for distinct market segments. Both customers and vendors can now define market segments and particularly diverse specifications, as well as new combinations of universal benefits, because of the growing experience base they have. Customers want special products with unique combinations of attributes, and vendors are anxious to find protected market niches, especially as growth in the core of the market abates. Product proliferation continues until a new technological breakthrough creates the opportunity for a new dominant design.

It is worthwhile to explore the rate at which these changes occur and the driving forces behind them. The relative importance of a close fit to the customer's product specifications on the one hand, and low price on the other, is a primary driving force. The more important the fit, as evidenced by the impact of product attributes on the customer's operating system, the faster the move to proliferate will be, and the slower will be the coalescing around a dominant design. On the other hand, a customer orientation toward price sensitivity will speed the move toward the dominant design and slow proliferation.

Another driving force is the possible differences among products: differentiability. The following circumstances tend to lead to more differentiability, and more and faster proliferation:

1. Number of relevant product attributes.
2. Range of variation across these attributes.
3. Importance of the attributes.
4. Difficulty in measuring the attributes and comparing products.
5. Inability of competitors to duplicate one another's attribute combinations.

A third driving force is the ratio of diverse specifications to universal benefits. By and large, diverse specifications with their discontinuous nature drive the process toward proliferation.

Technological opportunities in terms of the ability of product design engineers to develop a good compromise among universal benefits are a fourth driving force. Closely related is a fifth driving force: the technological opportunities for process engineers to develop scale economies and experience curve benefits. The greater the ability to develop a compromise product and the greater the economies of producing a limited line, the greater the speed to the dominant design and the slower the move to proliferation.

Finally, if the product can be customized in the field by manufacturer service centers, distributors, or the customer, the move toward proliferation will be slowed because the benefits of variety can be gained without proliferation in the factory. In many industries, combinations of short product lines and economical field customization have led to a good mixture of customer benefits.

It is useful to review the driving forces and to categorize them by customer or vendor so that the diversity of influences can be seen:

| *Force* | *Source* |
| --- | --- |
| 1. Relative importance of customer fit and price | 1. Customer |
| 2. Differentiability | 2. Customer and product |
| 3. Ratio of diverse specifications to universal benefits | 3. Customer and product |
| 4. Product design opportunities | 4. Vendor |
| 5. Economies of scale and experience curve benefits | 5. Vendor |
| 6. Field customization | 6. Customer/vendor |

It is also interesting to note the impact of the product itself on the driving forces. Differentiability is somewhat a function of the product. Computers have many attributes and ways to vary the attributes, while sand offers limited capabilities for differentiation.

A final note on the driving forces is the extent to which the vendors can affect the forces by communication and persuasion. A supplier who wants to encourage proliferation might do so by convincing customers of the importance of diverse specifications. Clearly, such an approach has limitations and is not easy, but it should be explored.

### Structural Impact on the Industry

The product evolution trajectory (PET) seems to be a continuing process in many industries and to have substantial impact on the way a company and, indeed, a whole industry develops and evolves. It is instructive to look at the impact of the PET on industry structure and on the way companies must operate to succeed.

The initial phase of the PET begins with the introduction of a few custom-designed and -built units that enable the customer to do tasks previously not feasible. This custom-product phase can last for between a few years and quite some years as the customers and suppliers seek ways to work together with a reasonable set of designs. A critical management skill at this point is the selection of profitable market opportunities. Custom designing, building, and installation is expensive. Vendors who are not careful in identifying the profitable opportunities in terms of market segments, customers, applications, and profits will fail. Pricing is also a critical skill. Many of the hungry pioneering vendors will price their wares too low because they are anxious to "buy into opportunities." Many of the early pioneering firms will invariably fail.

The custom-design phase eventually leads to the development of a smaller set of special-purpose items. They tend to focus around applications identified during the earlier stage. In general, the product is still sold very much on the basis of the fit between the product and its application. At this stage, the vendors must offer considerable sales and technical support. Successful vendors invariably succeed as much through field execution as product design. In fact, a close working relationship with customers is the *only* way to garner the applications and technological information necessary to improve designs. Careful choice of markets and customers remains critical during this phase as well as the first phase.

As the industry continues to grow, a standard dominant design appears. This design tends to make radical changes in the manufacturing, engineering, technical service, marketing, and sales functions of the vendor. The switch from the special-purpose units to the dominant design tends to be accompanied by a major shakeout in the industry. Customers find it much easier to compare different vendors because the dominant design provides an implicit industry standard. In addition, customers have grown more experienced in making good judgments and more confident in their judgments. Competitors have become more imitative of one another's successful design and service features.

During the dominant design phase, industry demand tends to coalesce around a few suppliers and their more or less comparable designs. The lower prices made possible by the lower costs of the shorter product line and resultant long runs, accompanied by substantial industry growth, tend to lead toward an emphasis on a more commoditylike approach to marketing. The ratio of performance to price becomes exceedingly important in the customer's decision-making process. This standard dominant design phase can be easily seen in the microprocessor, personal computer, and robot industries. (Some industries do not grow enough to justify the development of a dominant design, and forever stay oriented toward special-purpose designs.)

The critical skills change abruptly from phase II, special-purpose products, to phase III, the dominant design. Customer and application selection and custom-design skills cease to be important while cost-sensitive product and process engineering and manufacturing move to the fore. The successful vendors of the dominant design must be able to manage rapid unit growth because of both market size and market share growth. Organizations become large, more professional, and more specialized. The loose confederation around special customer needs gives way to a more disciplined approach to volume manufacture, distribution, and sales. The cost structure shifts as product lines narrow. "Commoditization is under way!"

Over time, the customers' interest in having their unique needs met and the vendors' constant search for ways to generate additional sales and profits lead to the development of special-purpose units for market segments of limited size. The fourth phase is driven as much by the vendor's search for market niches which offer growth and profitability as by customer needs. As phase III continues and the dominant design ages, unit volume growth abates and sometimes ends, perhaps even with declines. The drive for growth continues and various suppliers cut prices in attempts to spur growth and gain share. Eventually, market size does not respond to price cuts and costs go down more slowly than prices. Profit pressure grows to intense levels and vendors search for relief.

In this new phase, the market tends to fragment, with the emphasis being the provision of units that meet the unique needs of various market segments, as opposed to the coalescing which took place in the dominant-design phase. The fragmentation continues until a new design emerges which is so attractive to all customers, or to many customers, that it encourages demand to converge on another, dominant design, one that is more advanced. This convergence is again often accompanied by increasing concentration in the industry and a shakeout of marginal producers who cannot respond to the new dominant design.

As the industry continues to evolve, it will go through a series of cycles involving fragmentation followed by coalescing. The fragmentation tends to be driven by the amount of diversity in customer needs and by the ability of the industry to provide that diversity at a reasonable cost. Exhibit 4 shows the cycles in the PET.

Two industries demonstrate the continuing process of coalescing and fragmentation which can occur over a long period despite relative maturity in the industry.

## The Day the Dalmatian Cried

The fire engine industry has traditionally been terribly fragmented but now seems to be coalescing. In fact, the strength of the change was so great that American La France, once the strongest competitor in the industry, was forced to close. Apparently,

EXHIBIT 4    **Product Evolution Trajectory: Product Line Breadth**

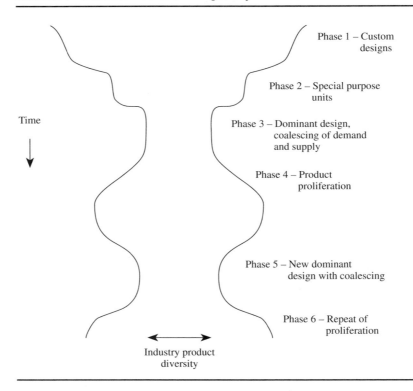

the coalescing was forced by a "shift from custom vehicles to cheaper commercial ones" (*American Metal Market,* January 28, 1985, p. 14). Commercial fire engines are of a much more standard design than the custom ones. Custom units cost between $250,000 and $450,000, while commercial trucks cost between $150,000 and $200,000. Current economic factors and pressures on municipal budgets have forced fire departments to be more cost conscious and less sensitive to their apparent unique needs in their purchase decisions.

The change in the customer buying process was accompanied by a major change in the competitive situation. A new competitor, Emergency One, arose. Emergency One builds its fire engines primarily from aluminum instead of the steel used by other older competitors. The aluminum assembly, combined with a more standard product, enables Emergency One to assemble a unit in 45 days versus six months for American La France. There are also other major differences in the way the two companies operate.

The change in competition often accompanies or causes the industry to move toward a dominant design. It is not unusual for the newest competitor to offer the dominant design and thus to energize the latent customer interest in high universal benefits per dollar. In the Emergency One example, the owner of the company did not even have industry experience.

Neither American La France, nor its parent, Figgie International, seemed to recognize the changes, or were able to move fast enough to incorporate them. It is interesting that when they did recognize change was necessary, they had to hire an outside design organization to develop new models. That relationship ended in a lawsuit.

### From Consolidation to Fragmentation

In clear counterpoint to the fire engine example is the current move in the integrated circuit business from general-purpose to custom and semicustom products. For example, Intel, previously a leader in the general-purpose, dominant-design part of the market, is making a "mad dash" to move into more customized products (*Business Week,* August 12, 1985, pp. 25 and 28). Here, the industry is changing in the opposite direction from the fire engine example. Customers are becoming increasingly sensitive to performance, and decreasingly sensitive to costs because of the general and strong degradation of integrated circuit prices. At the same time, various changes in manufacturing and engineering technology are enabling circuit vendors to offer more customization more easily at a lower price.

# International Marketing Implications

The variety-versus-value conceptualization can be applied to international marketing. Each country can be viewed as a single market segment. Then the variety-versus-value issue becomes the question of developing a unique product or product line for each separate country. The variety orientation would lead to a separate product or product line for each country, while the value orientation would lead to a more universal or world standard product. Professor Theodore Levitt has made an impassioned plea for greater standardization[4] because, he states, all people want pretty much the same thing. On the other hand, there are many examples of products failing in new foreign markets because the foreign customers rejected a product not customized to their situation and needs.

Probably the greatest experiential evidence in favor of Levitt's approach is Japan's success with limited product lines. Japanese manufacturers stress a universal product line with little customization. Even in automobiles, their products tend to be similar from one country to the next, offering a standard set of accessories as opposed to the custom-built orientation of American manufacturers. This approach builds well upon the renowned ability of Japanese manufacturers to upgrade competitive designs in small ways and to manufacture standard products with great efficiency.

---

[4]Theodore Levitt, "The Globalization of Markets," *Harvard Business Review,* May–June 1983, p. 92.

The original export mentality of the Japanese companies and the long distance (cultural as well as geographic) between them and their customers probably almost forced the approach on them. It also fit well with their background as a more subsistence economy and their willingness as a people to be more standardized than societies like the United States which grew richer earlier. I suspect that countries just emerging from or still in the economic development process have a greater interest in higher universal benefits per dollar than in more diverse specifications. Certainly Henry Ford's success with his Model T in the United States's days of intense economic development emphasized a value orientation at the sacrifice of variety ("You can have any color you want as long as it is black!").

The variety-versus-value issue will probably have to be carefully approached in each industry and perhaps in each country group. It certainly seems to me that a doctrinaire approach like Levitt's is unlikely to succeed in situation after situation despite the author's impressive credentials and colorful rhetoric. The variety-versus-value choice is more likely to be driven by the forces described above.

## Management Implications

There are two distinct sets of management implications of the variety-versus-value and product-evolution-trajectory thinking.

The concept of the product evolution trajectory emphasizes the importance of being able to identify the transition points in the industry. It is unpleasant to be a custom-oriented manufacturer (like American La France) when the industry goes to a dominant design. Often the shift to a dominant design is spurred by price sensitivity on the part of the customer industry which leads to a diminution of orders, as well as the emergence of the value-oriented dominant design.

The ability to enter with a dominant design at the right point can add considerably to corporate profits. Kearney & Trecker, for example, introduced its MM-180 numerically controlled machining center as a simple, limited variety unit to appeal to smaller machine shops as well as its traditional larger industrial manufacturing customers. The product met overwhelming success in 1979 and helped to move the industry substantially away from its earlier variety orientation based on special-purpose custom-built units. Demand for the MM-180 tripled company goals in the first two years after introduction.

It is just as painful to be a value-oriented supplier (like Intel) when the industry moves toward fragmentation. Common wisdom suggests that industries only consolidate. The striking example of the integrated circuit business shows that sometimes at least some industries go the other way.

Substantially different skills and a totally different orientation are needed to operate in the value and variety markets. The narrow-product-line orientation of the value approach requires the discipline not to proliferate the product line beyond a few economically produced items. The items must be well positioned to meet the needs of the largest market segments and to draw customers from other market segments. The strength of the line must revolve around maximum universal benefits per dollar. Effective process design and efficient manufacturing, logistics, service, and sales functions are necessities. Product designers must constantly fight to keep the product line narrow and economical (in terms of universal benefits per dollar) for the customer.

At the other extreme, the custom producer must be responsive to unique needs, particularly diverse specifications. It must identify and service many small segments with unique products. The sales force must be able to paint the picture of the benefits of custom products and must focus on the unique needs of customers. Applications engineers must be responsive yet efficient in meeting custom needs. The manufacturing function must be flexible so that it can accommodate the range of products needed. Since most custom-designed products are sold through a bidding process, the company must be able to set bid prices well; otherwise, it will lose bids that would have been profitable and win only those which lead to losses. Finally, because each order is a different item, functional integration among sales, marketing, manufacturing, engineering, and applications engineering is an absolute necessity. In custom producers, the profits are made at the interfaces of the functions, not in any single function.

The special-purpose product line is broad but not unlimited. Management must be sensitive to the need for variety without becoming a custom-oriented producer by accident. Product positioning and a total limitation on the number of items in the line is important. Of particular importance for this type of vendor is being close to the customer so that it can make the critical trade-offs between more items, perhaps at a lower unit volume per item, and not being responsive to a market segment. This approach requires management to walk a tightrope between the value-oriented limited product line and the custom-design supplier.

# What the Hell Is "Market Oriented"?

*This reading explains the concept of market orientation in a new, unconventional way. It helps the reader to understand that market orientation is an interfunctional process with distinct characteristics and much more than "being or getting close to the customer." It stresses data gathering, the nature of the decision-making process, and implementation.*

The air hung heavy in French Lick, Indiana. A tornado watch was in effect that morning, and the sky was black. In a meeting room in one of the local resort hotels, where top management of the Wolverine Controller Company had gathered, the atmosphere matched the weather. Recent results had been poor for the Indianapolis-based producer of flow controllers for process industries like chemicals, paper, and food. Sales were off, but earnings were off even more. Market share was down in all product lines.

As the president called the meeting to order he had fire in his eyes. "The situation can't get much more serious," he proclaimed.

As you all know, over the past couple of years everything has gone to hell in a handbasket. We're in deep trouble, with both domestic and foreign competition preempting us at every turn. The only way to get out of this mess is for us to become customer driven or market oriented. I'm not even sure what that means, but I'm damn sure that we want to be there. I don't even know whether there's a difference between being market driven and customer oriented or customer driven and market oriented or whatever. We've just got to do a hell of a lot better.

"I couldn't agree with you more, Frank," the marketing vice president put in. "I've been saying all along that we've got to be more marketing oriented. The marketing department has to be more involved in everything that goes on because we represent the customer and we've got an integrated view of the company."

This reading was prepared by Benson P. Shapiro.
Copyright © 1988 by the President and Fellows of Harvard College.
Reprinted from *Harvard Business Review* 66, no. 6 (November–December 1988), pp. 119–25.

The CEO scowled at him. "I said *market* oriented, not marketing oriented! It's unclear to me what we get for all the overhead we have in marketing. Those sexy brochures of yours sure haven't been doing the job."

There followed a lively, often acrimonious discussion of what was wrong and what was needed. Each vice president defended his or her function or unit and set out solutions from that particular standpoint. I will draw a curtain over their heedless and profane bickering, but here are paraphrases of their positions:

*Sales VP:* "We need more salespeople. *We're* the ones who are close to the customers. We have to have more call capacity in the sales force so we can provide better service and get new product ideas into the company faster."

*Manufacturing VP:* "We all know that our customers want quality. We need more automated machinery so we can work to closer tolerances and give them better quality. Also, we ought to send our whole manufacturing team to Crosby's Quality College."

*Research and development VP:* "Clearly we could do much better at both making and selling our products. But the fundamental problem is a lack of *new* products. They're the heart of our business. Our technology is getting old because we aren't investing enough in R&D."

*Finance VP:* "The problem isn't not enough resources; it's too many resources misspent. We've got too much overhead. Our variable costs are out of control. Our marketing and sales expenses are unreasonable. And we spend too much on R&D. We don't need more, we need less."

*The general manager of the Electronic Flow Controls Division:* "We aren't organized in the right way—that's the fundamental problem. If each division had its own sales force, we would have better coordination between sales and the other functions."

*Her counterpart in the Pneumatic Controls Division:* "We don't need our own sales forces anywhere near as much as we need our own engineering group so we can develop designs tailored to our customers. As long as we have a central R&D group that owns all the engineers, the divisions can't do their jobs."

As the group adjourned for lunch, the president interjected a last word.

You all put in a lot of time talking past each other and defending your own turf. Some of that's all right. You're supposed to represent your own departments and sell your own perspectives. If you didn't work hard for your own organizations, you wouldn't have lasted long at Wolverine, and you couldn't have made the contributions that you have.

But enough is enough! You aren't just representatives of your own shops. You're the corporate executives at Wolverine and you have to take a more integrated, global view. It's my job to get all of you coordinated, but it's also the job of each of you. I don't have the knowledge, and nothing can replace direct, lateral communication across departments. Let's figure out how to do that after we get some lunch.

## All Right, What Is It?

Leaving the Wolverine bunch to its meal, I want to make a start in dispelling the president's uncertainty. After years of research, I'm convinced that the term *market oriented* represents a set of processes touching on all aspects of the company. It's a great deal more than the cliché "getting close to the customer." Since most companies sell to a variety of customers with varying and even conflicting desires and needs, the goal of getting close to the customer is meaningless. I've also found no meaningful difference between "market driven" and "customer oriented," so I use the phrases interchangeably. In my view, three characteristics make a company market driven.

*Information on all important buying influences permeates every corporate function.* A company can be market oriented only if it completely understands its markets and the people who decide whether to buy its products or services.

In some industries, wholesalers, retailers, and other parts of the distribution channels have a profound influence on the choices customers make. So it's important to understand the trade. In other markets, nonbuying influences specify the product, although they neither purchase it nor use it. These include architects, consulting engineers, and doctors. In still other markets, one person may buy the product and another may use it; family situations are an obvious illustration. In commercial and industrial marketplaces, a professional procurement organization may actually purchase the product, while a manufacturing or operational function uses it.

To be of greatest use, customer information must move beyond the market research, sales, and marketing functions and "permeate every corporate function"—the R&D scientists and engineers, the manufacturing people, and the field-service specialists. When the technologists, for example, get unvarnished feedback on the way customers use the product, they can better develop improvements on the product and the production processes. If, on the other hand, market research or marketing people predigest the information, technologists may miss opportunities.

Of course, regular cross-functional meetings to discuss customer needs and to analyze feedback from buying influences are very important. At least once a year, the top functional officers should spend a full day or more to consider what is happening with key buying influences.

Corporate officers and functions should have access to all useful market research reports. If company staff appends summaries to regular customer surveys, like the Greenwich commercial and investment banking reports or the numerous consumer package-goods industry sales analyses, top officers are more likely to study them. That approach lets top management get the sales and marketing departments' opinions as well as those of less-biased observers.

Some companies that have customer response phones—toll-free 800 numbers that consumers or distributors call to ask questions or make comments—distribute selected cassette recordings of calls to a wide range of executives, line and staff. The cassettes stimulate new ideas for products, product improvements, packaging, and service.

Reports to read and cassettes to hear are useful—but insufficient. High-level executives need to make visits to important customers to see them using their industrial and commercial products, consuming their services, or retailing their consumer goods. When, say, top manufacturing executives understand how a customer factory uses their products, they will have a more solid appreciation of customer needs for quality and close tolerances. Trade show visits provide valuable opportunities for operations and technical people to talk with customers and visit competitors' booths (if allowed by industry custom and show rules).

In my statement on the first characteristic, I referred to "important" buying influences. Because different customers have different needs, a marketer cannot effectively satisfy a wide range of them equally. The most important strategic decision is to choose the important customers. All customers are important, but invariably some are more important to the company than others. Collaboration among the various functions is important when pinpointing the key target accounts and market segments. Then the salespeople know whom to call on first and most often, the people who schedule production runs know who gets favored treatment, and those who make service calls know who rates special attention. If the priorities are not clear in the calm of planning meetings, they certainly won't be when the sales, production scheduling, and service dispatching processes get hectic.

The choice of customers influences the way decisions are made. During a marketing meeting at Wolverine Controller, one senior marketing person said, "Sales and marketing will pick out the customers they want to do business with, and then we'll sit down with the manufacturing and technical people and manage the product mix." Too late! Once you have a certain group of customers, the product mix is pretty much set; you must make the types of products they want. If sales and marketing choose the customers, they have undue power over decisions. Customer selection must involve all operating functions.

*Strategic and tactical decisions are made interfunctionally and interdivisionally.* Functions and divisions will inevitably have conflicting objectives that mirror distinctions in cultures and in modes of operation. The glimpse into the meeting at French Lick demonstrates that. The customer-oriented company possesses mechanisms to get these differences out on the table for candid discussion and to make trade-offs that reconcile the various points of view. Each function and division must have the ear of the others and must be encouraged to lay out its ideas and requirements honestly and vigorously.

To make wise decisions, functions and units must recognize their differences. A big part of being market driven is the way different jurisdictions deal with one another. The marketing department may ask the R&D department to develop a product with a certain specification by a certain date. If R&D thinks the request is unreasonable but doesn't say so, it may develop a phony plan that the company will never achieve. Or R&D may make changes in the specifications and the delivery date without talking to marketing. The result: a missed deadline and an overrun budget. If, on the other hand, the two functions get together, they are in a position to make intelligent technological and marketing trade-offs. They can change a specification or extend a delivery date with the benefit of both points of view.

An alternative to integrated decision making, of course, is to kick the decision upstairs to the CEO or at least the division general manager. But though the higher executives have unbiased views, they lack the close knowledge of the specialists.

An open decision-making process gets the best of both worlds, exploiting the even-handedness of the general manager and the functional skills of the specialists.

*Divisions and functions make well-coordinated decisions and execute them with a sense of commitment.* An open dialogue on strategic and tactical trade-offs is the best way to engender commitment to meet goals. When the implementers also do the planning, the commitment will be strong and clear.

The depth of the biases revealed at the French Lick gathering demonstrates the difficulty of implementing cross-functional programs. But there's nothing wrong with that. In fact, the strength of those biases had a lot to do with Wolverine's past success. If the R&D vice president thought like the financial vice president, she wouldn't be effective in her job. On the other hand, if each function is marching to its own drum, implementation will be weak regardless of the competence and devotion of each function.

Serial communication, when one function passes an idea or request to another routinely without interaction—like tossing a brick with a message tied to it over the wall—can't build the commitment needed in the customer-driven company. Successful new products don't, for example, emerge out of a process in which marketing sends a set of specifications to R&D, which sends finished blueprints and designs to manufacturing. But joint opportunity analysis, in which functional and divisional people share ideas and discuss alternative solutions and approaches, leverages the different strengths of each party. Powerful internal connections make communication clear, coordination strong, and commitment high.

Poor coordination leads to misapplication of resources and failure to make the most of market opportunities. At one point in the meeting at French Lick, the vice president for human resources spoke up in this fashion:

> Remember how impressed everyone was in 86 with the new pulp-bleaching control we developed? Not just us, but the whole industry—especially with our fast response rate. Even though the technology was the best, the product flopped. Why? Because the industry changed its process so that the response rate was less important than the ability to handle tough operating conditions and higher temperatures and pressures. Plus we couldn't manufacture to the tight tolerances the industry needed. We wasted a lot of talent on the wrong problem.

Probably the salespeople, and perhaps the technical service people, knew about the evolving customer needs. By working together, manufacturing and R&D could have designed a manufacturable product. But the company lacked the coordination that a focused market orientation stimulates.

## Action at Wolverine

Just about every company thinks of itself as market oriented. It's confident it has the strength to compete with the wolf pack, but in reality it's often weak and tends to follow the shepherd. In marketing efforts, businesses are particularly vulnerable to this delusion. Let's return to French Lick to hear of such a sheep in wolf's clothing.

"Look at Mutton Machinery," the vice president of manufacturing was saying.

They've done worse than we have. And their ads and brochures brag about them being customer oriented! At the trade show last year, they had a huge booth with the theme "The Customer Is King." They had a sales contest that sent a salesperson and customer to tour the major castles of Europe.

The sales vice president piped up.

They should send their salespeople for technical training, not to look at castles. We interviewed two of their better people, and they didn't measure up technically. The glitzy trade show stuff and the sexy contest don't make them customer oriented.

No, slogans and glossy programs don't give a company a market orientation. It takes a philosophy and a culture that go deep in the organization. Let's take a look at Wolverine's approach.

It's unlikely that any company ever became market oriented with a bottom-up approach; to make it happen, you need the commitment and power of those at the top. In gathering everybody who mattered at French Lick, Wolverine was taking the right step at the start. And from what we have heard, clearly they were not sugar-coating their concerns.

By the end of the first day, the executives had decided that they knew too little about their own industry, particularly customers and competitors. After a mostly social dinner meeting and a good night's sleep, they began at breakfast on Day 2 to develop a plan to learn more. They listed 20 major customers they wanted to understand better. They designated each of the 10 executives at the meeting (CEO, 6 functional heads, and 3 division general managers) to visit the customers in pairs in the next two months; the sales force would coordinate the visits. All 10 agreed to attend the next big trade show.

They assigned the marketing vice president to prepare dossiers on the 20 customers plus another 10, as well as prospects selected by the group. Besides data on the customer or prospect, each dossier was to include an examination of Wolverine's relationship with it.

Finally, the group singled out seven competitors for close scrutiny. The marketing vice president agreed to gather market data on them. The R&D vice president committed herself to drawing up technical reviews of them, and the financial vice president was to prepare analyses of financial performance. The seven remaining executives each agreed to analyze the relative strengths and weaknesses of one competitor.

Spurred by the president, the group concluded on Day 2 that barriers had arisen among Wolverine's functional departments. Each was on its own little island. The human resources vice president took on the responsibility of scrutinizing cross-functional communication and identifying ways to improve it.

Back at headquarters in Indianapolis, the top brass did another smart thing: It involved all functional leadership so that line as well as staff chieftains would contribute to the effort. Top management quickly pinpointed the management information system as a major point of leverage for shaping a more integrated company view. Therefore, the president invited the MIS director to join the team.

Top management also decided that the bonus plan encouraged each function to pursue its own objectives instead of corporatewide goals. So the controller teamed up with the human resources vice president to devise a better plan, which won the approval of top management.

As a new interest in communication and cooperation developed, the president perceived the need to make changes in structure and process. Chief among these were the establishment of a process engineering department to help production and R&D move new products from design into manufacturing and the redesign of managerial reports to emphasize the total company perspective.

The management group, more sensitive now to the ways people deal with each other, awoke to the power of informal social systems. To make the salespeople more accessible to headquarters staff, the sales office at a nearby location moved to headquarters (over the objections of the vice president of sales). The effort to promote interfunctional teamwork even extended to the restructuring of the bowling league. Wolverine had divided its teams by function or division. Now, however, each team had members from various functions. Some old-timers snorted that that was taking the new market orientation too far. But in a conversation during a bowling league party, the head of technical field service and a customer-service manager came up with an idea for a program to improve customer responsiveness. Then even the skeptics began to understand.

The analyses of customers and competitors identified an important market opportunity for Wolverine. The management group diverted resources to it, and under the direction of the Pneumatic Controls Division general manager, a multifunctional task force launched an effort to exploit it. Top management viewed this undertaking as a laboratory for the development of new approaches and as a showcase to demonstrate the company's new philosophy and culture. Headquarters maintained an intense interest in the project.

As the project gained momentum, support for the underlying philosophy grew. Gradually, the tone of interfunctional relationships changed. People evinced more trust in each other and were much more willing to admit responsibility for mistakes and to expose shortcomings.

Unfortunately, some people found it difficult to change. The sales vice president resisted the idea that a big part of his job was bringing customers and data about them into the company as well as encouraging all functions to deal with customers. He became irate when the vice president of manufacturing worked directly with several major customers, and he told the president that he wouldn't stand for other people dealing with *his* customers. His colleagues couldn't alter his attitude, so the president replaced him.

Wolverine's sales and earnings slowly began to improve. The market price of its stock edged upward. Internally, decision making became more integrative. Some early victories helped build momentum. Implementation improved through cooperation very low in the ranks, where most of the real work was done.

# Imitate Larry Bird

A year after Wolverine's first meeting in the French Lick hotel, the management group gathered there again. A new sales vice president was present, and the newly promoted MIS vice president/controller was also there.

This time the executives focused on two concerns. The first was how to handle the inordinate demands on the company resulting from the new push to satisfy important customers. The second was how to maintain Wolverine's momentum toward achieving a market orientation.

Attacking the first item, the group agreed to set major customer priorities. At hand was the information gathered during the year via industry analysis and executives' visits to top accounts. Available to the executives also were several frameworks for analysis.[1] Some accounts fit together in unexpected ways. In some situations, a series of accounts used similar products similarly. In others, the accounts competed for Wolverine's resources.

It took several meetings to set priorities on customers. The hardest part was resolving a dispute over whether to raise prices drastically on the custom products made for the third largest account. Wolverine was losing money on these. "Maybe not all business is good business," the R&D vice president suggested. That notion was pretty hard for the team to accept. But the CEO pushed hard for a decision. Ultimately, the group agreed to drop the account if it did not accede to price increases within the next six to eight months.

On the second matter, the management group decided it needed a way to measure the company's progress. The approach, everybody understood, had to be grounded in unrelieved emphasis on information gathering, on interfunctional decision making, and on a vigorous sense of commitment throughout the organization. They recognized how easy it is to get complacent and lose detachment when examining one's own performance. Nevertheless, the executives drew up a checklist of customer-focused questions for the organization to ask itself (see table below).

---

**Self-Examination Checklist**

| 1. Are we easy to do business with? | 2. Do we keep our promises? |
| --- | --- |
| Easy to contact? | On product performance? |
| Fast to provide information? | Delivery? |
| Easy to order from? | Installation? |
| Make reasonable promises? | Training? |
|  | Service? |

---

[1]They used the account profitability matrix described by Benson P. Shapiro, V. Kasturi Rangan, Rowland T. Moriarty, and Elliot B. Ross in "Manage Customers for Profits (Not Just Sales)," *Harvard Business Review,* September–October 1987, p. 101.

**3. Do we meet the standards we set?**
  Specifics?
  General tone?
  Do we even know the standards?
**4. Are we responsive?**
  Do we listen?
  Do we follow up?
  Do we ask "why not?" instead of "why?"
  Do we treat customers as individual
    companies and individual people?

**5. Do we work together?**
  Share blame?
  Share information?
  Make joint decisions?
  Provide satisfaction?

---

Two years after the company changed its direction, a major customer asked the president about his impressions of Wolverine's efforts to become market oriented. Here is his response:

It's proved to be harder than I had imagined. I had to really drive people to think about customers and the corporation as a whole, not just what's good for their own departments. It's also proved to be more worthwhile. We have a different tone in our outlook and a different way of dealing with each other.

We use all kinds of customer data and bring it into all functions. We do much more interfunctional decision making. The hardest part of all was account selection, and that really paid off for us. It also had the most impact. Our implementation has improved through what we call the three Cs, communication, coordination, and commitment. We're getting smooth, but we sure aren't flawless yet.

Last night I watched the Pacers play the Boston Celtics on TV. The Celtics won. Sure they've got more talent, but the real edge the Celtics have is their teamwork. At one point in the game, the Indiana team got impatient with each other. They seemed to forget that the Celtics were the competition.

That's the way we used to be too—each department competing with each other. A few years ago we had a meeting down at French Lick where everything came to a head, and I was feeling pretty desperate. There's a real irony here because French Lick is the hometown of Larry Bird.

When I think about the Celtics and Bird, what working together means becomes clear. If each Wolverine manager only helps his or her department do its job well, we're going to lose. Back when the company was small, products were simple, competition was unsophisticated, and customers were less demanding, we could afford to work separately. But now, our individual best isn't good enough; we've got to work as a unit. Bird is the epitome. He subverts his own interest and ego for the sake of the team. That's what I want to see at Wolverine.

# Staple Yourself to an Order

*It's fashionable today to talk of becoming "customer oriented." But no matter how many companies flatten their organizations or empower frontline workers, the simple truth is that every customer's experience is determined by the order management cycle (OMC): the 10 steps, from planning to postsales service, that define a company's business system. The authors "stapled" themselves to an order in the 18 companies they studied, literally following it through each step of the OMC. Based on this practical, hands-on approach, they point out potential gaps throughout the order management cycle. The authors offer a process for streamlining order-cycle management.*

It's fashionable today to talk of becoming "customer oriented." Or to focus on that moment of truth when customers experience the actual transaction that determines whether or not they are completely satisfied. Or to empower frontline workers so they can delight the customer with their initiative and spunk.

None of this advice, however, focuses on the real way to harness the customer's interests in the operation of a company. The simple truth is that every customer's experience is determined by a company's *order management cycle* (OMC): the 10 steps, from planning to postsales service, that define a company's business system. The order management cycle offers managers the opportunity to look at their company through a customer's eyes, to see and experience transactions the way customers do. Managers who track each step of the OMC work their way through the company from the customer's angle rather than their own.

In the course of the order management cycle, every time the order is handled, the customer is handled. Every time the order sits unattended, the customer sits unattended. Paradoxically, the best way to be customer oriented is to go beyond cus-

---

This reading was prepared by Benson P. Shapiro, V. Kasturi Rangan, and John J. Sviokla.
Copyright © 1992 by the President and Fellows of Harvard College.
Reprinted from *Harvard Business Review,* July–August 1992, pp. 113–22.

tomers and products to the order; the moment of truth occurs at every step of the OMC, and every employee in the company who affects the OMC is the equivalent of a frontline worker. Ultimately, it is the order that connects the customer to the company in a systematic and companywide fashion.

Moreover, focusing on the OMC offers managers the greatest opportunity to improve overall operations and create new competitive advantages. Managers can establish and achieve aggressive goals—such as "improve customer fill rate from 80 to 98 percent," "reach 99 percent billing accuracy," or "cut order cycle time by 25 percent"—and force otherwise parochial teams to look at the entire order management cycle to discover how various changes affect customers. When the OMC substitutes for narrow functional interests, customer responsiveness becomes the overriding goal of the entire organization, and conflicts give way to systemic solutions. The best way for managers to learn this lesson and pass it on to their whole work force is, in effect, to staple themselves to an order. They can then track an order as it moves through the OMC, always aware that the order is simply a surrogate for the customer.

## A Realistic Walk Through the OMC

The typical OMC includes 10 activities that sometimes overlap or interact (see "The Order Management Cycle: Inside the Black Box"). While OMCs vary from industry to industry and are different for products and services, almost every business, from the corner ice cream stand to the global computer company, has these same steps. In the following discussion, a number of important lessons will emerge that explain both the customer's experience with a company and that company's ability to achieve ambitious cost and quality goals. For example, as we walk an order through the OMC, note the number of times that the order or information about it physically moves horizontally from one functional department to another. Since most companies are organized along vertical functional lines, every time an order moves horizontally from one department to another it runs the risk of falling between the cracks.

In addition to these horizontal gaps, a second lesson to be learned from tracking the OMC is the likelihood of vertical gaps in knowledge. In field visits to 18 different companies in vastly different industries, we invariably found a top marketing or administrative executive who would offer a simple, truncated—and inaccurate—description of the order flow. The people at the top couldn't see the details of their OMC; the people deep within the organization saw only their own individual details. And when an order moved across departmental boundaries, from one function to another, it faded from sight; no one was responsible for it or the customer.

A third lesson concerns the importance of order selection and prioritization. In fact, not all orders are created equal; some are simply better for the business than others. The best orders come from customers who are long-term, fit the company's capabilities, and offer healthy profits. These customers fall into the company's "sweet spot," a convergence of great customer need, high customer value, and good

fit with what the company can offer. But in most companies, no one does order selection or prioritization. The sales force chooses the customers, and customer service representatives or production schedulers establish the priorities. In these cases,
the OMC effectively goes unmanaged.

Finally, the fourth lesson we offer involves cost estimation and pricing. Pricing is the mediator between customer needs and company capabilities and a critical part of the OMC. But most companies don't understand the opportunity for or impact of order-based pricing. Pricing at the individual order level depends on: understanding the customer value generated by each order, evaluating the cost of filling each order, and instituting a system that enables the company to price each order based on its value and cost. While order-based pricing is difficult work that requires meticulous thinking and deliberate execution, the potential for greater profits is worth the effort. And by gaining control of their OMCs, managers can practice order-based pricing.

When we started our investigation of the order management cycle, we recognized first that the OMC, in fact, begins long before there is an order or a customer. What happens in the first step, *order planning,* already shows how and why bad customer service and fragmented operations can cripple a company: the people farthest from the customer make crucial decisions and open up deep disagreements between interdependent functions right from the start. The contention and internal gaming that we saw in order planning is an effective early warning sign of the systemwide disagreements that plague most order management cycles.

For example, people close to the customer, either in the sales force or a marketing group at company headquarters, develop a sales forecast. At the same time, a group in the operations or manufacturing function drafts a capacity plan that specifies how much money will be spent, how many people hired, and how much inventory created. And already these functional departments are at war. Lamented one production planner, "The salespeople and their forecasting 'experts' are so optimistic and so worried about late deliveries that they pad their forecasts. We have to recalculate their plans so we don't get sucked into their euphoria." From their side, marketing people counter distrust with equal distrust: "Production won't change anything, anyhow, anywhere." Ultimately, the people deepest in the organization and farthest from the customer—production planners—often develop the final forecast used to hire workers and build inventory.

The next step in the OMC is *order generation,* a stage that usually produces a gap between order generation, order planning, and later steps in the cycle. In our research, we saw orders generated in a number of ways. The sales force knocks on doors or makes cold calls. The company places advertisements that draw customers into distribution centers or retailers where they actually place an order. Or, increasingly, companies turn to direct marketing. But regardless of the specific marketing approach, the result is almost always the same: the sales and marketing functions worry about order generation, and the other functions get out of the way. Little coordination takes place across functional boundaries.

At the third step, *cost estimation and pricing,* battles erupt between engineers who do the estimating, accountants who calculate costs, a headquarters group that oversees pricing, and the field sales force that actually develops a price. Each group questions the judgment, competence, and goals of the others. Working through the organizational barriers takes time. Meanwhile, of course, the customer waits for the bid or quote, unattended.

*Order receipt and entry* comes next. It typically takes place in a neglected department called customer service, order entry, the inside sales desk, or customer liaison. Customer service representatives are usually either very experienced, long-term employees or totally inexperienced trainees. But regardless of their experience, customer service reps are, in fact, in daily contact with customers. At the same time, these employees have little clout in the organization and no executive-level visibility in either direction. That means customer service representatives don't know what is going on at the top of the company, including its basic strategy. And top management doesn't know much about what its customer service department—the function closest to customers—is doing.

This unlinked group of customer service reps are also often responsible for the fifth step in the OMC: *order selection and prioritization,* the process of choosing which orders to accept and which to decline. Of course, the more carefully companies think through order selection and link it to their general business strategy, the more money they stand to make, regardless of physical production capacity. In addition, companies can make important gains by the way they handle order prioritization—that is, how they decide which orders receive faster, more complete attention. However, these decisions are usually made not by top executives who articulate corporate strategy but by customer service representatives who have no idea what the strategy is. While customer service reps decide which order gets filled when, they often determine which order gets lost in limbo.

At the sixth step, *scheduling,* when the order gets slotted into an actual production or operational sequence, some of the fiercest fights erupt. Here sales, marketing, or customer service usually face off with operations or production staff. The different functional departments have conflicting goals, compensation systems, and organizational imperatives: production people seek to minimize equipment changeovers, while marketing and customer service reps argue for special service for special customers. And if the operations staff schedule orders unilaterally, both customers and their reps are completely excluded from the process. Communication between the functions is often strained at best, with customer service reporting to sales and physically separated from production scheduling, which reports to manufacturing or operations. Once again, the result is interdepartmental warfare.

Next comes *fulfillment*—the actual provision of the product or service. While the details vary from industry to industry, in almost every company this step has become increasingly complex. Sometimes, for example, order fulfillment involves multiple functions and locations: different parts of an order may be created in different manufacturing facilities and merged at yet another site, or orders may be manufactured in one location, inventoried in a second, and installed in a third. In some businesses, fulfillment includes third-party vendors. In service operations, it can mean sending individuals with different talents to the customer's site. The more complicated the assembly activity, the more coordination must take place across the organization. And the more coordination required across the organization, the greater the chance for a physical gap. The order is dropped and so is the customer. The order ends up on the floor, while different departments argue over whose fault it is and whose job it is to pick it up.

After the order has been delivered, *billing* is typically handled by people from finance who view their job as getting the bill out efficiently and making the collection quickly. In other words, the billing function is designed to serve the needs and interests of the company, not the customer. In our research, we often saw customers who could not understand a bill they had received or thought it was inaccurate. Usually the bill wasn't inaccurate, but it had been put together in a way more convenient for the billing department than for the customer. In one case, a customer acknowledged that the company provided superior service but found the billing operation a source of constant aggravation. The problem: billing insisted on sending an invoice with prices on it. But because these shipments went to subcontractors, the customer didn't want the actual prices to show. The finance function's response: How we do our invoices is none of the customer's business. Yet such a response is clearly self-serving and creates one more gap—and possibly a loss to the company—in the cycle.

In some businesses, *returns and claims* are an important part of the OMC because of their impact on administrative costs, scrap and transportation expenses, and customer relations. In the ongoing relationship with the customer, this ninth step can produce some of the most heated disagreements; every interaction becomes a zero-sum game that either the company or the customer wins. To compound the problem, most companies design their OMCs for one-way merchandise flow: outbound to the customer. That means returns and claims must flow upstream, against the current, creating logistical messes and transactional snarls—and extremely dissatisfied customers.

The last step, *postsales service,* now plays an increasingly important role in all elements of a company's profit equation: customer value, price, and cost. Depending on the specifics of the business, it can include such elements as physical installation of a product, repair and maintenance, customer training, equipment upgrading, and disposal. At this final step in the OMC, service representatives can truly get inside the customer's organization; because of the information conveyed and intimacy involved, postsales service can affect customer satisfaction and company profitability for years. But in most companies, the postsales service people are not linked to any marketing operation, internal product-development effort, or quality assurance team.

At company after company, we traced the progress of individual orders as they traveled the OMC, beginning at one end of the process where orders entered, concluding at the other end where postsales service followed up. What we witnessed was frustration, missed opportunities, dissatisfied customers, and underperforming companies. Ultimately, four problems emerged, which are tied to the four lessons discussed earlier.

- Most companies never view the OMC as a whole system. People in sales think that someone in production scheduling understands the entire system; people in production scheduling think customer service reps do. No one really does, and everyone can only give a partial description.

- Each step in the OMC requires a bewildering mix of overlapping functional responsibilities. As "Why Orders Fall Through the Cracks" on the next page illustrates, each step is considered the primary responsibility of a specific department, and no step is the sole responsibility of any department. But given the fact that responsibilities do overlap, many disasters occur.

# Why Orders Fall Through the Cracks

| Customer | Steps in the OMC | Sales | Marketing | Customer service | Engineering | Purchasing | Finance | Operations | Logistics | Top Management |
|---|---|---|---|---|---|---|---|---|---|---|
| Plans to buy | 1. Order planning | Supporting | **Leading** | Supporting | Supporting | Supporting | Supporting | **Leading** | Supporting | Coordinates |
| Gets sales pitch | 2. Order generation | **Leading** | Supporting | Supporting | | | | | | Sometimes participates |
| Negotiates | 3. Cost estimation and pricing | Supporting | **Leading** | Supporting | Supporting | Supporting | Supporting | Supporting | Supporting | Sometimes participates |
| Orders | 4. Order receipt and entry | Supporting | Supporting | **Leading** | Supporting | | | Supporting | Supporting | Ignores this step |
| Waits | 5. Order selection and prioritization | Supporting | **Leading** | Supporting | | | Supporting | Supporting | Supporting | Sometimes participates |
| Waits | 6. Scheduling | | Supporting | Supporting | | Supporting | | **Leading** | Supporting | Ignores this step |
| Waits | 7. Fulfillment | Supporting | | Supporting | | Supporting | | **Leading** | Supporting | Ignores this step |
| Pays | 8. Billing | | | Supporting | | | **Leading** | | Supporting | Ignores this step |
| Negotiates | 9. Returns and claims | **Leading** | Supporting | Supporting | Supporting | | Supporting | Supporting | Supporting | Sometimes participates |
| Complains | 10. Postsales service | Supporting | | **Leading** | Supporting | | | **Leading** | Supporting | Ignores this step |

Legend: ■ Leading role  ▨ Supporting role

The OMC is everybody's job, but overlapping responsibilities — and lack of management involvement — often lead to confusion, delays, and customer complaints.

- To top management, the details of the OMC are invisible. Senior executives at all but the smallest operating units simply don't understand the intricacy of the OMC. And people with the most crucial information, such as customer service reps, are at the bottom of the organization and can't communicate with the top.

- The customer remains as remote from the OMC as top management. During the process, the customer's primary activities are to negotiate price, place the order, wait, accept delivery, complain, and pay. In the middle of the OMC, they are out of the picture completely.

Of course, today top managers know that customer service and customer satisfaction are critical to a company's success. In one company after another, managers pursue the same solutions to problems that crop up with customers. They try to flatten the organization to bring themselves and nonmarketing people into direct contact with customers. But while flattening the organization is a fine idea, it's not going to solve the real problem. No matter how flat an organization gets, no matter how many different functions interact with customers face to face—or phone to phone—what the customer wants is something else. Customers want their orders handled quickly, accurately, and cost-effectively, not more people to talk to.

Here's what top managers *don't* do: they don't travel horizontally through their own vertical organization. They don't consider the order management cycle as the system that ties together the entire customer experience and that can provide true customer perspective. Yet all 10 steps are closely tied to customer satisfaction. Because the OMC is an intricate network that almost guarantees problems, top management's job is to understand the system so thoroughly it can anticipate those problems before they occur. That means managers must walk up and down and from side to side, every step of the way.

## What's Wrong with Their OMCs?

Consider two brief case studies. One is taken from a specialty materials producer, the other from a custom capital equipment company, but both exemplify the three most common and debilitating problems that plague OMCs.

At the specialty materials company, when customers complained about order cycle time, top managers responded by increasing the work-in-process inventory. As a result, the company could meet customer specifications from semifinished goods rather than starting from scratch. At the custom capital equipment company, when customers complained about slow deliveries, this company increased its manufacturing capacity. As a result, the company always had enough capacity to expedite any order.

Both solutions pleased customers. In addition, the first solution pleased that company's marketers and the second solution pleased that company's operations department. But neither solution pleased top management because, even after several quarters, neither produced economic returns to justify the investments. In fact, both solutions only made matters worse. At the specialty materials company, marketing staff took advantage of the increased work-in-process inventory to take orders and make sales that used up that inventory but didn't generate profits. And at the capital equipment company, manufacturing staff relied on the increased capacity to meet marketing demands but allowed productivity to slide.

The next step both companies took was predictable. Top management, frustrated by the failure of its solution and concerned over continuing squabbles between departments, called on managers across the organization to rally around "making superior profits by providing top quality products and excellent service." Top management translated *top quality* and *excellent service* into catchy slogans and posters that decorated office cubicles and factory walls. It etched the "superior profit" objective into the operating budgets of higher level managers. And it formed interfunctional teams so managers could practice participative decision making in pursuit of the new, companywide goal.

At the specialty materials company, a star sales manager who had been promoted to general manager set up an interfunctional executive committee to assess quarterly revenue and profit goals. We attended one meeting of this new committee. As the general manager sat down at the head of the table to begin the meeting, he expressed concern that the division was about to miss its revenue and profit goals for the second consecutive quarter. Committee members responded by pointing at other departments or making excuses. The vice president of sales produced elaborate graphs to demonstrate that the problem was not caused by insufficient order generation. The vice president of operations produced detailed worksheets showing that many orders had come in too late in the quarter to be completed on time.

However, given their new joint responsibility for profits, both sides agreed to put aside such arguments and focus on "how to make the quarter." All agreed to ship some customer orders in advance of their due dates because those items could readily be finished from available work-in-process inventory. While this solution would delay some long cycle-time orders, the committee decided to sacrifice these orders for the moment and take them up early in the next quarter. And immediately after the meeting, committee members started executing the plan: salespeople called their customers and cajoled them to accept early delivery; manufacturing staff rescheduled the shop floor.

Because of its small size, the custom capital equipment producer didn't need such a formal mechanism for coordinating activities. The CEO simply inserted himself into the daily workings of all functional areas and insisted on hearing all customer complaints immediately. While visiting this company, we heard a customer service representative talking on the telephone to a customer who had just been told her order would be late. The customer objected and asked for an explanation. After much hemming and hawing, the rep explained that her order had been "reallocated" to another customer who needed the product more. The customer on the phone, who purchased products from the company in a relatively large volume, demanded to speak to the CEO and, under the new policy, was connected right away. When the CEO heard this important customer's complaint, he instantly plugged the order back in at the top of the priority list.

In spite of such heroic efforts at both companies, however, customer service continued to slump, and financial results did not improve. At the materials company, customers who expected later delivery of their orders received them unexpectedly early, while those who needed them early got them late. At the capital equipment company, small customers who didn't know the CEO personally or didn't understand the route to him found their orders continuously bumped. At both companies, there was no real progress toward genuine customer satisfaction, improved service, or enhanced profits. Neither company had come to terms with the three critical problems embedded in their order management cycles: horizontal and vertical gaps, poor prioritization of orders, and inaccurate cost estimation and pricing.

The specialty materials company suffered from a fundamental horizontal gap: the marketing and manufacturing departments didn't share the same priorities for customer value, order selection, and order urgency. The real solution to this problem was to encourage and reinforce an understanding between these two critical OMC elements; both the marketing and manufacturing departments needed to address how their order management cycle generated customer value and where they were dropping customer orders in the horizontal handoff. Instead, the company introduced an expensive buffer to cover over the gap between the functions—a semifinished inventory—and, when that failed, it decided to sacrifice real customer service to serve its own short-term financial needs. The immediate solution, simply shipping orders based on the amount of time it would take to complete them, merely pushed the problem from one quarter to the next without addressing the system failure. When the next quarter rolls around, top management will still have to contend with horizontal gaps, a lack of order selection and prioritization, and the inability of their order flow to generate value for the customer.

The same underlying systemic problems existed at the custom capital equipment producer. However, because of the small size of the organization, this company took a simple, politically expedient solution—let the CEO decide—and superimposed it on an expensive financial solution—add manufacturing capacity. If the company suffered from vertical gaps before, where people down in the trenches failed to understand the strategy developed up in the executive suite, the CEO's intervention in customer orders only made the gaps worse. The CEO's involvement didn't address the systemic problems; he merely substituted his judgment and knowledge for that of lower-level employees. The detrimental effects on employee morale more than offset any immediate gains in customer appreciation. Had the CEO invested his energy in helping employees understand how each order creates customer value, has specific costs attached, and involves a certain amount of processing time—and communicated the importance of the whole OMC—he would have generated more customer satisfaction, greater employee morale, and higher profitability without adding expensive manufacturing capacity.

# How Can I Fix My OMC?

It takes hard work to improve a company's order management cycle. Most successful efforts involve three basic elements: analysis, system focus, and political strategy. Each plays a different role in overall upgrading of the OMC and requires different implementation techniques, so let's look at each in turn.

**1. Analysis: Draw Your OMC—and Chart the Gaps.**   In the course of our research, we visited a number of companies that were actively engaged in reviewing their OMCs with an eye to improvement. But only two companies had made progress; significantly, both had begun by trying to understand the whole OMC from start to finish. And they hadn't created a diagram on a single sheet of paper or a standard report format. Rather, one of these companies had built war rooms: two adjacent, bunkerlike offices. The walls of both rooms were made of poster board coated with color-coded sheets of paper and knitting yarn that graphically charted the order flow from the first step to the last, highlighting problems, opportunities, and potential action steps. With its multiple and overlapping sheets of paper, the entire chart easily exceeded 200 feet in length.

This visual tool made it possible for different people from different functions and levels in the organization to accept the OMC as a tangible entity. Everyone could discuss the order flow with a clear and shared picture in front of them. And by representing the OMC as a visible, tangible system, the chart guaranteed that disagreements over problems would focus on facts rather than on opinions about how the OMC worked.

A second type of successful analysis requires companies to look at the OMC from the customer's point of view. For example, at one company, the in-house measurement system found that 98 percent of all orders went out on time. But another detailed survey noted that only 50 percent of customers said they were satisfied with deliveries. The company was unable to reconcile the two reports until managers looked at the issue from the customer's angle and compared it with their own point of view. For instance, the customer survey measured the date when the customer actually received the order, but the company's internal system was based on the date when it shipped the order. If an order consisted of 100 items, and the company correctly shipped 99 of the items, the internal report recorded a 99 percent perfect shipment. But the customer, who needed all 100 items before work could begin, recorded the order as a complete failure. And if the order contained an incorrectly shipped item, the company did not register the mistake at all. Of course, the customer did because an incorrect item could easily interfere with his or her ability to get on with the job. Once this company recognized the difference between its perspective and the customer's, it switched to the customer's view as the basis for its tracking system.

Finally, successful companies have explicitly stated that their goals are satisfied customers, higher profits, and sustainable competitive advantage without compromising any of them. One company realized that, while it currently relied on extensive competitive bidding, it would have to start tracking its own win-loss percentages by type of customer, geography, type of order, and other relevant data to meet its larger goals. Managers could then use such data to analyze the relationship between the company's prices and its competitors as well as between volume and price. That, in turn, could translate into better price and market share and less effort wasted on unattractive or unattainable business.

**2. System Focus: Put the Pieces Together, Move across Boundaries.**    Analyzing the order management cycle should underline this fundamental point: the OMC is a system, and executives must manage it as a system. The goal, of course, is to fit together the horizontal pieces into a unified, harmonious whole. To encourage such alignment, managers have a number of tools at their disposal. For example, through the company compensation system, managers can introduce joint reward plans that encourage employees to take a systemwide view of company performance. Or in designing performance measurements, managers can include numbers that reflect performance across boundaries or throughout the system.

Perhaps the most powerful tool managers can use is interfunctional or interdepartmental investments in projects. These expenditures not only bring different units closer together but can also result in substantial financial returns to the company. Of course, in most companies, project champions drive the decisions in the capital budgeting process. Most project champions embrace projects in their own departments or functions. Projects that cross boundaries tend to be orphans because they lack champions; even with champions, such projects require difficult, time-consuming negotiations and are often deferred or fail outright. But precisely for this reason, projects that cross department boundaries can create an integrated atmosphere. When the CEO or chief operating officer personally back investments, the whole organization gets the message that these investments reflect a new perspective. Significantly, interdepartmental projects, usually underfunded for years, often deliver the greatest returns to the company in terms of real improvements and financial results.

A company's information technology system can also play an important role. Computer technology is a crucial tool for integrating many steps of the order management cycle. Direct computer links with customers and integrated internal computer systems, for example, typically result in lower costs and better analysis. And while order processing was one of the earliest activities to be computerized in many companies, it's now time to update and reengineer such systems. When managers walk through the entire OMC, they have the opportunity to ask whether each step can be improved with a computer or, perhaps, eliminated altogether given new technology and processes. With more reliable computer systems, for instance, is manual backup still required? Or can data be captured at the source to avoid repeat entry and inevitable clerical errors?

All of these human resource, management, and information technology tools reinforce the idea, represented by the OMC, that the basic work of the company takes place across boundaries. And because obsolete or unnecessary tasks hinder coordination, all pieces of the system must fit together to meet customer needs in a seamless fashion.

**3.  Political Strategy: Staple Yourself to an Order.**   Given that the order management cycle is critical to so many daily operating decisions, it is often at the center of all political maneuverings in a company. Realistically, OMC politics will never go away; working horizontally in a vertical organization is always difficult at best. In our research, we saw hardnosed CEOs and high-ranking divisional general managers forced to admit defeat when confronted with stonewalling functional staffs. We watched young, analytically focused managers with innovative ideas face lack of interest, distrust, and selfishness—and fail miserably. The only people who can succeed at interdepartmental management are usually hardened veterans who understand company politics and can cash in favors. But even they won't succeed without visible support from the top.

One way to improve the situation in any company is to close the loop between the service providers and the strategy setters or, in other words, to tie the company closer together through the order management cycle. Managers should try what we did in our research: we "stapled" ourselves to an order and literally followed it through each step of the OMC. When managers do this, descending from the executive heights into the organization's lower depths, they come into contact with critical people like customer service reps and production schedulers. Reps, schedulers, order processors, shipping clerks, and many others are the ones who know fine-grained information about customer needs. For example, customers might want the product delivered in a drum rather than a bag, or prefer plastic wrapping to Styrofoam.

For most executives in most companies, there is simply no organizational setup for listening and responding to people at all levels. The McDonald's policy of having executives regularly work behind the counter is a worthwhile example of creating such an opportunity. Requiring top managers to work as cashiers and cooks sends a message about the company's values to all staff and enables executives to experience the OMC firsthand.

However, this idea can degenerate into an empty gesture or just another management fad. Take, for example, CEO visits to customers that become official state visits in which corporate heads discuss company relationships at a level of abstraction that has little to do with reality. In most businesses, managers can learn more from salespeople, customer service representatives, production schedulers, and shippers than from a customer's CEO.

All too often, managers who try to focus on internal conflicts directly without charting the OMC find themselves thwarted by politics and recalcitrant employees. But the wall charts and interdepartmental measurements engendered by focusing on the OMC can create an overall vision that transcends vertical politics. The customer is not involved in organizational infighting, and when a company takes on the customer's perspective, politics must take a different and more productive turn.

# What Happens After I Fix My OMC?

When companies improve their order management cycles, there are three important benefits. First and foremost, they will experience improved customer satisfaction. Companies will fill orders faster, become more accurate, and generally keep their promises to customers. A well-run OMC has a huge impact on customers: Most OMCs perform worst when demand is greatest, which means that the largest number of customers experience service at its poorest quality. Fixing the OMC reverses that downward trend.

Second, interdepartmental problems will recede. When the OMC is not working well, it both reflects and causes monumental internal strife in a company. People in each department feel they are working hard to achieve their goals; they feel let down by other functions when customer service or financial performance fails to measure up. In the absence of unifying efforts and signs of improvement, the infighting can take on a life of its own and become even more divisive than the operating problems that started the battle. A systemic view helps everyone understand that all departments are interdependent.

Finally, companies will improve their financial performance. We saw companies lose sales, waste labor, and fumble investments because of poor order management cycles. Typically, companies throw money at their problems, building excess capacity, adding inventory, or increasing the body count, all of which are expensive and none of which solve the real problem. The simple fact is that when an OMC is poorly managed, greater sales, lower costs, higher prices, and smaller investments all seem impossible. But when the order management cycle works efficiently, a company can achieve these goals—and more.

# High-Tech Marketing: Concepts, Continuity, and Change

*The world of high technology is characterized by unusually high levels of market and technological uncertainty; this reading offers a thorough overview of how that uncertainty affects marketing strategies and tactics. The authors' pragmatic discussion focuses on the distinguishing characteristics of high-tech marketing, the issues that arise from those differences, and how managers can adapt fundamental marketing techniques to address those issues.*

Since the late 1970s, interest in "high-tech" marketing has skyrocketed. An industry of market research companies like International Data Corporation, Dataquest, and the Gartner Group has expanded rapidly to provide competitive intelligence and market forecasts for companies that buy and sell technology-intensive products. Regis McKenna, an eminent high-technology marketing consultant, and William Davidow, an Intel executive turned venture capitalist, have written best-selling books that address high-tech marketing issues. The academic community has also been caught up in the enthusiasm; professors have written textbooks and developed courses about high-tech marketing. Several universities now offer a high-tech MBA degree.

Articles about the marketing victories and defeats of companies in the computer, telecommunications, and biotechnology industries have flooded the business press. A generation of high-tech entrepreneurs with a flair for marketing has captured the imagination of the U.S. business community. People like Steve Jobs, founder of Apple Computer and NeXt, Bill Gates of Microsoft, and H. Ross Perot, founder of Electronic Data Systems (EDS), have achieved the celebrity status of rock stars and folk heroes. *High tech* has become synonymous with high excitement.

There has been plenty of hoopla about the fact that high-tech marketing is not the same animal as other product or service marketing. It would be easy to fill a

This reading was prepared by Rowland T. Moriarty and Thomas J. Kosnik.
Reprinted from *Sloan Management Review* 30, no. 4 (Summer 1989), pp. 7–17.

library shelf with books and articles that drive that point home. But sales and marketing professionals are not surprised that they might have to sell software, soap, and services three different ways. They are looking for pragmatic advice about how they should adapt their plans and practices, and how to avoid blind alleys and potholes as they drive their marketing machines into high-tech terrain.

The first objective of this article is to provide a framework that explains *why high-tech marketing is different.* The second is to *identify the key issues that arise from these differences.* The third is to assess implications for managers with specific suggestions about *how they should adapt their marketing policies* to increase their chances of success in the fast lane.

# Why Is High-Tech Marketing Different?

There is a great deal of confusion about the factors that differentiate high-tech marketing from other kinds of marketing. To clarify the issue, let's begin with the word *technology*—the easy part of high technology.

**Technology = Knowledge, Skills, and Artifacts.**   Technology has been defined as "the practical knowledge, know-how, skills, and artifacts that can be used to develop a new product or service and/or a new production/delivery system. Technology can be embodied in people, materials, cognitive and physical processes, plant, equipment, and tools."[1] This definition includes both product technology (which is embedded in the product itself) and process technology (which is part of the production/delivery system). It also encompasses "management technology," the knowledge of how to market the product and run the business.[2]

**High Tech = High Uncertainty about Technology and the Market.**   Now the hard part—the *high* in high technology. If we define technology as knowledge, skills, and artifacts, it becomes clear that every organization uses a variety of technologies to create and deliver value. What makes high-tech marketing unique? At first glance, there seems to be no consensus among the experts. Consider these three definitions from the marketing literature:

- The U.S. Bureau of Labor Statistics labels any industry having twice the number of technical employees and double the R&D outlays of the U.S. average as high tech.[3]

[1] R. A. Burgelman, T. J. Kosnik, and M. Van den Poel, "The Innovative Capabilities Audit Framework" in *Strategic Management of Technology and Innovation,* R. A. Burgelman and M. Maidique, eds. (Homewood, Ill.: Richard D. Irwin, 1987).

[2] N. Capon and R. Glazer, "Marketing and Technology: A Strategic Coalignment," *Journal of Marketing* 51 (July 1987), pp. 1–14.

[3] W. L. Shanklin and J. K. Ryans, Jr., *Marketing High Technology* (Lexington, Mass.: D. C. Heath, 1984).

- Regis McKenna asserts that high-tech industries are characterized by complex products, large numbers of entrepreneurial competitors, customer confusion, and rapid change.[4]

- William Shanklin and John Ryans apply the high-tech label to "any company that participates in a business with high-tech characteristics: the business requires a strong scientific/technical basis; new technology can obsolete old technology rapidly; and as new technologies come on stream their applications create or revolutionize demand."[5]

On the surface, these three definitions illustrate a divergence of opinion about what constitutes high technology. However, two underlying dimensions link the definitions and distinguish high-tech from low-tech marketing situations.

The first dimension is *market uncertainty*—ambiguity about the type and extent of customer needs that can be satisfied by the technology. Ted Levitt has argued powerfully that the difference between selling and marketing is that "selling concerns itself with the tricks and techniques of getting people to exchange cash for your product. . . . Marketing . . . view[s] the entire business process as consisting of a tightly integrated effort to discover, create, arouse, and satisfy customer needs."[6]

Unfortunately, using customer needs as the foundation for marketing in high-tech settings is problematic, because potential customers often cannot articulate what they need. McKenna's and Shanklin and Ryans's definitions of high-tech marketing both include elements of market uncertainty.

Why are the needs in the marketplace likely to be more uncertain in a high-tech situation? Figure 1 shows five questions that frequently raise market uncertainty. First, confronted with a radically new technology, customers may not understand what needs the technology could satisfy. A common example of this problem is the first-time purchase of a microcomputer. Many managers have been forced to choose between desktops and laptops, PCs and Macintoshes, without fully understanding how each would help perform various management tasks.

Second, customer needs, once known, may be subject to rapid and unpredictable changes as the environment evolves. Computer software to support income tax preparation in the face of changing federal tax codes is an example of a product facing a moving target.

Third, there may be questions about whether the market will eventually establish technical standards with which the products must be compatible if the buyer hopes to use them with other products, people, or organizations. The debate over VHS and Betamax formats in the early years of VCRs is an example of this type of market uncertainty.

---

[4]R. McKenna, *The Regis Touch: Million-Dollar Advice from America's Top Marketing Consultant* (Reading, Mass.: Addison-Wesley, 1985).

[5]W. L. Shanklin and J. K. Ryans, Jr., "Organizing for High-Tech Marketing," *Harvard Business Review,* November–December 1984, p. 164.

[6]T. Levitt, "Marketing Myopia," *Harvard Business Review,* September–October 1975, p. 26.

**FIGURE 1**

*Sources of market uncertainty*

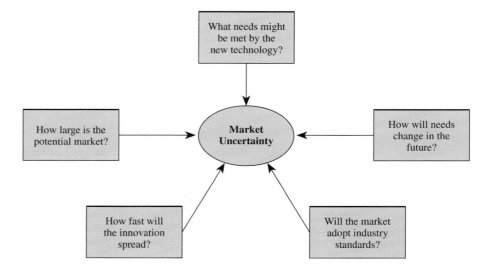

Fourth, predicting how fast a high-tech innovation will spread is difficult. An example is the difficulty market researchers have had predicting the future unit sales of innovations ranging from videocassette recorders to office automation systems.

Finally, all the preceding questions make it difficult to determine the size of the potential market. For example, in 1959, IBM turned down an offer from a startup called Haloid Corporation to invest in a new total xerographic technology because a consulting study predicted that the total market for the Xerox 914 was a mere 5,000 units. A decade later, Haloid (which became Xerox Corporation) had sold 200,000 of the 914s and was a billion-dollar company.

A second dimension that distinguishes high-tech marketing is *technological uncertainty.* Market uncertainty is not knowing what the customers want from the new technology. Technological uncertainty is now knowing whether the technology—or the company providing it—can deliver on its promise to meet needs, once they have been articulated. Technological uncertainty is higher where technology is new or rapidly changing. All three definitions cited above allude to this form of uncertainty.

Figure 2 shows five potential sources of technological uncertainty. The first is a lack of information about a product's functional performance—whether it will do what the seller promises. When computer time-sharing systems were being adopted in the 1970s, both buyers and sellers of computers often encountered this uncertainty when trying to establish the response time (how fast the computer responded to a user at a terminal) of different machines under different usage conditions. Vendors made glowing promises about response time that were difficult to compare across suppliers without the expensive benchmark testing that few customers had the time to conduct.

Second, the company supplying the technology may not have an established track record for delivery. Several situations may elicit uncertainty over delivery. The tendency of computer hardware and software manufacturers to miss promised

The good news is that certain high-tech organizations have discovered clever ways to adapt traditional marketing practices to their special situations. Paradoxically, they have discovered that focusing on marketing fundamentals is one of the best ways to provide the continuity in change so crucial to the long-term success of people and organizations.

The remainder of this section provides action recommendations for each of the five issues, with examples from leading high-tech companies.

### *Broadening and Deepening the Skill Set*

Successful high-tech marketers need to have a basic understanding of the technology, the customer's industry, and the customer's business functions. How do we increase the breadth and the depth of our marketing and sales teams' skills?

Part of the solution is *creative recruiting*. Many computer companies heavily emphasize a technical undergraduate degree for candidates seeking sales and marketing positions. While this deepens the sales force's technological skill, it leaves gaps in detailed knowledge of customers' industries and business functions. In contrast, a leading software and systems integration firm, American Management Systems (AMS), learned not to rely exclusively on people with education and experience in information technology. AMS has created a "functional specialist" career path and now hires fast learners with hands-on experience in their customers' business functions. Teaching functional specialists what they need to know about computers is easier than teaching computer scientists the intricacies of consumer loans or public-sector accounting.

Another part of the solution is *creative training that gets sales and marketing professionals closer to customers*. A training simulation widely adopted by computer hardware manufacturers has salespeople and sales managers live in a customer organization for a week and deal with a major technology purchase from the buyer's perspective. Various salespeople play the roles of a customer's division general manager and vice presidents of finance, marketing, sales, manufacturing, and management information systems. By walking in the customer's shoes, sales professionals gain insights not easily acquired by simply talking about, or even listening to, their clients.

Some high-tech marketers invite loyal customers and recent "rejectors" (buyers who recently selected a competitor's products over their own) to lead discussions about the buying process during marketing and management training. This approach is not recommended for those whose egos bruise easily. Candid criticism about product line flaws or mistakes made in the selling process can be painful in the short run. However, the lessons learned may reduce the pain of lost sales in the long run.

The third, and perhaps most enduring, way to broaden and deepen the skill set is through *creative job assignments*. While on-the-job training occurs in every company and industry, a few high-tech firms have used it in particularly clever ways to enhance the skills of those who create and market their products. One leading systems consulting firm routinely teams relatively new programmers and systems analysts with its most seasoned business developers in competing for new business. The new employee accompanies the veteran "rain maker" on calls to the prospective customer, is encouraged to ask questions in meetings to determine the client's needs, writes parts of the proposal, is involved in estimating the work's scope, and plays a key role in presenting the proposal to the prospective customer. If the business is won, the programmer or analyst becomes a member of the implementation team. He or she can communicate the subtleties of the business problem and the client organization more powerfully than if the partner handed the word down from on high. In the long run, letting employees taste the thrill of winning business and the agony of losing a sale early in their careers provides a sense of the big picture.

Another company, Manac Systems International, develops and markets software products to support law office functions such as time keeping, billing, and storage and retrieval of documents. Most of Manac's customer support is done via a telephone hot line. Clients call with a problem and are forwarded to one of the customer support staff, with whom they walk through the facts to solve the problem. Hot line support is not unique; virtually every computer company has such an organization. What *is* unique is the way Manac staffs this function. Unlike most companies, which hire full-time customer support workers, Manac has all its programmers and application consultants (who test the programs and write the documentation and training manuals) take turns on the telephone watch. Each programmer and application consultant has telephone consulting duty for two full workdays each week.

One advantage of having the software and manual writers on the phone is the customer's exposure to people with the best knowledge of the technology and its application. A second advantage is that the technical people develop a much deeper understanding of how law offices function. Ironically, although Manac does not have a separate marketing department, it is one of the most marketing-oriented high-tech companies we know.

### *Abandoning Knowledge That Has Lost Its Relevance*

How can we learn to recognize when the world has changed and to abandon once-successful marketing approaches that have outlived their usefulness?

One of the most powerful ways is to teach marketers to think in *future perfect* terms. Stanley Davis uses the term as the title of his book about linking strategy, science, technology, and organization. He suggests that implementing a strategy in a radically new context requires an organization's leaders to "lead from a place in time that assumes you are already there, and that is determined even though it has not happened yet." He cites an earlier definition of this new sense of time from Karl Weick:

> The actor projects this [future strategy] as if it were already over and done with and lying in the past. . . . The fact that it is thus pictured as if it were simultaneously past and future can be taken care of by saying that it is thought of in the *future perfect* tense.[9]

---

[9]S. M. Davis, *Future Perfect* (Reading, Mass.: Addison-Wesley, 1987).

For those who may think the suggestion that high-tech marketers be future perfect sounds far-fetched, consider these examples of future perfect behavior from successful high-tech marketing companies.

Between 1970 and the present, American Management Systems has successfully implemented numerous complex information systems. As they tackle each new custom-built system, they work closely with clients to develop the strategic concept of how the completed system will add value to the organization. Together, consultant and client create a "system concept" that describes in the present tense, *as though it already existed,* the tangible details of people and technology interacting in new ways to create information, respond to requests for changes, and perform new functions in the parts of the organization the system will support. AMS's future perfect visualization of the strategy for a high-tech product is unique. The founders have used future perfect projective techniques to articulate their own marketing strategy over five-year time horizons—a lifetime in the software and systems consulting business.

Apple Computer's corporate university, Apple University, recently introduced a series of learning programs for its managers, called Living Programs™, that also adopts a future perfect approach. At one of these programs, the Apple Management Seminar, groups of more than 100 managers spend four days living life at Apple five years in the future. They are formed into self-managing teams of 20 to 25 people and given the task of creating a product, using cutting-edge computer technologies, to help solve a problem that Apple will face in the future, or to communicate what Apple will be like in the future to new Apple employees. Apple senior managers, including CEO John Sculley, visit the seminar and conduct sessions. The learning and the concrete products Apple managers have developed during these programs are nothing less than astonishing compared with what other competent and dedicated marketers accomplish expending much more time and effort in management seminars and on the job.

In short, rapid change renders strategies based on the lessons of the past obsolete even before they can be implemented. High-tech managers can avoid becoming victims of their experience by thinking and acting in future perfect terms. This winning philosophy is captured by a recent quote from hockey star Wayne Gretsky: "I don't go where the puck is—I go where it is going to be!"

### Building Cross-Functional Collaboration and Communication

Product design, manufacturing, sales, and marketing professionals need to improve their cross-functional communication and understanding of customer needs if they are to design, make, and market products that provide value. Several methodologies show great promise of enhancing cross-functional activities and communication. For example, Quality Function Deployment (QFD) originated at Mitsubishi in 1972, and was piloted at Digital Equipment Corporation, AT&T, and ITT in the late 1980s.[10] Through a series of graphical forms, customer desires for intangible product

---

[10]J. R. Hauser and D. Clausing, "The House of Quality," *Harvard Business Review,* May–June 1988, pp. 63–73.

qualities are linked to a specific, physical product attribute. For example, customers' desires for sportiness in a car may be linked to the presence of bucket seats or the shape of the automobile. Then the physical product attributes are linked to design choices, technologies, components, or engineering specifications for the product.

Takeuchi and Nonaka and Hayes, Wheelwright, and Clark describe how well-managed companies have organized the development of new products to enhance cross-functional communication and reduce the time between conceiving and launching a new product.[11] Both approaches recommend a great deal of interaction among marketing, sales, field service, R&D, and manufacturing throughout the process. This degree of interaction contrasts with traditional approaches to new product development, in which one function dominates the process for one phase, and then passes the baton to another function at a later phase.

In addition to new methodologies for product design and project management, many high-tech firms are using management development and training to foster co-operation and communication across the borders traditionally erected between functions, business units, and countries. AMS and IBM use organizational and team-level simulations to give participants hands-on experience in developing group solutions to problems often encountered on high-tech project teams. Data General invites sales, field service, and R&D professionals to join its marketers as full participants during a series of marketing leadership development programs. As part of the Data General programs, cross-functional teams apply new tools and techniques to marketing problems currently faced by the organization.

## Using Interfirm Alliances Effectively

There are numerous examples of alliances in high-tech settings. In 1985, Digital Equipment Corporation established a Manufacturing Corporate Accounts Management (MCAM) program, in which manufacturing executives familiar with cutting-edge technology in Digital's operations met with their counterparts in the firm's leading customer organizations to exchange ideas on how to use new technology. The MCAMs also worked with Digital's manufacturing, marketing, sales, and product development organizations to cross-fertilize ideas in different functions.

Between 1985 and 1988, alliances between computer hardware and software vendors who constituted one "channel" to the customer markedly increased. For example, Tandem Corporation, the manufacturer of NonStop computers, built a group of 100 specialists responsible for developing relationships with third-party software manufacturers. In the following year, it tripled the number of alliances with software suppliers. *Systems Integration Age* has reported a significant rise in the number of relationships between computer software companies and consulting firms that specialize in customizing software, installing it, and training users.[12]

---

[11]H. Takeuchi and I. Nonaka, "The New New Product Development Game," *Harvard Business Review,* January–February 1986, pp. 137–46; R. H. Hayes et al., *Dynamic Manufacturing: Creating the Learning Organization* (New York: Free Press, 1988).

[12]"SIA Alliance Report," *Systems Integration Age,* February 1988, pp. 6–19.

Numerous biotechnology, semiconductor, and computer companies are also forming global strategic alliances to help match the financial strength of larger partners with the creativity of high-tech startups, or to marry the products and technologies of one partner with the market presence, access to customers, and knowledge of distribution channels of another.

As alliances proliferate, it is important to think carefully about how to select and then implement a portfolio of partnerships. Kosnik has pointed out five potential stumbling blocks of global alliances.

- Different partners are organized differently for making marketing and design decisions, leading to *problems in coordination.*
- A company with special competence may align itself with multiple firms that are bitter competitors, leading to *problems of cooperation and trust.*
- "Allies" with the best combination of complementary skills in one country may be ill equipped to help one another in other countries, leading to *problems in implementing alliances on a global basis.*
- The rapid pace of technological change virtually guarantees that the best partner tomorrow may be different from the best partner today, leading to *problems in maintaining alliances over a long time period.*
- The tendency of each partner to want as many allies and as few enemies as possible will make it difficult to say no to any alliance, leading to *problems in establishing unique competitive advantage.*[13]

A framework to compare what each partner "brings to the party" is summarized in Figure 4. Any venture requires a mix of:

- Resources (money, information technology, people, and time).
- Relationships (with customers, channels, and influential people).
- Reputation (breadth of a firm's visibility and depth of its credibility).
- Capabilities (technological expertise, industry experience, functional competencies, creative talent, managerial know-how, marketing skill, and knowledge of the countries in the target segment).
- Chemistry and culture (the compatibility of styles and values of the firms and people who work in them).

Each potential partner may offer a different mix of the above ingredients in each of the countries where the marketing will occur. This framework provides an approach to compare alternative partners and to assess the strengths and weaknesses of a proposed partnership in different country markets.

## *Focusing on Fundamentals to Provide Continuity in Change*

The rate of change in both technologies and markets has accelerated relentlessly in the last decade. High-tech products career from the uncertainty of development and

---

[13]T. J. Kosnik, "Stumbling Blocks to Global Strategic Alliances," *Systems Integration Age,* October 1988.

**FIGURE 4**

*What does each partner bring to the party? A framework for evaluating strategic alliances*

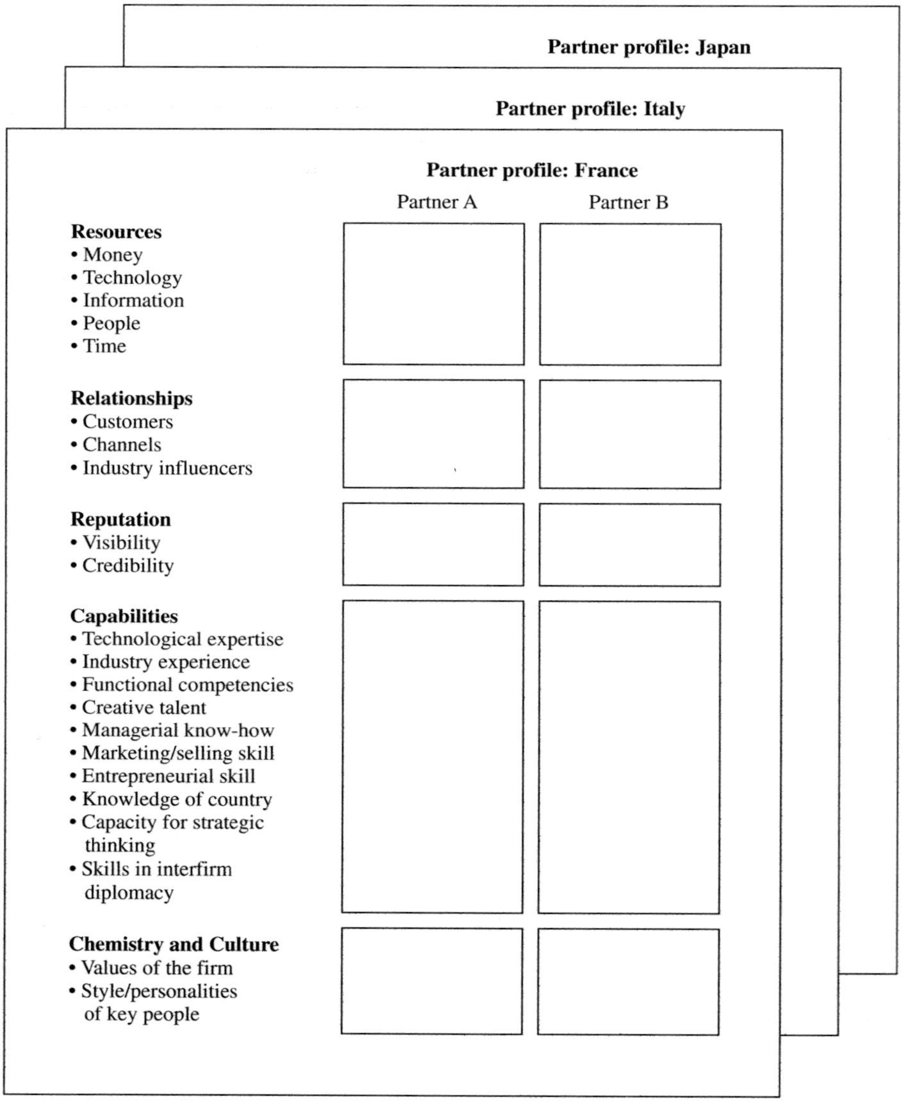

**Partner profile: Japan**

**Partner profile: Italy**

**Partner profile: France**

| | Partner A | Partner B |
|---|---|---|
| **Resources**<br>• Money<br>• Technology<br>• Information<br>• People<br>• Time | | |
| **Relationships**<br>• Customers<br>• Channels<br>• Industry influencers | | |
| **Reputation**<br>• Visibility<br>• Credibility | | |
| **Capabilities**<br>• Technological expertise<br>• Industry experience<br>• Functional competencies<br>• Creative talent<br>• Managerial know-how<br>• Marketing/selling skill<br>• Entrepreneurial skill<br>• Knowledge of country<br>• Capacity for strategic thinking<br>• Skills in interfirm diplomacy | | |
| **Chemistry and Culture**<br>• Values of the firm<br>• Style/personalities of key people | | |

launch through the phases of growth and product maturity in a span of months rather than years.[14] In the process, high-tech marketers experience both the excitement of a roller coaster ride and the stress of combat. In the midst of this chaos, some form of stability is needed if both people and companies are to achieve sustained success over the decades that mark the life cycles of organizations and marketing careers.

---

[14]G. Stalk, Jr., "Time—The Next Source of Competitive Advantage," *Harvard Business Review,* July–August 1988, pp. 41–51.

*To provide continuity in change, focus on the fundamentals.* The first element of this focus is a set of company values. IBM's values—respect for the individual, customer service, and commitment to excellence—are widely known by employees, customers, and others in the marketplace. So too are Hewlett-Packard's seven corporate objectives in the areas of profit, customers, fields of interest, growth, people, management, and citizenship. Unfortunately, corporate values have been trivialized in the 1980s; almost every company has drafted a statement of shared beliefs. In their rush to cover all the bases, many companies espouse such a large number of conflicting values that they lose their meaning. There are too many values to remember, and even if the mission statement is consulted, it is often impossible to determine how to make trade-offs between conflicting values. If corporate values are to provide continuity, they must be both memorable and meaningful for decisions in the trenches.

The second element of focus is targeting market segments and customers. Partly as a result of an engineering-driven heritage, many technology companies believe the key to success is in creating great products, then selling them to anyone who has the money. But the faster technology and markets change, the more impossible it is to be all things to all customers. Consider the market selection decision of Steve Jobs at NeXt, who developed a new generation of personal computers and focused its introduction on the college and university marketplace. Some industry observers scoffed that the focus was too narrow, but we think not. Undoubtedly financial institutions, manufacturing companies, and other target segments had potential uses for the NeXt machine. Few industry observers thought that NeXt would *always* confine itself to colleges and universities. But as a starting point, Jobs understood that trying to stretch a start-up company's marketing and sales resources across a broad range of customers was a recipe for failure. Focus rarely requires marketers to say "never" to opportunities; it often requires them to say "not now."

NeXt is an exception to the practice of most high-tech companies. In contrast, consider the segmentation strategy of a minicomputer manufacturer competing for market share with companies 10 to 50 times its size. The company recently announced it was confining itself to three target segments: government, manufacturing, and service industries around the world. The only specifically excluded segment is the scientific/engineering marketplace! Unless the company sharpens its focus considerably, it will be stretched too thin to achieve a dominant position in any segment. As competition intensifies, the company will risk being gradually overrun by larger competitors that can throw greater resources at any market opportunity. Carl von Clausewitz, a nineteenth century Prussian military strategist whose theories have become popularized by twentieth century business authors, stresses the importance of massing one's forces at the enemy's weakest point to achieve victory on the battlefield.[15] Focusing on target segments is the only way a small high-tech competitor can hope to win against much larger adversaries. In a global marketplace, even the largest companies are not large enough to be all things to all customers for all time.

---

[15]C. von Clausewitz, *On War* (Princeton, N.J.: Princeton University Press, 1976).

High-tech salespeople who have to make quarterly sales quotas, and high-tech entrepreneurs who are wondering if they can make the next payroll, often resist our advice to focus narrowly, since it means sacrificing some opportunities in the short run. We understand their dilemma. In fact, a certain amount of opportunism is not only acceptable but essential if marketers are to capitalize on the volatility of their environment. At the same time, however, maintaining discipline and composure in the heat of battle is essential for continued success.

The third element of focus is product policy. If focused market selection suggests that we can't be all things to all customers, focused product policy implies that most high-tech companies can't even be all things to *some* customers. Specific decisions that should be used to focus a company's product policy include the following.

• The amount of standardization versus customization—that is, the extent to which the marketer will adapt the physical product to meet special customer needs. Manac refuses to customize its software products to meet the needs of a single law firm. Many of its competitors customize, for a fee. However, Manac releases a new version of its software every six to twelve months. If customization were done, implementation of new releases would be a nightmare. Thousands of law firms would call to find out how to add the customized patches from their old versions to each new release.

• The amount of service to offer with the product. Computer hardware manufacturers offer widely varying amounts of education, service, and technical support. They also either charge customers separately for the service or bundle it with the product. Unfortunately, competitors who have not managed the service component carefully wind up bundling lots of free service with their products. This lack of focus squeezes their profits between competitors that give better-quality service and charge for it and those that give less service but offer lower prices.

• The breadth of product line—that is, the number of different types of product categories. Intel's decision to manufacture workstations, rather than limit itself to semiconductors, expanded the breadth of its product line.

• The depth of product line—that is, the number of models available within a product category. Apple recently announced new models of Macintosh computers but retained the existing models; this increased the depth of the Macintosh line.

• Industry standards versus proprietary technology. High-tech companies must decide between adhering to a voluntary set of technical standards for the industry and using a specialized, proprietary technology to solve customer problems. Debates on industry standards sometimes drag on for years, leaving companies that are trying to develop new products bewildered and behind schedule. Customer pressure for industry standards appears to be increasing. At the same time, the number of factions warring over which approach will become the standard is rising. The dilemma these conflicting trends pose for product policy is critical. Many companies are attempting to hedge their bets by simultaneously developing new products that adhere to differing technological standards. Unfortunately, playing it both ways is extremely expensive and tends to lengthen the time necessary for product development, as people, management attention, and finances are stretched to the limit. Only the largest competitors have the resources to pursue multiple industry standards at the same time.

We have limited our discussion of fundamentals to shared values, target market selection, and product policy. Other basic marketing tactics, such as pricing, advertising, sales force management, and distribution channel management, also merit the attention of high-tech marketers. However, if market selection and product policy are not focused, quality execution on the other marketing variables will rarely save the day. Conversely, if high-tech marketers clearly articulate their values, steadfastly commit to their customers, and are disciplined in their product policy decisions, they can make more than their fair share of mistakes elsewhere without suffering a fatal setback.

# Conclusion

This chapter began with a claim that high uncertainty about technology and the marketplace was the underlying difference between high-tech and other environments. This uncertainty gives rise to marketing problems that successful high-tech companies address with creative adaptation and a focus on fundamentals. Holding this delicate balance of flexibility and focus promises to be the foremost challenge facing high-tech company leadership in the 1990s.

# 23 Logic of Global Business: An Interview with ABB's Percy Barnevik

*Percy Barnevik, president and CEO of ABB Asea Brown Boveri, has boldly, yet simply, reorganized ABB as a model of competitive enterprise: an organization that combines global scale and world-class technology with deep roots in local markets. He offers a detailed guide to the theory and practice of building a "multidomestic" enterprise. He describes ABB's matrix system and a new breed of global managers.*

William Taylor: Companies everywhere are trying to become global, and everyone agrees that ABB is more global than most companies. What does that mean?

*Percy Barnevik:* ABB is a company with no geographic center, no national ax to grind. We are a federation of national companies with a global coordination center. Are we a Swiss company? Our headquarters is in Zurich, but only 100 professionals work at headquarters and we will not increase that number. Are we a Swedish company? I'm the CEO, and I was born and educated in Sweden. But our headquarters is not in Sweden, and only two of the eight members of our board of directors are Swedes. Perhaps we are an American company. We report our financial results in U.S. dollars, and English is ABB's official language. We conduct all high-level meetings in English.

My point is that ABB is none of those things—and all of those things. We are not homeless. We are a company with many homes.

*Are all businesses becoming global?*

No, and this is a big source of misunderstanding. We are in the process of building this federation of national companies, a multidomestic organization, as I prefer to call it. That does not mean all of our businesses are global. We do a very good business in electrical installation and service in many countries. That business is superlocal. The geographic scope of our installation business in, say, Stuttgart does not extend beyond a 10-mile radius of downtown Stuttgart.

We also have businesses that are superglobal. There are not more than 15 combined-cycle power plants or more than three or four high-voltage DC stations sold in any one year around the world. Our competitors fight for nearly every contract—they battle us on technology, price, financing—and national borders are virtually meaningless. Every project requires our best people and best technology from around the world.

The vast majority of our businesses—and of most businesses—fall somewhere between the superlocal and the superglobal. These are the businesses in which building a multidomestic organization offers powerful advantages. You want to be able to optimize a business globally—to specialize in the production of components, to drive economies of scale as far as you can, to rotate managers and technologists around the world to share expertise and solve problems. But you also want to have deep local roots everywhere you operate—building products in the countries where you sell them, recruiting the best local talent from the universities, working with the local government to increase exports. If you build such an organization, you create a business advantage that's damn difficult to copy.

*What is a business that demonstrates that advantage?*

Transportation is a good one. This is a vibrant business for us, and we consider ourselves Number 1 in the world. We generate $2 billion a year in revenues when you include all of our activities: locomotives, subway cars, suburban trains, trolleys, and the electrical and signaling systems that support them. We are strong because we are the only multidomestic player in the world.

First, we know what core technologies we have to master, and we draw on research from labs across Europe and the world. Being a technology leader in locomotives means being a leader in power electronics, mechanical design, even communications software. Ten years ago, Asea beat General Electric on a big Amtrak order for locomotives on the Metroliner between New York and Washington. That win caused quite a stir; it was the first time in 100 years that an American railroad bought locomotives from outside the United States. We won because we could run that track from Washington to New York, crooked and bad as it was, at 125 miles an hour. Asea had been pushing high-speed design concepts for more than a decade, and Brown Boveri pioneered the AC technology. That's why our X2 tilting trains are running in Sweden and why ABB will play a big role in the high-speed rail network scheduled to run throughout Europe.

Second, we structure our operations to push cross-border economies of scale. This is an especially big advantage in Europe, where the locomotive industry is hopelessly fragmented. There are two companies headquartered in the United States building locomotives for the U.S. market. There are three companies in Japan. There are 24 companies in Western Europe, and the industry runs at less than 75 percent of capacity. There are European companies still making only 10 or 20 locomotives a

# The Organizing Logic of ABB

ABB Asea Brown Boveri is a global organization of staggering business diversity. Yet its organizing principles are stark in their simplicity. Along one dimension, the company is a distributed global network. Executives around the world make decisions on product strategy and performance without regard for national borders. Along a second dimension, it is a collection of traditionally organized national companies, each serving its home market as effectively as possible. ABB's global matrix holds the two dimensions together.

At the top of the company sit CEO Percy Barnevik and 12 colleagues on the executive committee. The group, which meets every three weeks, is responsible for ABB's global strategy and performance. The executive committee consists of Swedes, Swiss, Germans, and Americans. Several members of the executive committee are based outside Zurich, and their meetings are held around the world.

Reporting to the executive committee are leaders of the 50 or so business areas (BAs), located worldwide, into which the company's products and services are divided. The BAs are grouped into eight business segments, for which different members of the executive committee are responsible. For example, the "industry" segment, which sells components, systems, and software to automate industrial processes, has five BAs, including metallurgy, drives, and process engineering. The BA leaders report to Gerhard Schulmeyer, a German member of the executive committee who works out of Stamford, Connecticut.

Each BA has a leader responsible for optimizing the business on a global basis. The BA leader devises and champions a global strategy, holds factories around the world to cost and quality standards, allocates export markets to each factory, and shares expertise by rotating people across borders, creating mixed-nationality teams to solve problems, and building a culture of trust and communication. The BA leader for power transformers, who is responsible for 25 factories in 16 countries, is a Swede who works out of Mannheim, Germany. The BA leader for instrumentation is British. The BA leader for electric metering is an American based in North Carolina.

Alongside the BA structure sits a country structure. ABB's operations in the developed world are organized as national enterprises with presidents, balance sheets, income statements, and career ladders. In Germany, for example, Asea Brown Boveri Aktiengesellschaft, ABB's national company, employs 36,000 people and generates annual revenues of more than $4 billion. The managing director of ABB Germany, Eberhard von Koerber, plays a role comparable with that of a traditional German CEO. He reports to a supervisory board whose members include German bank representatives and trade union officials. His company produces financial statements comparable with those from any other German company and participates fully in the German apprenticeship program.

The BA structure meets the national structure at the level of ABB's member companies. Percy Barnevik advocates strict decentralization. Wherever possible, ABB creates separate companies to do the work of the 50 business areas in different countries. For example, ABB does not merely sell industrial robots in Norway. Norway has an ABB robotics company charged with manufacturing robots, selling to and servicing domestic customers, and exporting to markets allocated by the BA leader.

There are 1,100 such local companies around the world. Their presidents report to two bosses—the BA leader, who is usually located outside the country, and the president of the national company of which the local company is a subsidiary. At this intersection, ABB's "multidomestic" structure becomes a reality.

year! How can they compete with us, when we have factories doing 10 times their volume and specializing in components for locomotives across the Continent? For example, one of our new plants makes power electronics for many of the locomotives we sell in Europe. That specialization creates huge cost and quality advantages. We work to rationalize and specialize as much as we can across borders.

Third, we recognize the limits to specialization. We can't ignore borders altogether. We recently won a $420-million order from the Swiss Federal Railways—we call it the "order of the century"—to build locomotives that will move freight through the Alps. If we expect to win those orders, we had *better* be a Swiss company. We had better understand the depth of the Swiss concern for the environment, which explains the willingness to invest so heavily to get freight moving on trains through the mountains to Italy or Germany and off polluting trucks. We had better understand the Alpine terrain and what it takes to build engines powerful enough to haul heavy loads. We had better understand the effects of drastic temperature changes on sensitive electronics and build locomotives robust enough to keep working when they go from the frigid, dry outdoors to extreme heat and humidity inside the tunnels.

There are other advantages to a multidomestic presence. India needs locomotives—thousands of locomotives—and the government expects its suppliers to manufacture most of them inside India. But the Indians also need soft credit to pay for what is imported. Who has more soft credit than the Germans and the Italians? So we have to be a German and an Italian company, we have to be able to build locomotive components there as well as in Switzerland, Sweden, and Austria, since our presence may persuade Bonn and Rome to assist with financing.

We test the borderlines all the time: How far can we push cross-border specialization and scale economies? How effectively can we translate our multidomestic presence into competitive advantages in third markets?

### *Is there such a thing as a global manager?*

Yes, but we don't have many. One of ABB's biggest priorities is to create more of them; it is a crucial bottleneck for us. On the other hand, a global company does not need thousands of global managers. We need maybe 500 or so out of 15,000 managers to make ABB work well—not more. I have no interest in making managers more "global" than they have to be. We can't have people abdicating their nationalities, saying "I am no longer German, I am international." The world doesn't work like that. If you are selling products and services in Germany, you better be German!

That said, we do need a core group of global managers at the top: on our executive committee, on the teams running our business areas (BAs), in other key positions. How are they different? Global managers have exceptionally open minds. They respect how different countries do things, and they have the imagination to appreciate why they do them that way. But they are also incisive, they push the limits of the culture. Global managers don't passively accept it when someone says, "You can't do that in Italy or Spain because of the unions," or "You can't do that in Japan because of the Ministry of Finance." They sort through the debris of cultural excuses and find opportunities to innovate.

Global managers are also generous and patient. They can handle the frustrations of language barriers. As I mentioned earlier, English is the official language of ABB. Every manager with a global role *must* be fluent in English, and anyone with regional general management responsibilities must be competent in English. When I write letters to ABB colleagues in Sweden, I write them in English. It may seem silly for one Swede to write to another in English, but who knows who will need to see that letter a year from now?

We are adamant about the language requirement—and it creates problems. Only 30 percent of our managers speak English as their first language, so there is great potential for misunderstanding, for misjudging people, for mistaking facility with English for intelligence or knowledge. I'm as guilty as anyone. I was rushing through an airport last year and had to return a phone call from one of our managers in Germany. His English wasn't good, and he was speaking slowly and tentatively. I was in a hurry, and finally I insisted, "Can't you speak any faster?" There was complete silence. It was a dumb thing for me to say. Things like that happen every day in this company. Global managers minimize those problems and work to eliminate them.

*Where do these new managers come from?*

Global managers are made, not born. This is not a natural process. We are herd animals. We like people who are like us. But there are many things you can do. Obviously, you rotate people around the world. There is no substitute for line experience in three or four countries to create a global perspective. You also encourage people to work in mixed-nationality teams. You *force* them to create personal alliances across borders, which means that sometimes you interfere in hiring decisions.

This is why we put so much emphasis on teams in the business areas. If you have 50 business areas and five managers on each BA team, that's 250 people from different parts of the world—people who meet regularly in different places, bring their national perspectives to bear on tough problems, and begin to understand how things are done elsewhere. I experience this every three weeks in our executive committee. When we sit together as Germans, Swiss, Americans, and Swedes, with many of us living, working, and traveling in different places, the insights can be remarkable. But you have to force people into these situations. Mixing nationalities doesn't just happen.

You also have to acknowledge cultural differences without becoming paralyzed by them. We've done some surveys, as have lots of other companies, and we find interesting differences in perception. For example, a Swede may think a Swiss is not completely frank and open, that he doesn't know exactly where he stands. That is a cultural phenomenon. Swiss culture shuns disagreement. A Swiss might say, "Let's come back to that point later, let me review it with my colleagues." A Swede would prefer to confront the issue directly. How do we undo hundreds of years of upbringing and education? We don't, and we shouldn't try to. But we do need to broaden understanding.

These are not hypothetical calculations. We bought Combustion Engineering in late 1989. I told the Americans that they had to go from 600 people to 100 in their Stamford, Connecticut, headquarters. They didn't believe it was possible. So I told them to go to Finland and take a look. When we bought Strömberg, there were 880 people in headquarters. Today there are 25. I told them to go to Mannheim and take a look at the German operation. In 1988, right after the creation of ABB, there were 1,600 people in headquarters. Today there are 100.

*Doesn't such radical decentralization threaten the very advantages that ABB's size creates?*

Those are the contradictions again—being simultaneously big and small, decentralized and centralized. To do that, you need a structure at the top that facilitates quick decision making and carefully monitors developments around the world. That's the role of our executive committee. The 13 members of the executive committee are collectively responsible for ABB. But each of us also has responsibility for a business segment, a region, some administrative functions, or more than one of these. Eberhard von Koerber, who is a member of the executive committee located in Mannheim, is responsible for Germany, Austria, Italy, and Eastern Europe. He is also responsible for a worldwide business area, installation materials, and some corporate staff functions. Gerhard Schulmeyer sits in the United States and is responsible for North America. He is also responsible for our global "industry" segment.

Naturally, these 13 executives are busy, stretched people. But think about what happens when we meet every three weeks, which we do for a full day. Sitting in one room are the senior managers collectively responsible for ABB's global strategy and performance. These same managers individually monitor business segments, countries, and staff functions. So when we make a decision—snap, it's covered. The members of the executive committee communicate to their direct reports, the BA managers and the country managers, and the implementation process is under way.

We also have the glue of transparent, centralized reporting through a management information system called Abacus. Every month, Abacus collects performance data on our 4,500 profit centers and compares performance with budgets and forecasts. The data are collected in local currencies but translated into U.S. dollars to allow for analysis across borders. The system also allows you to work with the data. You can aggregate and disaggregate results by business segments, countries, and companies within countries.

*What kind of information does the executive committee use to support the fast decision making you need?*

We look for early signs that businesses are becoming more or less healthy. On the 10th of every month, for example, I get a binder with information on about 500 different operations—the 50 business areas, all the major countries, and the key companies in key countries. I look at several parameters—new orders, invoicing, margins, cash flows—around the world and in various business segments. Then I stop to study trends that catch my eye.

Let's say the industry segment is behind budget. I look to see which of the five BAs in the segment are behind. I see that process automation is way off. So I look by country and learn that the problem is in the United States and that it's poor margins, not weak revenues. So the answer is obvious—a price war has broken out. That doesn't mean I start giving orders. But I want to have informed dialogues with the appropriate executives.

*Let's go back to basics. How do you begin building this kind of global organization?*

ABB has grown largely through mergers and strategic investments. For most companies in Europe, this is the right way to cross borders. There is such massive overcapacity in so many European industries and so few companies with the critical mass to hold their own against Japanese and U.S. competitors. My former company, Asea, did fine in the 1980s. Revenues in 1987 were 4 times greater than in 1980, profits were 10 times greater, and our market value was 20 times greater. But the handwriting was on the wall. The European electrical industry was crowded with 20 national competitors. There was up to 50 percent overcapacity, high costs, and little cross-border trade. Half the companies were losing money. The creation of ABB started a painful—but long overdue—process of restructuring.

That same restructuring process will come to other industries: automobiles, telecommunications, steel. But it will come slowly. There have been plenty of articles in the last few years about all the cross-border mergers in Europe. In fact, the more interesting issue is why there have been so *few*. There should be *hundreds* of them, involving *tens of billions* of dollars, in industry after industry. But we're not seeing it. What we're seeing instead are strategic alliances and minority investments. Companies buy 15 percent of each other's shares. Or two rivals agree to cooperate in third markets but not merge their home-market organizations. I worry that many European alliances are poor substitutes for doing what we try to do—complete mergers and cross-border rationalization.

*What are the obstacles to such cross-border restructuring?*

One obstacle is political. When we decided on the merger between Asea and Brown Boveri, we had no choice but to do it secretly and to do it quickly, with our eyes open about discovering skeletons in the closet. There were no lawyers, no auditors, no environmental investigations, and no due diligence. Sure, we tried to value assets as best we could. But then we had to make the move, with an extremely thin legal document, because we were absolutely convinced of the strategic merits. In fact, the documents from the premerger negotiations are locked away in a Swiss bank and won't be released for 20 years.

Why the secrecy? Think of Sweden. Its industrial jewel, Asea—a 100 year-old company that had built much of the country's infrastructure—was moving its headquarters out of Sweden. The unions were angry: "Decisions will be made in Zurich, we have no influence in Zurich, there is no codetermination in Switzerland."

I remember when we called the press conference in Stockholm on August 10. The news came as a complete surprise. Some journalists didn't even bother to attend; they figured it was an announcement about a new plant in Norway or something. Then came the shock, the fait accompli. That started a communications war of a few weeks where we had to win over shareholders, the public, governments, and unions. But strict confidentiality was our only choice.

*Are there obstacles besides politics?*

Absolutely. The more powerful the strategic logic behind a merger—the greater the cross-border synergies—the more powerful the human and organizational obstacles. It's hard to tell a competent country manager in Athens or Amsterdam, "You've done a good job for 15 years, but unfortunately this other manager has done a better job and our only choice is to appoint your colleague to run the operation." If you have two plants in the same country running well but you need only one after the merger, it's tough to explain that to employees in the plant to be closed. Restructuring operations creates lots of pain and heartache, so many companies choose not to begin the process, to avoid the pain.

Germany is a case in point. Brown Boveri had operated in Germany for almost 90 years. Its German operation was so big—it had more than 35,000 employees—that there were rivalries with the Swiss parent. BBC Germany was a technology-driven, low-profit organization—a real underperformer. The formation of ABB created the opportunity to tackle problems that had festered for decades.

*So what did you do?*

We sent in Eberhard von Koerber to lead the effort. He made no secret of our plans. We had to reduce the work force by 10 percent, or 4,000 employees. We had to break up the headquarters, which had grown so big because of all the tensions with Switzerland. We had to rationalize the production overlaps, especially between Switzerland and Germany. We needed lots of new managers, eager people who wanted to be leaders and grow in the business.

The reaction was intense. Von Koerber faced strikes, demonstrations, barricades—real confrontation with the unions. He would turn on the television set and see protesters chanting, "Von Koerber out! Von Koerber out!" After a while, once the unions understood the game plan, the loud protests disappeared and our relationship became very constructive. The silent resistance from managers was more formidable. In fact, much of the union resistance was fed by management. Once the unions got on board, they became allies in our effort to reform management and rationalize operations.

Three years later, the results are in. ABB Germany is a well-structured, dynamic, market-oriented company. Profits are increasing steeply, in line with ABB targets. In 1987, BBC Germany generated revenues of $4 billion. ABB Germany will generate twice that by the end of next year. Three years ago, the management structure in Mannheim was centralized and functional, with few clear responsibilities or accountability. Today there are 30 German companies, each with its own president, manufacturing director, and so on. We can see who the outstanding performers are and apply their talents elsewhere. If we need someone to sort out a problem with circuit breakers in Spain, we know who from Germany can help.

*What lessons can other companies learn from the German experience?*

To make real change in cross-border mergers, you have to be factual, quick, and neutral. And you have to move boldly. You must avoid the "investigation trap"— you can't postpone tough decisions by studying them to death. You can't permit a "honeymoon" of small changes over a year or two. A long series of small changes just prolongs the pain. Finally, you have to accept a fair share of mistakes. I tell my people that if we make 100 decisions and 70 turn out to be right, that's good enough. I'd rather be roughly right and fast than exactly right and slow. We apply these principles everywhere we go, including in Eastern Europe, where we now have several change programs under way. (See "Change Comes to Poland—The Case of ABB Zamech.")

Why emphasize speed at the expense of precision? Because the costs of delay are vastly greater than the costs of an occasional mistake. I won't deny that it was absolutely crazy around here for the first few months after the merger. We *had* to get the matrix in place—we couldn't debate it—and we *had* to figure out which plants would close and which would stay open. We took 10 of our best people, the superstars, and gave them six weeks to design the restructuring. We called it the Manhattan Project. I personally interviewed 400 people, virtually day and night, to help select and motivate the people to run our local companies.

*Once you've put the global pieces together and have the matrix concept working, what other problems do you have to wrestle with?*

Communications. I have no illusions about how hard it is to communicate clearly and quickly to tens of thousands of people around the world. ABB has about 15,000 middle managers prowling around markets all over the world. If we in the executive committee could connect with all of them or even half of them and get them moving in roughly the same direction, we would be unstoppable.

But it's enormously difficult. Last year, for example, we made a big push to squeeze our accounts receivable and free up working capital. We called it the Cash Race. There are 2,000 people around the world with some role in accounts receivable, so we had to mobilize them to make the program work. Three or four months after the program started—and we made it very visible when it started—I visited an accounts receivable office where 20 people were working. These people hadn't even *heard* of the program, and it should have been their top priority. When you come face-to-face with this lack of communication, this massive inertia, you can get horrified, depressed, almost desperate. Or you can concede that this is the way things are, this is how the world works, and commit to doing something about it.

*So what do you do?*

You don't inform, you *overinform*. That means breaking taboos. There is a strong tendency among European managers to be selective about sharing information.

We faced a huge communications challenge right after the merger. In January 1988, just days after the birth of ABB, we had a management meeting in Cannes with the top 300 people in the company. At that meeting, we presented our policy

# Change Comes to Poland—The Case of ABB Zamech

Last May, Zamech, Poland's leading manufacturer of steam turbines, transmission gears, marine equipment, and metal castings began a new life as ABB Zamech—a joint venture of ABB (76 percent ownership), the Polish government (19 percent ownership), and the company's employees (5 percent ownership). ABB Zamech employs 4,300 people in the town of Elblag, outside Gdansk. In September, two more Polish joint ventures became official—ABB Dolmel and Dolmel Drives. These companies manufacture a wide range of generating equipment and electric drives and employ some 2,400 workers.

The joint ventures are noteworthy for their size alone. ABB has become the largest Western investor in Poland. But they are perhaps more significant for their managerial implications, in particular, how ABB is revitalizing these deeply troubled operations. The company intends to demonstrate that the philosophy of business and managerial reform it has applied in places like Mannheim, Germany, and Muncie, Indiana, can also work in the troubled economies of Eastern Europe. That philosophy has at least four core principles:

1. Immediately reorganize operations into profit centers with well-defined budgets, strict performance targets, and clear lines of authority and accountability.

2. Identify a core group of change agents from local management, give small teams responsibility for championing high-priority programs, and closely monitor results.

3. Transfer ABB expertise from around the world to support the change process, without interfering with it or running it directly.

4. Keep standards high and demand quick results.

Barbara Kux, president of ABB Power Ventures, negotiated the Polish joint ventures and plays a lead role in the turnaround process. "Our goal is to make these companies as productive and profitable as ABB's operations worldwide," she says. "We don't make a 'discount' for Eastern Europe, and we don't expect the change process to take forever. We provide more technical and managerial support than we might to a company in the United States, but we are just as demanding in terms of results."

ABB Zamech has come the furthest to date. The change program began immediately after the creation of the joint venture. For decades, the company had been organized along functional lines, a structure that blurred managerial authority, confused product-line profitability, and slowed decision making. Within four weeks, ABB Zamech was reorganized into discrete profit centers. There are now three business areas (BAs)—the casting foundry, turbines and gears, and marine equipment—as well as a finance and administration department and an in-house service department. Each area has a leadership team that generates the business plans, budgets, and performance targets by which their operations are judged. These teams made final decisions on which employees would stay, which would go, what equipment they would need—tough-minded business choices made for the first time so as to maximize productivity (employee and capital) and business area profitability.

The reorganization was a crucial first step. The second big step was installing ABB's standard finance and control system. For decades, Zamech had been run as a giant overhead machine. Roughly 80 percent of the company's total costs were allocated by central staff accountants rather than traced directly to specific products and services. Managers had no clear idea what their products cost to make and thus no idea which ones made money. Tight financial controls and maximum capital productivity are critical in an economy with interest rates of 40 percent.

Formal reorganization and new control systems, no matter how radical, won't have much of an effect without big changes in who is in charge, however. ABB made two important decisions. First, there would be no "rescue team" from Western Europe. All managerial positions, from the CEO down, would be held by Polish managers from the former Zamech. Second, managers would be selected without regard to rank or seniority; indeed, there would be a premium on young, creative talent. ABB was looking for "hungry wolves"—smart, ambitious change agents who would receive intense training and be the core engine of Zamech's revival.

Most of the new leaders came from the ranks of middle management. The company's top executive, general manager Pawel Olechnowicz, ran the steel castings department prior to the joint venture's creation—a position that put him several layers below the top of the 15-layer management hierarchy. Employees had already elected him general manager shortly before the creation of ABB Zamech, so he looked like a good choice. The marine BA leader

# Change Comes to Poland

had been a production manager in the old Zamech, another low-level position, and the turbines and gears BA manager had been a technical director.

"We put in place a management team that lacked the standard business tools," Kux explains. "They didn't know what cash flow was, they didn't understand much about marketing. But their ambition was incredible. You could feel their hunger to excel. When we began the talent search, we told our Zamech contacts that we wanted to see the 30 people they would take along tomorrow if they were going to open their own business."

Next came the process of developing a detailed agenda for reform. The leadership team settled on 11 priority issues, from reorganizing and retraining the sales force to slashing total cycle times and redesigning the factory layout. Each project was led by a champion—some from top management ranks, some from the other "hungry wolves." A steering committee made up of the general manager, the deputy general manager, the business area managers, and Kux meets monthly to review these critical projects.

To support the change initiatives, ABB created a team of high-level experts from around the world—authorities in functional areas like finance and control and quality, as well as technology specialists and managers with heavy restructuring experience. Team members do not live in Poland. Kux says it is unrealistic to expect top people to spend a year or two in the conditions they would find in Elblag. But they visit frequently and stay updated on progress and problems.

The logistics of expertise transfer are more complicated than they sound. For example, most of the Polish managers spoke little or no English—a serious barrier to effective dialogue. So ABB began intensive language training. "If Polish managers want to draw from the worldwide ABB resource pool, they must speak English," Kux emphasizes. "Most communication doesn't happen face-to-face where you can have an interpreter. Last May, I couldn't simply pick up the phone and talk to the general manager. Today we speak in English on the phone almost every day."

Of course, speaking on the telephone in English assumes a working telephone system—a dangerous assumption in the case of Poland. Thus, another prerequisite for effective expertise transfer was creating the infrastructure to make it possible. ABB has linked Zamech and Dolmel by satellite to its Zurich headquarters for reliable telephone and fax communications. (It is now easier to communicate between Zamech and Zurich and Dolmel and Zurich than it is between Zamech and Dolmel.) In January, ABB Zamech began electronically transferring three monthly performance reports to Zurich—another big step to make communications more intensive and effective.

Once it created the communications infrastructure, however, ABB had to reckon with a second language barrier—the language of business. To introduce ABB Zamech's "hungry wolves" to basic business concepts and to enable them to transfer these concepts into the ranks, ABB created a "mini MBA program" in Warsaw. The program began in September, covers five key modules (business strategy, marketing, finance, manufacturing, human resources) and is taught by faculty members of INSEAD, the French business school. Sessions run from Thursday evening through Saturday noon, use translated copies of Western business school cases, and closely resemble what goes on in MBA classes everywhere else.

The change program at ABB Zamech has been under way for less than a year, and much remains to be done. But it is already generating results. The company is issuing monthly financial reports that conform to ABB standards—a major achievement in light of the simple systems in place before the joint venture. Cycle times for the production of steam turbines have been cut in half and now meet the ABB worldwide average. A task force is implementing a plan to reduce factory space by 20 percent—an important step in streamlining the operation. ABB will draw on the Zamech experience as it begins the reform process at Dolmel and Dolmel Drives.

"You can change these companies," Kux says. "You can make them more competitive and profitable. I can't believe the quality of the reports and presentations these people do today, how at ease they are discussing their strategy and targets. I have worked with many corporate restructurings, but never have I seen so much change so quickly. The energy is incredible. These people really want to learn; they are very ambitious. Basically, ABB Zamech is their business now."

—William Taylor

Customers; *see also* Buyers
    aggressive, 156–157
    benefits of strategic account
        relationships, 178–179
    classification of, 248–250
    cost-to-serve, 155–156
    evaluation of products by, 99–100
    hybrid channels and, 228–231
    industrial customer trade-offs,
        271–272
    management of, 152–163
    multiple channels and, 231–233
    net price realized, 155–156
    partnering with, in product
        development, 95
    product choice decisions, 272
    segmenting by size, 173, 190
    segmenting in mature industrial
        markets, 187–197
    sensitivity to price, 158
    sensitivity to service, 158
    for shadowed new products,
        52–53
    sophistication of, 280
    value, and, 274–275
    working relationship with, 259
Customers, analysis of
    for profitability, 152
    using MSP, 218
Customer satisfaction
    customer retention process and,
        262
    maximization of, 245
Customer segmentation
    in mature industrial markets,
        187–197
    by SIC code, 190
    by size, 173, 190
Customer segments, homogeneous,
    123
Customer service, 198–199
    accountability, 207
    description of, 199–203
    internal marketing and, 203–207
    management responsibility, 205
    managing customer retention,
        208–210
    meaning to customers, 201–203
    measurement and evaluation, 206
    order fulfillment and, 262
    plans and budgets, 205–206
Customer service workshops, 198
Customization, 7
    in integrated circuit business, 285

Database marketing, distribution
    channels and, 227
Davidow, William, 311
Davis, Stanley, 320
*Death of a Salesman,* 26, 164
Decentralization, global business,
    338–339
Deciders, 30–31
Decisionmaking, by executive
    committee, 339–340
Decision-making process, 193
    MSP and, 216
Dedication, 260–262
Delivery, uncertainty about time of,
    314–315
Delusionary new products, 54–55
Demand
    derived demand, 4–5
    estimation of, 5
Demand-side strategies, 149
Demographics, 15, 17–18
Demos, beta sites used as, 116–117
Derivative projects, 59
Derived demand, 4–5
Design in advance of market, 85–90
    challenges in, 90–96
Detailed market study, 44
Development map, 62–65
Development resources, 57–58
Development risks, 45
Differentiation of physical product,
    142–143
Differentiation strategies, 143–148
    market focus strategy, 147
    process innovation strategy, 146–147
    service innovation strategy, 148
    value-added strategy, 144–145
Digital Equipment, time-based
    competition, 75
Direct mail, for cost containment, 599
Direct mail and fulfillment, 214
    price for systems, 222
Direct marketing
    distribution channels and, 227
    MSP and, 216
Distinctive competencies of corporation,
    76
Distribution
    train of, traditional, 226–227
Distribution channels, 4, 9–10
    database marketing, effect of, 227
    design of, 122–134
    direct marketing, effect of, 227
    hybrid channels, 228–231

Distribution channels—*Cont.*
    multiple channels, 231–233
    reorientation of, 225–237
    shorter channels, 234–235
    strategic priorities, 225
    as vertical marketing systems,
        226–227
    vertical or horizontal, 225
Distribution costs, 154
Distribution industry, trends in, 225–237
Distributors, benefits of information
    technology to, 227–228
Diverse specifications, 271–272
    utility of, 277–278
Diversity
    different mixture of diverse
        specifications, 273–275
    in market maturity process, 257
    in Stage III, 262
    value-oriented product line, 274–275
    variety-oriented product line,
        273–276
Dominant design, 280
    demise of, 280–282
Dreyfuss, Henry, 94
DuPont, market segmentation by,
    187–188

Efficiency, 260–262
    MSP systems and, 216
Entrepreneurship, 258–260
Estimation, of demand for industrial
    products, 5
Evaluation, 206
Evolution of product to meet uncertain
    need, 89–90
Expansion, in Stage III, 262–265
Expert power, 31, 32
External linkages
    complex buying/selling process, 5–6
    concentrated customer base, 6
    derived demand, 4–5
    distribution channels, 4
    industrial marketing, 4–6

Final business plan, 44
Financial performance, new product
    development and, 56
Focus groups, 93
Follow-on services, 139
Franchised distributors, 173
Fry, Arthur, 52

Fulfillment, 308
Functional performance of product, uncertainty about, 314
Functional specialization, 260–261
Future need, determination of, 88–89

Gatekeepers, 29, 30
General Electric Plastics
    generation of consumer interest by, 91–92
    management of complexity, 265–269
General management orientation, 259
Geographic boundaries, 250
Geography
    effect on customer profitability, 152
    presale costs and, 153–154
Global business
    ABB Asea Brown Boveri reorganization, 328–346
    obstacles to global restructuring, 340–345
    politics of, 345–346
Global coordination, 334–334
Global manager, 331–332
GNP; *see* Gross national product
Gross national product (GNP), business-to-business activity as percentage of, 3–4

Headquarters, role in global business, 338–339
Health care industry, hybrid channels in, 229
Heavy equipment, 4
Herzberg, Frederic, 198–199
Hewlett-Packard
    immersion in environment of user, 94
    product definition project, 77–80
    Qualified Lead Tracking System (QUILTS), 219
    shortening product life cycles, 282
    tracking trends to determine future needs, 89
    user needs considered at, 86–88
High-cost channels, alignment with big customers, 245
High fashion marketing, 317
High-tech, defined, 312–313

High-tech marketing, 311–312, 311–327
    better mouse trap marketing compared with, 317
    broadening and deepening of skill set, 318–319
    continuity in change, 323–327
    creative job assignments, 319–320
    creative recruiting, 319
    creative training, 319
    critical issues, 317–318
    cross-functional collaboration and communication, 321–322
    customer needs, 313
    differentiating factors, 312–317
    high fashion marketing compared with, 317
    high-tech, defined, 312–313
    interfirm alliances, use of, 322–323
    literature about, 311
    low-tech marketing compared with, 316–317
    market uncertainty, 313–314
    recognizing obsolete marketing approaches, 320–321
    tactics, 318–327
    technical standards, 313
    technological uncertainty, 314–317
    technology, defined, 312
Homogeneous customer segments, 123
Human factors; *see* Buying psychology
Hybrid channels, 128–129, 228–231
Hybrid grid, 238, 242–247
Hybrid marketing systems, 238–254

IBM Corporation, hybrid marketing system, 238
Immersion in environment of user, 94
Incentives, in hybrid marketing systems, 251
Incremental products, relative importance of, 51
Industrial customer trade-offs, 271–272
Industrial marketing; *see* Business-to-business marketing
Industrial markets
    differentiated from consumer markets, 3
    products sold in, classification of, 4
    segmentation of, 15–25
Industrial pricing, 98–111
Industrial products and services, size of market for, 3–4
Industrial segmentation, 15–25

Industry knowledge, industrial segmentation and, 17
Industry life cycle, 65–66
Industry structure, PET and, 282–283
Influencers, 29–30
Information flow management from beta site, 118–119
Information technology
    distribution channels, effect on, 227–228
    MSP and, 214
Initial screening, 44
Initiators, 29, 30
Innovation
    incremental versus radical, 46, 47–51
    of product delivery system, 143
    relation to variety and value approaches, 279
*In Search of Excellence,* 198
Insurance industry, hybrid marketing systems, 599
Integration, market complexity and, 258–260
Interdepartmental coordination, 10
Interfirm alliances, use in high-tech marketing, 322–323
Internal linkages, 6–7
    customization, high level of, 7
    order fulfillment mechanism, 7
    research and development, 4
    technology, emphasis on, 6–7
Internal marketing, customer service and, 203–207
International marketing, variety versus value in, 285–286

Job assignments, creative, 319–320
Jobs, Steve, 46

Kleinschmidt, Elko, 81
Known need
    improved solution for, 86–87
    new solution for, 87–88
Kodak, time-based competition, 75–76

Labor, effect of automation on, 212
Laptop PCs, MSP and, 217
Launching of product; *see* Product launch
Levitt, Theodore, 102
Light equipment, 4

Logistics, generic channel function, 124
Lot size, generic channel function, 124
Low-cost channels, alignment with small
    customers, 245
Low-tech marketing, 316–317


McKenna, Regis, 311, 313
Major account management, 166–167
    justification of, 171–172
Mall studies, 93
Management challenges in business-to-
    business marketing, 7–10
Management of marketing
    industrial segmentation and, 16
    MSP and, 217–221
Managers, cross-functional
    responsibilities, 259
Manufacturing, order fulfillment and,
    262
Manufacturing resource planning
    system, 85
Map of tasks and channels in hybrid
    marketing system, 242–247
Mapping projects, 59–65
Market analysis
    industrial segmentation and, 15
    research on product success/failure,
        80–82
Market complexity
    case studies, 265–269
    efficiency and dedication, 260–262
    entrepreneurship and integration,
        258–260
    expansion and coordination,
        262–265
    GE Plastics, 265–269
Market coverage, increase of, 599
Market creation
    risk and, 91
    technology commercialization and,
        85–86, 90
Marketer, decisions regarding diverse
    specifications, 272
Market focus strategy, 147
Market growth, in Stage III, 262
Market identification, wrong market, 89
Marketing and sales productivity
    systems (MSP)
    customization of, 223–224
    direct mail and fulfillment, 214
    economies of scale and, 218
    estimation of financial benefit of,
        222

Marketing and sales productivity
    systems (MSP)—*Cont.*
    implementation guidelines, 221–224
    large companies as prospects for,
        213
    as management tool, 217–221
    MSP databases, 215–216
    PC-based, 215
    productivity improvement and,
        216–217
    ramp-up strategy, 223
    sales and marketing management, 214
    sales force automation, 217–218
    salesperson productivity tools, 214
    telemarketing, 214
    uses of, 213–216
Marketing automation, 212–224
Marketing inertia, MSP and, 217
Marketing mistakes, in new product
    development and
    commercialization, 46–55
Marketing resources, MSP for, 219
Marketing systems
    hybrid marketing systems, 238–254
Marketing tasks, analysis of, 242
Market knowledge, 193
Market launch, 44
Market life cycle, 257–258
Market oriented, 288–296
Market position, new product
    development and, 56
Market research
    beta testing, 112–121
    high-tech marketing, 311
Market segmentation, 8
    diverse specifications, 277
    in mature industrial markets,
        187–197
Market selection, industrial
    segmentation and, 16
Market share, 192
Market uncertainty, high-tech marketing,
    313–314
Market windows, 282
Mass marketing, 55
Master distributor, 234–235
Mature industrial markets
    product life cycle theory, 188
    segmenting customers in, 187–197
Measurement and evaluation, 206
Metal fabrication, hybrid marketing
    systems, 239
Micromanagement of project
    development, 58

Migration patterns, 158–159
Miller, Arthur, 26, 164
Motivation
    of buyers, 34–36
    for service, 198–199
Mowery, David, 80
MSP databases, 215–216
    as management tool, 217–221
Multidomestic enterprise, 329
    organization of, 333–338
Multiple channels, 231–233


Nested hierarchy, 16, 17, 23–25
Net price realized, 155–156
New core product, 48
New markets, technological potential
    requiring creation of, 85–86, 90
New product commercialization, 43–55
New products
    design of channels of distribution,
        122–134
    development and commercialization,
        7–8
    failure rates for, 43, 122
New product taxonomies, 46–48
Next generation product, 48
NutraSweet, joint marketing interests,
    178–179


Office supplies, hybrid marketing
    systems, 239
Operating variables, 15, 18–20
Opportunity costs, 45
Order fulfillment, 262, 308
    urgency of, 21–22
Order fulfillment mechanism, 7
Order generation, 300
Order management cycle (OMC),
    297–298
    analysis, 307–308
    benefits of, 309–310
    billing, 302
    case studies of, 303–306
    cost estimation and pricing, 300
    fulfillment, 308
    lessons regarding, 298–300
    order generation, 300
    order planning, 300
    order receipt and entry, 308
    order selection and prioritization,
        308
    political strategy, 309

Order management cycle (OMC)—*Cont.*
  postsales service, 302
  returns and claims, 302
  scheduling, 308
  system focus, 308
Order planning, 300
Order receipt and entry, 308
Orders, size of; *see* Order size
Order selection and prioritization, 308
Order size
  effect on customer profitability, 152
  industrial segmentation and, 22

Partnering with customers, in product
    development, 95
Passive customers, 156
Penalties, in hybrid marketing systems,
    251
Perceived quality index, 218
Personal buyer characteristics, 15, 23
Person to person relationships, in
    strategic account relationships, 179
Physical attributes of product, in analysis
    of customer perceptions, 102–104,
    105–106
Platform projects, 60–61
Platforms, 65–67
Post-It Notes, as example of shadowed
    new product, 52
Postsale service costs, 154
Postsales service, 302
Power, types of, 31–33
Powerful buyers
  identification of, 34
  types of, 31–33
Power structures, industrial
    segmentation and, 20
Power transformers, 334–334
Preliminary business analysis, 44
Preliminary market assessment, 44
Preliminary technical assessment, 44
Presale costs, 153–154
Price concessions, in mature markets,
    139
Price-performance ratio, 105–107
Price-sensitive customers, 157
Price strategy, 98, 99
Pricing
  based on marketing-related services,
    213
  diverse specifications and, 272
  market life cycle and, 257
  profitability and, 152

Pricing of products, 8–9
  analysis of customer perceptions in,
    100–107
  buying psychology and, 26–27
  cost structure and, 110–111
  customer needs considerations in,
    98–111
  product planning and, 109–110
Processed materials, 4
Process innovation strategy, 146–147
Process technology, 312
Product, type of, matching with
    development process, 44–45
Product application, industrial
    segmentation and, 22
Product attributes, 271
  price, trade-off with, 278
Product boundaries, 250
Product bundling, 200
Product choice decisions by customers,
    272
Product commercialization, new
    products; *see* New product
    commercialization
Product concept, communication of, 91–92
Product customization, generic channel
    function, 124
Product definition project, Hewlett-
    Packard, 77–80
Product development, 44
  acceleration of, 45
  beta testing, 112–121
  cross-functional team, 43–44
  failure rate of new products, 43
  Hewlett-Packard product definition
    project, 77–80
  new product commercialization, 43–55
  NeXT computers, 46
  research on product success/failure,
    80–82
  stages in, 44
  timing of beta testing, 118
Product development process
  flaws in, 43
  matching with product type, 44–45
Product differentiation strategy, 142
Product evaluation, by customers,
    99–100
Product evolution to meet uncertain
    need, 89–90
Product evolution trajectory (PET),
    279–285
  fire engine industry, 283–285
  integrated circuit business, 285

Product importance, 192
Product information
  channel function priority, 125
  generic channel function, 124
Production costs, 154
Production ramp up, 44
Productive sales calls, in buying
    psychology, 38
Productivity, MSP systems and,
    212–213, 216–217
Product launch
  failure of, 43
  Sony Walkman, 54–55
Product life cycles, 282, 139–140
Product life cycle theory, 188
Product line evolution, 270–287
Product planning, pricing and, 109–110
Product policy
  custom-designed item, 275–276
  different mixture of diverse
    specifications, 273–275
  diverse specifications and, 272
  price relationship with, 105–107
  product versus value, 270–287
  special-purpose products, 276–277
  variety-oriented product line,
    273–276
Product positioning, delusionary new
    products, 54–55
Product quality assurance, generic
    channel function, 124
Product status, industrial segmentation
    and, 18–19
Product technology, 312
Product warranty, channel function
    priority, 125
Profitability
  cost and price variation, effect on,
    152–153
  costs to suppliers, 152–153
  customer behavior, 155–159
  customer situation, effect of, 158
  migration patterns, effect of,
    158–159
  segmenting accounts and prospects,
    173–176
  strategy, focus of, 161
  support systems, 161–162
  variety product line, 274
Profitability dispersion, 152, 160–161
Profit dispersion analysis, 162–163
Profits, customer management for,
    152–163
Programmed buyers, 193–194, 196

Project development, micromanagement of, 58
Project mapping, 59–65
Project plans, 56–72
Project SAPPHO, 78–80
Purchase decision
people involved in, 28
powerful buyers, 31–34
Purchasers, 30, 31
impact of sales approaches on, 170
Purchasing approaches, 15, 20–21

Rabino, S., 117
Raw materials, 4
Recruiting, creative, 319
Reference accounts, beta sites used as, 116–117
Relationship buyers, 194, 196–197
Relative channel profile, 126
Relative price, 191
Relative service, 191–192
Repetitive tasks, MSP and, 216
Replacement motors, as commodity business, 138
Resale, goods purchased for, 3
Research
from basic to applied, 76–77
on product success/failure, 80–82
Research and development, 4, 61
from basic to applied research, 76–77
centrality in new product development, 262
shadowed new products and, 51–52
Returns and claims, 302
Reward power, 31
Risk, in product development, 91
Ryans, John, 313

Sales
automation and, 212–224
human side of; see Buying psychology
types of selling, 164–186
Sales and marketing management, 214
Sales approaches
application of different types, 169–171
comparisons of different types, 169–171
justification for different types, 171–173

Sales approaches—*Cont.*
major account management, 166–167
strategic account relationships, 167–169
systems sales, 165–166
transaction selling, 165
Sales audit, in buying psychology, 38–39
Sales force
productivity of, 216
raw leads, followup of, 219
Sales managers, 26
Salesperson productivity tools, 214
Sales promotion, beta testing used for, 116
Sales resources, coordination of, 219
Sales strategies, 26
Sales volume, income and, 152
Scale, management of, 260
Scheduling, 308
Secondary wave planning, –70
Segmentation criteria, 15, 16–23
Segmentation of industrial markets; *see* Industrial segmentation
Segmenting customers, 245
in mature industrial markets, 187–197
Seller, impact of sales approaches on, 170
Selling; *see* Buying/selling process
Selling approaches, based on buyer motivation, 35–36
Selling costs, 239
Service
after-sales-service, 124
high-technology, uncertainty about, 315
Service industries, hybrid marketing systems, 239
Service innovation strategy, 148
Services, 4
pricing of products and, 104
special services for selected accounts, 176–178
Shadowed new products, 51–53
shadowed, defined, 51
Shanklin, William, 313
Shorter channels, 234–235
SIC code, customer segmentation by, 190
Signaling properties of beta testing, 117
Site selection for beta testing, 117–118
Situational factors, 15, 21–22

Size of company, industrial segmentation and, 18
Social responsibility, management of, 10
Sony Walkman, launch process of, 54–55
Special account relationships, 176
Specialization, 260–261
Special-purpose products, 276–277
Stage-gate system, 45
Staples, Inc., hybrid marketing system, 253
Status power, 31, 32
Steady stream sequencing, 67–
Steel strapping, as commodity business, 138
Strategic account, defined, 176
Strategic account relationships, 167–169
benefits to customers, 178–179
choice of accounts, 182
customers applied to, 175–176
implementation, 183–186
integration in, 180
justification of, 172–173
management of, 184–186
nurturing of, 179–180
problems of, 181–183
rewards of, 180–181
Strategy, for managing accounts, 161
Strategy analysis, 162–163
Superglobal business, 329
Superlocal business, 329
Supplier-customer misperceptions, 46–47
Suppliers
costs to, 153–155
hybrid channels and, 228–231
reorientation of distribution channels, 225–237
shorter channels and, 234–235
Supply-side strategies, 149
Support systems, profitability and, 161–162
Support tasks, MSP and, 216
Surveys, 93
Switching potential, 193
Systems, 4
Systems sales, 165–166
customers applied to, 173–176
justification of, 171

Targeted selling, buying psychology and, 27
Task automation, 219–220

Taxonomies, new product, 46–48
Taylor, William, interview, 328–346
Technical standards, high-tech
    marketing uncertainty, 313
Technological obsolescence, 316
Technological potential
    alignment with current markets,
        85–86, 90
    development of products based on,
        87–88
Technological uncertainty
    defined, 314
    delivery date, 314–315
    obsolescence, 316
    product's functional performance,
        314
    service and repair, 315
    unanticipated side effects, 316
Technology
    of company; see Company
        technology
    defined, 312
    emphasis on, 6–7
    high-tech marketing, 311–327
    role in product development, 47–49
    strategic account relationships and,
        178
Technology commercialization
    design in advance of market,
        85–305
    distinctive competencies of
        corporation, 76
    Hewlett-Packard product definition
        project, 77–80
    market windows, 282
    research, 76–77
    statistics on, 73
    time-based competition, 75–76
    user needs, 80–85
Technology push, 89

Telemarketing, 214
    for cost containment, 239
    price for systems, 222
Telephone; *see* Phone systems
Test market, 44
Textiles, hybrid marketing systems, 239
Time-based competition, 75–76
Timing, of beta testing, 118
Training, creative, 319
Transaction buyers, 195, 196–197
Transaction costs, 200
Transaction selling, 165
    customers applied to, 173–176
Trial production, 44

Uncertain need, solutions for, 89–90
Uncertainty
    high-tech marketing, 313–314
    initial product introduction, 258–259
    in market maturity process, 257
    in product development, 91
    in Stage III, 262
    technological, 314–317
Universal benefits, 271
    diverse specifications versus trade-
        offs, 277–278
    dominant design and, 280
Urgency of order fulfillment, industrial
    segmentation and, 21–22
User evaluation of future products, 91–92
User needs, 80–85
    product development based on,
        86–90
    tools and mechanisms for
        understanding of, 92–96
User reaction, elicitation of, 91–92
Users, 30, 31
    as developers, 94–95
    myopia about needs, 84–85

Utility of product, 277–278
Utility pricing, 100

Value-added strategy, 144–145
Value-in-use, 199–200
Value-in-use strategy, 145
Value of purchase, 199
Value-oriented dominant design, 280
Value-oriented product line, 274–275
    dominant design and, 280
Value pricing, 100
Variety marketer, 274
Variety-oriented product line, 273–276
    custom-designed item, 275–276
    diverse specifications versus trade-
        offs, 278
    profitability of, 274
    special-purpose products, 276–277
Variety versus value, 270–287
    international implications, 285–286
    management implications, 286–287
Vendor relationships, in business-to-
    business marketing, 6
Vertical marketing systems, distribution
    channels as, 226–227
VideoDisc, as example of delusionary
    new product, 54
Von Hippel, Eric, 94

Warranty, channel function priority, 125
Weick, Karl, 320
Wholesaler, at risk, 234
Wilson, Edith, 69–80
Write Line, Inc., hybrid marketing
    system, 240–247

Zaltman, Gerald, 54